The Impact of the European Reformation

For Thomas Rowlands, born 6 June 2007

The Impact of the European Reformation

Princes, Clergy and People

Edited by

BRIDGET HEAL and OLE PETER GRELL

University of St Andrews, UK and the Open University, UK

ASHGATE

Published by
Ashgate Publishing Limited
Gower House
Croft Road
Aldershot
Hampshire GU11 3HR
England

Ashgate Publishing Company
Suite 420
101 Cherry Street
Burlington, VT 05401–4405
USA

Ashgate website: http://www.ashgate.com

British Library Cataloguing in Publication Data
The impact of the European Reformation : princes, clergy and people.
 – (St Andrews studies in Reformation history)
 1. Reformation 2. Europe – Civilization – 16th century
 3. Europe – Civilization – 17th century
 I. Heal, Bridget II. Grell, Ole Peter
 940.2'3

 ISBN 978–0–7546–6212–9

Library of Congress Cataloging-in-Publication Data
The impact of the European Reformation : princes, clergy, and people / edited by
 Bridget Heal and Ole Peter Grell.
  p. cm. – (St. Andrews studies in Reformation history)
 Includes index.
 ISBN 978–0–7546–6212–9 (alk. paper)
 1. Reformation – Influence.
 I. Heal, Bridget. II. Grell, Ole Peter.

BR307.I46 2007
274'.06–dc22

2007034440

ISBN 978–0–7546–6212–9

Printed and bound in Great Britain by MPG Books Ltd, Bodmin, Cornwall

Contents

Part III: People

List of Illustrations and Maps

List of Contributors

C. Scott Dixon (Queen's University, Belfast)

Kevin Gould (Nottingham Trent University)

Michael F. Graham (University of Akron)

Ole Peter Grell (The Open University)

Christopher Haigh (Christ Church, Oxford)

Bridget Heal (University of St Andrews)

Adam Mosley (Swansea University)

Christine Peters (Queen's College, Oxford)

Andrew Pettegree (University of St Andrews)

Bernd Roeck (Universität Zürich)

Luise Schorn-Schütte (Johann Wolfgang Goethe-Universität)

Tom Scott (University of St Andrews)

Margo Todd (University of Pennsylvania)

Alexandra Walsham (University of Exeter)

Acknowledgements

This volume springs from four one-day symposia organized by The Renaissance and Early Modern Research Group at the Open University, and St Andrews Reformation Institute, St Andrews University.

We should like to thank the Research Committee of the Arts Faculty of the Open University and St Andrews University for generous financial support of these successful events, which took place in Milton Keynes, Cambridge and St Andrews.

List of Abbreviations

ADHG   Archives départementales de la Haute-Garonne

ADLG   Archives départementales de Lot-et-Garonne

AMB   Archives municipales de Bordeaux

AMT   Archives municipales de Toulouse

BMB   Bibliothèque municipale de Bordeaux

BN   Bibliothèque nationale de Paris

ERO   Essex Record Office

ESPB   Helen Child Sargent and G.L. Kittredge (eds), *The English and Scottish Popular Ballads* (Boston, MA, 1904)

GRO   Gloucestershire Record Office

HRO   Hampshire Record Office

KGW   M. Caspar et. al. (eds), *Johannes Kepler Gesammelte Werke* (Munich, 1938–)

LA   Lincolnshire Archives

NAS   National Archives of Scotland

NLS   National Library of Scotland

NRO   Northamptonshire Record Office

ORO   Oxfordshire Record Office

RPC   *Register of the Privy Council of Scotland*, 1st series, ed. David Masson (11 vols, Edinburgh, 1877–98)

SRO   Somerset Record Office

StAUM   St Andrews University Muniments

TBOO   J. Dreyer (ed.), *Tychonis Brahe Dani Opera Omnia* (15 vols, Copenhagen, 1913–29)

WA   *D. Martin Luthers Werke. Kritische Gesamtausgabe* (67 vols, Weimar, 1883–1997)

WA Br.   *D. Martin Luthers Werke. Kritische Gesamtausgabe: Briefwechsel* (18 vols, Weimar, 1930–85)

WRO   Wiltshire Record Office

WSRO   West Sussex Record Office

Introduction

Bridget Heal

Recent decades have witnessed the fragmentation of Reformation studies. High-level research has tended to be confined within specific geographical, confessional or chronological boundaries. While authoritative surveys are still possible, few scholars would now be able to claim that research in their field is being driven forward by great works of synthesis. As a result, conferences, essay collections and even many undergraduate and graduate courses tend to focus on particular aspects of the long and complex process that constituted religious reform during the early modern period. By bringing together scholars working on a wide variety of topics, this volume aims to counteract this centrifugal trend and to provide a broad perspective on the impact of the European Reformation(s). The essays contained within it indicate the diverse directions in which Reformation scholarship is now moving, while reminding us of the need to understand particular developments within a broader European context.

The new research presented here from historians of politics, of the Church and of belief demonstrates that movements for religious reform left no sphere of early modern life untouched. While the main focus of this volume is on the Protestant Reformations, it is often impossible to understand the impact of these Protestant movements without considering the Catholic Church's responses to them. As the chapters by Luise Schorn-Schütte and Kevin Gould demonstrate, even in areas of Europe where the evangelical Reformation was ultimately unsuccessful, Protestantism had a tangible impact on Catholic religious and political culture. To view either Protestantism or Catholicism in isolation therefore inevitably detracts from our understanding of both.

The geographical scope of the contributions presented here is extensive, ranging from Scotland and England via France and Germany to Transylvania. This is a result of the editors' conviction that much of the most productive and exciting research in recent years has been, in part at least, the result of historians showing an increased awareness of the activities of scholars working on areas geographically remote from their own.[1] While

---

[1] See, for example, Margo Todd, *The Culture of Protestantism in Early Modern Scotland* (New Haven, CT and London, 2002), which makes extensive use of the techniques of historical anthropology pioneered by scholars such as Keith Thomas, Peter Burke and Bob Scribner.

regional differentiation will always be of paramount importance, in terms of the types of questions asked and the methodological approaches used, such intellectual exchanges can only deepen our understanding of early modern Europe.

The chronological span of the chapters in this volume is also considerable, staring in the 1520s and ending in the 1690s. Although specific political occurrences were, of course, key in instituting the Reformation in various parts of Europe, religious reform must be viewed as a process rather than an event. This process may have begun in the Holy Roman Empire during the 1520s, but in many parts of Europe its impact was felt only much later. Its political ramifications continued until well into the seventeenth century. Moreover, as work on both England and Germany has shown, the demands of providing a properly trained clergy to educate the populace meant that reform, in the sense of inculcating a true understanding of Protestant belief, took a very long time to achieve. For historians interested in questions of belief, it is therefore essential to look beyond the sixteenth century.

Princes

Part I of this volume considers the impact of the Reformation on political culture, investigating the extent to which Protestantism transformed traditional relationships between rulers and ruled. Three of the four chapters focus on the Holy Roman Empire, the heartland of the Reformation and, on account of its unique political structure, the site of some of the most interesting accommodations between governors and their subjects. One looks at southwest France, an area that witnessed some of the most extreme religious violence of the sixteenth century. The chapters demonstrate the extent to which, both at a macro and at a micro level, political life was transformed by the rise of the Reformation. For radical reformers, the traditional guarantors of political legitimacy were no longer sufficient: rulers had to uphold the true faith and protect the common weal if they were to retain their authority. Mainstream reformers – Luther, Calvin and Zwingli – accommodated themselves more successfully to existing secular authority, enabling their Reformations to survive. Yet even their more moderate demands brought about major changes in political life. In Germany, the authority of Lutheran princes within their own territories may have been strengthened, but the ideological unity of the Holy Roman Empire was compromised, and collapsed entirely with the onset of the Thirty Years' War. At a micro level, the Reformation might reinforce traditional social and political divisions, as it did in bi-confessional Augsburg, or it might provoke groups with divergent backgrounds and interests to present a united front, as it did in various cities in southwest France. Either way, rulers and ruled were required to adjust to a new political landscape in which the ideology and realities of government, from political theory to patronage and administration, were complicated by competing religious loyalties.

Part I opens with a chapter by Tom Scott, which explains how evangelical thought enabled certain reformers to contemplate and to legitimate the violent overthrow of the prevailing social and political order. In their campaigns to transform religious life, the first generation of evangelical reformers had to decide under what circumstances secular authority could legitimately be opposed. For Luther, revolt by the common man could never be justified. But as the extent of opposition to the Gospel became clear, Luther, Zwingli and Calvin had to formulate carefully defined rights of resistance and to propose methods of deposing unjust and tyrannical rulers. The ideas that the Continental reformers developed in the heartlands of the Reformation should therefore, Scott argues, be considered on a continuous gradient from Luther through Calvin and Zwingli to the 'so-called radicals', proponents of an 'applied or politicized theology' that countenanced social revolution. Scott explores in detail the views of three such radical reformers, all of whom were involved in the Peasants' War of 1524–26: Balthasar Hubmaier, Christoph Schappeler and Hans Hergot. His chapter demonstrates that for each of these men, social revolution could be understood and legitimized only through the prism of radical Christianity. They advocated godly justice and Christian equality: if the Gospel was suppressed and if the common man was made to suffer under the yoke of temporal oppression, then social revolution might justifiably follow. It was, Scott argues, their vision of divine justice, brotherly love and the common weal that enabled sixteenth-century 'radicals' to contemplate the violent overthrow of the prevailing order.

The practical threat from such 'applied or politicized theology' was largely eliminated in the wake of the Peasants' War in 1524–25 and the subsequent collapse of the Münster 'Anabaptist Kingdom' in 1533–34, but the Reformation none the less had, as Scott Dixon demonstrates in Chapter 2, a profound and long-term impact on the political development of the Holy Roman Empire. With the 1555 Peace of Augsburg, Lutheran princes won the right to reform the Church within their territories, precipitating, Dixon argues, a thoroughgoing transformation in relations between rulers and ruled. Protestant princes engaged in a process of domestic reform, whereby their power was extended right down to the level of the parish through, for example, Church orders and visitations. Prompted by fear of Anabaptist preaching in particular, reformers such as Luther and Melachthon called on their princes to protect the true Church. Secular intervention in religious affairs increased, and Protestant princes came to be seen as guardians of the faith. As a result, they were able to draw on religion to an unprecedented degree to consolidate and legitimize their rule. At an imperial level, however, the Reformation's impact was much less positive. Luther made effective use of nationalist discourse, and associated the empire with the corruption and tyranny of Rome. Moreover, by the mid-sixteenth century, Protestant princes had, Dixon writes, begun 'to define themselves *against* the Catholic emperor by drawing on the evangelical faith'. Since the time of the Schmalkaldic League, most Protestant territories had necessarily shared a general ideology of resistance. Thereafter, as Helen Watanabe-O'Kelly's work on the Wettin court in Dresden has shown, a distinctively Lutheran court culture emerged, which testified to its patrons' evangelical beliefs and affirmed their political claims through its art, literature and music.[2] Ultimately, of course, the empire survived as a system of political relations dealing with 'federal' issues such as taxation and defence. But its sacral legitimacy and its political integrity were, Dixon demonstrates, fatally compromised by the rise of confessionally determined blocs and divisions.

Despite these divisions it was sometimes possible, as Bernd Roeck shows in Chapter 3, for Protestants and Catholics to live side by side with a degree of equanimity. Germany's bi-confessional cities provide a unique opportunity for exploring the day-to-day realities of this *modus vivendi*. In a number of free and imperial cities within the empire, both Protestants and Catholics had the right to worship openly, their legal parity guaranteed by the Religious Peace of Augsburg.[3] Roeck's chapter focuses on one of the most important and richly documented of these cities, Augsburg in Swabia. Here, he argues, a new confessional structure developed alongside the city's pre-existing social structure. The religious division between Catholic and Protestant to a large extent mirrored the long-standing social division between rich and poor. Augsburg's pauperized craftsmen were keen proponents of the Reformation. In the early stages of Augsburg's Reformation, with the preacher Johann Schilling, social and religious discontent merged: Schilling attacked the rich, and said, according to one chronicler, that all things should be shared. The wealthy Fugger family, on the other hand, were bastions of the old Church, and it was largely thanks to their influence, Roeck argues, that Catholicism survived in Augsburg. As the sixteenth century progressed, these two different social and cultural *milieux* became entrenched. In general, bloody escalations were avoided, but Augsburg's religious peace was always precarious, as the conflict that broke out over the Gregorian calendar reform in 1583–84 demonstrates.

---

[2]   Helen Watanabe-O'Kelly, *Court Culture in Dresden: From Renaissance to Baroque* (Basingstoke, 2002).

[3]   See Paul Warmbrunn, *Zwei Konfessionen in einer Stadt. Das Zusammenleben von Katholiken und Protestanten in den paritätischen Reichsstädten Augsburg, Biberach, Ravensburg und Dinkelsbühl von 1548 bis 1648* (Wiesbaden, 1983).

The formation of separate confessional identities was accelerated by the Thirty Years' War, for, as Roeck points out, the co-existence that prevailed in Augsburg and in Germany's other bi-confessional cites was the product not of an ideology of toleration, but of prescribed pragmatism.

Elsewhere in Europe, it proved impossible to achieve even this degree of uneasy co-existence. France, for example, was wracked by four decades of religious warfare, despite the sporadic attempts of its rulers to promote conciliation between Catholics and Huguenots. The final chapter in Part I indicates that local studies of rulers and ruled may prove important in explaining France's patterns of religious warfare. Whereas in Augsburg the Reformation magnified a pre-existing social division, resulting in a lasting if uneasy balance of confessional power, in the cities that Kevin Gould studies in south-west France, the Protestant threat encouraged local Catholics of all classes to form a united front. Gould examines the struggles for control of three key urban sites: Bordeaux, Toulouse and Agen. In each case, despite some initial Protestant military success, Catholic defenders quickly regained and strengthened their positions, and by 1570 had established control over these cities to a degree that was unrivalled outside of Paris. In each city, Gould argues, the key to this success lay in a history of confessional conflict prior to 1562 that had encouraged local Catholics to form defensive organizations. The local *parlement*, communal authorities, clergy, urban bourgeosie and lesser social groups as well as members of the nobility joined together to defend their faith, both by pressuring for anti-Protestant policy and by supplying troops to fight. In these cities, Gould demonstrates, the Reformation provoked a Catholic revival that pre-dated any attempts at religious renewal inspired by Trent and its agents.

Clergy

Part II considers the Church and its personnel, another sphere of early modern life that was entirely transformed by the rise of the Reformation. In Protestant territories, the clerical estate, with its traditional privileges and immunities, disappeared, and was replaced by body of married clergymen who were, as Luise Schorn-Schütte points out, 'gradually integrated into the daily world of the faithful'.[4] Preaching and pastoral work, rather than, as in the medieval Church, the administration of the sacraments, were their most important duties. Recent research has emphasized the importance of this changing 'clerical paradigm', and has traced the evangelical Churches' prolonged struggle to produce men capable of fulfilling it. Until well into the early decades of the seventeenth century, Scott Dixon and Luise Schorn-Schütte suggest, 'the general level of learning among Protestant pastors

---

[4]   See page 121.

consistently remained much lower than has previously been assumed', especially in the countryside.[5] Gradually, however, through the provision of schools and universities offering a proper education in theology as well as practical ministerial training, the level of education among the Protestant clergy improved and they became more conscious of their calling and of the duties that their office entailed.

There has been a tendency to emphasize the distinctive nature of the Protestant pastorate, and to see its members as different from the traditional clergy because of their social and economic circumstances, their educational backgrounds, their relationships with the authorities and with local parishioners, and their sense of professional self-awareness. However, Luise Schorn-Schütte argues in Chapter 5 that by the seventeenth century, the evangelical ideal of a well trained, preaching pastor had shaped not only the Protestant but also the Catholic clerical body. The Protestant 'clerical paradigm' had a profound impact on the Catholic Church. The foundation of the Jesuit Order, of other reform orders and of the *Collegium Germanicum* in Rome was, Schorn-Schütte suggests, 'the Catholic response to the redefinition of clerical office within the Protestant church'.[6] Through these organizations, the Tridentine reform movement produced priests who, unlike the medieval pastoral clergy, were no longer concerned exclusively with assisting their congregations in the quest for salvation through the administration of the sacraments and an emphasis on good works, but were also leaders of parishes and proclaimers of God's word. In their socio-economic backgrounds, in their levels of education, in their material circumstances, and even, in many cases, in their relations with their parishioners, these men were often very like their Protestant counterparts.

Of course, crucial differences remained: while Catholic clerical office retained its sacral character, the ideal Protestant pastor was an exemplary family man. Moreover, he was engaged with moral discipline and with worldly affairs to a greater extent than his Catholic equivalent. Protestant pastors were not only preachers; they were also shepherds of souls, and were charged with watching over their parishioners' behaviour and ensuring their obedience to God's commands. While the exercise of excessive zeal in this sphere could provoke resentment, Christopher Haigh suggests in Chapter 6 that in England, one of the key expectations of a minister was that he should 'play a part in parish discipline, and seek to sustain peace and order among his people'.[7] Margo Todd has suggested that in Scotland, the services the Kirk could offer as a result of local sessions – in particular

---

[5]   C. Scott Dixon and Luise Schorn-Schütte (eds), *The Protestant Clergy of Early Modern Europe* (Basingstoke, 2003), pp. 3, 23.
[6]   See page 106.
[7]   See page 126.

discipline in such matters as domestic violence, arbitration of quarrels and administration of poor relief – help explain parishioners' acquiescence to the Calvinist system.[8] In England, Haigh argues, these services were equally significant, but their provision has been obscured by the nature of the written records. England may not have had local Kirk sessions, but court act books and deposition books offer plenty of evidence of clergy and churchwardens providing informal justice, arbitration and conciliation. Ecclesiastical discipline was imposed at a local level, with pastors using communion and the sanction of exclusion to promote the resolution of disputes and to enforce proper behaviour. Indeed, even once cases reached court, local ministers often remained engaged and interceded on behalf of parishioners. Haigh's archival evidence demonstrates that in England, as in Scotland, part of a pastor's duty was to restore communal harmony when it was threatened, and that the enforcement of discipline could be 'local, personalized, conciliatory and flexible'.[9]

Even in Lutheran Transylvania, Christine Peters argues in Chapter 7, local context was key in shaping pastors' relations with their congregations and in determining the nature of the emergent Protestant Church. Every evangelical Church had to make decisions about ritual and discipline: what should the new Church look like, and how should its ministers enforce proper behaviour? The lenient decisions the Saxon reformers took with regard to ritual seem at odds with their relatively harsh prescriptions concerning disciplinary matters such as marriage, the observance of the Sabbath and filial obedience. The 1547 *Reformation ecclesiarum saxonicarum* accommodated regional preferences in terms of ritual and imagery; indeed, some Saxon Lutheran Churches looked sufficiently traditional to deceive visitors into thinking that they were still Catholic. In matters of discipline, however, the Saxon Church was much more rigorous than other Lutheran Churches. Peters suggests that this apparent paradox can be resolved by paying proper attention to 'the logic of pre-Reformation religious and social instruction'.[10] Using the example of surviving late fifteenth-century wall paintings from the church at Honigberg near Kronstadt, she demonstrates that the region's traditional religious and social concerns, in particular its Christocentric Marian piety and its notion of individual Christian vocation, played a decisive role in determining the preoccupations of the evangelical Church that emerged there during the sixteenth century.

While Haigh's and Peters' chapters demonstrate the importance of local context in understanding the Reformation's impact on the Church and its personnel, the final chapter in Part II returns us to the realm of high

---

[8]   Todd, *The Culture of Protestantism in Early Modern Scotland*, ch. 5 and 6.
[9]   See page 140.
[10]   See page 154.

politics. As the Reformation became established, Church and state were bound more closely together. The self-governing hierarchy of the Catholic Church disappeared, and clergy found themselves dependent upon the state. This relationship was by no means always an easy one, as Michael Graham demonstrates in Chapter 8. Graham considers the Scottish clergy's engagement with the political sphere, drawing examples from the 1590s and 1690s, critical phases during which the clergy sought to test the extent of their influence by injecting religious discourse into the political arena. During the 1590s, James VI's godly ministers were concerned primarily with the threat of diabolism and with the king's religious backsliding (in particular with his dealings with Catholics at court). After the events of the revolutionary period of 1637–51 and of the Williamite revolution of 1688–89, the threats to the Kirk were of a different nature: primarily the religious laxity associated with Episcopalianism and growing tendency towards scepticism. There was an ongoing need for ministers to persuade magistrates to uphold the covenanted vision of Scottish society. The comparison between these two periods allows Graham to explore the nature of the clergy's relationship with political authority, and to illustrate the limits to the kings' toleration of the notion of 'Presbyterian political divinity' that, ministers felt, gave them the right to influence the policies of the kingdom.

People

Part III addresses issues of knowledge and belief. In his 1993 article 'The Reformation, Popular Magic and the "Disenchantment of the World"', Bob Scribner called for scholars to 'construct a new understanding of the Reformation ... which takes account of those dissonant elements which falsify the paradigm that has been hitherto accepted, and then to write a new history of Protestantism which includes the religious experience and practice of ordinary believers, with all of their contradictions and misunderstandings'.[11] The first two chapters in this part demonstrate the extent to which Reformation historians have responded to this call. Margo Todd and Alexandra Walsham explore the persistence of traditional beliefs in Protestant societies. These beliefs were sometimes, as in the case of Todd's Scottish fairies, at odds with the official teaching of the Church, but were sometimes, as in the case of Walsham's holy wells, successfully assimilated into Protestant piety. The second two chapters, which examine the elite intellectual world of natural philosophy and astronomy and the book trade, remind us that in our determination to recover the religious experiences of all social groups, we must avoid bifurcating popular and

---

[11]   R.W. Scribner, 'The Reformation, Popular Magic and the "Disenchantment of the World"', *Journal of Interdisciplinary History*, 23/3 (1993): 494.

elite belief. For all sixteenth-century people, religion was of paramount importance: the world was created and regulated by God, and both peasant and scholar lived with 'a cosmology still ordered principally by divinity rather than human reason' (Todd).[12] This was a world where natural philosophical investigations such as astronomy could be viewed as a branch of theology, and where printing and the book market developed, in part at least, according to the requirements of religious change.

In her 2002 study *The Culture of Protestantism in Early Modern Scotland*, Margo Todd analysed what she described as Scotland's 'cultural revolution', the process by which the country's late medieval religious cult, with its 'sensual and ceremonial spirituality', was replaced by Calvinist orthodoxy. She pointed out, however, that despite the imposition of uniform Calvinist belief and practice and the Kirk's vociferous condemnation of what it described as 'popish superstition', early modern Scots remained convinced that their world was populated by wizards and witches, fairies and demons, and angels and ghosts.[13] In Chapter 9, Todd focuses on one aspect of this surviving pre-Christian belief system: fairy belief. According to the accounts given by those who had met them, fairies lived under hills and appeared beside springs and streams; they were exotic in appearance, and behaved in a festive manner. They were capricious: they gave good gifts, but could also do harm. Stories concerning them therefore contradicted the Kirk's teaching on the rewarding of good and punishing of evil, yet belief in fairies was by no means confined to the level of the uneducated populace: educated and ignorant, rich and poor spoke of them and sought their aid. Moreover, for all its strident rhetoric, the Kirk rarely took decisive action against those who claimed to have received special powers of healing or second sight from the fairies. Such healers often operated for many years before some mishap led to their condemnation by their elders. Why did these beliefs, so much at odds with the providential view of the universe promulgated by Christian orthodoxy, persist for so long? Most importantly, Todd suggests, because fairies were an important part of the cosmology of a people always vulnerable to the arbitrary forces of nature. They were a manifestation of a 'nature religion', which reflected the powerful sense of place that characterized the lives of early modern communities and the obvious power that resided in natural phenomena such as rivers and storms. It was possible, Todd demonstrates, for this ancient cosmology to co-exist with Calvinist orthodoxy, which reminds us, as Scribner's work did, of the need to understand the early modern world in its own terms, contradictions and all.

---

[12]   Todd, *The Culture of Protestantism in Early Modern Scotland*, p. 318.

[13]   Ibid., Introduction and pp. 317, 355–7. For a recent discussion of the role of angels in Protestant piety, see Peter Marshall and Alexandra Walsham (eds), *Angels in the Early Modern World* (Cambridge, 2006).

The sense of place and the close relationship to the natural world that facilitated belief in fairies in seventeenth-century Scotland found another manifestation in pre-Reformation England, where sacred springs and wells attracted pilgrims seeking miraculous cures. These springs and wells, many of which had been connected since pre-Christian times with healing, were attacked by the Protestant reformers as part of their assault on idolatry and superstition. From the 1570s onwards, however, some of these sites were revived and promoted on account of their therapeutic powers by members of the medical establishment. Confirmation of the mineral content of the waters of these 'approved' springs distanced them from their superstitious past, but as Walsham points out in Chapter 10, this did not herald the triumph of 'scientific' rationalism. In fact, 'contemporary perception of such sites remained firmly locked within a framework of religious assumptions'.[14] Healing baths and springs were understood by the doctors who promoted them as gifts from God, and patients were encouraged to engage in prayer and repentance before and during their visits. The cures that occurred were not described in purely medical terms; indeed, on occasion they were even referred to as miracles. The quest for a proper understanding of the workings of nature was not, Walsham demonstrates, incompatible with a continued belief in the divine origins of healing. This belief survived into the post-Reformation era, not, as in the case of fairy belief, as part of a rival cosmology. Rather, English Protestant piety proved able to integrate holy wells and springs into its reformed, providential understanding of the universe. In this, it was not unique, as recent investigation into the role of holy springs in post-Reformation Denmark has shown.[15]

Adam Mosley's chapter on the reformation of astronomy also demonstrates that natural philosophical enquiries into the created world and a belief in divine providence often sat comfortably side-by-side together. The early modern period proved crucial in the history of astronomy: it witnessed the emergence of a new understanding of the cosmos, which began with Copernicus and culminated in Newton and the birth of modern 'classical' physics. Mosley considers the extent to which the emergence of this 'new astronomy' was shaped by the religious debates of the sixteenth century, thereby placing the narrative of the Copernican breakthrough firmly within the context of the Protestant Reformation. Organized religion should not, as recent studies have demonstrated, be seen as an obstacle to new undertakings and investigations in natural philosophy. On the contrary, Moseley argues that religious belief was in

---

[14] See page 218.
[15] Jens C.V. Johansen, 'Holy Springs and Protestantism in Early Modern Denmark: A Medical rationale for a Religious Practice', *Medical History*, 41/1 (1997): 59–69.

fact a motivating factor in the study of the created world. In Wittenberg, for example, Philip Melanchthon supported the study of astronomy and cosmology through his reforms of the university's educational curriculum. Melanchthon and his circle saw a religious and philosophical role for the study of the heavens: the movements of the stars and planets provided, they argued, evidence of God's providential ordering of creation, and moreover, God communicated with man through signs and portents in heaven. Natural philosophical study therefore complemented the study of the Bible, and astronomy could be regarded, as it was, for example, by Johannes Kepler, as a theological endeavour, a way of understanding divine providence. 'God is worshipped by my work,' Kepler wrote, 'even in astronomy'.[16] The work of Tycho Brahe was also, Moseley argues, stimulated by Melanchthon's legacy. As both Walsham's and Moseley's chapters demonstrate, if the history of natural philosophy is separated from the history of religion, our understanding of the former will remain at best incomplete.

The last chapter in this volume turns to printing and the book trade, another field closely bound up with the Reformation. As Andrew Pettegree argued in his *Reformation and the Culture of Persuasion*, 'there can be little doubt that the book did much to shape the Reformation; it must also be acknowledged that the Reformation did much to reshape the book'.[17] The Reformation emerged, Pettegree points out, when printing was still a developing industry, and its impact on the nascent book trade was huge. Wittenberg and Geneva, for example, became major centres of printing thanks entirely to Luther and Calvin. In Chapter 12 of this volume, Pettegree explores the international book market, focusing in particular on the Frankfurt Book Fair, which was so fundamental to its functioning. Surviving catalogues of books offered for sale at the Frankfurt fair allow us to trace the impact of religious and political changes on the production and sale of books. Despite Frankfurt's Protestant status, Pettegree notes, the fair saw a lively trade in Catholic as well as Protestant titles. During the second half of the sixteenth century, these catalogues reveal that in addition to the usual Latin and German titles, there were a significant number of French books for sale at the Frankfurt fair. After 1570, in particular, 'turbulent contemporary politics impact increasingly on the works offered for sale'.[18] Members of the French Huguenot movement forced to travel abroad, French nationals settled in Germany and interested foreign observers were able to purchase vernacular works on theology, history and contemporary politics to provide them with news and solace, and to guide them through

---

[16] See page 239.
[17] Andrew Pettegree, *Reformation and the Culture of Persuasion* (New York, 2005), p. 128.
[18] See page 257.

the difficult political choices facing France's Protestants during the Wars of Religion. During the 1590s, the character of the French books for sale at Frankfurt changed, and as peace appeared imminent, they disappeared entirely from the catalogues. Pettegree's chapter returns us, at the end of the volume, to the world of high politics, showing how the printing and book industry, one of the greatest innovations of the early modern period, responded to Europe's volatile political and religious history.

The chapters gathered together in the final part of this book demonstrate beyond doubt that there is no place left in Reformation studies for Max Weber's narrative that sees Protestantism as a crucial step in the 'disenchantment of world' and in the teleological triumph of rationalism over 'superstition'.[19] New medical theories and Copernicus' heliocentric universe may have been crucial developments in the so-called 'Scientific Revolution'; printing may be, as the Scottish philosopher Thomas Carlyle suggested, one of the 'three great elements of modern civilization' (the other two being gunpowder and Protestantism itself).[20] But we must not misinterpret these phenomena as moves towards secularization and modernization. In each, religion remained pre-eminent: for Protestants, the natural world, from healing spas to stars, could be read as a manifestation of divine providence, and the emergence of the printing industry was dictated to a large extent by the demands of religious reform. Moreover, as Margo Todd shows in Chapter 9, the Reformation certainly did not eliminate the 'magic' from everyday life. Seventeenth-century Scottish fairy belief draws our attention to the persistence of multiple and mutually contradictory cosmologies. It reminds us that in explaining the 'success' of the Reformation – the gradual transition to Protestant belief – we must pay proper attention to continuity with the past and to the reformers' willingness to accommodate or adapt traditional modes of behaviour and ways of thought.

---

[19]   See, for example, R.W. Scribner, 'Reformation and Desacralisation: From Sacramental World to Moralised Universe', in R. Po-Chia Hsia and R. Scribner (eds), *Problems in the Historical Anthropology of Early Modern Europe* (Wiesbaden, 1997).

[20]   Thomas Carlyle, 'The State of German Literature', in *The Works of Thomas Carlyle*, vol. 26, *Critical and Miscellaneous Essays I* (London, 1899), p. 28.

PART I
Princes

CHAPTER 1

Hubmaier, Schappeler and Hergot on Social Revolution

Tom Scott

The issue of social revolution in the Reformation cannot be separated from resistance theory; indeed, the leading reformers – Luther, Zwingli, Calvin – made a significant contribution to elaborating doctrines of resistance, usually *ex negativo*, it has to be admitted: that is, by setting strict limits to the legitimacy and appropriateness of opposition to secular authority. Luther's views are well known, from the time of *Eine treue Vermahnung* (1522) onwards, which ruled out any possibility of legitimate revolt by the common man.[1] And these views were of course reiterated and potentiated during the Peasants' War. But by the 1530s, doubtless alarmed at the threat to the Gospel posed by the hardening confessional antagonisms throughout Germany, Luther subtly changed his views. In his *Exposition of Psalm 101* (1534–35), he acknowledged the existence of those he termed the 'Wunderleute Gottes', those possessed of such supervening spiritual authority that they, as individuals, might depose an unjust ruler, provided that they derived no personal advantage therefrom. Because they possessed a direct line to God, they had no need of human advice on the configuration of righteous government. Such men, argued Luther, were extremely rare, and were certainly never to be found among the ranks of the peasantry.[2] Calvin, too, although resolutely opposed to revolutionary resistance, acknowledged the possibility of a human angel of retribution, an avenger of faith sent by God, but such persons were not only exceedingly rare: they could never be sure of their appointed role. Calvin looked rather to the Estates as guardians of right rule, who by their office had the right to resist tyranny (on the model of the ephors of Sparta or the Roman tribunes).[3]

---

[1]   *Eine treue Vermahnung an alle Christen, sich zu hüten vor Aufruhr und Empörung*, in WA, vol. 8, pp. 670–87. See Tobias Quilisch, *Das Widerstandsrecht und die Idee des religiösen Bundes bei Thomas Müntzer. Ein Beitrag zur politischen Theologie* (Beiträge zur politischen Wissenschaft, 113) (Berlin, 1999), p. 42.

[2]   *Auslegung des 101. Psalms*, WA, vol. 51, pp. 197–265; Quilisch, *Widerstandsrecht*, p. 49.

[3]   Jean Calvin, *Institutionis Christianae Religionis*, Lib. IV, cap. XX, p. 30, in *Ioannis Calvini opera quae supersunt omnia*, ed. Wilhelm Baum, Eduard Cunitz and Eduard Reuss, 59 vols (Braunschweig, 1863–1900), 2, p. 1115; Quilisch,

With Zwingli the accents were set somewhat differently. In common with the other reformers, Zwingli regarded evil rulers as sent by God as a punishment for the sins of mankind, but he did concede a carefully circumscribed right of resistance. In his *Exposition of the Sixty-Seven Axioms* of 1523, he identified unjust rule first and foremost with the suppression of the Gospel; what, he pondered, in those circumstances should faithful Christians do? His answer was clear – and I cite it in view of what I propose to discuss later: 'If Nero, Domitian, Maximinian, and others were unable to stop the teaching of Christ with their murdering, how much less can the angry, insane princes who rage in our time drive it out, as long as you stand firmly and without retreating?'[4] Of course, tyrannical rulers also oppressed the common people by their self-indulgence and wantonness, robbing the poor through duties, taxes, and by tolerating the holders of monopolies.[5] For Zwingli, therefore, the crux was not whether tyrants should be deposed, but how. If they had been elected by the common people, then they should be deposed following a collective decision of the people. If, on the other hand, the tyrant had been chosen by a few princes, then they should unseat him.[6] The difficulties were obvious enough: 'Here,' Zwingli conceded, 'the problem begins. For a despot will slaughter those who oppose him ... It is more comforting to be killed from doing right ... than to be destroyed later by the hand of God.' And, he concluded despairingly, if a despot rules by heredity, 'I do not know how

---

Widerstandrecht, pp. 38–40. In his last sermons, however, delivered against the background of increasing Huguenot persecution in France, Calvin did, albeit haltingly, countenance a limited right of resistance on the part of private citizens against a tyrannous monarch. Calvin instanced Abraham's victory over the four kings and the liberation of his nephew Lot, seeing in the patriarch as a private citizen not as ruler the special vocation of an avenger of faith. Willem Nijenhuis, 'The Limits of Civil Disobedience in Calvin's Latest Known Sermons: The Development of his Ideas of the Right of Civil Resistance', in Willem Nijenhuis (ed.), *Ecclesia Reformata. Studies on the Reformation*, vol. 2 (Kerkhistorische Bijdragen, 16) (Leiden, New York and Cologne, 1994), pp. 74–5, 84, 92. Although Nijenhuis concludes, 'If the honour of God is violated, resistance is required, even armed resistance by the private citizen' (ibid., p. 91), he is at all times careful to stress how exceptional this view was in the corpus of Calvin's thought. For drawing attention to this article, I am grateful to Prof. Andrew Pettegree.

4   'Exposition and Basis of the Conclusions or Articles Published by Huldrych Zwingli', Zurich, 29 January 1523, in *Selected Writings of Huldrych Zwingli*, vol. 1: *The Defense of the Reformed Faith*, ed. and trans. Edward J. Furcha (Pittsburgh Theological Monographs, n.s. 12) (Allison Park, PA, 1984), §38, p. 261. In all extracts from American translations of works cited, I have adopted British English conventions, and have silently amended infelicities and inaccuracies in these translations.

5   Ibid., §41, p. 275.

6   Ibid., §42, pp. 279–80.

such a kingdom is to have any foundation at all'.[7] I cite Zwingli verbatim, not only because there are clear echoes of the communal-collective and republican sentiments that we find in the manifestoes of the Peasants' War, but more especially to underscore the fundamental point that the views of the leading Reformers and the so-called radicals over questions of resistance or social revolution are located within a continuum. There was no caesura, merely a gradient, between Luther, Calvin or Zwingli, on one hand, and the proponents of an applied or politicized theology on the other. After all, Luke chapter 1 was normative for all the reformers: the words of the Magnificat sounded the knell of self-serving and vainglorious temporal rulers, in whose place the humble and meek should be exalted. What was at issue was agency (or, to put it more properly and in contemporary parlance, providence): who, and in what circumstances, was to initiate and carry through the transformation of the world?[8]

The choice of which radical reformers to interrogate on their views of social revolution was pragmatic: Balthasar Hubmaier, Christoph Schappeler and Hans Hergot were all involved in the Peasants' War of 1524–26, in different theatres of rebellion, and with differing theological assumptions and practical agendas. Hubmaier, whose chequered career from mariolater and instigator of an anti-Semitic pogrom in Regensburg in 1519 to Anabaptist exile in Moravia in 1526 is surely one of the most remarkable in the early history of the Reformation, offers himself as Zwinglian radical whose inchoate Anabaptist sympathies did not lead him to reject secular government or the sword; Schappeler, the Reformer of the Swabian imperial city of Memmingen, who glossed the *Twelve Articles* of the Upper Swabian peasantry, is here discussed as the author of the anonymous tract *To The Assembly of The Common Peasantry*; and lastly, the author of the utopia *On The New Transformation of A Christian Life* is considered, now presumed to have been the Nuremberg printer and colporteur Hans Hergot, who knew both Hans Denck and Hans Hut, and from whose press Müntzer's tract *A Highly Provoked Vindication and a Refutation of the Unspiritual Soft-living Flesh in Wittenberg* was issued in 1524. Though neither a cleric nor a lay preacher, Hergot's familiarity and identification with radical Reforming doctrines of Müntzerite provenance make him a suitable figure to set alongside Hubmaier and Schappeler. It may be asked: where are Müntzer and Gaismair? My decision to disregard

---

[7]   Ibid., §42, p. 279.

[8]   On resistance, see most recently Robert von Friedeburg (ed.), *Widerstandsrecht in der frühen Neuzeit. Erträge und Perspektive der Forschung im deutsch-britischen Vergleich* (Zeitschrift für historische Forschung, Beiheft 26) (Berlin, 2001); Robert von Friedeburg, *Widerstandsrecht und Konfessionskonflikt. Notwehr und Gemeiner Mann im deutsch–britischen Vergleich, 1530–1669* (Schriften zur europäischen Rechts- und Verfassungsgeschichte, 27) (Berlin, 1999).

them was, again, pragmatic. Their views – or at least their supposed views – have been well rehearsed in the existing literature, yet both men offer fragmentary and contradictory (or, at least, inconsistent) views both on the means of transforming the world, and of what a new Christian society should look like.[9] At various points in my remarks, however, I shall draw explicit comparisons with the thought of both these men as well that of other radicals.

Hubmaier

Hubmaier's involvement in the Peasants' War stemmed from his position as the Reforming preacher of the small Austrian town of Waldshut on the Rhine above Basel. From early 1523 onwards he was drawn into the controversy over true faith in Zürich, manifested in the two colloquies of January and October that year (the second of which he attended) which resulted in the defeat of the Catholic party and the Zürich magistracy's decision to throw its weight behind the Reforming cause. Hubmaier's debt to Zwingli, however, paled before the influence of more radical figures in the Zwinglian camp, notably Sebastian Hofmeister, the Reformer of Schaffhausen, but above all of a number of radicals in the Zürich countryside who advocated the application of Reforming theology to social issues, especially tithing. As the stirrings of peasant unrest gathered

---

[9]   There is no consensus on the role and function of Müntzer's leagues, or whether he was the author of the so-called *Constitutional Draft*. In addition to Quilisch, *Widerstandsrecht* (with bibliography), see Emidio Campi, '"*Foedus Christianitas causa adversus impios.*" Il concetto di patto in Thomas Müntzer', in Tommaso La Rocca (ed.), *Thomas Müntzer e la rivoluzione dell'uomo comune* (Turin, 1990), pp. 45–70. On the *Constitutional Draft*, see Tom Scott, *Thomas Müntzer. Theology and Revolution in the German Reformation* (Houndmills and London, 1989), pp. 133–7; Gottfried Seebaß, *Artikelbrief, Bundesordnung und Verfassungsentwurf. Studien zu drei zentralen Dokumenten des südwestdeutschen Bauernkrieges* (Abhandlungen der Heidelberger Akademie der Wissenschaften, phil.-hist. Klasse, 88/1) (Heidelberg, 1988). Recently, Michael Gaismair's Territorial Constitution for Tirol has likewise been caught in the crossfire of scholarly polemic: Giorgio Politi, *Gli statuti impossibili. La rivoluzione tirolese del 1525 e il 'programma' di Michael Gaismair* (Turin, 1995). See the review by Aldo Stella in *Rivista di storia della Chiesa in Italia*, 49 (1995), pp. 533–8, and his own monograph, *Il 'Bauernführer' Michael Gaismair e l'utopia di un repubblicanesimo popolare* (Annali dell'Istituto storico italo-germanico in Trento, Monografie 33) (Bologna, 1999); in addition, see Tom Scott, 'The Reformation and Modern Political Economy. Luther and Gaismair Compared', in Thomas A. Brady Jr (ed.), *Die deutsche Reformation zwischen Spätmittelalter und Früher Neuzeit* (Schriften des Historischen Kollegs: Kolloquien, 50) (Munich, 2001), pp. 173–202, esp. 184–91.

pace in the southern Black Forest in the summer of 1524, Hubmaier in Waldshut was pitched willy-nilly into the conflict.[10]

But that is where our difficulties begin. For there are no authentic Hubmaier testimonies from this period, except for the *Eighteen Axioms* of mid-1524, his explicit rejection of Catholic doctrine, liturgy and hierarchy.[11] The 'articles' supposedly composed by Hubmaier and sent by the bishop of Konstanz to the Outer Austrian government in Ensisheim were in reality a list of charges against him.[12] Instead, we are required to reconstruct his thought from the numerous writings he set down in exile in Nikolsburg from 1526 onwards, after the peasants' defeat, in circumstances where Hubmaier was not only keen to exculpate himself from charges of having fomented social unrest, but was also concerned to defend his Anabaptist doctrines against the rival interpretations of other Anabaptists, not least Hans Hut, whose brief appearance there in 1527 led to the Nikolsburg Disputation.[13] Above all, Hubmaier's *Apologia from Prison*, the account of his interrogation at Kreuzenstein Castle near Vienna in 1527 by Johann Fabri, the erstwhile vicar-general of the diocese of Konstanz and soon to be the bishop of Vienna, must be treated with caution.[14] Hubmaier was at pains to defend his views against the explicitly pacifist doctrines of Anabaptists such as Hans Hut. In his subsequent confession, extracted under torture, Hubmaier even retracted his rejection of infant baptism, and admitted to involvement in the Peasants' War. Nevertheless, he stood

---

[10]   Tom Scott, 'Reformation and Peasants' War in Waldshut: A Structural Analysis', part 1, *Archiv für Reformationsgeschichte*, 69 (1978), pp. 82–102; part 2, ibid., 70 (1979), pp. 140–69; repr. in Tom Scott, *Town, Country, and Regions in Reformation Germany* (Studies in Medieval and Reformation Traditions, 106) (Leiden and Boston, MA, 2005), pp. 3–56 (all following citations thence); Torsten Bergsten, *Balthasar Hubmaier. Anabaptist Theologian and Martyr*, ed. William R. Estep Jr and trans. Irwin J. Barnes and William R. Estep (Valley Forge, PA, 1978). The German original, *Balthasar Hubmaier. Seine Stellung zu Reformation und Täufertum 1521–28* (Acta Universitatis Upsaliensis: Studia Historico-Ecclesiastica Upsaliensa, 3) (Kassel, 1961) is vastly to be preferred.

[11]   *Balthasar Hubmaier. Theologian of Anabaptism*, ed. and trans. H. Wayne Pipkin and John H. Yoder (Classics of the Radical Reformation, 5) (Scottdale, PA and Kitchener, Ont., 1989), pp. 30–34; *Balthasar Hubmaier. Schriften*, ed. Gunnar Westin and Torsten Bergsten (Quellen und Forschungen zur Reformationsgeschichte, 29: Quellen zur Geschichte der Täufer, 9) (Gütersloh, 1962), pp. 69–74.

[12]   Carl Sachsse, *D. Balthasar Hubmaier als Theologe* (Neue Studien zur Geschichte der Theologie und der Kirche, 20) (Berlin, 1914; repr. Aalen, 1973), pp. 229–31; Scott, 'Reformation and Peasants' War in Waldshut', pp. 9, 16.

[13]   Bergsten, *Hubmaier*, ed. Estep, pp. 361–77.

[14]   *Hubmaier. Theologian*, pp. 524–62. The American editors unfortunately translate *Eine Rechenschaft des Glaubens* as *Apologia from Prison*, thereby not only obliterating the deliberate play on the reformers' 'justification by faith [alone]', but also creating potential confusion with *A Brief Apologia* (better put as *A Short Apology*).

by the views put forward in *On the Sword* (his last tract) and *The Christian Ban*, even though they sealed his fate at the stake.[15] We can therefore regard these tracts at least as authentic testimonies of Hubmaier's beliefs.

The 'articles' forwarded to Ensisheim in February 1524 are nevertheless of particular interest. They accuse Hubmaier of having preached against tithes, interest charges and rents, and of having rejected feudal lordship – even before the onset of peasant rebellion. And these charges were to dog Hubmaier throughout his career: can they be believed? After his flight to Moravia, Hubmaier composed a refutation, *A Brief Apologia*,[16] in which he affirmed that Christians should pay dues over and above what they owed rather than sow discord:

> I have never taught that subjects should not fulfil the duty and obedience due to their government. Since it is of God, who hung the sword at its side, one should without contradiction render to it tolls, duties, tribute, honour, and respect ....[17] A Christian does not quarrel or fight, rather he gives a fifth or a third, not to mention a tenth of his goods.[18]

Out of genuine brotherly love, interest should be given and taken, and the same applied to tithes. But his argument throughout was highly contingent, and in his defence of the sword – the most consistent theme in Hubmaier's Anabaptism *tout court* – he comes close to Müntzer's language:

> On the other hand I have also told the authorities to wield the sword according to the order of God for the protection of the righteous and punishment of the evil, or God will take away their mandate and mete out to them in like measure .... On the other hand I have also never taught that it is proper for the government, bishops, abbots, monks, nuns, and priests to overload their poor people, more than is godly and just, with unprecedented unchristian impositions, and to tear them away by force from the Word of God.[19]

When Hubmaier returned to the issue at the end of his career, he recounted in detail why he believed the sword was necessary:

> There are two kinds of sword in Scripture. There is a spiritual one which is used against the perfidious attacks of the devil .... In addition ... there is also an external sword which one uses for the protection of the righteous and for the terror of the evil persons here on earth. That is given to the government in order to maintain a common territorial peace .... It is also called a spiritual sword when one uses it according to the will of God. These two swords are not in opposition to each other.[20]

---

[15]   Ibid., pp. 563–5.

[16]   Ibid., pp. 296–313 ('A Brief Apologia').

[17]   Ibid., p. 304.

[18]   Ibid., p. 305.

[19]   Ibid., p. 304. On Müntzer, see *The Collected Works of Thomas Müntzer*, ed. and trans. Peter Matheson (Edinburgh, 1988): 'Sermon to the Princes (Exposition of the Second Chapter of Daniel)', p. 250; 'A Highly Provoked Vindication and Refutation', p. 335.

[20]   *Hubmaier. Theologian*, pp. 509–10 ('On The Sword').

In effect, Hubmaier believed that while only Christians were likely to exercise just government, the sword remained an imperfect instrument of rule in an imperfect world, and that it was the duty of the God-fearing to rid themselves of tyrants if that could be achieved without a serious breakdown of public order:

> However, if a government is childish or foolish, yea, if perchance it is not competent at all to reign, then you may escape from it legitimately and accept another, if it is good .... If the seeking of another cannot be done lawfully and peacefully, and also not without great damage and rebellion, then one must endure it, as the one which God has given us in his wrath, and as if he desires to chastise us on account of our sins.[21]

That is exactly what Zwingli had said, and indeed Hubmaier's verdict is couched in part word-for-word in the language of Zwingli's *Exposition*.[22]

Hubmaier was the only theologian of the early Reformation to place the Christian doctrine of the spiritual ban at the centre of his teaching, even though the ban was a fundamental aspect of Christian ministry, as set forth in Matthew 18:15–17, and echoed in many of Paul's epistles, and those of other apostles.[23] The reluctance of the reformers to embrace the ban is easily explained if we look at the situation in Strasbourg. There the radicals were pressing Bucer, who was not opposed to the use of the greater and lesser ban as such, since they lay with the logic of the priesthood of all believers, to make it the prime instrument of Church discipline. But the Anabaptists in the city wanted to go further: to use the ban as a means of separating themselves from the supervision of the city's magistrates into a gathered and autonomous community of the elect. As George Williams has sardonically observed, the evangelical magistrates, 'after being liberated from the menace of the papal ban', were not inclined to embrace this form of strict clericism. The ban, in other words, had largely been discredited by papal abuse; only among the Anabaptists, from the *Schleitheim Confession* onwards, did it become the hallmark of their separation and exclusiveness, especially in the case of Menno Simons, described by Williams as the 'theologian of the ban', and of the Dutch Anabaptists.[24]

Hubmaier's doctrine of the ban, expounded in Nikolsburg both in *A Christian Catechism* and *On the Christian Ban* and repeated in his *Apologia*

---

[21]   Ibid., p. 520.

[22]   James M. Stayer, *Anabaptists and the Sword*, 2nd edn (Lawrence, KS, 1976), p. 144; James M. Stayer, *The German Peasants' War and Anabaptist Community of Goods* (McGill-Queen's Studies in the History of Religion, 6) (Montreal, Kingston, Ont., London, Ont. and Buffalo, NY, 1991), p. 70.

[23]   The biblical references given in Hubmaier's Apologia, *Hubmaier. Theologian*, pp. 555–6, are: Matt. 18:15–18; 1 Cor. 5; 2 Cor. 2:7; 1 Tim. 1:20; 2 Thess. 3:6; Titus 3:10; 2 John 1:10.

[24]   George H. Williams, *The Radical Reformation* (Philadelphia, PA, 1962), pp. 250, 282, 396, 485–99.

from Prison,[25] is entirely conventional: the three stages, admonition by a fellow Christian in private, admonition in the presence of three witnesses, and finally admonition publicly before the congregation, correspond to the passage in Matthew. Our interest in Hubmaier's use of the ban lies elsewhere: in the fact that the peasant rebels in the Black Forest – from the spring of 1525 styling themselves the Christian Union of the Black Forest – adopted a secular version of the ban, most visibly in the so-called *Letter of Articles* which they sent to the town of Villingen on 8 May, exhorting it to join their Christian Union on pain of ostracism:

The secular ban runs as follows:

> All those who are in this Christian Union shall, by the honour and highest obligations which they have undertaken, hold and practise no communion of any kind with those who refuse and oppose admittance to this Christian Union and the furthering of the common Christian weal, to wit, by eating, drinking, bathing, milling, baking, ploughing, reaping, or by supplying or letting others supply them with food, grain, drink, wood, meat, salt, etc., or by buying from or selling to them. In those matters which do not promote, but rather retard, the common Christian weal and public peace they shall be treated as severed and dead limbs.

> They shall also be barred from all markets, forest, meadow, pasture, and water which does not lie within their jurisdictions.

> And whoever having joined the Union disregards these provisions shall himself henceforth be expelled, punished with the same ban, and with wife and children be handed over to the recalcitrant and obdurate.

The *Letter of Articles* concludes:

> Item, all those who shelter, abet, and support the enemies of this Christian Union shall likewise be called upon in a friendly manner to desist, but if they refuse, they too shall immediately be proclaimed as [falling] under the secular ban.[26]

Hubmaier's modern biographer, Torsten Bergsten, was at pains to dissociate him from any hand in composing either the *Letter of Articles* or the so-called *Constitutional Draft* (now ascribed to Thomas Müntzer), but as I have argued elsewhere, the diction of the secular ban so closely resembles Hubmaier's doctrine of the spiritual ban that is hard to see where else the peasants could have derived it. Bergsten's view that they were simply simultaneous phenomena based on a common New Testament source looks like special pleading.[27]

---

[25]   *Hubmaier. Theologian*, pp. 339–65, 409–25, 524–62. See also 'On Brotherly Punishment' (Nikolsburg, 1527), ibid., pp. 372–85, at 375, 378–9.

[26]   *The German Peasants' War: A History in Documents*, ed. and trans. Tom Scott and Bob Scribner (Atlantic Highlands, NJ and London, 1991), pp. 136–7.

[27]   Bergsten, *Hubmaier*, ed. Estep, pp. 213–14, 216–25 (German original, pp. 285–301); Scott, 'Reformation and Peasants' War in Waldshut', p. 33.

This is not the place to explore the notorious problems of sources and interpretation surrounding the *Letter of Articles* and *Constitutional Draft* in any detail. James Stayer has pointed to the verbal parallels between the description of the secular ban and Hubmaier's subsequent *A Christian Catechism*, where to the rhetorical question 'What is the ban?' came the reply: 'No fellowship, either in word, eating, drinking, grinding, baking, or any other form.'[28] It is true that the phrase 'severed and dead limbs' (*abgeschnittene gestorbene Glieder*) is not Hubmaier's, who speaks rather of 'offensive, disorderly, and poisonous persons' (*unordenliche, ärgerliche und aussätzige Menschen*): here, 'leprous' would be a much more pointed translation than 'poisonous'![29] 'Severed and dead limbs', however, echoes a formula common to ecclesiastical excommunications, and in any case has biblical connotations.[30]

Given the indisputable connection between Hubmaier's spiritual ban and the peasants' invocation of the secular ban – those selfsame peasants who under their fiery commander Hans Müller of Bulgenbach had twice the previous autumn staged demonstration marches to Waldshut in a show of solidarity[31] – it perhaps matters less whether Hubmaier actually composed the *Letter of Articles*. Nevertheless, there is an emerging consensus in recent scholarship that Hubmaier was indeed their author, and those who dissent do so because they believe instead that he had a hand in the *Constitutional Draft*![32] Certainly, a theologian as composer of the secular ban is rendered more likely by the fact that the peasants, as Gottfried Seebaß has remarked, could perfectly well have had recourse to a simple declaration of outlawry (*Acht*), an entirely commonplace device:[33] no other peasant troop apart from the Christian Union of the Black Forest ever invoked the secular ban.[34] From early April 1525, however, the Black

---

[28]   Stayer, *German Peasants' War*, p. 71; *Hubmaier. Theologian*, p. 353. 'Grinding' could equally well be rendered as 'milling'.

[29]   Ibid., p. 353 ('A Christian Catechism'); cf. *Hubmaier. Schriften*, p. 316.

[30]   Seebaß, *Artikelbrief, Bundesordnung und Verfassungsentwurf*, p. 150.

[31]   Scott, 'Reformation and Peasants' War in Waldshut', pp. 16–20.

[32]   Seebaß, *Artikelbrief, Bundesordnung und Verfassungsentwurf*, pp. 175–7; Stayer, *German Peasants' War*, p. 69; Scott, 'Reformation and Peasants' War in Waldshut', pp. 33–4. Hubmaier is advanced as the author of the *Constitutional Draft* by Peter Blickle, *Die Revolution von 1525*, 4th edn (Munich, 2004), pp. 226–8. Seebaß's view that Hubmaier must have known the *Constitutional Draft* (which also mentions the secular ban) is not compelling, since the doctrine of the ban could just as easily have been communicated by Hubmaier to Müntzer during the latter's stay on the Upper Rhine over the winter of 1524/25, with Müntzer then recasting it in a more radical fashion; Seebaß, *Artikelbrief, Bundesordnung und Verfassungsentwurf*, pp. 158, 177.

[33]   Ibid., p. 150.

[34]   Several peasant troops not only threatened their lords with *Heimsuchung* (the equivalent in Scots law of hamesucken, though directed here against things, not persons), but also with *Verpfählung*, banning by driving a stake before their

Forest peasants were already acting in a way which went well beyond the provisions of the secular ban. Rather than isolating or ostracizing the renitent, they were compelling them to join the Christian Union.[35] Moreover, the provisions of the so-called 'castle article' in the *Letter of Articles*, which ostensibly extended fellowship to those who joined the Christian Union as common brothers,[36] were quickly overtaken by events, as the rebels set about destroying the castles and convents that lay on their march route.[37]

Although Hubmaier cannot be regarded in any sense as a direct champion of the peasants' cause – he neither drew up articles of grievance nor furnished biblical glosses to support the same – it is clear that in his ministry he was an outspoken advocate of godly justice and Christian equality, and that he was prepared to offer the peasants an instrument with which to advance their cause, namely the concept of the secular ban, whether or not he actually composed the *Letter of Articles*. Since he regarded the spiritual and temporal swords as two sides of the same coin, is it implausible to suggest that Hubmaier may have viewed the spiritual and secular bans in the same light, given that his *A Christian Catechism* came close in its language to the secular ban?

Schappeler

When we turn to Christoph Schappeler, we are able to draw upon the results of very recent research. It is well known that Schappeler had preached

---

doors, and that could be directed at peasants as well. However, *Verpfählung*, a commonplace medieval practice, is not the same as the secular ban, a verbally proclaimed form of excommunication. The only instance of a coupling of 'Bann und Acht' in the peasants' actions comes in a letter by the officials of Bregenz to Archduke Ferdinand of Austria, 21 March 1525; Günther Franz (ed.), *Der deutsche Bauernkrieg. Aktenband*, 2nd edn (Darmstadt, 1968), p. 174, no. 36. See Stephan Nitz, 'Handlungsfähigkeit im Deutschen Bauernkrieg. Vorstellungen des gemeinen Mannes von den Bedingungen des Aufstandes' (PhD, Frankfurt am Main, 1979), pp. 138–9. The secular ban may have struck a chord with peasants already familiar with the custom of *Verpfählung*. I am grateful to Dr H.J. Cohn for drawing my attention to this reference.

[35]   Seebaß, *Artikelbrief, Bundesordnung und Verfassungsentewurf*, p. 174.

[36]   *German Peasants' War: Documents*, p. 137: 'Concerning castles, convents, and clerical institutions: Whereas all treachery, coercion and depravity befalls us and stems from castles, convents, and clerical institutions, they shall from this hour hence be placed under the ban. If, however, nobles, monks, or priests are willing to quit their castles, convents, and foundations and take up residence in common houses, as other foreign persons, and join this Christian Union, they shall be cordially and righteously admitted with all their goods and chattels. Thereafter everything which befits and belongs to them by godly law shall be accorded to them faithfully and honourably without let or hindrance.'

[37]   Cf. Seebaß, *Artikelbrief, Bundesordnung und Verfassungsentwurf*, p. 174.

against tithes on his return from the Second Colloquy of Zürich in October 1523, over which he had presided, and that he provided the introduction and conclusion to the *Twelve Articles* of the Upper Swabian peasants, and the biblical citations to support the individual articles.[38] What has emerged (after several half-baked attempts to attribute the tract to Karlstadt)[39] is that Schappeler was almost certainly the author of the anonymous *To The Assembly of The Common Peasantry*, composed at the height of the conflict in late April or early May 1525.[40] Those who have studied this tract have always identified themes that suggest Schappeler as the likely author, as well as noting obvious echoes of the *Twelve Articles*.[41]

---

[38]   *Akten zur Geschichte des deutschen Bauernkrieges aus Oberschwaben*, ed. Franz Ludwig Baumann (Freiburg im Breisgau, 1877), pp. 1–2 (no. 2); Martin Brecht, 'Der theologische Hintergrund der Zwölf Artikel der Bauernschaft in Schwaben von 1525. Christoph Schappeler und Sebastian Lotzers Beitrag', *Zeitschrift für Kirchengeschichte*, 85 (1974), pp. 174–208; Blickle, *Revolution von 1525*, pp. 166–9.

[39]   Christian Peters, 'An die Versammlung gemeiner Bauernschaft (1525). Ein Vorschlag zur Verfasserfrage', *Zeitschrift für bayerische Kirchengeschichte*, 54 (1985), pp. 15–28; Siegfried Hoyer, 'Karlstadt: Verfasser der Flugschrift "An die Versammlung gemeiner Bauernschaft"?', *Zeitschrift für Geschichtswissenschaft*, 35 (1987), pp. 128–37; Christian Peters, 'An die Versammlung gemeiner Bauernschaft (1525). Noch einmal – zur Verfasserfrage', *Zeitschrift für bayerische Kirchengeschichte*, 57 (1988), pp. 1–7.

[40]   The best modern German edition is in the appendix to Horst Buszello, *Der deutsche Bauernkrieg von 1525 als politische Bewegung. Mit besonderer Berücksichtigung der anonymen Flugschrift An die Versamlung gemayner Pawerschafft* (Studien zur europäischen Geschichte, 8) (Berlin, 1969), pp. 150–92. Further editions: *Flugschriften der Bauernkriegszeit*, ed. Adolf Laube and Hans Werner Seiffert, 2nd edn (Cologne and Vienna, 1978), pp. 112–34, 582–5; *An die Versammlung gemeiner Bauernschaft. Eine revolutionäre Flugschrift aus dem deutschen Bauernkrieg (1525)*, ed. Siegfried Hoyer and Bernd Rüdiger (Leipzig, 1975). This edition contains a useful linguistic analysis of the text by M.M. Guchmann, pp. 57–78. English trans. in *The Radical Reformation*, ed. and trans. Michael G. Baylor (Cambridge, 1991), pp. 101–29; excerpts in *German Peasants' War: Documents*, pp. 269–76.

[41]   Buszello, *Der deutsche Bauernkrieg*; Siegfried Hoyer, 'The Rights and Duties of Resistance in the Pamphlet *To the Assembly of the Common Peasantry (1525)*', in Bob Scribner and Gerhard Benecke (eds), *The German Peasant War: New Viewpoints* (London, 1979), pp. 123–36. Schappeler had hitherto been disqualified as the author on textual grounds, inasmuch as the one supposedly authentic text by him, *Auflösung etlicher argument*, is linguistically inconsistent with *To The Assembly of The Common Peasantry*. Now that the former tract has confidently been ascribed to Lazarus Spengler (*Lazarus Spengler. Schriften*, 1, ed. Bernd Hamm and Wolfgang Huber, Heidelberg, 1995, p. 354), the way is free for Schappeler to be brought into the frame as the true author. See Peter Blickle, 'Republiktheorie aus revolutionärer Erfahrung (1525)', in Peter Blickle (ed.), *Verborgene republikanische Traditionen in Oberschwaben* (Oberschwaben – Geschichte und Kultur, 4) (Tübingen, 1998), pp. 195–210, esp. 206–7. See also Peter Blickle, '*Es sol der Schwanberg noch mitten in Schweitz ligen*. Schweizer

The main objection to Schappeler as author – aside from an alleged linguistic incompatibility, now resolved – is that he must have changed his views radically between glossing the *Twelve Articles* and drafting a tract which is held to disavow the legitimacy of peasant rebellion. This view is based on a false contrast. From the outset, Schappeler was a committed adherent of Reforming doctrines, especially in so far as they challenged the position of the Catholic Church,[42] but unrest within Memmingen's own dependent rural territory confronted both Schappeler and the council with difficult decisions: the latter believed that it could not prevent an alliance between its peasants and sections of the citizenry.[43] In this context, Schappeler's counsel, to defend only if attacked, makes perfect sense, but his exhortation to the peasantry took a different tack.[44]

The subtitle of *To The Assembly of The Common Peasantry* sets out the tract's purpose: whether the rebellion (which had already broken out) was justified, and what obligations the peasants owed to the authorities, based on Scripture. In point of fact, the tract invokes three ancient histories: besides the Old Testament, we read of Babylon under King Ninus, and of imperial Rome, though Schappeler confuses the history of the hereditary rulers of Babylon from its founders, Semiramis and Ninus, with the Old Testament, for he equates Ninus with Nimrod, and Babylon with Babel. It has been assumed that Schappeler derived his material from Hartmann Schedel's *World Chronicle*, published by Anton Koberger in Nuremberg in 1493.[45] It seems likely, however, that Schappeler drew upon, and conflated,

---

Einflüsse auf den deutschen Bauernkrieg', *Jahrbuch für fränkische Landesforschung*, 60 (2000), pp. 113–25 (Festschrift Rudolf Endres).

[42] Barbara Kroemer, 'Die Einführung der Reformation in Memmingen. Über die Bedeutung ihrer sozialen, wirtschaftlichen und politischen Faktoren', *Memminger Geschichtsblätter*, 1980, pp. 3–226, esp. 87ff., 93ff; Justus Maurer, *Prediger im Bauernkrieg* (Calwer Theologische Monographien, 5) (Stuttgart, 1979), pp. 386–99. (Maurer strongly rejects Schappeler as author of *To The Assembly of The Common Peasantry*.)

[43] Kroemer, 'Einführung der Reformation in Memmingen', p. 128; cf. Rolf Kießling, *Die Stadt und ihr Land. Umlandpolitik, Bürgerbesitz und Wirtschaftsgefüge in Ostschwaben vom 14. bis ins 16. Jahrhundert* (Städteforschung. Veröffentlichungen des Instituts für vergleichende Städtegeschichte in Münster, A 29) (Cologne and Vienna, 1989), pp. 776–81.

[44] The approach of the forces of the Swabian League at the beginning of June 1525 caused Schappeler to flee across the border to his hometown of Sankt Gallen in Switzerland, after which he became a loyal and conventional follower of Huldrych Zwingli. Kroemer; 'Einführung der Reformation in Memmingen', pp 130–31.

[45] Hartmann Schedel, *Das buch der Cronicken und gedechtnus wirdigern geschichtgen von anbegynn bis auf dise vnßere zeit* (Nuremberg, 1493). See Thomas A. Brady Jr, 'German Civic Humanism? Critique of Monarchy and Refashioning of History in the Shadow of the German Peasants' War (1525)', in Michael Erbe, Hans Füglister, Katharina Furrer, Andreas Staehelin, Regina Wecker and Christian

several different accounts, including the Strasbourg chronicler, Jakob Twinger von Königshofen, all of which, in narrating of the history of the early Roman emperors as persecutors of Christians, derived ultimately from Orosius.[46]

Schappeler begins his tract, it is true, by exhorting the peasants to remain at peace, to render under Caesar that which is Caesar's, and to remember that authority is ordained by God. For that reason, the tract has usually been dismissed as disavowing social revolution. But, for Schappeler, these are merely the necessary preliminaries to a discussion of what true rulership entails. Only the unChristian way of life, as the heading to chapter 2 declares, requires human authority. Schappeler then develops a subtle dialectic: all lordship is stewardship, and therefore contingent upon its rightful exercise, while obedience is due to authority as a duty to the common weal and brotherly love; there is no justification for obedience other than this service. Having cleared the decks to avoid any misunderstanding – the accusation of provoking illegitimate rebellion – Schappeler turns in chapter 4 to his essential theme, 'On false and unlimited power, which one is not obliged to obey':

> Therefore whichever prince or lord invents and sets up his own self-serving burdens and commands rules falsely, and he dares impudently to deceive God, his own lord .... This year a labour-service is voluntary, next year it becomes compulsory .... In what dementia or disguise did God, your lord, give you such power that we poor people have to cultivate your lands with labour-services? But only in good weather, for on rainy days we poor people see the fruits of our sweat rot in the fields. May God in his justice not tolerate the terrible Babylonian captivity in which we poor people are driven to mow the lords' meadows, to make hay, to plough the fields, to sow flax in them, to pull it, hackle it, ret it, wash it, break it, and spin it – yes, even to sew their underpants on their arses. We also have to pick peas and harvest carrots and asparagus.

> God help us! Where has such misery ever been heard of! They tax and tear out the marrow of the poor people's bones, and we have to pay interest on that! Where are they, with their hired murderers and horsemen, the gamblers and

---

Windeler (eds), *Querdenken: Dissens und Toleranz im Wandel der Geschichte. Festschrift zum 65. Geburtstag von Hans R. Guggisberg* (Mannheim, 1996), pp. 41–55, esp. 53.

[46]   Schappeler states that there were 76 emperors from Julius Caesar to Charlemagne, whereas Schedel lists 92 (or rather 91, since he lists Lucius Aurelius Commodus twice). The figure of 76 comes much closer to the enumeration given by Jakob Twinger von Königshofen, who counts 71 emperors up to Leo, ignores the subsequent Byzantine emperors, but then loses his thread, describing Charlemagne's son Louis as 72nd emperor, and Charles the Fat, son of Louis the German, as 76th; Karl Hegel (ed.), *Die Chroniken der oberrheinischen Städte: Straßburg*, 2 (*Die Chroniken der deutschen Städte vom 14. bis ins 16. Jahrhundert*, 8) (Leipzig, 1870; repr. Göttingen, 1961), pp. 331ff., 408, 413. For Orosius, see *Pauli Orosii Historiarum adversum paganos libri VII*, ed. Karl Zangmeister (Corpus Scriptorum Ecclesiasticorum Latinorum, 5) (Vienna, 1882).

whoremasters, who are stuffed fuller than puking dogs? In addition, we poor people have to give them taxes, renders, and interest. And at home the poor should have neither bread, salt, nor lard for their wives and small children. Where are they with their entry-fines and heriots? ... Where are the tyrants and raging ones, who appropriate taxes, customs-dues, and excises, and waste and squander shamefully and wantonly what should go into the common chest or purse to serve the needs of the territory?[47]

The echoes of peasant grievances, especially those of the Stühlingen and Kißlegg peasants,[48] are impossible to ignore, and the language is as intemperate as Müntzer's. Princes both ecclesiastical and temporal feel the lash of Schappeler's tongue: bishops as sheep-biters (a pun on *bischoff/ beyßschoff*) and secular tyrants as werewolves.[49] Indeed, the origins of the Swiss Confederation, the tract argues, lay in the unlimited, tyrannical power of the nobility.

The theme of Swiss republican liberty – for Schappeler, the ideal polity – is taken up in chapter 5, where he dwells upon the atrocities of the early Roman emperors – not merely the well-known tyrants Caligula and Nero, but more obscure ones as well, Vitellius and Galba, alongside Zwingli's chosen Domitian and Maximinian – to make the point that the republican virtue of Rome had been irredeemably corrupted by the institution of hereditary imperial rule. Why is the example of Rome so significant? Because, says Schappeler: 'I am showing all this here only because all the great lords usually pride themselves on their ancient, pre-eminent descent from Rome. Yes, they pride themselves on an ancient, heathen descent.'[50] Chapter 5 is the pivot of *To The Assembly of The Common Peasantry* because it creates the ideological pedigree from Scripture and ancient history for the practical – and burning – question of how tyrants should be deposed. After a somewhat discordant excursus in chapter 6 on whether game belongs to the common man, Schappeler begins chapter 7 with the ringing declaration:

> Now to the heart of the matter! ... [T]o knock people such as Moab, Agag, Ahab, and Nero from their thrones is God's highest pleasure.

---

[47]   *Radical Reformation*, ed. Baylor, pp. 108–9. 'Dementia and disguise' (*dementin und lodex*) repeats the pun on 'the blabbering scribes with their *Clementin und codex*', first mentioned at p. 103. *Lodex* is a blanket; Baylor prefers to translate it as 'camouflage'. Laube and Seiffert bizarrely suggest that *Lodex* should be construed as *Lotterigkeit* ('slovenliness'): *Flugschriften der Bauernkriegszeit*, p. 583.

[48]   *German Peasants' War: Documents*, pp. 65–72, 82–5.

[49]   *Radical Reformation*, ed. Baylor, p. 110.

[50]   Ibid., pp. 112–14, here at 114. Cf. Brady, 'German Civic Humanism?', p. 51.

I will prove that a territory or community has the power to depose its pernicious lords by introducing thirteen sayings drawn from divine law, which the gates of hell with all their knights cannot destroy.[51]

Citing Joshua, and numerous passages from the New Testament, Schappeler insists that the command that 'those whom Christ upbraided ... as dogs and swine should be thrown from their thrones' does not refer merely to spiritual matters.[52] In chapter 8 he urges the common people to depose their tyrannous lords, provided 'you dear brothers do not engage in this insurrection in order to enrich yourselves with the property of others, or your hearts will turn false .... Come together only for the sake of the common peace of the land and to practise Christian freedom.'[53]

Schappeler is concerned that the peasants be not deterred from their duty by specious charges of rebellion: 'No rebellion has ever taken place among the subjects of a Christian lord who rules well. It has only occurred under wastrels and godless tyrants.'[54] But he avers that recent revolts in central Europe – he instances the revolt in Hungary under György Dózsa in 1514 as well as the Wendish revolt in Carniola the following year, and not least on their own doorstep the Poor Conrad revolt in Württemberg (1514) – have all failed and brought misery and hardship to the rebels 'through their own equivocating disloyalty'. Their maxim must be to keep 'brotherly fidelity with one another' – exactly as the *Federal Ordinance* of the Upper Swabian peasantry, the sister document to the *Twelve Articles*, enjoined.[55] Indeed, in the final chapter, chapter 11, Schappeler even gives detailed instructions on how to maintain discipline in the peasant troops:

> In truth, necessity requires good order. Always establish a platoon-leader over every ten men and a centurion over every ten platoon-leaders. Also establish a captain over every ten centurions, and over every ten captains a general, and so forth. In truth, such an order often brings good fruits to a common band.

> Again, everyone should be diligent and obedient to his authority [in the peasant army]. Hold general assemblies among yourselves often, for nothing strengthens and holds together the common band more heartily.[56]

These communal-corporative or federal motifs are the hallmark of peasant republican consciousness on the Swiss borderlands.

In sum, it is the Swiss who offer the model of valour and piety to which the peasants should aspire:

---

[51] *Radical Reformation*, ed. Baylor, pp. 118–19.

[52] Ibid., pp. 120, 121.

[53] Ibid., p. 122.

[54] Ibid., p. 124.

[55] Ibid., p. 127. See Buszello, *Der deutsche Bauernkrieg*, pp. 115–16; Hoyer, 'Rights and Duties', pp. 125–8.

[56] *Radical Reformation*, ed. Baylor, pp. 126–7.

[H]ow often great, ineffable deeds have been performed by that poor little band of peasants, your neighbours, the Swiss. How often their enemies have bragged when in their cups of defeating them .... But in most cases their enemies have been put to flight everywhere. And king, emperor, princes, and lords have turned themselves into laughing-stocks, no matter how mighty and how well-armed was the great force they sent into the field against them. And as often as these aforesaid Swiss fought for themselves, for their country, wives, and children, and had to protect themselves from proud power, in most cases they always triumphed and gained great honour. Without a doubt all this has occurred through the power and providence of God. Otherwise, how could the Swiss Confederation, which still increases daily, have grown constantly from only three simple peasants?[57]

Yet Schappeler cautions against triumphalism: the lowing of the famous cow on the Schwanberg may confirm the saying 'What increases the Swiss but the greed of the lords?':

But the present-day Swiss, on the contrary, have won very few victories since they left the paths of their forefathers. Rather, they have become a mockery, for they have marched out of their land and into the armies of other lords for money. Thus, he who does not want to recognize that both the victory and the defeat of the Swiss are God's work, is blind with seeing eyes and deaf with open ears.[58]

Not only does Schappeler echo Zwingli's theology, he endorses his condemnation of mercenary service as well!

The anonymity of the author of *To The Assembly of The Common Peasantry* until its recent ascription to Schappeler has undoubtedly contributed to its relative neglect by modern scholars. All serious collections of sources on the Peasants' War naturally include the tract, but even Horst Buszello's analysis of political ideas in the War, which was keen to identify Schappeler as author, has little to say about the thrust and ideology of the work as such.[59] That is perhaps understandable: its structure and its diction are somewhat uneven. In Tom Brady's words, as a treatise on republicanism it has neither the rhetorical polish nor the neo-Ciceronian Latin of a Leonardo Bruni.[60] Yet the recent identification of Schappeler as author pitches the tract into the centre of political discourse about communalism and republicanism in Upper Germany. Schappeler *is* an advocate of social revolution, in exactly the same manner as Zwingli: that is, the right of the guardians of the common weal to depose collectively unchristian and unjust rulers. Unlike Hubmaier, who lent comfort from a distance, Schappeler actively defends the peasants' uprising, viewing it as

---

[57]   Ibid., p. 128. Baylor entirely misconstrues the phrase 'Wie oft hatt man sy mit grossem pracht hyndter dem wein geschlagen' to imply that their enemies *did* defeat them!

[58]   Ibid., pp. 128–9.

[59]   Buszello, *Der deutsche Bauernkrieg*, pp. 92–125.

[60]   Brady, 'German Civic Humanism?', p. 52.

both equitable and justified in the light of the suppression of the Gospel and of the temporal oppression of the common man.[61]

Among recent writers, only Victor Thiessen has fully acknowledged the radicalism of the tract; though still handicapped by ignorance of Schappeler as author, he recognized the affinities with the *Twelve Articles*.[62] While Thiessen insists that Schappeler's remarks on military discipline rested upon a doctrine of legitimate defence rather than active aggression, it is hard to believe that Schappeler – in the context of open hostilities – disavowed the armed struggle, not least since unjust rulers were not only to be deposed, but slaughtered. But even Thiessen does not quite have the confidence of his own arguments:

> Only unity would give the resistance a chance of victory. Bold strokes of military derring-do were not possible, given the strength of the opposing forces. The resistance had not begun as a violent revolution, and our author had no intention of calling for bloody aggression by the commoners. He knew well, however, that compromise was out of the question. All bluffs had been called, and the stakes had been set. The conflict was upon them, and the outcome was by no means assured.[63]

This argument is surely contradicted by the invocation of the valiant Swiss in defence of their homeland. As long as they remained united, they prevailed; only the lure of pensions from mercenary service had led them astray. Thiessen nevertheless concludes:

> Our pamphlet professed a most radical rejection of the established feudal system. That this categoric rejection of the status quo was not followed up by a call to armed insurrection need not be interpreted as a lack of revolutionary insight. Instead, our author's approval of defensive military action reflects the realistic approach of a disillusioned reformer whose hopes for change rested on the outcome of an undesirable civil war.[64]

These views, it strikes me, have no basis in the tract itself. Schappeler had been closely involved from the outset in the legitimization of peasant revolution; his flight into Switzerland and subsequent Zwinglian loyalism may attest to his lack of mettle (or disillusion), but there is no reason to

---

[61]   I cannot therefore agree with Buszello's all too cautious verdict: 'Dem Autor ist es in seinem Anruf an die Bauern nur um die Bewahrung vor Tyrannei und Vergewaltigung von seiten der Obrigkeiten zu tun. Von allen Bestrebungen genereller wirtschaftlicher Neuordnung (Gütergleichheit, Gütergemeinschaft) setzt er sich ab' – a classically Marxist verdict from a bourgeois historian! Buszello, *Der deutsche Bauernkrieg*, p. 116.

[62]   Victor D. Thiessen, '*To the Assembly of Common Peasantry*: The Case of the Missing Context', *Archiv für Reformationsgeschichte*, 86 (1995), pp. 175–98. Thiessen also seems to regard the tract as Franconian in origin, following Christian Peters, rather than Swabian, which on dialect grounds alone is implausible; ibid., p. 175.

[63]   Ibid., pp. 193–4.

[64]   Ibid., p. 197.

think that he saw the peasants' cause as anything other than righteous until defeat stared them in the face with the advance of the forces of the Swabian League.

Hergot

Hubmaier and Schappeler were both concerned to detail the appropriate means of resistance to feudal authority and the circumstances in which such resistance could be justified. Hans Hergot, by contrast, has strikingly little to say about either issue. Instead, *On The New Transformation of A Christian Life*, which can confidently be ascribed to him, is a tract that seems to fall into two halves.[65] The first section sketches Hergot's vision of a Christian utopia and the place of the common man within it, while the second, rather disjointedly composed, seeks to apportion blame for the present misery of the common people and to describe how retribution will unfold.

For Hergot, the legitimacy of social revolution and the use of force are taken for granted, or rather, they are located within a historical teleology that makes revolution immanent and ineluctable. The very first lines of *On The New Transformation*, with their Joachite vision of the three ages of the world, set the metaphysical and intellectual framework for the entire tract:

> Three transformations have taken place. God the Father brought about the first with the Old Testament. God the Son brought about the second transformation of the world in the New Testament. The Holy Spirit will bring about the third change with a future transformation of the wickedness of them that dwell therein.[66]

Hergot's vision, however, was also conditioned by being written in the wake of the peasants' defeat. From his encounters with both Hans Denck and Hans Hut, and as the printer of Müntzer's *Vindication and Refutation*, Hergot inhabits a world of visionary spiritualism far removed from that of Huldrych Zwingli. Nevertheless, Hergot is not a chiliast; rather, he offers a blueprint for the transformation of human society which, while utopian, contains proposals both detailed and in some particulars realizable that

---

[65]   The ascription is shared by all modern scholars, though it cannot be proven. The tract was printed in Leipzig in 1527, where Hergot was arrested and executed.

[66]   *Radical Reformation*, ed. Baylor, p. 210. Baylor's translation of this tract is semantically and syntactically at sea, and I have frequently been obliged to alter his style. For instance, in this extract he translates 'wandlung von yhrem argen do sie yetzo ynnen seynd' as 'transformation of the bad situation in which people now find themselves', thereby failing to see that *Argen* is in fact a quotation from Jeremiah 12:4. The German text is contained in *Flugschriften der Bauernkriegszeit*, pp. 547–57, 642–3.

bring him close to Eberlin von Günzburg's *Wolfaria*, or indeed to Michael Gaismair's *Territorial Constitution for Tirol* with its unmistakable Zwinglian influences.[67]

Several scholars have argued that *On The New Transformation* is incoherent, or at least inconsistent, since the utopian blueprint precedes the polemic against the prevailing social order, whereas one might have expected the running order to have been reversed; Peter Blickle has even argued that the two sections are not connected at all.[68] In actual fact, the argument of the tract is entirely logical, for if the God-directed transformation of world is not achieved, then God's wrath will no longer be vented on the oppressors by his chosen agents, a 'nobility of virtue' and the common people, but by an avenger altogether more terrible, namely those unvirtuous outcasts, the Turks and the heathens. Hence, what appears to be inconsistent in fact follows a logical sequence to its inexorable conclusion. Such confusion as may be discerned comes rather from the tract's muddled composition, for already in the first, utopian, section Hergot addresses the crucial issue of *how* the transformation is to be achieved, only to elaborate it in the second, polemical, section. The establishment of a classless society without private property will be accomplished by force, as Hergot indicates when he urges the common people not to destroy the fabric of convents, since they are subsequently to be turned into hospitals:

> [N]o part of these buildings is [to be] destroyed in this insurrection of the people …. To construct this order will be a praiseworthy task of the 'nobility of virtue'; the great cities will be instruments of the countryside; and the master of the construction will be God and the common people. Thus all sectional interests will be overthrown and forged into a single unity … Thereat the people will be moved by fear and love of God to begin to destroy selfish interests and to elevate the common good.[69]

Still, a taint of imprecision remains. God and the common people will bring about the transformation, but how are the latter to co-operate with the 'nobility of virtue' (who will replace the nobility of birth)? Are we to assume that the 'nobility of virtue' (whoever they may be) should act as leaders of the common people, or are we to envisage a league between them, in the manner of Müntzer's leagues, where the feudal nobility were to be admitted if they surrendered their castles and joined as common brothers?[70] Hergot does not provide an answer.

---

[67]   The comparisons, which can be extended to Thomas More, are drawn out by Ferdinand Seibt, *Utopica. Modelle totaler Sozialplanung* (Düsseldorf, 1972), pp. 90–104.

[68]   Blickle, *Revolution von 1525*, p. 233.

[69]   *Radical Reformation*, ed. Baylor, pp. 217–18.

[70]   See Scott, *Müntzer*, esp. pp. 157–8; Seibt, *Utopica*, p. 92.

In his second section, Hergot indeed seeks, deliberately in the light of their defeat, to downplay the impact of the peasants' revolutionary violence: 'People say that the peasants are responsible for the upheaval, but I reply "no". Peasants armed with flails certainly do not destroy walls.'[71] Hergot then attempts, in a bold stroke, to turn the charge of insurrection levelled against the peasants on its head (who have in any case already paid a heavy price):

> The Lord says in the Gospel, 'But the very hairs of your head are all numbered'; since that is God's will, then it has always been so ordained. Since the peasants rather than others have acted, so must it always have been ordained. But if it [the rebellion] did not come of God, verily I would affirm that the scribes were more responsible than the peasants.[72]

Hergot's tirade against the scribes, which he then develops at length and with vehemence, is the least coherent passage of his tract. Who are these scribes who are the cause of unrest, and why should they be so fractious? Is Hergot merely echoing Müntzer's denunciation of the learned biblicists such as Luther in his *Manifest Exposé of False Faith* and again in his *Vindication and Refutation*?[73] If so, is he laying a positive charge – that the Gospel was a Gospel of social unrest (to borrow Heiko Oberman's term: surely inconceivable!), or a negative charge – that the promised freedom of a Christian had been frustrated by the main reformers' exhortation to renounce rebellion and violence? And if the latter, has Hergot's vision become so distorted, a charge justly levelled at Müntzer, that he chooses ultimately to lay the blame at the door of the learned biblicists rather than the Catholic Church and the feudal nobility? – 'But God, who is a true field commander, is now upon them and will smite them [the scribes] more powerfully than the peasants.'[74] Again, the question is left unanswered. Rather, Hergot teases out his teleological reading of history to its conclusion:

> I believe that God will never again stir up the peasants against their overlords, for God has dealt too leniently with the nobility and the scribes by entrusting his task to the peasants. And since they in their thanklessness have not recognized that he treated them so leniently, God has raised the Turks and the hosts of the infidel against them for the blood which the peasants shed for him. That will bring about the true conflict, as is plain before our eyes, and not only with the Turks, but also with our most holy father the Pope and the prelates, riven amongst themselves, each lusting after the other's blood.[75]

---

[71]   *Radical Reformation*, ed. Baylor, p. 221.
[72]   Ibid., p. 221.
[73]   Hergot at one point cites Luther's *Against the Robbing and Murderous Hordes of Peasants* directly; ibid., p. 222.
[74]   Ibid., p. 223.
[75]   Ibid.

Hergot concludes sombrely: 'My pamphlet does not induce insurrection. Rather, it exposes those who dwell in wickedness that they may know themselves for what they are and beg God for mercy; for he will not allow himself to be smitten as the peasants were smitten.'[76]

It is not germane to the purposes of this chapter to discuss the details of Hergot's utopia. Suffice it to say that it is pervaded by exactly the same spirit of bureaucratic rationalism (duodecimal tiers of government, for instance), the elevation of agriculture and rural society above towns, burghers and trade, and strong monastic or puritanical strains (quite explicit in Hergot's case) that can be found not only in the thought of the Protestant reformers, but of the Catholic and imperial reformers of the fifteenth century before them (Nicholas of Cusa, the author of the *Reformation of Emperor Sigismund*, or the so-called Revolutionary of the Upper Rhine), and indeed in Renaissance utopias in general.[77] What should be noted is that Hergot is no pacifist. He may protest:

> I have not written this pamphlet because I am angry, or want anyone else to get angry, or because I somehow want to move the world to wrath. Rather, I have written it to create benevolent peace and benevolent unity. Where there is unrest, more unrest is generated, but where there is benevolent peace, this also creates benevolent peace.[78]

But even after the 'new transformation of a Christian life', the possibility of the commonwealth having to wage war – in self-defence, of course – is expressly countenanced; indeed, Hergot develops a scheme of rotating recruitment very similar to that deployed in the Peasants' War itself: 'If the lord wants to wage war, he will be given every third man in each village community, provided that the war accords with the honour of God or the common good.'[79]

In practice, Hergot's Christian commonwealth is a republican theocracy whose configuration – though not its derivation – echoes both Schappeler and Hubmaier, albeit that it is more radical than either of these men's vision. The one element that is missing, perhaps surprisingly, in Hergot's tract is any explanation of why the peasants had been defeated. Unlike Müntzer, Hergot does not attribute the failure of the peasant rebels to their pursuit of creaturely ends rather than God's will[80] – and, equally, he has no truck with Schappeler's 'equivocal disloyalty'. The matter is left hanging – very possibly because Hergot's Joachite view of history made

---

[76]   Ibid., p. 224.
[77]   Seibt, *Utopica*, passim; Miriam Eliav-Feldon, *Realistic Utopias: The Ideal Imaginary Societies of the Renaissance, 1516–1630* (Oxford, 1982).
[78]   *Radical Reformation*, ed. Baylor, p. 222.
[79]   Ibid., p. 214; Blickle, *Revolution von 1525*, p. 236.
[80]   See Scott, *Müntzer*, p. 168.

such an issue redundant: where the peasants had failed, the Turks and infidels would shortly succeed.

Conclusion

It is self-evident that for all three men, social revolution could only be understood – and legitimized – through the prism of radical Christianity: secular communism would have been incomprehensible to them. Under the triple sign of divine justice, brotherly love and the common weal, Hubmaier, Schappeler and Hergot were all prepared to contemplate not merely the overthrow of the prevailing social order, but its overthrow, under strictly defined conditions, by violent means. None of our authors, however, viewed bloodshed as anything other than a regrettable necessity, a transitional cleansing which would usher in a new age of peace. They were certainly no Jacobins, and would have recoiled in horror from any reign of terror. Yet an impending sense of the transformation of the world, even if not couched explicitly as eschaton, encouraged them to see tyranny not merely as an evil in itself, a corruption of the right order of the world, but expressly as a signal that the corrupt and unChristian order was about to be swept away. All three men start from the assumption that a Christian society is to be defined by immanence: that is, by what it shall become under God's will.[81] Whether the rebellious peasants understood their message in that sense is, of course, quite another matter, and one which has always remained contentious in the scholarly literature; likewise the question how far possessing peasants and village chieftains were disposed to embrace the expropriation of private property, the radical egalitarianism of the Christian commonwealth or the pervasive disavowal of commerce, crafts and capital, so indispensable to their ability to pay feudal dues or to survive in an increasingly market-oriented economy.

---

[81]   A suggestion made by Rev. Prof. Peter Matheson, to whom I am indebted for helpful comments on an earlier draft of this chapter. I also acknowledge with gratitude the help of Prof. Dieter Mertens and Dr Klaus Lauterbach.

CHAPTER 2

The Politics of Law and Gospel: The Protestant Prince and the Holy Roman Empire

C. Scott Dixon

In describing the aspects of power at the heart of the German princely state, the seventeenth-century historian and political theorist Veit Ludwig von Seckendorff did not hesitate to include the rule of public religion among them, for the defence of the faith and the preservation of Christian morality was one of the duties entrusted to the higher secular authorities by God. As Seckendorff noted: 'the main purpose of all [rule] is the salutary maintenance of *Polizey*, that is [maintenance of] the whole realm in its justice, power, sovereignty, and religion, the final aim being the honour of God'.[1] This is a quality of early modern rule that has sometimes been overlooked by historians interested in the making of the German territorial state. Traditional approaches have emphasized the secular features of the process, in particular the evolution of centralized governance, the growth of bureaucracy, the rise of the military, the onset of written records, and the rationalization of rule; but in the majority of these models, confessional change has been viewed as a parallel or a secondary development.[2] Constitutional histories have approached the theme from the same perspective. The point of origin in the history of the German state

---

[1] Veit Ludwig von Seckendorff, *Teutscher Fürsten-Stat* (Frankfurt, 1660), pp. 138–9; Michael Stolleis, 'Veit Ludwig von Seckendorff', in Michael Stolleis (ed.), *Staatsdenker in der frühen Neuzeit* (Munich, 1995), pp. 152–60.

[2] See the discussions in Wim Blockmans, 'Les origines des états modernes en Europe, XIIIe–XVIIIe siècles: état de la question et perspectives', in Wim Blockmans and Jean-Philippe Genet (eds), *Visions sur le développement des états Européens. Théories et historiographies de l'état moderne* (Rome, 1993), pp. 1–14; Wolfgang Reinhard, 'Das Wachstum der Staatsgewalt: historische Reflexionen', *Der Staat*, 31 (1992): 59–75. On the rise of German monarchy and the conditions of its growth, see Robert von Friedeburg, 'The Making of Patriots: Love of Fatherland and Negotiating Monarchy in Seventeenth-Century Germany', *The Journal of Modern History*, 77 (2005): 881–916. For a sovereign overview of European developments, see Hillay Zmora, *Monarchy, Aristocracy and the State in Europe 1300–1800* (London, 2001).

is the fifteenth century, with the crucial period running from 1450 to 1570, for this is when the central features of the modern territorial powers began to take shape. Confessional developments have been imagined within the parameters of this process, and while religious belief is clearly seen as a central feature of early modern social and political life, the religious upheavals have not been viewed as a catalyst.[3]

In recent years, however, religion has made a comeback, and indeed to the point where confessional change is now considered by some historians to have been the 'heuristic indicator' of broader patterns of change.[4] In part, this new perspective is due to a gradual shift in historiographical priorities, a turn away from the grand inclusive vision to a concern with simultaneous narratives based on local contexts and distinct spheres of experience. Models of state growth and political power now speak in terms of different levels of development, starting at the level of interaction between individuals and groups (where the power of religion was most in evidence), and reaching to the macro level and the rise of nations.[5] Even more significant in German historiography has been the influence of the idea of confessionalization.[6] In this model, religious change is not

---

[3]   Ernst Schubert, 'Die Umformung spätmittelalterlicher Fürstenherrschaft im 16. Jahrhundert', *Rheinische Vierteljahrsblätter*, 63 (1999): 209: 'Zu betonen ist: Diese Veränderung hängt mitnichten mit der Reformation zusammen, sondern ist Folge einer Vielzahl von innerterritorial endogenen und exterritorial exogenen Einwirkungen auf die bestehenden Verhältnisse'; compare Fritz Hartung, *Deutsche Verfassungsgeschichte vom 15. Jahrhundert bis zur Gegenwart* (Stuttgart, 1950), pp. 53–80; Dietmar Willoweit, 'Allgemeine Merkmale der Verwaltungsorganisation in den Territorien', in Kurt G.A. Jeserich, Hans Pohl and Georg-Christoph von Unruh (eds), *Deutsche Verwaltungsgeschichte: Vom Spätmittelalter bis zum Ende des Reiches* (Stuttgart, 1983), vol. 1, pp. 289–345.

[4]   The expression comes from Heinz Schilling, 'Confessional Europe', in Thomas A. Brady, Heiko Oberman and James D. Tracy (eds), *Handbook of European History, 1400–1600: Late Middle Ages, Renaissance and Reformation* (Leiden, 1995), vol. 2, p. 643.

[5]   Wolfgang Reinhard, 'Croissance de la puissance de l'état: un modèle théorique', in André Stegmann (ed.), *Pouvoir et institutions en Europe au XVIième siècle* (Paris, 1987), pp. 173–86; Wolfgang Reinhard, 'Power Elites, State Servants, Ruling Classes, and the Growth of State Power', in Wolfgang Reinhard (ed.), *Power Elites and State Building* (Oxford, 1996), pp. 1–18; for new models at the macrohistorical level, see Thomas Ertman, *Birth of the Leviathan: Building States and Regimes in Medieval and Early Modern Europe* (Cambridge, 1997), pp. 1–34.

[6]   Fundamental for the original conceptualization of the idea: Wolfgang Reinhard, 'Zwang zur Konfessionalisierung? Prolegomena zu einer Theorie des konfessionellen Zeitalters', *Zeitschrift für historische Forschung*, 10 (1983): 268–77, trans. as 'Pressures towards Confessionalization? Prolegomena to a Theory of the Confessional Age', in C. Scott Dixon (ed.), *The German Reformation: The Essential Readings* (Oxford, 1999), pp. 169–92; Heinz Schilling, 'Die Konfessionalisierung im Reich. Religiöser und gesellschaftlicher Wandel in Deutschland zwischen 1555

viewed as derivative or subordinate to the forces at work in the secular sphere. On the contrary, religious reform, both the Catholic and the Protestant variants, is thought to have had an ordering function in the process of social and political change.[7] By the end of the sixteenth century, large German territories such as Brandenburg, Saxony and Bavaria had evolved into powerful and sophisticated sovereign states, with systems of governance that made little or no distinction between the secular and the spiritual, notions of identity rooted in the symbols, ritual and language of religion, and a philosophy of rule that sought its final justification in works of theology. To an extent without precedent in German history, the secular and the spiritual joined together in common purpose.[8]

Speaking in such broad terms, however, tends to elude some of the more subtle questions relating to the Reformation and political change. The idea of confessionalization, for instance, projects a model of historical development that in its essentials applies to all of the territories of the empire, whether Catholic, Lutheran or Reformed, and it tends to view developments from a statist perspective, using the relative wealth of normative sources to project an inclusive historical dynamic.[9] Moreover, explanatory theories that tie so many developments together – both secular and spiritual – often make it difficult to distinguish between cause and effect. In this case, to what extent can we attribute political developments to religious factors, and to what extent was the Reformation itself brought into being by the shifts in late medieval relations of power? In what follows,

---

und 1620', *Historische Zeitschrift*, 246 (1988): 1–45, trans. as 'Confessionalization in the Empire: Religious and Societal Change in Germany between 1555 and 1620', in Heinz Schilling (trans.) Stephen Burnett, *Religion, Political Culture, and the Emergence of Early Modern Society: Essays in German and Dutch History* (Leiden, 1992), pp. 204–45. The literature on confessionalization is now legion. For a synthesis of recent research, see Stefan Ehrenpreis and Ute Lotz-Heumann, *Reformation und konfessionelles Zeitalter* (Darmstadt, 2002), pp. 62–81.

[7]   Schilling, 'Die Konfessionalisierung', p. 5; Schilling, 'Confessionalization', p. 208; Ehrenpreis and Lotz-Heumann, *Reformation und konfessionelles Zeitalter*, pp. 64–5.

[8]   Martin Heckel, *Deutschland im konfessionellen Zeitalter* (Göttingen, 2001), p. 13.

[9]   Recent critical discussions of the idea can be found in Heinz Schilling, 'Die Konfessionalisierung von Kirche, Staat und Gesellschaft – Profil, Leistung, Defizite und Perspektiven eines geschichtswissenschaftlichen Paradigmas', in Wolfgang Reinhard and Heinz Schilling (eds), *Die katholische Konfessionalisierung* (Münster, 1995), pp. 419–52; Walter Ziegler, 'Altgläubige Territorien im Konfessionalisierungsprozeß', in Anton Schindling and Walter Ziegler (eds), *Die Territorien des Reichs im Zeitalter der Reformation und Konfessionalisierung* (Münster, 1997), vol. 7, pp. 67–90; Anton Schindling, 'Konfessionalisierung und Grenzen von Konfessionalisierbarkeit', in ibid., pp. 9–44; Heinrich Richard Schmidt, 'Sozialdisziplinierung? Ein Plädoyer für das Ende des Etatismus in der Konfessionalisierungsforschung', *Historische Zeitschrift*, 265 (1997): 639–82.

I would like to take up some of the issues relating to the Reformation and the rise of the confessional principality in sixteenth-century Germany, but with more of a view to the particulars than the overarching vision. At the centre of the analysis will be the following questions: To what extent did the Reformation affect the actual praxis of rule in the German territories? Was the movement a catalyst for political change and if so how did this influence the methods and the philosophy of princely sovereignty? Did Protestantism have an impact on the sense of political community in the German lands, whether at the level of the empire or the level of the territory? And finally, what is the best way to conceptualize these developments – as a chain of interconnected events, or a more sweeping and seamless process of change?

Process and Event in the Princely Reformation

The foundation stone for the rise of the Protestant state in Germany was the principle *ius reformandi* ('right of reformation'), a term first used with frequency during the seventeenth century, but which in fact described a state of affairs that had been put in place by the Peace of Augsburg (1555). The right of reformation, as the name suggests, made it possible for the Lutheran and later Calvinist princes to determine the religion of their lands and influence the workings of the Church. This was not entirely without precedent. Historians working on late medieval Germany have drawn attention to the powers already exercised over the Church by the princes of the larger territories.[10] To do this, the medieval prince had two legal means at his disposal: the right of patronage, and the right of guardianship or advocacy (*Vogtei*), both of which enabled some rulers – the electors of Saxony being the best examples – to dominate the institutional Church and its higher clergy in their territories. (To use the words of the historian Manfred Schulze, the medieval bishops of Saxony were little more than the 'spiritual officials' of the prince.)[11] But the princes never claimed the right

---

[10]   See Enno Bünz and Christoph Volkmar, 'Das landesherrliche Kirchen-regiment in Sachsen vor der Reformation', in Enno Bünz, Stefan Rhein and Günther Wartenberg (eds), *Glaube und Macht. Theologie, Politik und Kunst im Jahrhundert der Reformation* (Leipzig, 2005), pp. 89–109.

[11]   Manfred Schulze, *Fürsten und Reformation. Geistliche Reformpolitik weltlicher Fürsten vor der Reformation* (Tübingen, 1991), p. 133; Wilhelm Dersch, 'Territorium, Stadt und Kirche im ausgehenden Mittelalter', *Korrespondenzblatt des Gesamtvereins der deutschen Geschichts- und Altertumsvereine*, 80 (1932), pp. 32–51; Isnard W. Frank, 'Kirchengewalt und Kirchenregiment in Spätmittelalter und Früher Neuzeit', *Innsbrücker historische Studien*, 9 (1987), pp. 33–60; Justus Hashagen, 'Die vorreformatorische Bedeutung des spätmittelalterlichen landesherrlichen Kirchenregiments', *Zeitschrift für Kirchengeschichte*, 41 (1922), pp. 63–93.

to influence matters touching on religious belief. On occasion, and always with papal dispensation, they could oversee a visitation of the monasteries, but this was with a view to reforming discipline or administration. Moreover, it was always done on the basis of papal privilege within the framework of canon law. The *ius reformandi* that emerged with the Reformation was fundamentally different in kind. With the Augsburg settlement, the Protestant princes were granted the right to introduce the Reformation, the right to determine the religion of the subject population in their lands (with a clause allowing emigration to avoid problems of conscience), the right to maintain the Church property in their possession, and the suspension of all jurisdiction – ecclesiastical and imperial – that impeded the sovereignty of the Protestant Church.[12]

All of this was completely new, and not just the entitlement to establish the Lutheran faith, which obviously had no precedent, but the legal stipulations as well. New formulations had been forced on the empire by historical circumstance, for none of the medieval privileges extended far enough to justify the Protestant rejection of Catholic teaching and canon law. In his study of the evolution of the *ius reformandi*, Bernd Christian Schneider has shown in detail how the settlement was pieced together to deal with the crises of mid-century (paramount being the wars between Charles V and the German princes).[13] Even the famous formula *cuius regio, eius religio* ('his the rule, his the religion'), the later juridical standard of the confessional state, was forced by events. Indeed, a similar idea was first proposed by the Catholic minorities threatened by Protestant advances, who saw the solution for each of the parties in Ephesians 4:5: 'There is one body, and one Spirit, even as ye are called in one hope of your calling.' The end result was confirmed with the Peace of Augsburg (1555), a settlement that was in large part an affirmation of changes already in train, but also a clear point of division between the piecemeal advances of the embryonic evangelical powers and the rise of the confessional state. After the mid-century Peace, the Lutheran territories began to build.[14]

---

[12] On the Peace of Augsburg, see Axel Gotthard, *Der Augsburger Religionsfrieden* (Münster, 2004); on the relationship between sovereignty and the growth of the territorial Church, see Dietmar Willoweit, *Rechtsgrundlagen der Territorialgewalt. Landesobrigkeit, Herrschaftsrechte und Territorium in der Rechtswissenschaft der Neuzeit* (Cologne and Vienna, 1975), pp. 34–110; Jörn Sieglerschmidt, *Territorialstaat und Kirchenregiment. Studien zur Rechtsdogmatik des Kirchenpatronatsrechts im 15. und 16. Jahrhundert* (Cologne and Vienna, 1987), pp. 8–23; Burkhard von Bonin, *Die praktische Bedeutung des ius reformandi* (Stuttgart, 1902).

[13] Bernd Christian Schneider, *Ius Reformandi. Die Entwicklung eines Staatkirchenrechts von seinen Anfängen bis zum Ende des Alten Reiches* (Tübingen, 2001), pp. 51–170.

[14] Compare Holger Thomas Gräf, *Konfession und internationales System. Die Außenpolitik Hessen-Kassels im konfessionellen Zeitalter* (Darmstadt and

With the right of reformation and the rise of the Protestant Church, a new matrix of rule emerged, reaching from the higher councils of princely sovereignty down to the office of village schoolmaster.[15] Dioceses and chapters were absorbed into the state and partitioned according to secular boundaries. In some areas, this resulted in the restructuring of parishes, as Catholic clergy were dismissed, evangelical clergy were put into office, and district officials took stock of local affairs. Overnight, parishes could be reduced in size, property could change hands, and fees and dues could devolve to a new lord.[16] More ominous for the actual exercise of local power was the extension of princely rule to the parish level. In the Lutheran margraviate of Brandenburg-Ansbach-Kulmbach, for instance, a clear chain of command emerged stretching from the higher offices of the state through the institutions and individuals responsible for rule at the level of the administrative districts to the Lutheran pastors, and finally, through them, to the parishioners in the villages. Each level was tied to the next through the mandates and Church orders. The yearly visitation process, for instance, was overseen by the special superintendent and the consistory in the capital; regional superintendents implemented the visitations, travelling from parish to parish accompanied by margravial officials; once in the villages, the local servants of the Church reported to the superintendents, while separate hearings were held for the village officials. With the progress complete, the results were compiled and then forwarded to the consistory for the officials to act on the information.[17]

All of this restructured relations of power in the principality. Not only did the local officials have much less political independence, but the rural parishioners, by virtue of the reforming mission of the Protestant Church, were necessarily bound up in the same compact. As Ernst Walter Zeeden

---

Marburg, 1993), pp. 73–7; on the Peace of Augsburg, see Gotthard, *Der Augsburger Religionsfrieden.*

[15]   See Werner Freitag, 'Konfessionelle Kulturen und innere Staatsbildung. Zur Konfessionalisierung in westfälischen Territorien', *Westfälische Forschung,* 42 (1992): 74–191.

[16]   Joachim Conrad, 'Die Umstrukturierung des Pfarreisystems durch die Reformation in Nassau-Saarbrücken', *Monatshefte für Evangelische Kirchengeschichte des Rheinlandes,* 51 (2002): 47–66; Eberhard Fritz, 'Reformation als Prozeß. Verlauf und Fortgang im Amt Urach und den angrenzenden Herrschaften unter besonderer Berücksichtigung der Schwäbischen Alb', *Blätter für Württembergische Kirchengeschichte,* 92 (1992): 34–58.

[17]   C. Scott Dixon, *The Reformation and Rural Society: The Parishes of Brandenburg-Ansbach-Kulmbach, 1528–1603* (Cambridge, 1996), pp. 60–65, 129–31; for the rise of the territorial state in Brandenburg-Ansbach, see Rudolf Endres, 'Die Reformation im fränkischen Wendelstein', in Peter Blickle (ed.), *Zugänge zur bäuerlichen Reformation* (Zurich, 1978), pp. 127–46; Rudolf Endres, 'Stadt und Landgemeinde in Franken', in Peter Blickle (ed.), *Landgemeinde und Stadtgemeinde in Mitteleuropa* (Munich, 1991), pp. 101–17.

once remarked, even during the church service the parishioners were now reminded that they were subjects of the state.[18] Little wonder that historians have begun to draw attention to the process of centralization and consolidation in the German territories that gathered momentum from the second half of the sixteenth century onward, thus precisely at the stage when the second generation of Protestant princes was able to establish an equilibrium of rule in the empire. More interested in internal consolidation than external advance, and with much less to fear from the Habsburgs in light of the legalization of the faith, the Lutheran rulers, drawing on their perceived role as God's agents on earth and *Landesväter* over their subjects, embarked on a campaign of domestic reform that has often been viewed as a first stage in the rise of the modern state.[19]

Given the implications of this process for the course of German history, it is easy to overlook the fact that it was more the result of necessity than calculation. In this sense, the princely Reformation was more the consequence of a series of events than the outcome of a process reaching back to the medieval period. And two events in particular dictated the terms – the Peasants' War of 1525, and the rise of the Anabaptists. Both incidents forced the hands of the authorities at a stage when there was not yet a sense of vision or resolution, and both provided a basis for secular intervention into religious affairs by equating false faith with civil disobedience. The Peasants' War worked as a catalyst, as it required the princes to take a political stand on issues that had primarily been a war of words. The immediate consequence was the diet of Speyer (1526) and the compromise formula of its recess (that each ruler, with reference to the Edict of Worms, should conduct his affairs 'as [they] hope and trust to answer to God and his imperial majesty'), which has often been considered a turning point in the German Reformation.[20] But even more significant was the threat posed by the Anabaptists, for they not only provided the authorities with ample evidence of the worldly dangers of false religion. Unlike the rebels of 1525, the Anabaptists had not been defeated in battle. This required the secular authorities to develop more permanent methods of dealing with religious affairs, and in order to do this, the princes turned to the theologians. It was out of this dialogue that the Church orders, the religious mandates and the reform process began to take shape.

---

[18]   Ernst Walter Zeeden, *Die Entstehung der Konfessionen. Grundlagen und Formen der Konfessionsbildung im Zeitalter der Glaubenskämpfe* (Munich, 1965), p. 119.

[19]   See the discussion and the literature in Manfred Rudersdorf, 'Patriarchalisches Fürstenregiment und Reichsfriede. Zur Rolle des neuen lutherischen Regententyps im Zeitalter der Konfessionalisierung,' in Heinz Duchhardt and Matthias Schnettger (eds), *Reichsständische Libertät und Habsburgisches Kaisertum* (Mainz, 1999), pp. 309–27.

[20]   Peter Blickle, *Die Reformation im Reich* (Stuttgart, 1992), pp. 154–5.

We can follow the course of this development in Electoral Saxony. In the beginning, Luther resisted the intervention of the secular arm; he even came to the defence of Thomas Müntzer with appeals to freedom of conscience. His main concern at the outset was establishing clear lines of demarcation between the secular and the spiritual, and in particular keeping the Church free of manipulation by the state, an idea he spelled out in some detail in his work *On Secular Authority* (1523). With the rise of the radicals and the Anabaptists, however, first in Zwickau, Wittenberg and Allstedt, and then throughout the lands of northern and western Thuringia, he began to appeal to the secular authorities to intervene in the course of reform.[21] As early as 1524, Luther had changed his mind and was advising the elector to act against Thomas Müntzer, and gradually he broadened the extent of the prince's commission, to the point where he claimed the ruler was the 'instrument' of God with the obligation to see through the reform of the Church in the absence of any initiative from the bishops.[22] He feared that the radical preachers were leading the faithful to their own destruction, proof that the Devil 'intends through these emissaries to create rebellion and murder (even if for a while he carries on peacefully), and to overthrow both spiritual and temporal government against the will of God'.[23]

Remaining true to the two-kingdoms format, Luther simply enlarged the scale of secular responsibility until it embraced the activities of the radical preachers and allowed for the secular magistrate to impose order on the movement. For instance, after the Peasants' War, Luther began to make a distinction between matters of conscience and instances of blasphemy, the latter being a public concern as it affected the entire congregation. With the publication of the *Instructions for the Visitors of Saxony* (1528), blasphemy or unrest (*Aufruhr*) was defined as anything that deviated from the faith as stipulated in the *Instructions*. As John Oyer has remarked, 'Luther developed the idea that blasphemy, the open proclamation of a heretical view, constituted a form of sedition.'[24] As a consequence, the activities of the radical reformers fell subject to the secular arm. Luther now began to support the idea of secular involvement in religious affairs, and he forwarded letters to the chancellery with advice and calls for a visitation. With one eye on the radicals, Luther and the Saxon reformers

---

[21]   Paul Wappler, *Die Täuferbewegung in Thüringen von 1526–1554* (Jena, 1913), pp. 5–89.

[22]   Hermann Kunst, *Evangelischer Glaube und politische Verantwortung. Martin Luther als Berater seiner Landesherrn und seine Teilnahme an den Fragen des öffentlichen Lebens* (Stuttgart, 1976), pp. 191–206.

[23]   Quoted in James M. Estes, *Peace, Order and the Glory of God: Secular Authority and the Church in the Thought of Luther and Melanchthon, 1518–1559* (Leiden, 2005), p. 190.

[24]   John S. Oyer, *Lutheran Reformers against Anabaptists. Luther, Melanchthon and Menius and the Anabaptists of Central Germany* (The Hague, 1964), p. 136.

proclaimed that all public religion that was not fully in accordance with the teaching of Wittenberg and its approved preachers was blasphemy and destructive of the civil peace. And given that the Church was in the grip of the Antichrist, it was the duty of the prince to root it out.[25]

The process against Hans Mohr is illustrative of this development. In 1528, Mohr, captain of the castle of Coburg, fell suspect due to his sacramentarian beliefs. Acting on the directives coming from Wittenberg, the local authorities sent the details of the case to Elector Johann, who then forwarded them to Luther for advice on how he should deal with the man, who to that point had been considered an honourable and valuable soldier. Luther feared Mohr might try to win others to his views, and thus ordered in the first instance that 'his mouth should be stopped'. Once it became clear, however, that Mohr would not abandon his beliefs, harsher measures proved necessary, and ultimately the secular officials relieved him of his post and placed him in prison.[26] The entire process was carried out in accordance with the *Instructions*, with both secular and spiritual authorities working together to bring Mohr to account.

Philipp Melanchthon, who drafted the *Instructions*, would later provide the theological legitimization for this relationship and in the process partly eclipse Luther's earlier caveats about keeping the secular and the spiritual at a distance.[27] According to Melanchthon, the prince had a God-given obligation to intervene and introduce reform, partly due to the fact that as 'chief member of the church' (*praecipuum membrum ecclesiae*) he had inherited this charge, but also because Melanchthon maintained, as did Erasmus and many commentators before him, that the state itself was a Christian entity with a religious purpose. In working out his ideas, Melanchthon built on Luther's theological foundations. He developed a theory of Church–state relations that remained faithful to the two-kingdoms framework while drawing on the idea of the priesthood of all believers and the commands of brotherly love in order to provide the justification. Unlike the early Luther, however, Melanchthon spoke openly about the positive obligation to watch over the Church that inhered in secular rule. In essence, he was the first of the magisterial reformers to offer a defence of the *cura religionis* of the emerging Protestant princes. Without usurping the authority of the ministry or offending the glory of God, and

---

[25] Paul Wappler, *Inquisition und Ketzerprozesse in Zwickau zur Reformationszeit* (Leipzig, 1908), pp. 1–69; 85–95.

[26] WA Br., vol.4 (1933), pp. 347–50.

[27] Though, as James Estes has recently illustrated, in the fundamentals Luther and Melanchthon were essentially in agreement; see Estes, *Peace, Order and the Glory of God*.

without trespassing on theological terrain, the state and its sovereign had the duty to preserve the earthly Church and oversee the faith.[28]

The main features of Melanchthon's thought on this theme were already present in the second edition of the *Loci Communes* (1535), where he argued openly that the secular authorities, as 'Gods' and 'guardians' of the Church, had the obligation to uphold true religion and watch over the Church. This not only repeated the obligation to preserve the public peace for the sake of earthly order; it also evoked the divine commission, which inhered in earthly rule, to realize the True Church on earth. As James Estes has observed, by the 1530s, in his interpretation of 1 Timothy 2:2, Melanchthon's emphasis had shifted from the beginning to the end of the passage: that is, let us pray and give thanks for all men, 'for kings and all those in authority, that we may live peaceful and quiet lives in all *godliness and holiness*'.[29] At this stage Melanchthon was also stressing the necessity for the secular authorities to watch over both tables of the Decalogue, not just the final seven commands dealing with worldly relations, but the first three as well, those which concerned the externals of the faith and thus the proper public worship of God.

Melanchthon synthesized his mature views on the powers of the secular arm in *De officio principum* (1539), one of the final works in his corpus of thought on the theme, and one that proved extremely influential in Lutheran Germany.[30] And while it had its own intrinsic logic, a fusion of Erasmian ideals and Lutheran insight, like Luther he too developed much of his thought in response to the threats posed by the activities of the Anabaptists. Much of the 1535 *Loci Communes*, for instance, was revised with the radicals in mind, and in particular his defence of the *cura religionis* of the secular magistrates and the divine origins of secular rule. Moreover, as he worked out his ideas, he continued to press the prince and his advisors to act against the Anabaptist communities and bring them to justice. Indeed, to a much greater extent than Luther, Melanchthon never lost the scent of Anabaptist blood, and he called for the death penalty for all instances of blasphemy. As he wrote in the final edition of the *Loci Communes* (1559):

> the authorities [princes] must watch over the second table of commandments, and the first even more so. For the rulers have to serve the honour of God

---

[28]   Ralph Keen, *Divine and Human Authority in Reformation Thought: German Theologians on Political Order, 1520–1555* (Nieuwkoop, 1997), p. 49; James M. Estes, 'The Role of Godly Magistrates in the Church: Melanchthon as Luther's Interpreter and Collaborator', *Church History*, 67 (1998): 463–83.

[29]   Estes, *Peace, Order and the Glory of God*, p. 126. NIV translation.

[30]   Ibid., p. 177: 'So clear and persuasive to adherents of the magisterial Reformation were those arguments that it is difficult to find a German Protestant theologian from 1535 onward (until well into the following century) who did not take them over virtually unchanged.'

above all things. They are the guardians of the church. And whoever has taken the name of God in vain, he should be punished by death.[31]

The Protestant Church orders of the sixteenth century formalized this relationship. Most opened with a preface elevating the prince to the status of guardian over the faith. The sovereign had been placed in office 'not only to preserve the common peace, and with it all honour and discipline', but also to defend true religion, and this meant enforcing the requirements of the Decalogue. In the words of one Lutheran order, it was the prince's duty 'to safeguard God's name and his Word' and to ensure that the faithful 'were protected from error in pure, healthy teaching and proper belief'.[32] Throughout the German lands in the sixteenth century, the princes defined the nature of acceptable belief in Church orders, secular mandates and educational programmes. Margrave Georg of Brandenburg-Ansbach, for instance, empowered Johannes Brenz to work alongside Nuremberg's Andreas Osiander in drafting the *Brandenburg-Nuremberg Church Order* (1533). Once it was published, all clergy and all parishioners were obliged to honour this Lutheran statement of the faith. It was introduced into the churches, taught in the schools, and Osiander's catechism (appended to the order) was used to indoctrinate the young. The margrave thus determined the religion of his subjects; all other faiths (Catholicism, Anabaptism, Calvinism) were anathema. In essence, the Protestant prince was acting like a bishop, legislating what people might believe and how they should come to believe it. Such was the nature of Church rule in all of the Protestant territories in Germany, from Württemberg to Pomerania, Albertine Saxony to the Rhine Palatinate. The Reformation had invested the sovereigns with the right to police their subjects' thoughts as they previously policed their actions.[33]

Of course, claims to be God's agent on earth did not separate Protestant from Catholic rulers, nor did the emphasis placed on morals, piety, or indeed the prominent role of the prince within the Church. The essential difference was the extent to which the Protestant prince was both an active participant in the shaping and defending of the faith (as the *princeps*

---

[31] Wappler, *Inquisition und Ketzerprozesse,* p. 95.

[32] Heinrich Schmidt, 'Kirchenregiment und Landesherrschaft im Selbstverständnis niedersächsischer Fürsten des 16. Jahrhunderts', *Niedersächsisches Jahrbuch für Landesgeschichte,* 56 (1984): 31–58; Hans-Walter Krumwiede, 'Reformation und Kirchenregiment in Württemberg', *Blätter für Württembergische Kirchengeschichte,* 68/69 (1968/69): 81–111; Emil Sehling (ed.), *Die evangelischen Kirchenordungen des XVI. Jahrhunderts* (16 vols, Tübingen, 1902–), vol. 15, *Württemberg I,* (1977), pp. 55–6.

[33] Ibid., vol. 15, pp. 55–6; Dixon, *Reformation and Rural Society,* pp. 47–54, 143–62; on the rise of the Protestant princely state in general, see C. Scott Dixon, 'The Princely Reformation in Germany', in Andrew Pettegree (ed.), *The Reformation World* (London, 2000), pp. 146–68.

eruditus) and, as a consequence, the extent to which he could draw on religion to legitimize and consolidate his rule.[34] By way of analogy, in medieval Catholic thought, kingship was defined against the backdrop of two cognate traditions, that of the mystical corpus of the Church and the corpus of the secular realm. Out of this dualism arose the theory of the two bodies of the king.[35] In the Protestant scheme, with the sacral dimension abolished and religion bound so closely to the secular in the compact of the territorial Church, the two worlds were united in the figuration of the prince. There was a single corpus.

Faith, Sovereignty and Identity

The image of the Protestant prince was first captured in the flood of *Fürstenspiegel* ('princely mirrors') written for the second generation of Reformation sovereigns.[36] The central purpose of the Protestant mirror was to demonstrate the dangers of the secular world (often referred to as the *regnum diaboli*) and the inability of fallen man to establish any sort of order without complete trust in the Word of God. Thus, when the evangelical authors spoke of the learned prince, they meant something more than the *rex philosophus* of the humanist tradition. The Protestant prince had to be versed in Scripture, not only capable of defending the Church in his lands and watching over the salvation of his subjects, but theologically astute enough to recognize that there could be no rule on earth without proper faith and fear of God.[37] In this sense, the Protestant prince was not marked out by the gift of sanctity (as in the medieval mirrors), but rather by his unique potential for sin. As Luther noted, 'a prince is a man as any other, but one surrounded by ten devils whereas an average man has just the one. [For this reason] God must provide him with special guidance and place his angels by his side.'[38]

---

[34]   Heinz Duchhardt, 'Das protestantische Herrscherbild des 17. Jahrhunderts im Reich,' in Konrad Repgen (ed.), *Das Herrscherbild im 17. Jahrhundert* (Münster, 1991), pp. 33–4.

[35]   Ernst H. Kantorowicz, *The King's Two Bodies: A Study in Medieval Political Theology* (Princeton, NJ, 1997).

[36]   Rainer A. Müller, 'Die deutschen Fürstenspiegel des 17. Jahrhunderts. Regierungslehren und politische Pädagogik', *Historische Zeitschrift*, 240 (1985): 571–98.

[37]   Michael Philipp, 'Regierungskunst im Zeitalter der konfessionellen Spaltung. Politische Lehren des mansfeldischen Kanzlers Georg Lauterbech', in Hans-Otto Mühleisen (ed.), *Politische Tugendlehre und Regierungskunst. Studien zum Fürstenspiegel der Frühen Neuzeit* (Tübingen, 1990), pp. 85–92.

[38]   WA, vol. 36, p. 245; Michael Götz, 'Gottes Wort als Anleitung zum Handeln für den lutherischen Fürsten. Thomas Bircks Fürstenspiegel', in Mühleisen (ed.), *Politische Tugendlehre*, pp. 118–39. The importance of the Word of God for the rule and conduct of a prince is commonly the central message of the Protestant

This shift in emphasis had a number of implications for the perception of the ruler and the expectations of rule. To begin with, the prince, as God's first vassal on earth, was now responsible for the care of the earthly Church; he had to preserve the true faith and the preaching of the Word. Theoretically, as later commentators pointed out, this was a much more dynamic conception of rule than the medieval variant, as the ruler and his court were much more personally engaged with all aspects of the godly commonwealth.[39] In addition, given that the prince was a sinner like all other men and stood in the same relationship to the divine as all other men, it followed that he was subject to the same laws of the Christian commonwealth. In the end, as Luther implied, the only thing that distinguished a prince was the quality of sins he might commit – and yet it was exactly this, in the Protestant scheme of things, that invested the sovereign with such importance for the political and religious order. For if a ruler, surrounded by temptation, could remain true to the faith, what lesser man might not be inspired by this example of 'the living law'? Moreover, given that he was so highly attuned to the temptations, what better man than the prince had the authority and the legitimacy to dictate the terms of the compact? As Leonhard Werner wrote in his *Mirror of Princely Consolation* (1562):

> For precisely because all authority and its orders are in the service of God, so too must all such works that rightly belong to a prince in his office of rule be good works, for he serves God in his stead – just as a preacher preaches the holy gospel and ministers the holy sacraments according to the express intentions of our Lord Jesus Christ.[40]

With the culture of good works discredited and earthly deeds distanced from the idea of the ever-present threat of the Last Judgement and the related notion that secular rulings figured in the final reckoning, the prince was perceived as less of a judge of the Old Testament type and more of a counsel for the teaching of Christ. More emphasis was placed in the princes (or the authorities in general) in their roles as overseers of the divine commission, which was to preserve the secular realm in accordance

---

Fürstenspiegel. Examples include: Johann Schuwardt, *Regententaffell* (1583); Thomas Sigfrid, *Aulicus Praeceptor* (1594), fol. B^r–D^v; Friedrich Glaser, *Oculus Principis* (1595), fol. Biii^v–Fviii^r; Johann Schramm, *Fasciculus Historiarum* (1589), fol. 30^v–31^r.

[39] Horst Dreitzel, *Monarchiebegriffe in der Fürstengesellschaft: Theorie der Monarchie* (Cologne, 1991), vol. 2, p. 499: 'Der Fürst und sein Hof sollen also als Vorbild wirken – nicht, wie in der katholischen *Politica christiana*, durch ihre "Majestät".'

[40] Leonhard Werner, *Fürstlicher Trostspiegel* (1562), p. 5.

with the laws of the Scripture, to which they themselves – above all men – were bound.[41]

Despite the tenor of the language in works of this kind, there was no place for the *rex et sacerdos* of medieval theology. The combination of the priesthood of all believers and the Lutheran insistence that each worldly office had equal validity in the eyes of God undermined the idea of the ruler being invested with a higher degree of sacramental authority. Johannes Bugenhagen made this point in his coronation sermon for Christian III, the Lutheran king of Denmark. Although little of the liturgy had been changed for the event, Bugenhagen stressed that the royal consecration had no effect in the sense of a sacrament; the significance of the rite was symbolic, a means of making sensible the pledge made by the sovereign to uphold the trust placed in him by God.[42] And while this did not have a direct impact on the standing of the German princes, as they were never objects of a sacramental rite of coronation (only the emperor had a ritual anointment), the explicit desacralization of the rite – and, by implication, rulership – in the teaching of the reformers undoubtedly contributed to a shift of perception. Paradoxically, however, rather than weakening the standing of the prince, it tended to invest him with even greater authority. No longer reliant on the mediation and legitimation of the Catholic Church, the princes could assume rule with the claim that they had been placed directly in office by God. Heirs of a divine commission, and thus to an extent above the laws of the secular realm, the Protestant rulers began to develop their own notions of sacral sovereignty, speaking in terms of the majesty and the charisma of kingship and stressing their unmediated proximity to the will and the Word of the divine. Indeed, in this sense the standing of the Protestant prince outweighed that of his medieval predecessor, for he did not just represent a sacramental instance of divine favour: the prince had become the mediator of the divine covenant, entrusted with the enforcement of his laws and the preservation of his honour, and all with a view to the sacral welfare of the land.[43]

The idea of a German prince assuming such eminence within an imagined community of the elect was legitimized by the Reformation, but it was made possible by decades of nationalist discourse. When the Luther affair first surfaced, two medieval notions of German identity were in flux.

---

[41]   Compare Kirstin Eldyss Sorensen Zapalac, '*In His Image and Likeness*': *Political Iconography and Religious Change in Regensburg, 1500–1600* (Ithaca, NY, 1990), pp. 55–91, esp. 83.

[42]   Hans Liermann, 'Untersuchungen zum Sakralrecht des protestantischen Herrschers', *Zeitschrift der Savigny-Stiftung für Rechtsgeschichte. KA*, 30 (1941): 329–38; on this theme in general, see Jens Ivo Engels, 'Das "Wesen" der Monarchie? Kritische Anmerkungen zum "Sakralkönigtum" in der Geschichtswissenschaft', *Majestas*, 7 (1999): 3–39.

[43]   Seckendorff, *Teutscher Fürsten-Stat*, p. 25.

On the one hand there was the idea of the *Imperium Romanum*, the sacral empire bequeathed to the German kings, and on the other the notion of the German Nation, a community defined primarily by language, custom, history and political reality. Despite this dual inheritance, there was a fairly consolidated impression of national self-perception on the eve of Reformation. Politically, the Estates had become much more aware of the unique system which marked out the land and its people, and they began to speak of the need to secure the German Nation in the face of external threats.[44] At the same time, a latent sense of identity began to find expression in the works of the theologians and the humanists. From the work of Nicholas of Cusa and Gregor Heimburg to the *Grievances of the German Nation* (*Gravamina nationis Germanicae*), the underlying thread remained the desire to invest the German Church with its own legitimacy and remove Rome from national affairs. Prophecies and prognostications spoke of the fall of the Catholic Church and the rise of a heroic emperor, while tracts and pamphlets appeared projecting a new social order (largely taken from the *Germania* of Tacitus) based on the supposed primal virtues of the German race – honesty, piety, a love of liberty and fatherland – which, according to the humanists, once flourished in the land.[45]

The Reformation movement borrowed from this nationalist spirit, but it also reworked and reconfigured it at two levels: at the level of the *Reich*, and the level of the territory. From the outset, the integrity of the Holy Roman Empire was necessarily weakened by the attack on the Catholic Church. The main author of this revaluation was Martin Luther, who contributed to the making of German identity by unmasking the papacy as the Antichrist

---

[44]   Peter Moraw, 'Bestehende, fehlende und heranwachsende Voraussetzungen des deutschen Nationalbewußtseins im späten Mittelalter', in Joachim Ehlers (ed.), *Ansätze und Diskontinuität deutscher Nationsbildung im Mittelalter* (Sigmaringen, 1989), p. 107; Heinrich Lutz, 'Die deutsche Nation zu Beginn der Neuzeit. Fragen nach dem Gelingen und Scheitern deutscher Einheit im 16. Jahrhundert', *Historische Zeitschrift*, 234 (1982): 529–59; Heinz Thomas, 'Die Deutsche Nation und Martin Luther', *Historisches Jahrbuch*, 105 (1985): 426–54; Ulrich Nonn, 'Heiliges Römisches Reich Deutscher Nation. Zum Nationen-Begriff im 15. Jahrhundert', *Zeitschrift für historische Forschung* 9 (1982): 129–42; Georg Schmidt, 'Luther und die frühe Reformation – ein nationales Ereignis?', in Bernd Moeller (ed.), *Die frühe Reformation in Deutschland als Umbruch* (Gütersloh, 1998), pp. 54–75. For a recent reinterpretation of the development of the German Nation, see Georg Schmidt, *Geschichte des Alten Reiches. Staat und Nation in der Frühen Neuzeit 1495–1806* (Munich, 1999); for the debate it has aroused, see Heinz Schilling, 'Reichs-Staat und frühneuzeitliche Nation der Deutschen oder teilmodernisiertes Reichssystem', *Historische Zeitschrift*, 272 (2001): 377–95; Georg Schmidt, 'Das frühneuzeitliche Reich – komplementärer Staat und föderative Nation', *Historische Zeitschrift*, 273 (2001): 371–99.

[45]   A.G. Dickens. *The German Nation and Martin Luther* (London, 1974), pp. 1–48; Hans Kloft, 'Die Germania des Tacitus und das Problem eines deutschen Nationalbewußtseins', *Archiv für Kulturgeschichte*, 72 (1990): 93–114.

and severing all association with Rome. Two theological insights provided the foundation. First, in identifying the Antichrist, he ignored the corpus of medieval speculation and located the proofs in Scripture – it was solely a theological claim; and second, he made the Antichrist a collective rather than an individual threat. As he wrote in the *Babylonian Captivity*, the final antagonist was not a person but an institution.[46] This had the effect of locating and pluralizing the enemy. Luther's Antichrist, unlike medieval notions of the Antichrist, was physically present. In his view, the prophecy of Daniel, which associated the Antichrist with the fourth monarchy (Roman Empire) had been fulfilled, leaving Luther to conclude that the present empire was a mere counterfeit of the original, a deception invented by the papacy and entrusted to the Germans. 'For the Emperor is not the Emperor at all,' he wrote, 'but rather the Pope, to whom the Emperor is as submissive as a slave.'[47] In nationalistic discourse, this tended to make the German rulers even more unique, in that God had invested them with the task of defending the faith while both Rome and the empire succumbed to corruption.

The other contribution of the Reformation to the making of German identity was more profane, and more in the manner of an event. With the appearance of Martin Luther, the vague sense of expectation assumed an immediacy. He worked as a catalyst for public perception, convincing people that the time to act had finally arrived. In large part, this was due to his own skills as a publicist. In his reforming tract *Address to the Christian Nobility* (1520), Luther announced that a new age had dawned. 'The time for silence is over,' he wrote, paraphrasing *Ecclesiastes*, 'and the time for speech has come.' In the *Address*, Luther wrote directly to the princes of the German Nation and outlined a programme of reform that was little less than the manifesto for a national movement. Moreover, unlike previous (medieval) proposals, the *Address* spoke in a much more direct and aggressive tone. Luther did not just list the grievances and hope for better days; he targeted the cause of Germany's misery (the Papacy) and called for immediate action.[48] Borrowing from the traditional themes in the grievances and various conciliar tracts, he also seems to have made use

---

[46]   On Luther's ideas of the Antichrist, see Hans Preuss, *Die Vorstellungen vom Antichrist im späteren Mittelalter, bei Luther und in der konfessionellen Polemik* (Leipzig, 1907), pp. 83–144.

[47]   Arno Seifert, *Der Rückzug der biblischen Prophetie von der neueren Geschichte. Studien zur Geschichte der Reichstheologie des frühneuzeitlichen deutschen Protestantismus* (Cologne, 1990), p. 9. In making this claim, Luther was thus suggesting that the actual recipient of imperial power was the pope himself. See Jean Schillinger, 'Luther et l'idée d'empire', in Jean-Marie Valentin (ed.), *Luther et la Réforme. Du Commentaire de l'Epître aux Romains à la Messe allemande* (Paris, 2001), pp. 116–17.

[48]   Thomas, 'Die Deutsche Nation und Martin Luther', pp. 449–52.

of more activist clerical works such as the *Reformatio Sigismundi* and the report on the reform of the German Church drawn up by Jacob Wimpfeling at the request of Emperor Maximilian. The *Address* was infused with the popular anti-papal language of the day, and it was clearly (and openly) indebted to the work of the humanists. The result was a work, to cite its most exact interpreter, with an 'extremely lively relationship to the present',[49] and thus a text which offered both a point of origin and a fresh horizon for the creation of German identity. After decades of waiting for a new age to commence, Luther simply proclaimed that it had begun.

We can get a sense of this transformation by looking at the shifts in Protestant dynastic self-understanding. In Hesse, the history of the ruling house was reworked in the wake of the Reformation. In medieval accounts, in addition to important founding figures such as Saint Boniface, Charles Martel and the early Ludowinger rulers, the roots of the ancestral tree were traced back to Saint Elisabeth of Thuringia, medieval countess, daughter of the king of Hungary, and grandmother of Heinrich of Brabant, this latter role affording her the status of the mediatrix of legitimacy as rule passed to the Brabant lineage. Hessian genealogy was thus grounded in the twelfth century, and the main point of the association with Elisabeth was to invest the ruling princes with sacral authenticity. After Philipp of Hesse introduced the Lutheran faith, however, the history was rewritten. Elisabeth was cast as the pious wife of a landgrave, an unwitting exemplar of Lutheran sanctification, but nothing more. Philipp had her reliquary opened and her bones profaned, he replaced her image on all coins and medallions with his own, and stipulated that his final resting place would be Kassel rather than Marburg (where his ancestors had been interred beside the saint). In place of a line of descent associated with Elisabeth the saintly Hungarian, the Hessian chroniclers now fashioned a narrative which privileged Sophia, daughter of Elisabeth and mother of Heinrich, and traced a genealogy which began with the dukes of Brabant but reached back to Charlemagne – thus a family with German origins and vestiges of the imperial bloodline, but no sacral ancestry.[50]

---

[49]   Walther E. Köhler, *Luthers Schrift 'An den christlichen Adel deutscher Nation' im Spiegel der Kultur- und Zeitgeschichte* (Halle, 1895), p. 94.

[50]   A process recently illustrated in a series of articles by Thomas Fuchs. See Thomas Fuchs, 'Fürstliche Erinnerungspolitik und Geschichtsschreibung im frühneuzeitlichen Hessen', in Werner Rösener (ed.), *Adelige und bürgerliche Erinnerungskulturen des Spätmittelalters und der Frühen Neuzeit* (Göttingen, 2000), pp. 205–26; Thomas Fuchs, 'Transformation der Geschichtsschreibung im Hessen des 16. Jahrhunderts', *Hessisches Jahrbuch für Landesgeschichte*, 48 (1998): 63–82; Thomas Fuchs, 'Ständischer Aufstieg und dynastische Propaganda. Das Haus Hessen und sein Erbrecht auf Brabant', *Hessisches Jahrbuch für Landesgeschichte*, 52 (2002): 19–53; see also Karl E. Demandt, 'Verfremdung und Wiederkehr der Heiligen Elisabeth', *Hessisches Jahrbuch für Landesgeschichte*, 22 (1972): 112–61.

A similar exercise in confessional revisionism occurred in the duchy of Anhalt, where in mid-century the Lutheran Duke Georg III commissioned Ernst Brotuff to compile a new account of the origins of the house. Brotuff's *Genealogia und Chronica*, which included a preface by Melanchthon, who had already published a short work on Georg III praising his piety and learning, redirected the history of the dynasty. Tracing the origins back to the sixth century, the main focus of the work was devoted to the German origins of the line, and in particular the close relations with Brandenburg and Saxony, while the narrative made a gradual ascent from the depths of medieval Catholicism to the arrival of the Reformation, which comes to a close with the apotheosis of the three pious princes of Anhalt, Georg, Johann and Joachim.[51] In Caspar Peucer's later history, the trajectory was similar. All medieval speculation linking the house with Italian forefathers was rejected; the Anhalt dynasty came from German stock (proven by onomastic association: Ascanes, Thuiscones, Teutsche). Moreover, the entire narrative was written with one outcome in mind – the Reformation – and the contribution of the various princes to this event. In this history, the dynasty reaches its culmination with the three Lutheran princes of mid-century and their defence of the Word of God. This was projected as Anhalt's greatest contribution to the history of the German lands (by which Peucer meant the duchy itself).[52]

Perhaps the most potent reflection of this change can be viewed with reference to Luther's own land of Electoral Saxony. In the medieval period, the dynastic imagination of the Wettin princes was closely tied to two sacral communities: the Roman Catholic Church and the Holy Roman Empire. The former was made most manifest in the famous relics collection in the castle church, while the latter, the imperial realm, was expressed through the artwork in the churches and the residence as well as the literary and historical works, paramount being the *Chronicle of the Saxons* (1492), which was essentially a register of Saxon relations with the various

---

[51] Martin Hecht, 'Hofordnung, Wappen und Geschichtsschreibung. Fürstliches Rangbewusstsein und dynastische Repräsentation in Anhalt in 15. und 16. Jahrhundert,' in Werner Freitag and Michael Hecht (eds), *Die Fürsten von Anhalt. Herrschaftssymbolik, dynastische Vernunft und politische Konzepte in Spätmittelalter und Früher Neuzeit* (Halle, 2003), pp. 103–9; Ernst Brotuff, *Genealogia und Chronica, des Durchlauchten Hochgebornen, Königlichen und Fürstlichen Hauses, der Fürsten zu Anhalt* (Leipzig, 1556), Ci^r–Cvi^v; Philipp Melanchthon, *Von des hochlöblichen, Christlichen Fürsten und Herrn, Georgen Fürsten zu Anhalt* (Wittenberg, 1554), fol. Bv^v–Bvi^r; later histories largely followed the narrative established by Brotuff, among them the work by Bartholomäus Clamorin, *Descriptio Historica, praeclarae, magnificae et antiquae stirpis, principum Anhaldinorum* (Dresden, 1587).

[52] Caspar Peucer, *Kurtze Historische Erzelung, Von dem Fürstlichem Hause zu Anhalt.* (Wittenberg 1572), fol. Bi^r–Ci^r.

emperors and their subsequent rewards.[53] A century and a half later, as Johann Meisner described the land in an anniversary sermon, a different sense of community had evolved. Wittenberg was now eulogized as the very centre of the world, 'because it was in this place,' claimed Meisner, 'as out of Zion, as it were, that the light of [God's] gospel was set aflame'.[54] The relic collection that had once made Wittenberg such an important site of pilgrimage no longer existed. Save a chalice that had been gifted to Luther, the collection had been dismantled and sent to Nuremberg, where it was melted down to pay off the debts of Elector Johann.[55] Many of the medieval paintings and the portraits had been removed or destroyed; in their place was a series of portraits of the electors, now with German verse celebrating their contributions to the land of Saxony. Visitors travelled to the city in order to take in the display of artefacts associated with the Reformation, including Cranach's portraits of Luther and Melanchthon, together with their tombs in the church, and the statues and memorials devoted to Friedrich and Johann Friedrich, the two great champions of the Lutheran faith.

When Balthasar Menz visited Wittenberg at the end of the sixteenth century, he noted how rebuilding had covered up the traces of the past. Even the gold lettering Elector Friedrich had embossed over the gate of the residence referring to his role as marshal of the empire now sat beneath layers of chalk left during recent renovations.[56] The old notions of sacral

---

[53]   On the origins of the relic collection, see Enno Bünz, 'Zur Geschichte des Wittenberger Heiltums. Johannes Nühn als Reliquienjäger in Helmarshausen und Hersfeld', *Zeitschrift des Vereins für Thüringische Geschichte*, 52 (1998): 135–58; on late medieval Saxon identity, see Günter Werner, *Ahnen und Autoren. Landeschroniken und kollektive Identitäten um 1500 in Sachsen, Oldenburg und Mecklenburg* (Husum, 2002), pp. 57–129.

[54]   Johann Meisner, *Jubilaeum Wittebergense* (Wittenberg, 1668), p. 6; the full range of Old Testament types had been explored a few years earlier in Caspar Schmidt, *Wittenbergisches Jerusalem* (Wittenberg, 1640).

[55]   Ernst Müller, 'Die Entlassung des ernestinischen Kämmerers Johann Rietesel im Jahre 1532 und die Auflösung des Wittenberger Heiligtums. Ein Beitrag zur Biographie des Kurfürsten Johann des Beständigen von Sachsen', *Archiv für Reformationsgeschichte*, 80 (1989): 228–31. The evangelical objection to the relic collection was neatly summarized by a sixteenth-century reader in the margin of a copy of the *Dye Zaigung des hochlobwirdigen hailigthums der Stifft Kirchen aller hailigen zu Wittenburg* (Wittenberg, 1509), presently in the Herzog August Bibliothek, Wolfenbüttel (154.2 Theol.), fol. Aiii: 'die ewige selikeit kan niemant erwerben noch erehrben, Sie ist eine gabe Gottes'. The *Zaigung* (along with the inventory of the Halle collection) was reissued as part of the Reformation centenary celebrations, though this time with a preface pointing out how they were testimony to the deceit and corruption of the Roman Catholic Church. See Wolfgang Franz, *Historischer Erzehlung Der Beyden Heiligthümen* (Wittenberg, 1618).

[56]   Balthasar Menz, *Stambuch und kurtze Erzehlung* (Wittenberg, 1598), fol. Mii[v]–Miii[r]. Until it perished in the fire of 1760, the door of the Castle Church itself became something of a relic. Matthaeus Faber included an engraving in

community had given way to a more localized and secularized sense of identity.

The Rise of Confessional Politics

Scripture enabled the evangelical princes to imagine the religious conflict in terms of root dichotomies – law versus Gospel, good versus evil, Christ versus the Antichrist – and thereby serve as the template for an early sense of confessional identity. This first became apparent at the diet of Speyer (1526), when Protestant princes such as Philipp of Hesse and Johann Friedrich of Saxony arrived at the gathering with the letters VDMIE (*verbum domini manet in aeternum*) stitched onto the sleeves of their livery. Within a few years this slogan had spread throughout the Protestant camp in a variety of media (clothes, banners, coins, swords, powder flasks, horse muzzles, cannon bores and halberds), and it was clearly meant to distinguish the community of the godly from the rest of the Catholic lands.[57] In the art and imagery of the courts as well, the symbolism changed by mid-century: from portraits to public theatre to music, the Protestant princes began to define themselves *against* the Catholic Empire by drawing on the evangelical faith.[58] Protestant imagery became brazenly anti-Catholic, often evoking figures or types from Scripture to portray local history, as did the Old Testament studies commissioned by Moritz of Saxony for the walls of the loggia, or the more personal visual histories of the Ernestine princes devised with a view to their heroic struggle against the forces of the Antichrist in the early years of the Reformation. Indeed, the new sense of Protestant identity that evolved in Saxony was deliberately and meticulously fashioned, and it was nothing less than an attempt to re-imagine the recent past within the framework of sacral history. Thus in a range of paintings and engravings, Johann Friedrich, defeated and imprisoned by Emperor Charles V after the Battle of Mühlberg, became the wounded Protestant warrior, with the scar on his cheek as stigma and biblical verse on the edge of the portrait testifying to his role as the new Daniel. More direct was the series of woodcuts depicting the baptism of

---

his bicentenary history that depicted tourists stopping before the door. He also provided a rather brief and embarrassed history of the relic collection for the 'curious reader'. See Matthaeus Faber, *Kurtzgefaste Historische Nachricht von der Schloß- und Academischen Stiffts-Kirche zu Aller-heiligen in Wittenberg* (Wittenberg, 1717), pp. 192–94.

[57]   F.J. Stopp, '*Verbum Domini Manet in Aeternum*. The Dissemination of a Reformation Slogan, 1522–1904,' in Siegbert S. Prawer, R. Hinton Thomas and Leonard Forster (eds), *Essays in German Language, Culture and Society* (London, 1969), pp. 123–35; Meisner, *Jubilaeum Wittebergense*, p. 107.

[58]   For the rise of Protestant court culture, see Helen Watanabe-O'Kelly, *Court Culture in Dresden: From Renaissance to Baroque* (Basingstoke, 2002), pp. 5–36.

Christ in the Elbe, with the Ernestine princes and their families, joined by Martin Luther, bearing witness to the event.[59]

Mühlberg and its aftermath, however, remind us that these shifts in perception had profound consequences for political relations. The fault lines became apparent in the immediate wake of the defeat, as the Protestants, forced to kneel before Emperor Charles V and effect the traditional act of supplication, began to express public pangs of conscience. Some of the princes were unable to divorce the ritual from its sacramental (and thus idolatrous) overtones and expressed their reservations about this type of 'Egyptian adoration'.[60] The political ideology behind this aversion had been worked out years before in the theories of resistance formulated to justify the creation of the League of Schmalkald, a military alliance with the explicit purpose of resisting the emperor. Realizing that the faith could not survive long isolated and defenceless, the Lutherans had been compelled to join forces and develop a theory of resistance that pitched the German princes against the Habsburg emperor. The theoretical foundations differed: while the Hessians drew on a notion of constitutional resistance grounded in the belief that the emperor did not rule as a monarch, but rather shared sovereignty with the imperial estates, the Saxon jurists built on theories of private law, claiming that when an authority went beyond the bounds of his office, he was no longer a rightful judge but a private citizen, and hence no longer a lawful magistrate. In this case, the emperor was abusing his office by legislating in matters of belief.[61] Notwithstanding the different approaches, the end result was a general ideology of resistance shared by

---

[59] Even within a biblical landscape on this scale, there was a place for local history. For those with a keen eye, the townscape of Wittenberg could be seen in the background, its towers, having fallen victim to imperial forces, deprived of their gothic points. See Carl C. Christensen, *Princes and Propaganda: Electoral Saxon Art of the Reformation* (Kirksville, MO, 1992), pp. 92–101; Ingrid Schulze, *Lucas Cranach d. J. und die protestantische Bildkunst in Sachsen und Thüringen* (Jena, 2004), pp. 87–102; on more general themes relating to the rise of territorial identity in Saxony, see the contributions in Michael Beyer, Andreas Gößner and Günther Wartenberg (eds), *Kirche und Regionalbewußtsein in Sachsen im 16. Jahrhundert. Regionenbezogene Identifikationsprozesse im konfessionellen Raum* (Leipzig, 2003); for the development of a Protestant princely iconography, see Naima Ghermani, 'Une difficile représentation? Les portraits de princes calvinistes dans l'Empire allemand à la fin du XVIe siècle', *Revue Historique*, 635 (2005): 561–91.

[60] Barbara Stollberg-Rilinger, 'Knien vor Gott – knien vor dem Kaiser. Zum Ritualwandel im Konfessionskonflikt', in Gerd Althoff (ed.), *Zeichen – Rituale – Werte. Internationales Kolloquium des Sonderforschungsbereichs 496 an der Westfälischen Wilhelms-Universität Münster* (Münster, 2004), pp. 501–32.

[61] Eike Wolgast, *Die Religionsfrage als Problem des Widerstandsrechts im 16. Jahrhundert* (Heidelberg, 1980), pp. 9–27; Quentin Skinner, *The Foundations of Modern Political Thought: The Age of Reformation* (Cambridge, 1996), vol. 2, pp. 189–225.

most of the Protestant powers and a general readiness to view the emperor as an enemy of the German people. Moreover, this was clearly affiliated with the emerging sense of fatherland (*patria*) and its association with justice, political order and the preservation of the faith within a given jurisdictional area.[62] The empire was beginning to turn in on itself.

By mid-century, the idea of the papal Antichrist and its association with the emperor had become a central topos in the language of German liberty.[63] And it sounded a clear political note. Even the Catholic princes could agree that Charles's efforts to force through a religious settlement smacked of Roman tyranny. And even in the most candid of the Lutheran theories of resistance, such as the work *About Defence and Self-Defence* (1547) by Regius Selinus, tutor to the children of the Saxon Elector, the main issue was not only one of religious conscience, but rather the liberties of 'our dear Fatherland of the German Nation' and how they had been threatened by Spanish domination and papal tyranny.[64] Little wonder rumours began to surface at the diet of Augsburg (1530) that the Protestant princes were planning to oppose Ferdinand's succession to the imperial crown and replace the Habsburg with a king of their own. Some spoke of Johann Friedrich as the natural choice, but most hope was placed in the candidature of Philipp of Hesse, who emerged as a serious threat after the restitution of Württemberg (1534). As Zwingli prophesied in open letters after the meeting in Marburg, Philipp of Hesse 'has been chosen [by God] to do great things', though the time was not yet ripe to speak openly about what this might mean.[65]

Of course, despite the tensions and crises, and the German wars of mid-century, the empire survived the Reformation, even though over time many of its foundation principles and its higher organs of rule no longer commanded Protestant assent. As Georg Schmidt has remarked: 'while the flawed effectiveness of the empire was repeatedly criticized, its legitimacy as a state was never called into question'.[66] In part this was due to the change of guard: with Charles V retiring to the monastery in Yuste and the deaths of Johann Friedrich and Philipp of Hesse, a generation that thought in extremes passed away. Their successors – Ferdinand and Maximilian, August of Saxony, William IV of Hesse – were more interested in

---

[62]   Von Friedeburg, 'The Making of Patriots', pp. 895–6.

[63]   Schmidt, *Geschichte des Alten Reiches*, pp. 75–99.

[64]   Robert von Friedeburg, *Self-Defence and Religious Strife in Early Modern Europe. England and Germany, 1530–1680* (Aldershot, 2002), p. 82.

[65]   Heinz Duchhardt, *Protestantisches Kaisertum und altes Reich. Die Diskussion über die Konfession des Kaisers in Politik, Publizistik und Staatsrecht* (Wiesbaden, 1997), p. 20.

[66]   Georg Schmidt, 'Konfessionalisierung, Reich und Deutsche Nation', in Schindling and Ziegler (eds), *Die Territorien des Reichs*, vol. 7, p. 193.

conservation and consolidation than winning new ground.[67] In part it was due to the nature of the empire and how it actually functioned. Confessional division put an end the idea of a consolidated monarchy, especially once it came into conflict with an idea of German Liberty charged by religious sentiment and embraced by the territorial prince. But as a system of political relations (what Schmidt has likened to a composite monarchy) that dealt with 'federal' concerns such as forms of taxation, the defence of the realm against the Turks, and the general peace and commonwealth, it was not seriously endangered by the process of Reformation.[68]

What did not survive unshaken, however, was the political *integrity* of the empire, and not just the higher ideals, such as its sacral legitimacy and subsequent claims to universal dominion, but its inner constitution. The full range of impact of the Reformation would require an analysis that takes into account the crises and settlements of the seventeenth century, but as two brief examples of the beginnings of this process, we might look at the shift in patterns of patronage effected by religious change and the restructuring of international and inter-territorial relations.

In medieval Germany, both the Catholic Church and the empire provided 'channels of mobility' for the aristocracy of the realm.[69] Indeed, the status of a German prince was more or less defined by his degree of proximity to the Roman king. After the Reformation, due to the centrifugal effects of the confessional dynamic, Protestant princes preferred men of the same religious convictions, a logical preference in an age when the confession of a territory could be perceived as little less than a declaration of war. Viewed in this light, it is little wonder that the prince of Hesse was so interested in men 'who understood matters, and will stick with us against the papists and others ... and will resolutely defend our Christian religion against the Jesuits and their like ...'.[70] In the duchy of Württemberg, the

---

[67]   Manfred Rudersdorf, 'Die Generation der lutherischen Landesväter im Reich. Bausteine zu einer Typologie des deutschen Reformationsfürsten', in Schindling and Ziegler (eds), *Die Territorien des Reichs*, vol. 7, pp. 137–70.

[68]   Rudersdorf, 'Die Generation', p. 32: 'Man sah die trennenden konfessionellen Faktoren, fühlte sich aber auf dem festen Boden des Religionsfriedens und hatte überhaupt keinen Grund, eine radikale neue Herrschaftsordnung zu konzipieren – das Reich war Rahmen und Ideologie genug, in ihm konnte sich jeder, der protestantische wie der katholische Fürst, als Pater Patriae fühlen – was gewisse Unterschiede im Selbstverständnis nicht ausschloß.' In later years, as Protestants began to discuss the legitimacy of assuming the imperial throne, emphasis was placed on the 'catholicity' of the evangelical faith. See Duchhardt, *Protestantisches Kaisertum*, pp. 4ff., 329, 126ff.

[69]   Wolfgang Reinhard, 'Kirche als Mobilitätskanal der frühneuzeitlichen Gesellschaft', in Winfried Schulze (ed.), *Ständische Gesellschaft und soziale Mobilität* (Munich, 1988), pp. 331–51.

[70]   Thomas Klein, *Der Kampf um die zweite Reformation in Kursachsen, 1586– 1591* (Cologne, 1962), p. 98; Volker Press, *Calvinismus und Territorialstaat. Regierung*

state ordinance stipulated that state ministers show evidence of 'zeal in the [evangelical] religion' – which essentially meant that Catholics needed to look elsewhere for patronage.[71]

In the search for power and favour, many thus turned to the Habsburg lands, where the Catholic faith was so closely tied to the ideology of rule.[72] Throughout the confessional age, a number of suspect conversions (what contemporaries termed 'court conversions') saw members of the elite rise in imperial favour, including Wolf Siegmund von Losenstein, who was elevated to the rank of Count of the Empire after his conversion, Karl von Liechtenstein, who, once an 'ardent Protestant', became a member of the Privy Council as a Catholic, and Franz Christoph Khevenhüller, whose change of heart saw him rise in imperial service.[73] Protestants could serve the empire as well, and in fact many second-generation Lutheran princes had little difficulty serving both the Catholic Empire and their Protestant subjects. Post-Augsburg Protestant rulers moved freely between imperial and territorial politics, and they made skilled use of the networks and the institutions of the *Reich* to achieve their territorial aims.[74] But this political necessity notwithstanding, it was clearly an advantage in the eyes of the emperor to be a son of the Catholic Church, and there is little doubt that the traditional imperial matrix of power and patronage was transformed by the religious developments of the sixteenth century.

Of course, even more detrimental to the integrity of the empire was the confessionalization of German politics, the gradual disintegration of the unity (or the ideal of unity) of the realm, and the rise of blocs and divisions generated by the new religious order. Historians have traced this process in detail, from the first phase of mid-century theological consolidation as religious ideas began to impact social and political development to the outbreak of the Thirty Years' War, which was, in effect, the final stage of the confessional dynamic and the harvest of decades of political and theological division.[75] The impact was clear to see: the fragmentation of imperial and international relations, the further decentralization and particularization of the *Reich*, the rise of territorial identity and the eclipse of the idea of the

---

und Zentralbehörden der Kurpfalz 1559–1619 (Stuttgart, 1970), pp. 181–266; Georg Schmidt, 'Die zweite Reformation in den Reichsgrafschaften. Konfessionswechsel aus Glaubensüberzeugung oder aus politischem Kalkül?', in Meinrad Schaab (ed.), *Territorialstaat und Calvinismus* (Stuttgart, 1993), pp. 97–136.

[71] Walter Bernhardt, *Die Zentralbehörden des Herzogtums Württemberg und ihre Beamten 1520–1629* (Stuttgart, 1972), vol. 1, p. 80.

[72] R.J.W. Evans, *The Making of the Habsburg Monarchy 1550–1700: An Interpretation* (Oxford, 1979), pp. 157–308.

[73] Thomas Winkelbauer, *Fürst und Fürstendiener. Gundaker von Liechtenstein, ein österreichischer Aristokrat des konfessionellen Zeitalters* (Vienna, 1999), pp. 66–158, 103.

[74] Rudersdorf, 'Patriarchalisches Fürstenregiment', pp. 309–15.

[75] Schilling, 'Confessionalization in the Empire'.

sacrum imperium, the disintegration of the traditional legal and political bonds (dynastic conventions, unions and alliances, laws and precedents), and the rise of political associations and leagues based upon the principles of a common Protestant faith.[76] The old concerns of imperial statecraft did not just disappear, and even the most pious sovereigns continued to weigh the concerns of the faith against the realities of rule (whether defined against a backcloth of German liberties or the practical necessities of governance); but by the latter decades of the sixteenth century, religion had emerged as one of the central foundations (and in many instances, *the* central foundation) of the strategies and policies that determined political relations between territories and nations. As Holger Thomas Gräf has remarked, with the onset of confessional divisions, 'religious affiliation now formed the basis for political cooperation, which was no longer guaranteed through dynastic affinity or traditional feudal relations and friendships'.[77] Although it did not have a fatal effect on the workings of the *Reich*, confessional plurality did work to undermine the integrity of the late medieval empire.

Conclusion

In the end, it should not come as a surprise that the Reformation gave rise to such a complex landscape of political change in the German lands of the empire. With the introduction of the Peace of Augsburg and the underlying legal principle of the right of reformation, the empire adopted a political and juridical framework that was predisposed to give rise to tension, conflict and plurality.[78] Moreover, due to the nature of the political setting, there was no inevitable pattern to the rise of the confessional state in sixteenth-century Germany, no unobstructed triumph of the confessional will as secular and spiritual authorities joined in common purpose. On the contrary, the introduction of religion into political affairs 'brought both centripetal and centrifugal forces to bear on early modern state building'.[79] For every proof that could be offered in support of the notion that religion

---

[76]   Compare Heinrich Lutz, *Christianitas afflicta. Europa, das Reich und die päpstliche Politik im Niedergang der Hegemonie Kaiser Karls V. (1552–1556)* (Göttingen, 1964), pp. 31ff.

[77]   Gräf, *Konfession und internationales System*, p. 333.

[78]   Axel Gotthard, *Das Alte Reich 1495-1806* (Darmstadt, 2003), pp. 48–85, esp. 61; Schmidt, *Geschichte des Alten Reiches*, pp. 113–49; Heckel, *Deutschland im konfessionellen Zeitalter*, pp. 75–85; Moriz Ritter, *Deutsche Geschichte im Zeitalter der Gegenreformation und des Dreißigjährigen Krieges (1555–1648)* (Stuttgart, 1895), vol. 2, pp. 213–32.

[79]   Joel F. Harrington and Helmut Walser Smith, 'Confessionalization, community, and state building in Germany, 1555–1870', *The Journal of Modern History*, 69 (1997): p. 84.

was a central pillar of absolutism, another could be flourished in defence of the idea that it was one of its most profound constraints.

Yet in substantial respects, the Reformation movement did effect an evident transformation of political culture in the Protestant territories. Church and state formed a closer union, a process with consequences for both the systems and the ideologies of sovereignty; the evangelical prince inherited increased powers of rule and a more profound language of legitimacy; Protestant territories fashioned a new sense of community, new ideas of origins and identity, while relations between the German princes and the empire began to suffer strains and ruptures that had not existed in any previous age. None of this was enough to bring imperial politics to the ultimate breaking point. For Protestant and Catholic alike, the empire remained the only legitimate state. But within the territories, changes had taken place that would have serious implications for later stages of German history. For as Seckendorff remarked in the work cited at the outset:

> even though the German principalities are not monarchies in the strict sense, they contain within them the same broad tracts of land, the same babel of tongues and nations, the same countless customs and mores of diverse peoples, the same unruly subjects and powerful, ill-intentioned neighbours, and in general the same profound and weighty conditions as any of the great kingdoms of the world.[80]

Any change of religion in such a setting would necessarily have implications that reached deep into political life.

---

[80]   Seckendorff, *Teutscher Fürsten-Stat*, p. 85.

CHAPTER 3

Rich and Poor in Reformation Augsburg: The City Council, the Fugger Bank and the Formation of a Bi-confessional Society

Bernd Roeck

A German 'Montaillou'

In recent years, the city of Augsburg has come to be seen as a kind of 'Montaillou' in early modern German history – I need only mention the studies of Claus Peter Clasen on the history of the weavers in the city,[1] Lyndal Roper's *Holy Household* (and latterly her books *Oedipus and the Devil* and *Witch Craze*)[2] and the network analysis of Katharina Sieh-Burens[3] – but would like to refer especially to Etienne François's *La frontière invisible*, where the extraordinary mixed confessional society of this imperial city is described and analysed.[4] The reason Augsburg has gained such prominence in the early modern history of Germany (and for that matter of Europe) is not only due to its importance as a centre for finance and trade, as a regular meeting-place for Imperial diets and for that matter its position as a central *lieu de mémoire* for the Reformation. It is also due to the existence of an outstanding set of records in the municipal archives of Augsburg which in turn have become a major attraction to historians from around the world.

---

[1]   Claus Peter Clasen, *Die Augsburger Weber. Leistungen und Krisen des Textilgewerbes um 1600* (Augsburg, 1981).

[2]   Lyndal Roper, *The Holy Household: Women and Morals in Reformation Augsburg* (Oxford, 1989); Lyndal Roper, *Oedipus and the Devil: Witchcraft, Sexuality and Religion in Early Modern Europe* (London and New York, 1994); Lyndal Roper, *Witch Craze. Terror and fantasy in Baroque Germany* (New Haven, CT and London, 2004).

[3]   Katharina Sieh-Burens, *Oligarchie, Konfession und Politik im 16. Jahrhundert. Zur sozialen Verflechtung der Augsburger Bürgermeister und Stadtpfleger 1518–1618* (Munich, 1986).

[4]   Etienne François, *Die unsichtbare Grenze. Katholiken und Protestanten in Augsburg, 1648–1806* (Sigmaringen, 1991).

An unbroken series of city tax records starts in 1346 and continues well into the late seventeenth century.[5] They provide enough information to make a reasonable assessment of the economic situation of most burghers, while informing us about the social topography of the city, not to mention other aspects. The wedding and punishment books, the wills, *Pflegschaftsbücher* ('tutelage books') and other sources permit the historian to reconstruct social networks based on family relations, sponsorships by godparents, friendships, not to mention the significance of neighbourhoods.[6] The council's minutes can be used to retrace and elucidate political decisions. An outstandingly important group of sources is the *Urgichtensammlung*, an uninterrupted series of interrogation records of male and female delinquents, starting in the sixteenth century. They contain detailed information, often amounting to several pages; some exceptional examinations even run to several hundred pages. They not only deal with every crime from homicide to theft, rape, insult and tavern scraps, but also with all kinds of religious issues – suspicion of heresy, black and white magic, witchcraft and confessional affairs.[7] Combined with other sources, especially the tax records, they make it possible to reconstruct an extremely polymorphic picture of life in this early modern city – even down to the level of the 'common man'. Moreover, no other German city has produced such a rich late medieval and early modern historiography which provides us with detailed information about events and contemporary discourses.

Augsburg as a Paradigm

There are good reasons for choosing Augsburg as a Reformation paradigm. The surviving sources allow considerable insight into the 'structures' of the Reformation and make it possible to compare long-term processes with single events, as well as offering insight into the thinking and acting of individuals. The pertinence of the example of Augsburg for Reformation history is enhanced by the bi-confessional nature of the city.[8]

---

[5]   See Claus Peter Clasen, *Die Augsburger Steuerbücher um 1600* (Augsburg, 1979).

[6]   See Bernd Roeck, 'Neighbourhoods and the Public in German Cities of the Early Modern Period: A Magician and the Neighbourhood Network', in Anton Schuurman and Pieter Spierenburg (eds), *Private Domain, Public Inquiry. Families and Life-styles in the Netherlands and Europe, 1550 to the Present* (Hilversum, 1996), pp. 193–209.

[7]   Bernd Roeck, *Eine Stadt in Krieg in Frieden. Studien zur Geschichte der Reichsstadt Augsburg zwischen Kalenderstreit und Parität*, 2 vols (Göttingen, 1989).

[8]   See François, *Unsichtbare Grenze*, and Paul Warmbrunn's excellent study, *Zwei Konfessionen in einer Stadt. Das Zusammenleben von Katholiken und*

The mechanisms of confessionalization are easy to identify here, especially the growth of confessional identity, the formation of confessional groups through means of conflict and the development of specific ritual systems.

In terms of bi-confessionalism, Augsburg was something of a special case. Most of the large imperial cities had turned exclusively protestant; the only – very interesting – exception being Cologne.[9] Besides Augsburg, a couple of smaller southern German cities such as Ravensburg, Biberach and Dinkelsbühl also allowed the coexistence of two confessions within their walls: the Catholic and the Lutheran.[10] This was the situation in 1555, and one hundred years and many painful experiences later, the parity of Lutheranism and Catholicism in Augsburg was confirmed by the Peace of Westphalia.

The Peace ordered in its city-clause that complete equality should prevail in religious affairs in Augsburg.[11] Future religious disputes were to be settled by law; laws were introduced to deal with controversies. Indeed, this served to generate a host of narrow-minded quarrels concerning all sorts of petty questions – but it prevented bloody escalations. This kind of coexistence had little to do with tolerance. In the city, a specific type of society developed which split into two separate social and cultural milieus. In the nineteenth century, the cultural historian Wilhelm Heinrich Riehl provided an account of how this process might end: 'Shall the Protestant buy his meat at a Catholic butcher? Shall the Catholic go to a Protestant carpenter when his chair is broken? For some people in Augsburg these are still scrupulous questions.'[12]

The intention of this chapter is to trace the origins of this bi-confessional structure. This in turn will reveal why Augsburg did not become an exclusively Protestant bastion, as most other imperial cities did. An important factor, but far from the only one, was the presence of the wealthy merchant banking house of the Fugger family, with Jacob Fugger II (1459–1525) as its central character. In what follows, I shall focus on the social history of the Reformation. It will not be possible to understand the Reformation in Augsburg if the extremely pronounced economical imbalance in Augsburg during the late Middle Ages and the early modern

---

Protestanten in den paritätischen Reichsstädten Augsburg, Biberach, Ravensburg von 1548 bis 1648 (Wiesbaden 1983).

[9] See Bob Scribner, 'Why was there no Reformation in Cologne?', *Bulletin of the Institute of Historical Research*, 49 (1976): 217–41, and Manfred Groten, 'Die nächste Generation: Scribners Thesen aus heutiger Sicht', in Georg Mölich and Gerd Schwerhoff (eds), *Köln als Kommunikationszentrum. Studien zur frühneuzeitlichen Stadtgeschichte (Der Riss im Himmel*, vol. IV) (Cologne, 2000), pp. 110–13.

[10] See Warmbrunn, *Zwei Konfessionen*.

[11] Instrumentum Pacis Osnabrugense, V, pp. 3–10.

[12] Wilhelm Heinrich Riehl, 'Augsburger Studien' (1857), in *Culturstudien aus neun Jahrhunderten* (Stuttgart, 1862), pp. 261–330, p. 319.

period is ignored. In Augsburg, a small elite, which grew richer and richer, was counterbalanced by the mass of impoverished craftsmen, day labourers and so on. It was from within these circles that the first followers of Luther, Zwingli and other evangelical leaders emerged, guaranteeing that social and religious questions remained closely intertwined.

A Centre for Social Unrest: The Suburb of St Jacob

Already by the late Middle Ages Augsburg was one of the most important centres for the textile industry in the Holy Roman Empire. A huge part of the population made their living from the production and refinement of textiles.[13] We do not have exact numbers for the fifteenth century, but it is a fair assumption that about half the craftsmen of Augsburg depended directly or indirectly on this key area: being tailors, cloth cutters, dyers, spinners, and last but not least, weavers living within the city and its surrounding areas. By the fifteenth century, Augsburg was characterized by a mono-structured economy. The textile economy fed the population, but disturbances within the market, especially export problems, immediately affected the Augsburg economy. The textile production was not only extremely susceptible to economic cycles; in Augsburg, the whole city was affected when the weavers faced difficulties. Around 1600, about two thirds of the weavers in Augsburg depended on support from the public purse.[14] During the period leading up to the Reformation, the situation was probably less dramatic, but it is noticeable that weavers constantly participated in social riots. Even so, it is impossible to quantify or measure the social discontent of this group.

Similarly, the topography of urban riots on several occasions points to the weavers and other textile workers as particularly discontented. Often, these riots seem to have started in the suburb of St Jacob, the centre of Augsburg's cloth manufacture.[15] A closer inspection of this quarter of the city is crucial for an understanding of the Reformation of Augsburg, since it was here that evangelical ideas made their first and most significant impact.

To comprehend these developments fully, it is necessary to start right after the Black Death of the fourteenth century. The plague seems to have

---

[13] See Rolf Kiessling, 'Augsburgs Wirtschaft im 14. und 15. Jahrhundert', in Gunther Gottlieb (ed.), *Geschichte der Stadt Augsburg von der Römerzeit bis zur Gegenwart* (Stuttgart 1985), pp. 171–81.

[14] See Clasen, *Die Augsburger Weber* and Bernd Roeck, '"Arme" in Augsburg zu Beginn des 30jährigen Krieges. Untersuchungen zu Wohn- und Vermögensverhältnissen der städtischen ‚Unterschicht' und zur Sozialtopographie der Reichsstadt anhand einer Getreideverteilungsliste aus dem Jahr 1622', *Zeitschrift für bayerische Landesgeschichte*, 46 (1983), pp. 515–58.

[15] See Roeck, *Stadt in Krieg und Frieden*, pp. 836–8.

caused a significant accumulation of capital. The fortunes of the dead were handed over to the survivors.[16] Accordingly, the plague resulted in a concentration of capital among a rich elite of traders and bankers. Like elsewhere, the 'dynamics of the shrinkage' strengthened the trade guilds. It also resulted in a shortage of qualified craftsmen: at the time, a popular phrase stated that two masters were running after one craftsman to win him for their workshop.[17] The demand for high-quality handcrafted products and luxury goods from the merchant elite guaranteed that earnings among the skilled craftsmen rose.

However, this was only half of the story. Hand in hand with the accumulation of capital among the upper class, and the rise of the craft guilds, went a considerable expansion in the number of destitute in the city.[18] Like elsewhere, the people from the surrounding areas migrated into the depopulated city of Augsburg. As a result, the population density grew, in particular in the suburbs. It is noteworthy that the suburb of St Jacob was legally incorporated into the city of Augsburg during the second half of the fourteenth century. In this part of Augsburg, the population density was high, and people lived in often desperate and unhygienic circumstances conditioned by extreme poverty. The capital redistribution in the wake of the Black Death was now a distant memory. To the new burghers, often only low and badly paid employment was available. It is not surprising that the recurring epidemics claimed most of their victims here.[19] Among these new immigrants, we find the first member of the Fugger family to arrive in Augsburg: a tax book from 1367 simply states 'Fucker advenit'. The weaver Hans Fugger had arrived from a village south of Augsburg, taking the first steps towards the creation of one of wealthiest merchant banking houses of the early modern period.

By the seventeenth century, rural traditions still characterized life in the suburb of St Jacob. People addressed each other by their forenames, as explicitly stated by a chronicler.[20] At that time, even the sexual habits of the population corresponded more rural than urban patterns, with

---

[16]   Regarding Augsburg, there is no thorough survey of this develpment. See Kießling, *Augsburger Wirtschaft*; Bernd Roeck, *Geschichte Augsburgs* (Munich, 2005), pp. 75–9.

[17]   Eberhard Weis, 'Gesellschaftsstrukturen und Gesellschaftsentwicklung in der frühen Neuzeit', in Karl Bosl and Eberhard Weis, *Die Gesellschaft in Deutschland I* (Munich, 1976), p. 144.

[18]   Joachim Jahn, 'Die Augsburger Sozialstruktur im 15. Jahrhundert', in Gottlieb (ed.), *Geschichte*, pp. 187–93, p. 188.

[19]   Roeck, *Eine Stadt*, pp. 643–8.

[20]   Ibid., p. 837.

exceptionally few births during the summer harvest months.[21] Likewise, traditional magical practices remained prominent within this quarter.[22]

Magic is the attempt, not only to pray to God and the saints for good health and fortune, but according to Marcel Mauss, to *force* health, wealth and luck by applying rituals.[23] That is not to say that magic can be interpreted exclusively as an answer to precarious life conditions (it is known that the use of magical practices was by no means limited to the lower classes), but the use of magic is an indication that the people did not exclusively believe in the power of religion and that they considered the Church to be deficient. The 'wise woman' or the magician could give an answer if the priest and his holy books had none.

Popular beliefs and culture within the suburb of St Jacob was clearly strong, and formed a subculture outside the control of the Catholic Church. Similarly, the district appears to have been a centre of social and economic dissatisfaction already in the fourteenth century. Thus, shortly after the epidemic of 1352, some Augsburg burghers were put on trial by the city authorities. They were named Jacobites due to the place of their meetings, and were accused of sedition and revolutionary ideas.[24]

Clearly, the weavers, many of whom lived in the suburb of St Jacob, could draw on inspiration for their social and religious dissatisfaction from the actions of their forefathers, and their participation in social riots and religious opposition during the late fourteenth and fifteenth centuries belongs to a long tradition of unrest and resistance.[25] A weaver was the speaker for the craftsmen who took power in the Augsburg during the so-called 'guild revolution'. Cloth (*Loden*) weavers are named explicitly as the core group of a heretic movement discovered in 1393. Most likely, the cloth workers known as the 'grueblins lewt', of whom six were burnt in public, were Waldensians or followers of John Wycliffe.[26] In 1397, tax revolts broke out in Augsburg, leading a chronicler to make this statement: 'There are a lot of unsound weavers in the city and one could well imagine that they would love to kill somebody in the city if they could get rid of their debts through this.' The fifteenth-century economic boom, leading to

---

[21]   Ibid., pp. 836–44.
[22]   Ibid., pp. 446, 551, 836–7.
[23]   See Marcel Mauss, *Sociologie et anthropologie* (Paris, 1950).
[24]   Wolgang Zorn, *Augsburg. Geschichte einer deutschen Stadt* (Augsburg, 1972), p. 128; Rolf Kießling, *Bürgerliche Gesellschaft und Kirche in Augsburg im Spätmittelalter* (Augsburg 1971), p. 316.
[25]   See Bernhard Schimmelpfennig, 'Religiöses Leben im späten Mittelalter', in Gottlieb (ed.), *Augsburg*, pp. 220–24, 224 (n. 18: sources); Friedrich Roth, *Augsburger Reformationsgeschichte*, 4 vols (Munich, 1901–11); Roeck, *Augsburg*, pp. 83–4.
[26]   Kießling, *Bürgerliche Gesellschaft*, p. 317.

the era of 'Golden Augsburg', as some historians have termed this period, did not benefit the people of Augsburg across the board.

The Fuggers

As we have seen, clear correlations between social deprivation and religious excitement existed in Augsburg for more than a century and a half before the Reformation. The dominant groups in Augsburg, the bankers and long-distance traders, were aware of the threat to the political order presented by the large number of poor and discontented citizens, constantly inflated by the influx of people from the countryside. It was no coincidence that Jacob Fugger 'the wealthy' built his most famous foundation for the poor, the so-called 'Fuggerei', in the St Jacob's quarter of the city. It became a 'city within the city', modelling itself on the Dutch *Beginenhöfe*.[27] Since 1514, Jacob Fugger had been purchasing land in this part of the city, and by 1523, 53 uniform houses had been built, each consisting of two dwellings – this 'village', a Christian utopia, was constructed around straight streets. The houses were leased to poor day labourers and craftsmen for one Rhine florin a year.

Fugger's foundation coincided with the beginning of the Reformation. While the construction workers built the first houses in the suburb, Luther was interrogated by Cardinal Cajetan at the diet of Augsburg, probably in the Fugger palace close to the wine market. The contemporary visitor Antonio de Beatis claimed that this house was one of the most beautiful in Germany.[28]

The meteoric rise of the Fugger merchant house to become the most influential merchant banking organization of the early sixteenth century depended on several factors: on its ability to dominate the traditional trade in goods, on the sophistication of its banking and exchange business, but especially on its involvement in mining and the related trade in copper and silver in particular.[29] Such dominance was only feasible due to the Fuggers' almost symbiotic alliances with the political masters of the day. The contact with the ruler of Tyrol, Sigmund 'dem Münzreichen' ('rich in money') was of major importance for the growth of the merchant house. The Fuggers financed Sigmund's expensive foreign policy and his lavish court; in return, they were given control of the Tyrolean silver and copper

---

[27]   See Marion Tietz-Strödel, *Die Fuggerei in Augsburg. Studien zur Entwicklung des sozialen Stiftungsbaus im 15. und 16. Jahrhundert* (Tübingen, 1982).

[28]   Roeck, *Augsburg*, p. 101.

[29]   For an overview, see Götz von Pölnitz, *Die Fugger*, 6th edn (Tübingen, 1999); Olaf Mörke, 'Die Fugger im 16. Jahrhundert. Städtische Elite oder Sonderstruktur?', *Archiv für Reformationsgeschichte*, 127 (1983), pp. 141–62.

mines. Later, Jacob Fugger was involved in the abdication of the heavily indebted Sigmund; he then transferred his sponsorship to Sigmund's successor, Archduke Maximilian, who succeeded his unhappy nephew in 1490. When Maximilian was elected king in 1493, Jacob Fugger became the most important banker to the Habsburgs. From then on, the fates of the Fuggers and the Habsburg dynasty became ever closer intertwined.

By then, the Fuggers not only controlled all the Tyrolean mines; bit by bit they also began to take charge of the silver and copper production in Carinthia, Thuringia and Hungary. In 1498, Ulrich Fugger together with the families Gossembrot and Herwart set up a Tyrolean company, in effect the first copper ore syndicate ever to be established. Through the creation of similar cartels, the Fuggers ensured their monopolistic position in the European metal trade.

Through their branch office in Nuremberg, the Fuggers also became significant financiers to the popes; in the jubilee year 1500, the extremely profitable business of selling indulgences became a new commercial line of the Fuggers. Furthermore, the merchant house took over the management of the Zecca, the papal coin, for a couple of years. Consequently, papal coins became marked with the trading sign of the Fuggers: the trident and the ring.

This aggressive and spectacularly successful business strategy was the creation of an almost legendary figure: Jacob Fugger II (1459–1525), also known as 'the wealthy'. Under his direction, the Fugger company developed into a worldwide business. Gradually, after the death of the brothers Ulrich and Georg (1506 and 1510 respectively), the co-operative structure of the company changed and became controlled by one man, Jacob Fugger, who had the final word in all matters.

Despite his far-reaching business activities, Jacob Fugger retained a strong interest in local affairs. He had had property deeds and sovereignty rights transcribed to him as securities; based upon these, he acquired titles: in 1511 he was ennobled, soon thereafter he was made a count. His acquisition of real estate was not caused solely by social ambition, it also made sense in business terms. The estates, *latifundia*, were well managed and generated a good profit, while simultaneously serving to diversify the business. What a Fugger started usually turned out to be very successful.[30]

It is generally accepted that the election of Charles V as the Roman-German emperor in 1519 would not have been possible without the money of the Fuggers. Jacob Fugger organized a syndicate which collected the sum needed: exactly 851,918 guilders, an exceptionally large amount

---

30   See Robert Mandrou, *Les Fugger, propriétaires fonciers an Souabe, 1560–1618. Étude de comportements socio-économiques à la fin du 16ᵉ siècle* (Paris, 1969).

of money, of which nearly 544,000 guilders were provided by the Fuggers. This undoubtedly represents the pinnacle of the Fuggers' politico-economic influence.

The Turbulent Years of the Augsburg Reformation

The development of the Augsburg Reformation illustrates the significance of timing for the success of the evangelical movement.[31] Luther's doctrines were spread while both the emperor and the pope were otherwise engaged. Augsburg with its unique publishing scene was the second most important printing location after Wittenberg for Luther's writings during the early years of the Reformation.[32]

Luther quickly gained more and more followers in the city; the mendicant orders in particular favoured his teachings, and most notably he gained adherents within the so-called 'Barfüsserkloster' ('bare-foot monastery') that was situated on the periphery of the unruly suburb of St Jacob. At the Feast of Corpus Christi in 1521, the new ideas reached the heart of the old Church, when the cathedral preacher Urbanus Rhegius began to espouse evangelical ideas. The chapter forced him to resign. When the pope's bull announcing Luther's ban was published later that year, the cathedral preachers demanded from the pulpit that those among the laity who owned copies of Luther's writings hand them over to the cathedral authorities. This had an explosive effect, and caused significant numbers of craftsmen to riot; once more, the sources explicitly refer to the weavers as playing a prominent part in the disturbances.

The city council surprisingly stood aloof and did not intervene. The reason for this may well be found in the fact that within the deciding organs of the city, a fine balance existed between those who sympathized with Luther and other evangelical leaders, and their Catholic opponents. Another possible explanation for the city council's inaction could be fear. The governing elite and the majority of wealthy craftsmen were united in their fear of major riots by their social inferiors, going to great lengths in times of crisis to quell anything that might develop into a major riot or rebellion. The failed harvest of 1517 came close to causing a hunger

---

[31] On the Reformation in Augsburg, see Roth, *Reformationsgeschichte*; Sieh-Burens, *Oligarchie* ; Herbert Immenkötter, 'Kirche zwischen Reformation und Parität', in Gottlieb (ed.), *Geschichte*, pp. 391–412; the relevant articles in Günther Grünsteudel, Günther Hägele and Rudolf Frankenberger (eds), *Augsburger Stadtlexikon*, 2nd edn (Augsburg, 1998); Josef Kirmeier, Wolfgang Jahn and Evamaria Brockhoff (eds), '*... wider Laster und Sünde*'. *Augsburgs Weg in die Reformation* (Cologne, 1997), and Carl A. Hoffmann et al., *Als Frieden möglich war. 450 Jahre Augsburger Religionsfrieden* (Munich, 2005).

[32] See Helmut Gier and Johannes Janota (eds), *Augsburger Buchdruck und Verlagswesen. Von den Anfängen bis zur Gegenwart* (Wiesbaden, 1997).

revolt, yet another indication of the fragile social peace which reigned in Augsburg. The evangelical sermons of the Reader of the 'bare-foot' or discalced monks, Johann Schilling, proved popular.[33] Schilling proved something of a social radical, attacking the churchly hierarchy and the power of the city council. Apparently, he also attacked the wealthy, and a contemporary chronicler claimed to have heard him say 'that all things should be shared'.[34]

In the summer of 1524, matters grew more acute. The council banned Schilling from Augsburg. This was too little too late, and on 6 August the craftsmen took collective action when a thousand of them, or perhaps even more, gathered in front of the town hall and won the right of Schilling to return. Shortly afterwards, the Catholic priests left the city; Jacob Fugger also fled; only the council's deployment of mercenaries controlled the situation. A month later, the city council quietly had the two leaders of the revolt beheaded.

Later in 1524, the Peasants' War broke out. Upper Swabia was in a state of turmoil; cloisters and manors were burnt down. The council of Augsburg hired 400 lansquenets, who not only guarded the city walls, but were also expected to keep the riotous citizenship under control. On 16 October, it published an imperial mandate against the possession of and distribution of Lutheran writings. The council was in a situation where it could not act. An expression of this can be seen in the fact that Rhegius could once more appear in public.[35] In fact, the preacher started on St Nicholas' day in 1524 with a reading of Paul's letters in German. There is no doubt about his interpretation of these central passages for the understanding of Luther.

Monks and nuns began to leave their cloisters in the areas surrounding Augsburg. In the middle of March, the revolting peasant armies arrived before the city walls. The peasants tried to get in contact with revolutionaries within the city, amongst whom were many poor weavers. An assault would have been without any chance of success. The situation became extremely menacing: 'Outside of the city fear and fright, inside the city worry, anguish and misery,' noted the chronicler Clemens Sender.[36]

---

[33]   See Wilhelm Vogt, 'Johann Schilling der Barfüßer-Mönch und der Aufstand in Augsburg im Jahre 1524', *Zeitschrift des Historischen Vereins für Schwaben*, 6 (1879): 1–32.
[34]   See Roeck, *Geschichte Augsburgs*, p. 108.
[35]   See Maximilian Liebmann, *Urbanus Rhegius und die Anfänge der Reformation* (Münster, 1980).
[36]   Roeck, *Geschichte Augsburgs*, p. 109.

The Preservation of the Old Faith

By then, the Fuggers had become a bulwark of the Catholic Church, and they shared a common destiny with the Catholic Habsburgs, since their financial involvement in the election of Charles V as emperor. Furthermore, the faith of the Fuggers was grounded in the belief that good deeds led to salvation. The foundation of the 'Fuggerei' is a spectacular proof of this, as are other foundations such as the creation of a preacher's prebend at the church of St Moritz and the building of St Anna's Chapel.[37] The Fugger company also generated considerable sums of money from the sale of indulgences. They must have considered Luther's sermon on usury as a declaration of war, particularly since the discussion concerning trade monopolies was revived at the diet of Worms; soon, this escalating conflict threatened to become menacing for the major trading companies.

The Fuggers invested heavily in halting both the progress of the Reformation and the Peasants' War. Thus, it was the Fuggers who helped finance the army of the Swabian League, which in April 1525 moved against the rebellious peasants. The peasant army proved no match for the professional soldiers of the League. In the region of Wurzach, thousands of peasants were killed, while the Treaty of Weingarten on Easter Monday 1525 brought a halt to the fighting in Swabia. In Tyrol and in some Hungarian mining cities, however, the peasants' and miners' rebellion escalated. They felt particularly aggrieved by the larger trading companies. They plundered and destroyed the agencies of the Fugger company. Only during the following year did the forces of the princes prevail.

Living through his last days, Jacob Fugger cannot but have had the feeling that his world was falling apart. He died in his palace at the Augsburg wine market on 30 December 1525. His nephew Anton succeeded him as 'director', and under his leadership the Fugger company peaked.[38]

During these years, Augsburg became a centre of heterodoxy. It was not only Luther who gained adherents in the city, but also other reformers, such as Zwingli. The 'tolerant' attitude of the council encouraged many religious refugees from Switzerland and elsewhere to seek refuge in Augsburg. Already around 1524 a Baptist community was in existence.[39] Against the backdrop of the Peasants' War, the council finally decided to take some drastic measures. It was a congregation of southern German

---

[37] See Benjamin Scheller, *Memoria an der Zeitenwende. Die Stiftungen Jakob Fuggers des Reichen vor und während der Reformation (ca. 1505–1555)* (Berlin, 2004); on the chapel, see Bruno Bushart, *Die Fuggerkapelle bei St. Anna in Augsburg* (Augsburg, 1994).

[38] See Götz von Pölnitz, *Anton Fugger*, 4 vols (Tübingen, 1958–71).

[39] See Friedwart Uhland, *Täufertum und Obrigkeit in Augsburg im 16. Jahrhundert*, PhD thesis (Tübingen, 1972), pp. 65–80; Roth, *Reformationsgeschichte*, vol. 1, pp. 218–271, vol. 4, pp. 612–18.

Baptists, the so-called 'martyrs' synod' in the summer of 1527, which finally caused the council to take action.[40] The leaders were thrown into prison and subsequently expelled from the city; some had their tongues pulled out or were branded. The radical preacher Hans Hut died while in prison – according to the authorities, killed during an attempt to escape. In 1528, a further member of the Baptists was executed. Henceforth, the Baptists, commonly known as the 'garden brethren' because of their preferred meeting place, where either expelled or driven underground. Another prominent evangelical group, the spiritualists, proved more tenacious and still maintained a presence in the city as late as 1600.[41] Without the support of the Fuggers, it is questionable whether the Catholic Church in Augsburg would have managed to survive the turbulent years of the early Reformation.

The Road to Bi-confessionalization

Members of the council plutocracy were far from unified in confessional matters. The Herbrot family and the Seitz family wanted a Reformation along Zwinglian lines; the Zurich reformer was very popular among the Augsburg craftsmen, too.[42] The Welsers, however, initially refrained from committing themselves to the teaching of any of the reformers, eventually opting for Luther. The confessional structure of Augsburg then developed within the framework of existing social relations. The Fuggers remained firm defenders of the old faith.

After the dramatic events of 1527, Augsburg remained a comparatively peaceful place and the iconoclastic movement in 1529 was quickly stamped out.[43] It proved significant that not only the bourgeoisie, but also the oligarchy was religiously divided. Endeavours to mediate failed. Among them were the efforts of the humanist Conrad Peutinger to create a middle way.[44] However, a firm and distinctive confessional policy proved impossible to introduce, due to the split in the existing power structure. Augsburg did not even join the 'Protestation' at the diet in Speyer which

---

[40]   See Albrecht Hege, 'Märtyrersynode', in *Mennonitisches Lexikon*, III (Frankfurt am Main, 1958), pp. 53–6.

[41]   See Roeck, *Stadt*, pp. 117–19; Bernd Roeck, 'Spiritualismus und Groteske. Religiosität, Lebenswelt und Kunst eines Goldschmieds im 16. Jahrhundert', *Zeitschrift für Kunstgeschichte*, 70 (2007): 69–88.

[42]   For details, see Sieh-Burens, *Oligarchie*.

[43]   On iconoclastical movements in Augsburg, see Jörg Rasmussen, 'Bildersturm und Restauratio', in Städtische Kunstsammlungen, Augsburg and Zentralinstitut für Kunstgeschichte, Munich (ed.), *Welt im Umbruch. Augsburg zwischen Renaissance und Barock*, vol. 3 (Augsburg 1980), pp. 95–114.

[44]   On Peutinger, see Heinrich Lutz, *Conrad Peutinger. Beiträge zu einer politischen Biographie* (Augsburg, 1958).

gave the Protestants their name. The process of confessionalization in Augsburg resulted in the formation of Protestant and Catholic groups within the city. Gradually, these two groups withdrew behind more and more clearly defined barriers separating them while taking care that no third party emerged.

By then, the Protestants had the initiative. Evangelically inspired priests ascended the pulpits of the St Anna Chapel, the *Barfüsserkirche* and other churches like those of the Holy Cross and St George. Simultaneously, the number of monasteries and convents diminished.

The construction of a Protestant confessional identity received a more solid foundation at the famous diet of Augsburg in 1530; Augsburg itself admittedly did not embrace the Lutheran *Confessio Augustana* instantly. However, the city withstood the pressure of emperor Charles V and refused to sign the so-called *Reichsabschied* ('conclusive legislation'), which contained all matters regulated by the imperial diet. The city council wanted to prove its obedience to the emperor and the empire in secular matters, and did too much rather than too little in this respect; however, when it came to the question of faith, it begged to differ and insisted on a Christian's right to freedom of conscience.

Meanwhile, the evangelical temperature was rising among the growing number of Protestant sympathizers within the city, forcing the city council to take action. A growing number of Protestant preachers were employed, the majority of whom turned out to be Zwinglians. A further step towards turning Augsburg into a Protestant city was taken in 1531 with the foundation of the Latin school situated in the former monastery of St Anna.[45] Gradually, the school developed into a prominent scholarly Protestant centre of learning, becoming a centre for philological scholarship and astronomical research.

On 22 July 1534, after considerable debate, the Augsburg council passed a law which finally provided the legal foundation for the city's Reformation.[46] The most significant decision was that in future, only preachers employed by the council and therefore controlled by them were allowed to preach within the walls. Catholic services were allowed to continue only within eight endowments or chapels. Churches and monasteries were closed, and some buildings were demolished. Within a year, all Church land and property that did not specifically belong to the bishop was confiscated and used to finance new educational and charitable initiatives. The book collections of the various monasteries were amalgamated, and came to

---

[45]   See Karl Köberlin, *Geschichte des humanistischen Gymnasiums bei St. Anna in Augsburg von 1531–1931. Zur 400 Jahrfeier der Anstalt* (Augsburg, 1931).

[46]   For details, see the literature mentioned in note 31 above.

form the basis for a new urban library, which later employed the famous scholar Hieronymus Wolf as its director.

The year 1537 proved a low point for Catholics in Augsburg when all Catholic services were outlawed.[47] Consequently, the bishop and his cathedral chapter, and the monks and the nuns who had persevered, went into exile. Having achieved control over matters of faith, the city council proceeded to establish the godly city, as envisaged in the ideal of the later Middle Ages – the theopolis. Disciplinary and police orders came to regulate rigidly the daily life of the people of Augsburg. A marriage court controlled compliance with the regulations, six correctors or castigators (*Zuchtherren*) were appointed to make sure that the citizens of Augsburg lived moral and upright lives, and a Censorship Board was created to make sure that the printers were kept under control. Informers were encouraged to turn in their fellow citizens so that the authorities could intervene.

The cultural climate in the city changed. The colourful abundance of late medieval ecclesiastical ornaments gave way to the plainness represented by the Zwinglians, whose simple service helped prevent pious thoughts from being distracted. The artists found themselves short of new orders. Some reacted to the changes in demand and began to depict profane subjects. Worldliness now had its place. Until then, strict rules had applied to the sacral field. A *Monatsbild* ('picture of the month'), representing the months of October, November and December, probably painted by Heinrich Vogtherr the Younger around 1540, by no means gives the impression that Augsburg society had totally dispensed with the traditional, good life.[48] However, the urban environment lost significant aspects of its sacral importance in this period; characteristic was the removal of the city's patron, St Ulrich, from his position next to the city hall. Instead, his place was taken by the classical but heathen god Neptune: the result was the creation of a humanist public sphere in place of what had been a sacral site.[49]

The Schmalkaldic War and the 'Armed Diet' of Augsburg

Despite the pressure from the reformers and their supporters, the Catholics in Augsburg did not find themselves totally excluded from influence, not least because of their economic and commercial significance. In 1538, the

---

[47] See Gottfried Seebaß, 'Die Augsburger Kirchenordnung von 1537 in ihrem historischen und theologischen Zusammenhang', in Reinhard Schwarz (ed.), *Die Augsburger Kirchenordnung von 1537 und ihr Umfeld. Wissenschaftliches Kolloquium* (Gütersloh 1988), pp. 2–58.

[48] See Roeck, *Geschichte Augsburgs*, p. 128.

[49] Bernd Roeck, 'Der Brunnen der Macht', in Michael Kühlental (ed.), *Der Augustusbrunnen in Augsburg* (Munich, 2003), pp. 13–50.

number of families classified as patricians was expanded in Augsburg. This served to enlarge the elite from which the city leaders were chosen. Other Catholic families besides the Fuggers, such as the Imhofs and Baumgartners, became part of the city elite, thus confirming that the guild regulation of 1368 still carried weight.

The foreign policy scenario remained precarious. Augsburg had joined the Schmalkaldic League in 1536, but the city remained threatened from the east by the duke of Bavaria – its traditional enemy. From the outset of the Reformation, the dukes of Bavaria had been staunch supporters of the old Church. They had no sympathy for the heretics beyond the River Lech. The bishop of Augsburg, Otto Truchsess von Waldburg, a Counter-Reformation hardliner who had succeeded the mediating humanist Christoph von Stadion as bishop, constituted another dangerous enemy.[50]

During the summer of 1546, it all came to a head when Charles V began what became known as the Schmalkaldic War after extensive diplomatic preparations.[51] Meanwhile, in Augsburg the Protestant fanatics supporting the guild mayor Jacob Herbrot gained the upper hand. This pro-war party was primarily motivated by religion: they hoped to spread the Protestant revolution, and had no doubt that they acted with the blessing of God. Catholic financiers to the Habsburgs, such as the Fuggers, went into exile despite attempts by the council to prevent this. Not surprisingly, Anton Fugger provided Charles V with considerable sums of money for his campaign to secure the empire and the Catholic Church.

Augsburg's decision to fight with the Schmalkaldic League proved costly. Having shared in the Protestants' defeat, the city had to face the consequences. In the wake of his victory, Charles V called a diet to settle the religious issues that had plagued the empire. That he chose Augsburg, a city closely linked to the fortune of the Reformation, as the meeting place is hardly a surprise, bearing in mind its symbolic significance.

The 'armed diet', as it became known, which assembled in the city in 1547/48 proved significant.[52] No one could doubt who controlled not only the empire but also the city of Augsburg. The presence of imperial mercenaries reminded the citizens of their predicament with the clang of their arms. It was decided that until a general Church council reached a decision about the true faith, the 'Interim' had to be forced upon the Protestants; Protestant ministers retained the licence to marry, and the

---

[50] See Ferdinand Siebert, *Zwischen Kaiser und Papst. Kardinal Truchseß von Waldburg und die Anfänge der GegenReformation in Deutschland* (Berlin, 1943).

[51] Heinrich Lutz, 'Augsburg und seine politische Umwelt 1490–1555', in Gottlieb (ed.), *Geschichte*, pp. 413–33, esp. pp. 425ff.

[52] See Horst Rabe, *Reichsbund und Interim. Die Verfassungs- und Religionspolitik Karls V. und der Reichstag von Augsburg 1547/48* (Cologne, 1971); see generally Axel Gotthard, 'Der Reichstag', in Hoffmann (ed.), *Als Frieden möglich war*, pp. 84–8.

communion cup for laymen was granted, but at the same time the Catholic doctrines were confirmed and the Catholic services re-established.

In Augsburg, some churches were immediately returned to Catholic use. The constitutional changes introduced by the emperor proved of paramount importance for what followed in the city. The Lesser Council fell under the control of the patricians, while the Secret Council, consisting of two *Stadtpfleger* ('curators') and five *Geheime* ('secret councillors'), came to function as a board of management.[53] Even within this council, the 'epicentre' of power, the patricians came to play a decisive part. The Major Council was supposed to have 300 members, including 140 craftsmen. The guilds from which the craftsmen had been elected were dissolved, and instead 'craftsmen' amenable to the patricians took their place.[54] According to the ruling patricians, the fact that such an 'ancient, powerful and famous city' had been ruled by plebeians had caused it to fall into disrepute.[55]

The new city government demonstrated its political and religious awareness by granting equal rights to Catholics and Protestants. It became the norm that one of the *Stadtpfleger* was Catholic, while the other was a Protestant. The Major Council took on a central role, communicating the measures and new initiatives to the city's Protestant subjects; it became a mediator between the city government and the burghers. By then, however, the confessionalization of the citizens had already reached levels that prevented the introduction of the Interim in an unadulterated form.[56] During the Augsburg diet of 1550–51, the Imperial Council unexpectedly ordered an inspection of the preachers in the city. This proved that hardly any of the Protestant preachers in Augsburg were prepared to accept the Interim. Consequently, most of the Protestant preachers and schoolteachers in the city were dismissed.

Confessional Peace

Once again the tide turned for Augsburg when, in the spring of 1552, some territorial princes led by Moritz of Saxony took up arms against Emperor Charles V in what became known as the Second Schmalkaldic

---

[53] For details, see Warmbrunn, *Zwei Konfessionen*, and Roeck, *Stadt*.

[54] See Eberhard Naujoks (ed.), *Kaiser Karl V. und die Zunftverfassung. Ausgewählte Aktenstücke zu den Verfassungsänderungen in den oberdeutschen Reichsstädten (1547–1556)* (Stuttgart, 1985); Eberhard Naujoks, 'Vorstufen der Parität in der Verfassungsgeschichte der schwäbischen Reichsstädte (1555–1648). Das Beispiel Augsburg', in Jürgen Sydow (ed.), *Bürgerschaft und Kirche* (Sigmaringen, 1980), pp. 38–66.

[55] See Roeck, *Geschichte Augsburgs*, p. 116.

[56] See Rolf Kießling, 'Augsburg in der Reformationszeit', in … *wider Laster und Sünde*, pp. 17-43, esp. pp. 37–8.

War.[57] Augsburg took part in this 'revolution of the princes', and one of its consequences was the restoration of the guilds to their former power and glory (*Zunftherrlichkeit*).[58] However, this proved short-lived. By the end of August, Emperor Charles V, whose forces had been financed by loans from Anton Fugger, marched into Augsburg and restored the patrician regime. This time, however, Charles V failed to suppress and defeat the territorial princes opposed to him.

The Treaty of Passau had already signalled the confessional peace to come,[59] and this was subsequently confirmed by the Peace of Augsburg in 1555, which legally recognized the Lutheran confession.[60] In the imperial cities, where both confessions existed, people were supposed to continue 'friedlich und ruhig bei und nebeneinander wonen, und kein Teil des anderen Religion, Kirchengepreuch und Ceremonien abzutun oder ine darvon zu tringen understen' ('to live peacefully and quietly side by side; and not to force anyone from their religion, ceremonies or ecclesiastic customs'). On 25 September 1555, the religious peace of Augsburg was announced during a ceremony in the Guildhall. One of its immediate consequences was the development of narrow Protestant dogmatism, not least because only the Lutheran confession was given legal recognition. Consequently, Augsburg's Protestantism turned increasingly Lutheran.[61]

For Augsburg, this proved to be the beginning of a long period of external peace matched by a more precarious internal peace.[62] Catholic patricians gradually managed to occupy an increasing number of key positions within city government, although the population remained predominantly Protestant. The ratio was two to one until the middle of the seventeenth century. This circumstance explains the reluctance of the

---

[57]   See Karl Erich Born, 'Moritz von Sachsen und die Fürstenverschwörung gegen Karl V.', *Historische Zeitschrift*, 191 (1960), pp. 18–67.

[58]   Roth, *Reformationsgeschichte*, IV, pp. 413–52.

[59]   Ibid., pp. 474–5; Lutz, *Augsburg*, p. 429; Bernhard Sicken, 'Der Heidelberger Verein (1553–1556). Zugleich ein Beitrag zur Reichspolitik Herzog Christophs von Württemberg', *Zeitschrift für Württembergische Landesgeschichte*, 32 (1973), pp. 320–435; Albrecht Luttenberger, 'Landfriedensbund und Reichsexekution. Erster Teil: Friedenssicherung und Bündnispolitik 1552/53', *Mitteilungen des Österreichischen Staatsarchivs*, 35 (1982), pp. 1–34; Winfried Becker, *Der Passauer Vertrag von 1552. Politische Entstehung, reichsrechtliche Bedeutung und konfessionsgeschichtliche Bewertung* (Neustadt an der Aisch, 2003).

[60]   On the Peace of 1555 and Augsburg, see Hoffmann (ed.), *Als Frieden möglich war ...*, with exhaustive bibliography, and esp. Axel Gotthardt, *Der Augsburger Religionsfrieden* (Münster, 2004).

[61]   See Irene Dingel, 'Evangelische Lehr- und Bekenntnisbildung im Spiegel der innerprotestantischen Auseinandersetzungen zur Zeit des Augsburger Religionsfriedens', in Hoffmann (ed.), *Als Frieden möglich war ...*, pp. 51–61.

[62]   See Warmbrunn, *Zwei Konfessionen*, Roeck, *Stadt*, and Dietrich Blaufuß, 'Das Verhältnis der Konfessionen in Augsburg 1555 bis 1648', *Jahrbuch des Vereins für Augsburger Bistumsgeschichte*, 10 (1976), pp. 27–56.

ruling elite to intervene in religious matters until the first years of the Thirty Years' War. Similarly, the Jesuits did not set up shop in the city until 1584 – comparatively late. The foundation of the Jesuit college of St Salvator was enabled by Fugger money.[63]

Augsburg in the Age of Confessionalization

When the French philosopher Michel de Montaigne visited Augsburg in October 1580, he could witness regular weddings between Catholics and Protestants[64]; his comments are often quoted as proof of the peaceful coexistence of the two confessions. A few years after Montaigne's stay in Augsburg, the conflict over the Gregorian calendar proved that the two confessions were far from well integrated.[65] This turned out to be the most dramatic crisis of bi-confessional Augsburg between 1555 and the years of the *Restitutionsedikt* and the Swedish occupation during the Thirty Years' War.

The initial failure of Gregor XIII's calendar reform was due solely to the fact that it was backed by papal authority. Accordingly, it found a hostile reception among Protestants, including the Protestant preachers of Augsburg. When the city council banished one of the agitators against it, the superintendent Dr Georg Mylius, by the end of May 1584, the mob (and among them once more the poor weavers) rose; the suburb of St Jacob became once more a centre of social and religious riots.

An armed insurrection nearly followed, but by then some of the Lutheran preachers had belatedly realized the dangers of social revolt and withdrew their support from the rebels. An imperial commission eventually restored peace in the city, expelling the rioters. At first the citizens boycotted the meetings of their replacements, who were appointed by the council, and whom they contemptuously labelled 'hirelings'.

The Augsburg conflict over the Gregorian calendar had its roots in social misery and confessional resentment; soon, however, the opposition of the wider citizenship crumbled. The conflict was eventually settled years later by a compromise, which made it possible for those expelled to return to the city. From then on, life in Augsburg was characterized by peaceful

---

[63]   Wolfram Baer and Hans-Joachim Hecker (eds), *Die Jesuiten und ihre Schule St. Salvator in Augsburg* (Munich, 1982); Peter Rummel, *Katholisches Leben in der Reichsstadt Augsburg (1650–1806)* (Augsburg, 1984).

[64]   See François, *Unsichtbare Grenze*, p. 192, for a discussion of mixed marriages in Augsburg.

[65]   Warmbrunn, *Zwei Konfessionen*; Roeck, *Stadt*, pp. 125–84; Max Radlkofer, 'Die volkstümliche und besonders dichterische Literatur zum Augsburger Kalenderstreit', *Beiträge zur bayerischen Kirchengeschichte*, 7 (1901), pp. 1–32, 49–71; Ferdinand Kaltenbrunner, 'Der Augsburger Kalenderstreit', *Mitteilungen des Instituts für österreichische Geschichtsforschung*, 1 (1880), pp. 497–540.

coexistence until the beginning of the Thirty Years' War. Catholics and Protestants came to tolerate each other, and everyday life in the city proved unproblematic, while the foreign policy of the council followed a confessionally neutral course. The confessional problems in Augsburg seemed to have been solved even though the Catholics demonstrated an increasing willingness to fly their own flag – literally and, especially after the turn of the century, by organizing processions with banners.[66] The creation of confessionally split cemeteries can be seen as a clear indication of growing demarcation dynamics.[67] In other words: the confessions began to mark out their territories.

The process of confessionalization accelerated because of the Thirty Years' War. Augsburg was chosen as a test case for the implementation of the Edict of Restitution, enacted by the emperor on 6 March 1629.[68] Based on a rigid interpretation of the Ecclesiastical Reservation (*reservatum eccliasticum*), the edict ordered the return of Church property that had been secularized since 1552, the year of the Passau treaty. However, the measures taken went far beyond that. The Protestants in Augsburg lost their freedom of worship, while a 'cleansed' city council consisting entirely of Catholics was installed. Civil servants unwilling to convert to Catholicism were dismissed; few if any gave in and converted. When an armed force was deployed to escort the children from the Lutheran orphanage to attend mass, it was prevented by an enraged crowd of Protestant citizens.

It was no exaggeration when the merchant Jacob Wagner, contemplating these events, wrote in his diary that 'this was the beginning of the downfall of this city'.[69] The Edict of Restitution became an important focus for Protestant militants within and without the city, all hoping for a reversal of their fortunes; they did not have to wait long, for on 20 April 1632, Augsburg opened its gates for Gustavus Adolphus of Sweden.[70] The situation was reversed, and the Protestants in the city once more gained possession of their churches while all Catholics were forced to resign from the council. Gustavus Adolphus took the opportunity to ennoble 13 Protestant merchant families, who became known as 'increasers', thereby simultaneously expanding the Protestant patrician class from amongst whom the city's rulers were chosen, while neatly tying the new nobles to his regime. Symbolically, it was from a window in the Fugger palace that Gustavus Adolphus received the homage of the citizens.

Even if the Swedish occupation resulted in some limited religious toleration – some Protestant Augsburgers were so enthusiastic about their

---

[66] Roeck, *Stadt*, p. 180, 184–5.
[67] Ibid., p. 186.
[68] Ibid., pp. 665–80.
[69] Ibid., p. 657.
[70] Ibid., pp. 680–767.

perceived saviour as to name their newborn sons Gustav Adolph – it also entailed confinement and heavy taxation. As a result of the many soldiers garrisoned in the city, Augsburg witnessed a series of outbreaks of plague and other epidemic diseases.

The period of Swedish occupation, however, remained a short intermezzo. After the defeat of Gustavus Adolphus and his allies in the battle of Nördlingen at the beginning of September 1634, southern Germany was exposed to the might of the imperial forces. Augsburg came under siege, and during the winter of 1634/35 the city was completely blocked off and suffered widespread famine. Reports about cannibalism in the city appear credible. At the end of March 1635, all the city's resources had been spent, and the city gates were opened to the besieger, Count Ottheinrich Fugger, who took up residence as governor. Once more, the political circumstances of the city had come full circle. Despite their defeat, the Protestants were allowed to build their own church. Lacking the resources, they held their services outside, in the courtyard of St Anna. The result of a census from these years shows that of 16,422 inhabitants, nearly three quarters (12,017) were Protestants and a quarter (4405) were Catholics.

Parity

At the Peace Convention of Westphalia the delegates of the Augsburg Protestants managed to have denominational parity introduced into the treaty. Their last-minute success was mainly achieved because of Swedish support. The regulations in article V, paragraph 3 of the Peace Treaty of Westphalia followed the logic of the Peace of Augsburg in 1555.[71]

By the beginning of 1649, the regulations of the peace treaty were being introduced in Augsburg. In St Anna, St Ulrich and the other Lutheran churches in the city, Lutheran services took place again. Lessons were given in the Lyceum at St Anna. Protestants from across the empire, and as far away as Denmark and Sweden, provided generous donations towards the rebuilding of the evangelical church of the Holy Cross which had been torn down in the wake of the Edict of Restitution in 1629. A symbol of the new order can be seen in the fact that the Protestant parish church of St Ulrich was established in a former Benedictine church next door to the Catholic St Ulrich Basilica.

In March, the new council was constituted. A Catholic *Stadtpfleger* ('curator') was matched by a Protestant, the Minor Council, then the city council, the city's court, the censorship office, and even the most

---

[71] See Hermann Vogel, *Der Kampf auf dem westfälischen Friedenskongreß um die Einführung der Parität in der Stadt Augsburg* (Munich, 1890); Hermann Vogel, *Die Exekution der die Reichsstadt Augsburg betreffenden Bestimmungen des Westfälischen Friedens* (Augsburg, 1890).

unimportant posts such as the lantern lighters or the chimney sweepers were filled according to the parity doctrine.[72] Where an unequal number of positions was to be occupied, the two denominations took it in turn to fill the vacancy. It was a simple, mechanical solution, uncomplicated and efficient.

While the Catholics of Augsburg considered the results of the negotiations in Osnabruck to be disappointing and a novelty, which would create difficulties for their community, the Protestants exulted. For the first time, on 8 August 1650, they celebrated the anniversary of the expulsion of the Lutheran preachers as a salvation from the utmost misery, with a 'glorious and joyous festival of thanksgiving and peace'. The Protestants of Augsburg did not celebrate quietly, but with martial sounds from trumpets, kettledrums and gun salutes.[73] The festival of peace has continued to be celebrated in the city; even today, 8 August remains a public holiday in Augsburg, while people beyond the city have to work.

The most significant effect of the Thirty Years' War was the change it brought to the denominational composition of Augsburg, reversing the balance between a Protestant majority and a Catholic minority. The war caused people from the surrounding Catholic countryside to seek safety within the city walls, and due to their much higher birth rate, the Catholic population of the city gradually gained the upper hand again. By the end of the war, the population of Augsburg, which had picked up rapidly, amounted to 20,000 inhabitants, of whom 70 per cent were Protestant; by the end of the eighteenth century, the number of Protestants had fallen to 40 per cent. This development has continued, and today Protestants only constitute 20 per cent of the city's population.

Summary: Rulers and Subjects

As we have seen, the confessionalization of Augsburg became explicit only during the Thirty Years' War and during the subsequent period of confessional parity, in the seventeenth and eighteenth centuries (and even into the nineteenth century). During the war, confessionally distinctive Christian names came into use in the city, while during the parity period,

---

[72]   See François, *Unsichtbare Grenze*.

[73]   See Claire Gantet, 'Das Augsburger Friedensfest im Rahmen der Feier des Friedens', in Johannes Burkhardt and Stefanie Haberer (eds), *Das Friedensfest. Augsburg und die Entwicklung einer neuzeitlichen Toleranz-, Friedens- und Festkultur* (Berlin, 2000), pp. 209–33; Claire Gantet, *Discours et images de la paix des villes d'Allemagne du sud aux XVIIe et XVIIIe siècles* (Paris 2001); Bernd Roeck, 'Die Feier des Friedens', in Heinz Duchardt (ed.), *Der Westfälische Friede. Diplomatie, politische Zäsur, kulturelles Umfeld, Rezeptionsgeschichte* (Munich 1998), pp. 633–60; Ulrike Albrecht, *Die Augsburger Friedensgemälde* (Munich, 1983).

the two confessions started to develop distinguishing features in terms of dress, social mores and rites.[74] The wealth and quality of the Augsburg sources allow us to take a closer look at this development. The formation of a confessional identity was characterized by a process of group dynamics and interactive influences, in which the political system had crucial importance. In the period after the Religious Peace of Augsburg (1555), in the second half of the sixteenth century, the city council acted as a *pouvoir neutre* ('neutral power') which preferred to stick to a confessionally neutral course; however, during the Calendar controversy, the limitations of this policy became evident. This becomes apparent, for example, when we consider the patronage of art in Augsburg:[75] the city's 'liberal' attitude changed around 1600, and a clear Counter-Reformation trait began to emerge. The upheavals of 1629, 1632 and 1635 made it clear to the citizens that faith and confession could determine all aspects of their existence. Suddenly, their lives and existences were defined by their confession. It could determine whether or not they had work and food, any political influence, and sometimes whether or not they could practise their religion. Those dates mark deep caesurae, for the council, which ruled the city and its citizens, was homogenously Catholic during the period between 1629 and 1648, then Lutheran, finally again Catholic. All the while, it tried to force its confession(s) on the citizenry. Faith became paramount for the authorities. This, however, was an area where rulers were not always able to act voluntarily: the worst political mistake made by the 'Catholic Party' in the empire during the seventeenth century – the Edict of Restitution – was forced upon the citizens of Augsburg by Elector Maximilian of Bavaria and their own Bishop Henry V von Knöringen. Then the pikes and canons of the Swedish army returned Protestantism to Augsburg, and after them, the Bavarians and the Imperialists caused the return of Catholicism to the city in 1635. After these *bouleversements* ('upheavals'), the confessional split of Augsburg society turned out to be final in political, social and cultural terms. The parity between the confessions which was introduced by the Peace of Westphalia forced the city council to return to a kind of confessional neutrality that it had already adopted before 1600. Then, it had been dictated primarily by reasons of state, even if irenic leanings, nourished by a humanist outlook, may have encouraged the council to choose the *via media*. Now, in the wake of the Thirty Years' War, the political circumstances were different. In the end, the regulations of 1648 were imposed on the city; after the experiences during the years of war, they had become unavoidable. They were a pragmatic solution that had little if anything to do with genuine toleration.

---

[74]   Roeck, *Stadt*, pp. 858–66; François, *Unsichtbare Grenze*.
[75]   Roeck, 'Der Brunnen der Macht'.

CHAPTER 4

The Contest for Control of Urban Centres in Southwest France during the Early Years of the Wars of Religion

Kevin Gould

On 21 November 1561, Protestant forces attempted an assault on the château Trompette, the impressive fort that guarded the northeast approaches to Bordeaux.[1] The move was tactically astute, as the château was known to be the key to the town's defences; capture the château, and the town would surely fall. The attempt failed, though, as stubborn resistance from the fort's Catholic garrison allowed time for the town guard to rally to its defence; Bordeaux would remain in Catholic hands for the time being. The offensive is significant for other reasons, however, as it offers insight into what would become the primary goal of Protestants during the early stages of the French Wars of Religion: the seizing of key urban centres so as to secure control over local and regional administrative, fiscal, judicial and military functions. Nowhere was this policy more evident than in the turbulent southwest, a region that witnessed a ferocity of sectarian clashes rarely seen elsewhere during the 1560s. Denis Crouzet has labelled this region 'a laboratory of violent experiences',[2] contending that it was the scale and intensity of Protestant initiatives within the southwest that engendered such explosive tensions. This is confirmed by studies of military activity within the region, as James B. Wood has noted that of the 17 dioceses of France worst affected by the Wars, 12 (71 per cent) were located in or on the borders of Guyenne and Western Languedoc, with the southwest witnessing especially high levels of abuse against Catholic priests and canons throughout the decade.[3]

The notion that Protestants were intent on capturing and controlling urban centres is not merely an observation of twentieth-century historians; contemporary Catholic testimony also identified such purposes: a report

---

[1]   Archives municipales de Bordeaux (hereafter AMB), ms 768, fos 133–40.
[2]   Denis Crouzet, *Les guerriers de Dieu* (Seyssel, 1990), vol. 1, p. 524.
[3]   James B. Wood, 'The impact of the Wars of Religion: A view of France in 1581', *Sixteenth Century Journal*, 15 (1984): 148–53.

from the Toulouse *parlement* to the Crown in January 1562 asserted that 'by violence and insidious means, the reformers are conspiring to be dominant in this kingdom',[4] while the governor of Narbonne, Raymond de Pavie, *sieur* de Fourquevaux, informed the French ambassador in Spain six months later that 'the seditious of Guyenne are the worst of all'.[5] Several factors exacerbated these tensions: the southwest had a large reformed population – almost 13 per cent of the region by 1560; a high percentage of urban centres across Guyenne and Western Languedoc included substantial Protestant communities – many would subsequently fall under Protestant control; and there was a discernable willingness among large numbers of reformed landholding nobles to deploy their personal retinues in the service of Protestant policy, and against local Catholic forces, throughout the 1560s. If the attempt on the château Trompette offered a taster of Protestant tactics, the outbreak of war in April 1562 signalled the start of a concerted programme to gain control of the region's major urban centres. Over the next year, Catholic citadels across the southwest became the focus of intense military activity, their defences tested severely by well-marshalled Protestant forces. Many assaults were two-pronged: well-armed corps would besiege the walls and gates at strategic points, while substantial numbers of fifth columnists sought to cause distractions within, and so divert defenders from their primary role. The results of these onslaughts were mixed: at Montauban, Protestant forces achieved their goal, and gained control of the town in rapid time, holding their prize for several decades to come; at Condom, the Protestant attack was checked effectively by co-ordinated and unified Catholic defences, comprised of varying social groups not known for affable relations, let alone effective interaction or integrated military activity; and at Castres, early Protestant successes were soon reversed as concerted counter-thrusts from Catholic forces combined with better-organized town defences to expel reform fighters from the town and its environs.

The contest for dominion over the urban centres of the southwest would prove pivotal to sectarian fortunes over the coming decades, with the failure to gain control of strategic bases ultimately weakening the long-term prospects of the French Huguenot movement in this fraught region. The critical nature of this struggle was most evident in the battles for control of the three key centres of the southwest: Bordeaux, Toulouse and Agen. Protestant strategy had clearly identified each town as a priority

---

   [4]   *Parlement* of Toulouse to Charles IX (7 January 1562). A. de Ruble, *Jeanne d'Albret et la guerre civile* (Paris, 1897), p. 101.
   [5]   Fourquevaux to Saint-Sulpice, ambassador of Charles IX in Spain (17 June 1562), Edmond Cabié, *Guerres de religion dans le sud-ouest de la France et principalement dans le Quercy, d'après les papiers des seigneurs de Saint-Sulpice de 1561 à 1590. Documents transcrits, classés et annotés* (Paris, 1906), pp. 5–6.

long before the wars, and substantial resources of manpower and finances were employed to facilitate their capture. While limited breakthroughs were made, in each case Catholic defenders managed to regain authority within months of the insurrection. Furthermore, in the process of re-evaluating and invigorating urban defences, and of revitalizing and reorganizing defensive capabilities, Catholic powers at each centre were able to greatly enhance the town's military potential, so that by 1570, each citadel was not only able to defend itself so much more successfully, but effective counter-offensives were now possible. Most common was the implementing of severe punitive measures against Protestant residents, ranging from the sequestration of property and goods to the imposition of large fines, and the expulsion of certain elements from the town. The Catholic hierarchies of Bordeaux, Toulouse and Agen, empowered by success, now became more militant, so that by 1570, their authority was unchallenged, and their control over their towns unrivalled across France outside of Paris. This chapter will examine the Protestant challenge at each citadel, the measures taken to repulse the assaults, and the subsequent counter-offensives and retaliatory programmes employed by Catholic powers against their reformed communities.

Bordeaux

The preparedness of Bordeaux's defences against assault and insurrection by 1562 owed much to recent experience in dealing with sectarian tensions within the town. Clashes between Bordeaux's Catholic majority and evangelical minority had been prevalent since the 1540s, most notably in the confrontations between the players of the *basoche*, and the *écoliers* of the collège de Guyenne.[6] The *basoche*, the affiliated actors and musicians of the Confraternity of Saint-Yves – the representative corporation of the advocates and procurers of the *parlement* – combined legal apprenticeship with performing at religious processions and feast day celebrations, and so assumed the role of promoters of Catholic orthodoxy at Bordeaux.[7] The *écoliers* of the collège de Guyenne – the foremost Humanist centre in the southwest – proffered the evangelical voice; their function as the only other troupe permitted to stage plays, ballads and processional songs in Bordeaux during this period providing them with opportunities to articulate and

---

[6]   It is estimated that over 7000 (around 14 per cent) of Bordeaux's 50,000 inhabitants were sympathetic to *la nouvelle réligion* by 1561; see Géralde Nakam, *Montaigne et son temps. Les évènements et les essais* (Paris, 1982), p. 47; Robert Boutrouche, *Bordeaux de 1453 à 1715* (Bordeaux, 1966), p. 243.

[7]   The origins of the *basoche* in France date back to 1303, when Philippe le Bel authorized the institution of a community of *clercs du parlement de Paris*; Howard Graham Harvey, *The Theatre of the Basoche: The Contributions of the Law Societies to French Medieval Comedy* (Cambridge, MA, 1941), p. 17.

advance reform ideology through their performances.[8] Both groups had moved away from traditional biblical tales and devotional songs in favour of the new but controversial morality plays and farces, which allowed them to ridicule the confessional affiliation of their opponents. It did not take long for this provocative content to incite vocal outbursts from attending partisans, and this soon escalated to more violent retorts, with stones thrown and sticks, swords and even guns brandished to intimidate and disrupt proceedings. The Bordeaux *parlement* was forced to intervene: in 1550, both groups were ordered to submit their material before the court to be censored before performance, with members of the *jurade* and town guard dispatched to maintain order at each event;[9] in 1555, a ban was placed on 'any pieces relating to religion, the Christian faith, the veneration of the saints, and the institutions of the church',[10] while in May 1560, the court moved to censure all illegal *basochien* activity, and to prohibit the *écoliers* from assembling outside the walls of their collège.[11]

The rivalry between the *basoche* and *écoliers* captured in microcosm the growing tension between Catholics and Protestants across the southwest. It also demonstrates the fact that the growth of Catholic resistance to the rise of the evangelical movement did not wait for the outbreak of the Wars of Religion, but had manifested itself as direct – albeit ad hoc – confrontation to Protestant expansion at its earliest opportunity. Catholic reaction to the reformers' offensive against the château Trompette could be seen, therefore, as a continuing, evolving response to decades of enmity, made all the more potent by the escalating hostility between the faiths immediately prior to the assault: November 1561 had witnessed widespread aggression against Catholic communities across the Bordelais and Agenais, most notably the razing to the ground of the convent of the Cordeliers at Marmande,[12] and the murder of the Catholic baron de Fumel in his home by a Protestant mob.[13] Yet the attempt to seize the château was a seminal moment in these clashes: if this fortress had fallen, then so would the town, with the likelihood that many lesser Catholic satellites across the region would soon follow. Potentially, the Protestant

---

[8]   For the formation of the Collège du Guyenne at Bordeaux, see Bernard Chevalier, *Les bonnes villes de France du XIVe au XVIe siècle* (Paris, 1982), p. 231; Gaston Zeller, *Les institutions de la France au XVIe siècle* (Paris, 1948), p. 211.

[9]   Bibliothèque municipale de Bordeaux (hereafter BMB), ms 367, fo. 81. For wider moves to censor the content of *basochien* performances across France at this time, see Harvey, *The Theatre of the Basoche*, p. 34.

[10]   Arrêt du parlement (April 1556), *Archives historiques du département de la Gironde*, III, p. 466.

[11]   AMB, ms 766, fos 452–8.

[12]   AMB, ms 768, fos 184–5.

[13]   Ibid., fos 202–4.

forces could have sealed victory in the southwest with this one gambit. The gravity of the situation for Catholic authorities is made evident by their immediate and forceful response. A syndicate of militant officers of the *parlement*, headed by the advocate, Jean de Lange, was duly formed within the environs of the palais de l'ombrière to lobby for the introduction of anti-Protestant policy at Bordeaux.[14] The grievances of the syndicate were made public in a harangue delivered before the court by Lange and fellow Catholic militant, Thomas de Ram, on 18 December 1561. The two launched fierce condemnations of recent Protestant violence, asserting that the crown's policy of accommodating rather than censuring the reformers was hampering effective local governance and breeding discontent and disunity. They then turned on moderates within the *parlement*, claiming that a number of officials had been spotted attending local *prêches*, and that certain *parlementaires* had been seen taking weapons from the town hall and distributing them among the Protestant community.[15] As a result, they argued, Catholics had little option other than to take independent measures to defend themselves, and, as such, permission would be sought immediately to co-opt greater numbers of Catholic militia into the guard to bolster the town's defences.[16]

The informal, ad hoc resistance to the Protestant presence in Bordeaux, as practised by the *basoche*, had now given way to formal, organized militancy. Activists would no longer simply confront their opponents on the streets in the defence of their faith, but would lobby for the promulgation of anti-Protestant policy, so as to secure Catholic hegemony. In essence, the syndicate was a hybrid of communal (*basochien*) and *parlementaire* militancy, drawing on the co-operative relations forged between the two parties during the various Catholic ceremonials and functions, some of which – such as the ritual administrative assembly of the confraternity of St Yves – had been presided over by leading Catholic magistrates of the *parlement*, each now declared supporters of the syndicate.[17] It also received wholehearted support from the clergy and urban bourgeoisie of Bordeaux, and significant contributions from the lesser social groups within the town, such as the *confrères*, *basochiens*, artisans and guildsmen. Thus, within weeks of its creation, the syndicate was able to offer the authorities the use of four thousand armed men to augment the town guard to bolster patrols of the streets and secure the town gates, many of which had experience

---

14   The king was alerted to the presence of a syndicate in Bordeaux on 16 December 1561; ibid., fo. 346. See also Lecler, 'Aux origines de la Ligue: premiers projets et premiers essays (1561–1570)', *Études*, 227 (1936): 193.

15   AMB, ms 768, fos 369–403.

16   Ibid., fos 448–62.

17   Kevin Gould, *Catholic Activism in South-west France, 1540–1570* (Aldershot, 2006), pp. 25–33.

of street fighters, active in the recent clashes with the *écoliers*.[18] The final piece of the jigsaw that would secure Catholicism at Bordeaux, and so deny Protestants the foothold their military policy for the region demanded, was the support offered to the town by the local Catholic nobility of the Bordelais, many of whom deployed their armed retinues in the service of the Catholic generals in order to counter any further threat of assault and insurgency. Thus, when a second attempt on the château Trompette was undertaken on 26 June 1562, the town's reinvigorated defences were more than a match for massed Protestant forces. Catholicism was now secured at Bordeaux; the activism of the *basoche*, the militancy of the syndicate and the potent forces deployed by the elites had combined with the pre-eminence of Catholic magistrates to ensure the dominance over administrative and military affairs of the Catholic hierarchy within the town.

Toulouse

The second major Catholic centre targeted by Protestant forces in 1562 was Toulouse, the fortified capital of Western Languedoc. The spread of evangelical fervour across this region had been dramatic – by 1560, 18 per cent (approximately 9000) of the population of Toulouse was thought to adhere to or sympathize with the reform movement[19] – and just as at Bordeaux, confrontations between Catholic communities, especially local Spanish residents, and the evangelical *écoliers* of the University of Toulouse had been noted long before the outbreak of the religious wars.[20] The clashes were at their most violent in the 1550s, with armed bands of *écoliers* roaming the streets of Toulouse, disrupting Catholic ceremonials and damaging property. Those members of the community whose day-to-day activities brought them into contact with the reformers, and whose rituals were most often disrupted by the *écoliers*, were at the vanguard of the Catholic reaction, most notably the clergy, *confrères* and players of the *basoche*. The spring of 1560 saw especially brutal clashes, with Catholic May Day and *jour des jeux floral* processions targeted by Protestant gangs.[21] Confrontations became so unruly over the next months that the

---

[18]   Ibid., pp. 44–6.

[19]   Robert A. Schneider, *Public Life in Toulouse, 1463–1789: From Municipal Republic to Cosmopolitan City* (Ithaca, NY, 1989), pp. 12–43.

[20]   See, for example, Arrêt du parlement (27 February 1534), Archives municipales de Toulouse (hereafter AMT), AA 17, no. 55; Arrêt du parlement (14 May 1540), AMT, AA 18, no. 35; Archives départementales de la Haute-Garonne (hereafter ADHG), B 37, fo. 458ᵛ (31 May 1544).

[21]   For the unrest of 4 May 1560, see AMT, CC 1705, fo. 22. For the unrest during the Toulouse *jour des jeux floral* in 1560, see AMT, BB 11, fo. 182ᵛ. For the illegal assembly of *écoliers* at a *prêche* on rue des Vigoreux on 10 March 1560,

Toulouse *parlement* was forced to intervene, with the town's governor, George, cardinal d'Armagnac, informing the Crown that even the local villains, in an attempt to take advantage of the poor reputation of the *écoliers*, were now dressing in scholastic robes.[22]

Matters were not helped by the inflammatory rhetoric emanating from Calvinist ministers and psalm-chanting students on the one hand, and Catholic preachers, including several Jesuits, on the other. The open hostility shown towards pro-reform *capitouls* by Catholic radicals within the *parlement* did little to lessen the tensions, especially as Catholic magistrates now questioned the legitimacy of allowing suspect *capitouls* to preside over such contentious issues as the deployment of the guard and the validation of sites of reformed worship – jurisdiction of which would soon be removed from the *parlement* and given to the council by the conciliatory edict of January 1562.[23] In response to such turbulent relations, a syndicate of Catholic clergy, judges and lawyers was formed at Toulouse early in the same year. Two leading activists within the *parlement*, *Présidents* Latomy and du Tournoir, assumed leadership over the syndicate, with numerous councillors, advocates, procurers and captains enlisting and pledging to join in the extirpation of 'all those of the new religion'.[24] Unfortunately, little is known of the structure or conduct of this militant presence, as, unlike at Bordeaux, where the political and financial machinations of Lange's association left a discernible trail within the town's *registres du parlement*, the paucity of surviving archival material relating to the Toulouse syndicate makes a detailed survey of its actions less achievable. What is pertinent here, though, is that, once again, a formal Catholic association had been founded to confront the Protestant menace well before the open conflict of April 1562, and that it drew on popular and communal, not just elite, militancy.

The existence of the syndicate would prove important to Catholic fortunes once fighting broke out across France. With the Crown's carefully nurtured policy of conciliation and coexistence in tatters following Condé's declaration at Orléans, sectarian tensions escalated at Toulouse. In an attempt to maintain order, the court granted Catholic and Protestant communities permission to deploy 'security forces' onto the streets, so long as they remained unarmed.[25] This expedient failed for two

---

see Germain de Lafaille, *Annales de la ville de Toulouse* (2 vols, Toulouse, 1687, 1701), vol. 2, p. 207.

[22] AMT, BB 269, fo. 89ᵛ.

[23] Ibid., fo. 81.

[24] See Philippe Tamizey de Larroque, 'Lettres inédites du Cardinal d'Armagnac', *Collection Méridionale*, V (Paris, Bordeaux, 1874), p. 26; Mark Greengrass, 'The anatomy of a religious riot in Toulouse in May 1562', *Journal of Ecclesiastical History*, 34 (1983): 370–77.

[25] Ibid., pp. 373–4.

reasons. Firstly, Catholic captains proved unwilling to take orders from 'heretic' *capitouls*, and so refused to place their men under the control of the authorities.[26] Secondly, the *sénéchal* and *parlement* of Toulouse had moved to convoke the *ban-et-arrière ban* in order to reinforce the militia and prevent insurrection. This decision was contested by Protestant and moderate *capitouls* alike, who cited clauses within the civic charter that prevented armed soldiers from being assembled at Toulouse without their consent – undoubtedly, many feared the presence of a large Catholic host on the streets of Toulouse. The *parlement*, however, refused to back down, and on 10 May, over two hundred armed Catholic elites and their retinues entered the town through its main gate.[27]

However, the initiative would be wrenched back by Protestant forces days later. In the early hours of 13 May 1562, barricades were erected at strategic points across Toulouse by reformers, who quickly seized the maison de ville and broke into the arsenal to distribute arms and munitions among supporters.[28] The rebels were close to gaining control of the town, a coup that would enhance Protestant military potential in the region enormously. That Catholics were able to rally owed much to established militant organization within the town. The *parlement* was first to react, requesting assistance from leading Catholic captains of the region, most notably Blaise de Monluc, the king's lieutenant-general to Guyenne, and his captains, Bellegarde, Terride and Negrepelisse. While Monluc and Bellegarde moved to intercept Protestant reinforcements travelling south, Terride and Negrepelisse deployed their troops outside Toulouse to prevent Protestant forces entering or leaving the town.[29] Neighbouring Catholic nobles rallied in support of their co-religionists, and attempts were made by these combined forces to break into the town and link up with the *ban* forces stationed within.[30] With Catholic troops engaging with the rebels, the internal counter-offensive was directed by a council of war, headed by the *premier président* of the *parlement*, Mansencal, and *Présidents* Latomy and de Paulo. A number of ad hoc committees were established so as to secure finances, to distribute arms to Catholic troops, and to gather

---

26   Théodore de Bèze, *Histoire ecclésiastique des églises réformées au royaume de France*, ed. G. Baum and E. Cunitz (Nieuwkoop, 1974), vol. 3, p. 8.
27   AMT, BB 104, fo. 530.
28   ADHG, B 55, fos 414ᵛ–15; AMT, GG 824, fos 22–7. For details of the insurrection at Toulouse in May 1562, see Emile Connac, 'Troubles de mai 1562 à Toulouse', *Annales du Midi*, 3 (1891): 310–39; Joan Davies, 'Persecution and Protestantism: Toulouse, 1562–1575', *Historical Journal*, 22 (1979): 31–51; Greengrass, 'The anatomy of a religious riot', pp. 367–91.
29   Bibliothèque nationale de Paris (hereafter BN), nouv. acq. français, 6001, fos 136–7.
30   Lafaille, *Annales de la ville de Toulouse*, vol. 2, pp. 226–8.

intelligence on the movements of Protestant fighters.[31] Perhaps the most significant development was the decision to reorganize the town guard. Sixty additional Catholics were levied to boost its numbers, and a number of experienced military veterans appointed to command each section, thereby replacing the civilian officers who had been in charge during peacetime. The main body of the guard was then divided into smaller sections, so that individual units could be deployed to trouble spots more rapidly. Precise patrol routes were devised, with passwords required for each checkpoint and barricade, and all Catholics of the town were required to wear a white cross, sewn onto their garments, to indicate their confession. Finally, strict regulations were drawn up to govern the conduct and discipline of the guard, with disobedience punishable by death.[32]

The syndicate played a decisive role here. Just as at Bordeaux, the Toulouse corpus was a heterogeneous entity, comprised of members of the clergy, merchants and bourgeoisie, as well as lawyers, judges, confrères and basochiens. Many of these men had been active in the confrontations with the écoliers and other evangelical elements over preceding years, so their experience at the barricades, and in rousing the citizenry to action, proved invaluable during the fighting.[33] Soon, the combination of sound organization, astute guard deployment, intervention from local noble retinues and popular activism from syndicate and citizens alike turned the tide in favour of the Catholic forces. On 19 May, the Catholic leadership felt confident that the battle had been won, and turned its attention to cleansing the town of insurgents. Once the streets were safe, the parlement focused on the administrative machinery of Toulouse, summarily dismissing those Protestant capitouls and magistrates who had not yet fled the town, filling the vacant offices with trusted Catholics.[34] This policy had an immediate benefit. Before the insurrection, any sizeable deployment of Catholic troops and militia on the streets of Toulouse elicited determined complaints from the capitouls, who cited the ubiquitous civic charter in

---

[31]   The Histoire ecclésiastique attributes this response to the Catholic syndicate; Bèze, Histoire ecclésiastique, vol. 3, pp. 20–40. George Bosquet also alludes to this Catholic collective, but does not give it a formal title. See AMT, GG 1022 (15 May 1562).

[32]   For these developments, see AMT, EE 26 (May 1562). See also AMT, AA 14, no. 4.

[33]   Greengrass, 'The anatomy of a religious riot', pp. 380–81.

[34]   The parlement appointed Guillaume La Laine, bourgeois, Jehan de Borderia, avocat, Pierre Madron le jeune, François de Saint-Felix, docteur, Ramon Alies, avocat, Etienne de Rabestans, seigneur de Colomiers, Gaston du Pin, bourgeois, and Laurent de Puybisque, seigneur de la Landelle. Their oaths of office were sworn the same day, 19 May, before the premier président, Jehan de Masencal, and Présidents Antoine de Paulo, Jehan Daffis, Nicolas Latomy and Michel Dufaur; AMT, AA 18, no. 88.

support of their claims. Now, with much of the civic corporation peopled by staunch Catholics, protestations against such deployment fell away.[35]

Recrimination and retribution now followed. In June, the *capitoul*, Mandinelli, became the first consul to be condemned for his part in the unrest; his goods were confiscated and sold off to contribute towards the repair of the town.[36] Further purges ensued, with seven more *capitouls* condemned in absentia, their effigies hung in the Place Saint-George before a vociferous Catholic crowd. Each was banished from Toulouse in perpetuity, fined 100,000 *livres*, and excluded from the nobility – a punishment also visited on their immediate family members.[37] As a warning, the court ordered that their sentences be read out each 17 May to remind the citizens of Toulouse of the ever-present threat posed by Protestantism to society.[38] Such was the new mood of fanaticism at this time that even moderate Catholics came under suspicion, the most prominent being the *président*, Dufaur, who was accused of aiding and abetting the insurrectionists. In fact, Dufaur was only saved from the ignominy of arrest and prosecution by the personal intervention of Monluc, who vouched for his long-time friend's orthodoxy.[39]

The Catholic victory against the rebellion of May 1562 owed much to the willingness of the nobility, magistrates, bourgeoisie and minor officials of Toulouse to unite in defence of the town. The experience and fervour of activists such as the *basoche* and the syndicate helped ensure that Catholic tactics were carried out effectively and forcefully, and with the full support of the 'grassroots' community. Catholics at Toulouse, then, had survived a most stern test. Moreover, they had achieved a degree of supremacy by the summer of 1562 that far exceeded the political situation of their compatriots at Bordeaux, who were still fighting against the intransigence of moderates within the court. This success would act as a springboard for more confident militant action, so that by 1570 Toulouse had established itself as an unassailable Catholic stronghold of the southwest.

---

[35]　ADHG, 1B 55, fo. 569. Henri Ramet observed that by August 1562, the *parlement* had redefined the town council as a tool of the Catholic party, rather than the irritant it had tended to be in former years. See Henri Ramet, *Le capitole et le parlement de Toulouse* (Toulouse, 1926), p. 29.

[36]　AMT, AA 18, no. 89.

[37]　AMT, AA 14, no. 1.

[38]　AMT, AA 18, no. 96.

[39]　Jean-Baptiste Dubédat, *Histoire du parlement de Toulouse* (Paris, 1885), vol. 1, p. 398. Dufaur had served as a *juge au présidial* at Toulouse (1531–35), *juge-mage* at Toulouse (1535–47), *président du parlement* at Toulouse (1557–72), and was appointed *conseiller au grand'conseil* in May 1556. See Blaise de Monluc, *Commentaries 1521–1576*, ed. Paul Courteault and J. Giono (Paris, 1964), p. 1249, n. 3. For accusations and subsequent enquiry into the role of Dufaur in the insurrection of May 1562, see AMT, GG 826 (17 May 1562).

Agen

The third major target of Protestant forces was the compact though robustly walled town of Agen. Although smaller than Bordeaux and Toulouse (its population numbered 7000 by 1560), stout defences and a dominant position overlooking the river Garonne ensured Agen would be prized as a command centre by both faiths during the religious wars. For Catholics, the town's location, equidistant between sister bastions of Bordeaux and Toulouse, made it an important staging post for the distribution of troops, munitions and resources across the region, and a hub for communication between dispersed Catholic communities. For reformers, the capture of Agen would provide a significant satellite for its regional army, and perhaps more importantly, sever the umbilical cord between Catholic forces at Bordeaux and Toulouse. Predictably, then, this strategic prize became the focus of Protestant attention the moment war was declared. The assault on Agen was launched in late April 1562, under the command of Generals Caumont and Duras. Concerted attacks were launched against predetermined locations along the town's walls, while supporters within engaged key defensive units so as to draw them away from these pressure points. Within the day, Protestant forces had broken through the defences and occupied the town; Agen's Catholic hierarchy was captured and imprisoned – though some managed to effect an escape – and its many churches and cathedral were sacked.[40] With the fall of Agen, numerous neighbouring centres across the Agenais also succumbed; Lectoure, Tonneins, Villeneuve-d'Agenais and Nérac all fell into Protestant hands within the week.[41]

How had this success been possible? Protestant expectations on the eve of the assault must have been minimal, given the strength of Agen's fortifications, and the nature of the improvements made to the town's defensive capabilities over recent years. The enhancement of the defences had been the initiative of two Catholic councillors – Martial de Nort, consul of the jurade, and Clément de Lalande, canon of the church of Saint-Caprais – in preparation for just such an eventuality. They had commenced the reorganization of the guard and militia as early as February 1560, enlisting Monluc to help identify areas that required improvement. Monluc had observed that civil stability was a primary concern for the town, and had recommended that Catholics on the town council maintain a watchful eye over the town's reformed community, so as to pre-empt agitation and

---

[40]   A comprehensive Catholic account of the seizure and occupation of Agen by Protestants in April 1562 exists in the records of the jurade, written in November of that year. See Archives départementales de Lot-et-Garonne (hereafter ADLG), E Sup. Agen, BB 30, fos 96–9.
[41]   ADLG, E Sup. Agen, BB 30, fos 88–91.

unrest.[42] As incidences of Protestant violence rose across the Agenais, de Nort and Lalande moved to establish a coalition council to formulate Catholic responses. The council convened in June 1560, attended by prominent Catholic officials of the *jurade*, *sénéchaussée* and *présidial*, with Monluc present to advise on military affairs.[43] The coalition promulgated two significant directives: a *conseil militaire* was to be created to monitor Huguenot activity within Agen, and a sizeable Catholic militia force was to be established, under the direct authority of Lalande. This unit would be commanded by experienced Catholic captains, and provisioned with arms and artillery from the town arsenal.[44] Further initiatives followed. Monluc recommended that the coalition deploy the town's consuls, attired in their formal robes of office, to guard the gates,[45] while consuls were also deployed to head militia patrols of the streets at night.[46] These were more than mere gestures: by employing elites as well as citizens to guard and patrol the town, and by making them conspicuous to all in their robes, Monluc was reminding everyone of the symbolism and traditions of the town, and emphasizing the value of collective responsibility and communal defence.[47]

The coalition was soon bolstered by increased support from the local Catholic nobility, who endorsed the measures implemented by the council, and offered their mobilized retinues as a police force to patrol the region. The impetus for such elite endorsement stemmed from the activism of the *états d'Agenais*. The assemblies of 1560 and 1561 were both dominated by concerns expressed at the increasing levels of Protestant violence across the Agenais, with Catholic delegates advocating confrontation with the reformers rather than acceptance of the conciliatory policies being promoted by the Crown.[48] Following the 1561 assembly, the *états* drafted an extensive remonstrance, calling upon the Crown to finance military action that would force Protestant troops to disarm, and compel reformed communities to refrain from civil disobedience.[49] All the region's prominent Catholics signed this request, including Monluc, the *comte* de Villars, and the *sieurs* de Lauzun, d'Estissac, Caumont, Negrepelisse, Tonneins and Biron, revealing the degree of consensus behind such a militant action. Its two main pledges – that all 'Catholic gentlemen' devote their lives to the

---

42   Paul Courteault, *Blaise de Monluc. Historien* (Geneva, 1970), p. 388.
43   ADLG, E Sup. Agen, FF 31 (1 June 1560; 4 June 1560).
44   ADLG, E Sup. Agen, FF 31 (4 June 1560).
45   ADLG, E Sup. Agen, FF 31 (no folio).
46   Ibid.
47   For a similar requirement of Bordeaux magistrates to wear their formal robes while on guard duty in June 1562, see BMB, ms 369, II, fo. 421; BMB, ms 370, fo. 654.
48   ADLG, E Sup. Agen, AA 43.
49   BN Dupuy, 588, fo. 106.

defence of orthodoxy, and that the Crown would be better served utilizing the local Catholic nobility of the southwest to maintain the peace, rather than continuing with its ineffective policy of legislating for concord – would become the staple of militant Catholic manifestos over the next years.[50]

Given Catholic preparedness, then, it would appear that the element of surprise was key to initial Protestant success at Agen. However, the integrated nature of the various Catholic military and militant bodies meant that the Catholic powers were able to initiate a plan to recover the town soon thereafter. Monluc played a significant role here. Despite being ordered to defend Bordeaux as a matter of priority, the Catholic general and his troops determined to secure Agen before departing.[51] Assuming command of the relief effort, Monluc implemented a series of extraordinary military decrees. Six new commissions were created to direct the large number of noble retinues that rallied to his command, and a *conseil militaire* was established at Faudouas to co-ordinate the various military bodies gathered within the town.[52] It is interesting to note that the assembled Catholic gentlemen swore to *faire amis*, a pledge of fraternity that would be common in later, larger Catholic leagues.[53] This suggests that Monluc's council of war was more than a simple ad hoc arrangement, but that it constituted a formal association.[54] The Catholic relief force was able to move against the rebels at Agen in August 1562, regaining control of the town with little resistance. With the coalition restored to power, and the local elite fraternity providing potent military support, Catholic dominance over Agen was re-established.

The repercussions were immediate and decisive. Lalande was appointed military governor of the town, and set about implementing a series of reprisals. Under the auspices of Monluc's *prévôt*, Hélie de Penchéry, *sieur* de la Justinie, Lalande ordered over a thousand Protestant suspects be arrested and tried for insurrection, with around half hanged on town gibbets between August 1562 and March 1563.[55] The coalition then turned its attention to the sequestering of Protestant goods. In September

---

[50]   Ibid.

[51]   Monluc, *Commentaires 1521–1576*, p. 498; Georges Tholin, 'La ville d'Agen pendant les guerres de religion du XVIe siècle', *Revue de l'Agenais et des anciennes provinces du sud-ouest*, 14 (1887): 506–7.

[52]   Present at the *conseil militaire* in May 1562 were leading Catholic activists of the southwest: *seigneurs* Bajaumant, Cancon and Montferrand; *sieurs* de Terride, Tilladet, Besoles, Gondrin and Jean de Narbonne, the *marquis* de Fimarcon and 'plusieurs autres gentilzhommes'; Monluc, *Commentaires 1521–1576*, p. 499.

[53]   Ibid.

[54]   J.-F. Samazeuilth supports this assumption, noting that all the leading associates at Faudouas would go on to play key roles in Catholic activism across the Agenais over the coming decade; J.-F. Samazeuilth, *Histoire de l'Agenais, du Condomois et du Bazadais* (Auch, 1847), vol. 2, p. 99.

[55]   Jules Andrieu, *Histoire de l'Agenais* (Agen, 1893), vol. 1, p. 226.

1562, the Catholic-dominated *jurade* ordered the homes of all prominent reformers to be searched 'in the name of the king ... [the harvests] used to repair and fortify the town',[56] while in January 1563, the order was extended to encompass the sale of household furniture and even wine cellars belonging to the reformers.[57] When the coalition began to expel suspicious persons from the town, it was evident that a watershed had been reached. From meagre beginnings, Catholic militants had transformed their ad hoc alliances into a single, authoritative coalition, which enjoyed the support of the *états* and local nobility. These elements were about to fuse in the formation of an oath-bound, elite-led Catholic league at Agen, an association that would move Catholic militancy from a defensive to an offensive posture. The town of Agen had emerged from the shadows of its sister citadels, Bordeaux and Toulouse, to stand proud as one of three bastions of orthodoxy in the southwest.

Conclusion

It is evident, then, that the contest for control of urban centres was fundamental to sectarian fortunes in the southwest during the early stages of the Wars of Religion. Catholics were able to remain in power at Bordeaux, Toulouse and Agen because the coalitions formed between civic authorities, urban militants and local nobility proved effective buttresses against Protestant incursions. Had these three bastions of orthodoxy succumbed, the ability of neighbouring Catholic communities to resist would have been severely compromised. Conversely, the failure of the reform movement to capture such key citadels proved a fatal flaw in its struggle for hegemony over the region. Not only were Protestant forces denied strategic platforms from which to orchestrate their campaigns, but the Catholic resistance gained time to regroup and plan its counter-offensives.[58] The various activists deserve most of the credit for this resurgence. At Bordeaux, Catholics were able to draw on lessons learned during repeated confrontations with evangelicals over the previous decades, allowing them to be better prepared for insurrection in 1562. At Agen, it was the urban patricians who staved off initial Protestant aggression through adept political manoeuvring, and the astute use of coalition committees to secure control of administrative functions. The local nobility was then marshalled

---

[56]   ADLG, E Sup. Agen, CC 65 (9 September 1562). For list of prominent victims of this confiscation, see ADLG, E Sup. Agen, CC 304 (Comptes des Consuls).

[57]   ADLG, E Sup. Agen, CC 302 (1563).

[58]   David Bryson also states that the Protestant failure to take Bordeaux in 1562 weakened their position in Guyenne. See David Bryson, *Queen Jeanne and the Promised Land. Dynasty, Homeland, and Religion and Violence in Sixteenth-century France* (Brill, 1999), pp. 147, 311–14.

in support of the town, as were an eager populace, keen to participate in the unified defence of their homes. At Toulouse, committees were formed to co-ordinate Catholic defiance, with the local nobility, magistrates and populace engaged in integrated resistance, much like at Agen. At all three centres, uncompromising militant figures assumed greater control within local government during this period, and once Catholic authority had been consolidated, radical agendas were often employed, most notably the punitive measures taken to restrict, censor and penalize Protestant minorities within the towns through repressive legislation.

The interconnectedness of the various syndicates, leagues and coalition councils, then, both underpinned Catholic defensive policy and facilitated Catholic counter-offensives. The contribution of 'grassroots' activism in support of the Catholic cause, as embodied in the bitter conflict between the *basoche* and the emerging evangelical movement on the streets of Bordeaux and Toulouse throughout the 1540s and 1550s, should not be overlooked. Participation by such 'popular' elements bolstered and augmented Catholic militancy, and showed that spontaneous communal activism was not a phenomenon solely of the war years, but was instead a feature of the region's urban landscape from earlier times. John Bossy's assertion that the persistence of French Catholicism through the crises of the Reformation was 'largely the result of the voluntary association of French Catholics' has resonance here.[59] Significantly, this study indicates that Catholic revival in the southwest pre-dated the influence of the Council of Trent and proceeded largely independently of it.

---

[59] John Bossy, 'Leagues and associations in sixteenth-century French Catholicism', *Studies in Church History*, 23 (1986): 171.

PART II
Clergy

The 'New Clergies' in Europe: Protestant Pastors and Catholic Reform Clergy after the Reformation

Luise Schorn-Schütte

The long-prevailing division of the history of the European Reformation into 'Reformation' and 'Counter-Reformation' has been overtaken by more recent research. The older model has been replaced by that of a single reform movement, one which resulted in the formation of Protestant Churches on the one hand and a deferred Catholic reform movement on the other. At times parallel and at times interdependent, these developments are vividly illustrated by the history of confessional office holders – both the Protestant clergy and the Catholic 'reform clergy'. Strong arguments suggest that from the mid-seventeenth century on, there remained few significant differences, in terms of educational and/or socio-economic backgrounds, between Protestant pastors and the Catholic pastoral clergy. This effectively contradicts Max Weber's thesis that Protestants enjoyed an educational advantage over Catholics.[1]

Medieval Traditions

Visitation reports from a number of European regions, dating back to the mid-sixteenth century and offering an insight into the educational levels of the clergy on the eve of the Reformation, record an urgent need for improvement. The theological training of both the lower clergy and those theologians who, although ordained to higher orders, served merely as holders of benefices and failed to carry out their spiritual duties, left much to be desired. Similar deficits existed concerning their pastoral abilities and preaching skills. In addition, the personal conduct of all clergy groups remained a constant bone of contention in the eyes of the congregation as well as of secular and ecclesiastical authorities. Most of

---

[1]   See Luise Schorn-Schütte, 'Priest, Preacher, Pastor: Research on Clerical Office in Early Modern Europe', *Central European History*, 22 (2000): 1–39.

these deficiencies clashed with even the medieval ideal of a priest. Yet theological competence and preaching skills were not part of the 'job description' for pastoral clergy: 'Their main functions were sacramental and disciplinary, not doctrinal.'[2] Thus, the majority of pre-Reformation clergy did not need profound theological training; their task was to facilitate the accomplishment of good works as a path towards spiritual salvation – a task requiring primarily practical and technical skills. Only the higher clergy were expected to perform theological duties. Technical skills and theological knowledge were supposed to be taught at schools and theological seminaries and faculties; in reality, however, this was not done adequately, if at all, in the late fifteenth and early sixteenth centuries. After all, appointment to a clerical office was closely tied to the assumption of a benefice, and only in the rarest of cases did this selection depend on spiritual-pastoral abilities. Rather, in the late Middle Ages, the pursuit of personal income and patronage were the decisive factors in these decisions. All pre-Reformation efforts to redress these deficiencies were aimed at the full realization of the clerical ideal. Thus, they were not anti-clerical, but rather were marked by a singular esteem for the sanctity of priesthood.

But it was exactly this sanctity of office that was brought into question by Luther's doctrine of justification. There was no longer a need for powerful assistants in the quest for salvation by way of good works; hence, Luther's teachings on the priesthood of all believers. With this doctrine, the Wittenberg reformer was actually building on medieval traditions (among others, those of the Lollards and the followers of Wyclif). In sum, the reformist cause can be seen as the sacralization of the secular and the secularization of the sacral; the separate clerical estate was to be abolished. Social historians have found that the first two generations of the new Protestant clergy were recruited largely from the clerical estate (former monks or priests), and moreover, that numerous pastors' wives had previously been their illicit companions, or were, as in the famous case of Katharina von Bora, former nuns.[3] A complete replacement of the

---

[2]   Richard N. Swanson, 'Before the Protestant Clergy: The Construction and Deconstruction of Medieval Priesthood', in Scott Dixon and Luise Schorn-Schütte (eds), *The Protestant Clergy of Early Modern Europe* (Basingstoke, 2003), pp. 39–59, p. 40.

[3]   Despite the large volume of social-historical studies, an unevenness of sources has meant that the depth of coverage varies greatly from one territory to the next: for the Old Reich, see Luise Schorn-Schütte, *Evangelische Geistlichkeit in der Frühneuzeit. Deren Anteil an der Entfaltung frühmoderner Staatlichkeit und Gesellschaft (16.–18. Jahrhundert)* (Gütersloh, 1996), and Andreas Wahl, *Lebensplanung und Alltagserfahrung. Württembergische Pfarrerfamilien im 17. Jahrhundert* (Mainz, 2000); for England, see Rosemary O'Day, *The English Clergy: The Emergence and Consolidation of a Profession 1558–1642* (Leicester, 1996); for France, see Joseph Bergin, *The Making of the French Episcopate 1589–1661* (New Haven, CT, 1969); for central Europe, see Joachim Bahlcke, 'Geistlichkeit

clerical personnel in all the territories where the Reformation had taken hold would have led to a total breakdown of spiritual care, and was therefore out of the question.

Basic Outlines of a Social Biography of the 'New Clergy'

Few historical studies compare the European clergy across confessions and regions. In large measure, this reflects the unevenness of the sources, as not all records provide mass data of equal significance. But it also reflects a problem of interpretation, as it is still generally assumed that an unbridgeable gap existed between Protestant pastors and Catholic clerics, both in their perception and execution of office and in their social backgrounds. However, more recent regional studies in social history – including those dealing with confessionally mixed regions – clearly show that both the Protestant clergy and the majority of the Catholic pastoral clergy belonged to the European bourgeoisie. This chapter takes these insights as its starting point.

We must, however, bear in mind that there were other possible social origins (such as peasant backgrounds), particularly at the outer edges of Europe (in the south and central east), which need to be taken into account as exceptions to the rule. And the high clergy in the Catholic Church still came from the European nobility.

Social and Regional Origin and Integration

The common image of the peasant origin of Catholic priests has given way to a much more differentiated one as a result of numerous studies of the pastoral clergy in the Old Reich since the late sixteenth century.[4] The term 'pastoral clergy' applies to the lower secular and regular clergy at the parochial level, which – as a result of the reform of clerical education

---

und Politik. Der ständisch organisierte Klerus in Bömen und Ungarn in der Frühen Neuzeit', in Joachim Bahlcke, Hans-Jürgen Bömelburg and Norbert Kersken (eds), *Ständefreiheit und Staatsgestaltung in Ostmitteleuropa* (Leipzig, 1996), pp. 161–86; for southern Europe, see José Pedro Paiva, 'The Portuguese Secular Clergy in the Sixteenth and Seventeenth Centuries', in Eszter Andor and István Toth (eds), *Frontiers of Faith: Religious Exchange and the Constitution of Religious Identities 1400–1750* (Budapest, 2001) pp. 157–66; for Switzerland, see Albert Fischer, *Reformatio und Restitutio. Das Bistum Chur im Zeitalter der tridentinischen Glaubenserneuerung. Zugleich ein Beitrag zur Geschichte der Priesterbildung und Pastoralreform 1601–1661* (Zürich, 2000); Amy Burnett, *Teaching the Reformation. Ministers and their Messages in Basel 1529–1629* (Oxford, 2006). For an European overview from a Catholic perspective, see Peter Hersche, *Muße und Verschwendung. Europäische Gesellschaft und Kultur im Barockzeitalter* (2 vols, Freiburg, 2006) pp. 267–73.

[4]   For more literature, see Schorn-Schütte, *Evangelische Geistlichkeit in der Frühneuzeit*.

launched by the Council of Trent (1545–63)[5] – increasingly had to take on spiritual responsibilities that went beyond the technical-practical task of pastoral care (*Seelsorge*). Despite inadequate sources, the following can be said about the sixteenth and early seventeenth centuries: just like Protestant pastors of the second and third generations, the majority of the Catholic pastoral clergy appear to have come from the urban or territorial bourgeoisie. The evolution of this social pattern was probably closely related to the introduction of ordination titles (proof of financial security in terms of money or landholdings as a prerequisite for ordination) at the end of the sixteenth and beginning of the seventeenth century. Thus, entrance into clerical office was barred to the great majority of poor, independent peasants, while it remained open for the more affluent urban bourgeoisie and wealthier peasants, as well as for the territorial civil servants (drawn from the court, administration and universities).[6] These findings are confirmed by the Jesuit Order's tendency to recruit its members from the more affluent and/or highly educated bourgeoisie.[7] The foundation of the Jesuit Order (1540), as well as that of other reform orders (such as the Capuchin Order in 1525/28) and the *Collegium Germanicum* in Rome (1552)[8], was the Catholic response to the redefinition of clerical office within the Protestant Church and to its strong pedagogical influence on the secular sphere. The debates about a more specialized education of boarding students in the *Germanicum* that arose at the end of the sixteenth century confirm this conclusion about social origins. While the first generation of pupils still partly came from the bourgeoisie, after the 1670s a new practice prevailed: the *Germanicum* was now dedicated exclusively to the

---

[5]   The education of the clergy was one of the main topics on the agenda of the first session of the Council, 1545–47. For the ideal of the reform priest formulated at the Council, see Hubert Jedin, 'Das Leitbild des Priesters nach dem Tridentinum und dem Vaticanum II', in *Theologie und Glaube*, 60 (1970): 102–24.

[6]   Cf. Thomas P. Becker, *Konfessionalisierung in Kurköln. Untersuchungen zur Durchsetzung der katholischen Reform in den Dekanaten Ahrgau und Bonn* (Bonn, 1989); Alois Hahn, *Die Rezeption des tridentinischen Pfarrerideals im westtrierischen Pfarrklerus des 16. und 17. Jahrhunderts. Untersuchungen zur Geschichte der katholischen Reform im Erzbistum Trier* (Publication de la Section Historique de l'Institut G.-D. de Luxembourg, vol. 90), (Luxembourg, 1974); Werner Freitag, *Pfarrer, Kirche und ländliche Gesellschaft. Das Dekanat Vechte 1400–1803* (Bielefeld, 1998); Andreas Holzem, *Religion und Lebensformen. Katholische Konfessionalisierung im Sendgericht des Fürstbistums Münster* (Paderborn, 2000).

[7]   Cf. Ronnie Po-Chia Hsia, *Social Discipline in the Reformation. Central Europe 1550–1750* (London and New York, 1989), pp. 48–50.

[8]   For the history of the *Germanicum*, see Peter Schmidt, *Das Collegium Germanicum in Rom und die Germaniker. Zur Funktion eines römischen Ausländerseminars 1552–1914* (Tübingen, 1984).

education of the nobility in order to reform the higher echelons of the territorial Church.[9]

These observations on the social origins of the new pastoral clergy apply to France and Italy as well. According to Joseph Bergin, 'one of the most significant features of the French Counter-Reformation parish clergy is how large a proportion of it was drawn from the bourgeoisie of town and country'.[10] In the mid–seventeenth century, the bourgeoisie supplied up to 85 per cent of all secular and regular clerics who were employed as parish pastors. This 'bourgeois' dominance found in France from the late sixteenth century on can be explained at least in part by the material incentives involved. Exempted from taxes and dues, the parish clergy enjoyed a privileged status in an economically overburdened society.[11] Moreover, the French Catholic Church itself contributed to social change through persistent efforts to improve standards of education.

Developments in Italy were very similar to those in France. A number of recent studies have shown that members of the urban elites turned towards clerical office for economic reasons. This applies to both the pastoral clergy and the clerical elite; numerous bishops of the seventeenth century were patricians from large Italian cities.[12] From the mid seventeenth century on, this development was reinforced by the fact that the episcopal seminary-colleges that had been founded exclusively for the education of future clergy opened their doors to the affluent urban bourgeoisie, as well as to interested aristocratic laymen.[13]

Just as before the Reformation, the aristocracy remained the social recruiting pool for the higher clergy (such as bishops and cardinals) within the old Church throughout Europe. In contrast to Protestantism, the Catholic clergy remained an independent social and political estate, retaining its political function in the estate assemblies in the Catholic regions of Europe.[14] Since these structures no longer existed within the Protestant

---

[9] Ibid., pp. 44ff as well as pp. 78ff and fig. 3 on p. 79.

[10] Joseph Bergin, 'Between Estate and Profession: The Catholic Parish Clergy of Early Modern Western Europe', in M.L. Bush (ed.), *Social Orders and Social Classes in Europe since 1500: Studies in Social Stratification* (London and New York, 1992), pp. 76–7.

[11] Ibid., pp. 77–8.

[12] Cf. Martin Papenheim, *Karrieren in der Kirche: Bischöfe in Nord- und Süditalien 1676–1903* (Tübingen, 2001), pp. 221–3.

[13] Cf. Dominique Julia, 'Il prête', in Marc Novelle (ed.), *L'uomo dell' Illuminismo* (Rome and Bari, 1992), pp. 399–443; Carlo Fantappiè, 'Istituzioni ecclesiastiche e istruzione secondaria nell' Italia moderna: I seminari-collegi vescovili', *Jahrbuch des deutsch-italienischen historischen Instituts in Trient*, 15 (1989): 186–240.

[14] Ronald G. Asch, '"Lumine solis". Der Favorit und die politische Kultur des Hofes in Westeuropa', in Michael Kaiser und Andreas Pečar (eds), *Der zweite Mann im Staat. Oberste Amtsträger und Favoriten im Umkreis der Reichsfürsten in der*

Church, the Catholic clergy were far more diverse; that is, membership was recruited from a much wider social scale. The number of aristocratic boarding students educated in the above-mentioned *Germanicum* rose to a good 60 per cent by the middle of the seventeenth century, and to 70 per cent by the middle of the eighteenth century.[15]

A glance at the regional backgrounds of the Catholic pastoral clergy in the Old Reich confirms the above conclusions regarding social origins. From the late sixteenth century on, the pastoral clergy in the countryside came only rarely from rural areas or the parish itself. In the case of the diocese of Würzburg, it has been shown that the country pastors predominantly came from neighbouring cities, often the seats of the court and territorial administrations or of the military.[16] Even for such ecclesiastical territories as the prince-bishopric of Münster or the bishoprics of Hildesheim and Chur – in which the Tridentine reforms requiring that the pastor reside in his parish had proven hard to implement – this pattern of regional origin holds true.[17] The confessionally reliable candidates needed for the stabilization of a Catholicism renewed by the Tridentine measures – figures who often were members of the new reform orders[18] – came from distant regions and were mostly of urban background. From the mid-seventeenth

---

Frühen Neuzeit (Zeitschrift für Historische Forschung Beiheft 32) (Berlin, 2003), pp. 21–38; Hélène Millet and Peter Moraw, 'Clerics in the State', in Wolfgang Reinhard (ed.), *Power Elites and State Building* (New York, 1996), pp. 173–207; Luise Schorn-Schütte, 'Die Geistlichen vor der Revolution. Zur Sozialgeschichte der evangelischen Pfarrer und des katholischen Klerus am Ende des Alten Reiches', in Helmut Berding, Etienne François and Hans Peter Ullmann (eds), *Deutschland und Frankreich im Zeitalter der französischen Revolution* (Frankfurt am Main, 1989), pp. 216–44; Wolfgang Reinhard, *Geschichte der Staatsgewalt. Eine vergleichende Verfassungsgeschichte Europas von den Anfängen bis in die Gegenwart* (Munich, 1999), p. 187.

[15]   Schmidt, *Das Collegium Germanicum in Rom und die Germaniker*, pp. 80–89. For the bishopric of Chur as an example, see Fischer, *Reformatio und Restituito*; for the Old Reich in general, see Karl Otmar Freiherr von Aretin, *Heiliges Römisches Reich 1776–1806*, vol. 1 (Wiesbaden, 1967), pp. 76–82; for similar results in France, see Joseph Bergin, *The Making of the French Episcopate 1589–1661*, p. 196 and passim.

[16]   Georg Knetsch, 'Die Geistlichen in Frickenhausen/M. Grundlagen und Personen', in Karl W. Wittstadt (ed.), *Kirche und ländliche Gesellschaft in Mainfranken von der Reformation bis zur neuesten Zeit* (Würzburg, 1988), p. 159.

[17]   For more information, see Werner Freitag, *Pfarrer, Kirche und ländliche Gesellschaf*, pp. 185–7 and table 8; Renate Dürr, *Kirchenräume. Handlungsmuster von Pfarrern, Obrigkeiten und Gemeinden in Stadt und Kleinem Stift Hildesheim 16.–18. Jahrhundert* (unpublished Habilitation, Johann Wolfgang Goethe-Universität Frankfurt am Main, 2003), pp. 196–202; Fischer, *Reformatio Restitutio*, pp. 544–52.

[18]   Dürr, *Kirchenräume*, p. 200; evidence for the Grisons can be found in Andreas Wendland, 'Träger der Konfessionalisierung und spiritueller Habitus.

century on, the so-called 'local' clergy continued to be of mainly urban origin. It can therefore be asserted for Catholic Germany as well that the cultural gap 'between the urban-minded priest and the rural environment of the faithful' helped widening 'the gulf between pastor and parishioners' over the course of the seventeenth century.[19] Only seldom was there an actual family connection between the village community and the pastor's relatives. In areas where the parish office was filled by members of orders, their short-term residence exacerbated this situation.[20] Still, this did not necessarily make the pastor an outsider.[21]

As early as the seventeenth century, the regional mobility of the Catholic parish clergy in France was apparently more pronounced than that of the pastoral clergy in the Old Reich.[22] There was a clear disparity between the various church provinces in terms of supply of clergy members, which could be described as over- or undersourcing. The conclusion that from the early seventeenth century on the rural parish clergy came largely from cities applies to France as well. Thus, here – as in other European regions – the gulf between laymen and pastoral clergy was growing. Whether this led to mistrust and rejection, however, is not at all certain.[23]

Despite the reform decrees of the Council of Trent, in the Italian regions, more than anywhere else, clerical office continued to be regarded as a private domain and could be filled according to private law. This custom was facilitated and further promoted by the great diversity of Church patrons who were endowed with different local privileges. The families of prebends saw clerical benefices as a legitimate way to provide for their own.[24] Thus, the extent of regional mobility among the pastoral clergy remained rather limited.

The social integration of the Protestant clergy has been much better documented, at least for the period since the late sixteenth century.[25] As a result of comparative research on the Old Reich, the Swiss Confederation and the Polish aristocratic republic, the commonly accepted idea of self-recruitment to clerical office must be thoroughly revised for the late sixteenth and the seventeenth centuries. Instead, it has been shown that the urban and territorial administrations played a rather important role

---

Betrachtungen zur Kapuzinermission in den Drei Bünden im 17. Jahrhundert', *Wissenschaft und Weisheit*, 67 (2004), pp. 71–95.

[19] Becker, *Konfessionalisierung in Kurköln*, p. 82.

[20] Dürr, *Kirchenräume*, pp. 198 and 201–2.

[21] Ibid. This revises the predominant opinion in existing research.

[22] Bergin, 'Between Estate and Profession', pp. 72–4.

[23] For more on this, see Hsia, *Social Discipline in the Reformation*, pp. 163–4.

[24] Cf. Julia, 'Il préte'.

[25] *Pfarrerbücher* are a good source of relevant documents for the German-speaking areas.

both in the recruitment of pastors and their wives, and promoted the Church as an occupational field for their sons or sons-in-law. In some regions, craftsmen and merchants still played a major part in recruiting the pastors.[26] This illustrates that the Protestant clergy became integrated into the group of (often legally trained) non-aristocratic office holders in the service of territorial or city authorities, a group that was becoming increasingly influential from the late sixteenth century on. A growing network of personal and familial relations connected these different groups'.[27] Upward mobility within this group of civic office holders was possible over the course of two or three generations; clerical office proved to be a 'springboard profession' (*Plattformberuf*). This trend was even more pronounced in the case of pastors' wives. By using marriage as a means for social integration, the clergymen merely followed established social patterns. Aside from the financial advantages that it offered both spouses, marriage promoted social establishment and ascent.[28]

Developments in the Protestant cantons of the Swiss Confederation did not differ much from those in the Old Reich. The oft-cited occupational continuity among the clergy is not to be found here either. In some of the researched areas, clergy members proved even less willing to remain in their profession over a long period of time than did artisans. What is remarkable here is the consistently high proportion of craftsmen recruited to the clergy in the Swiss cities. From the mid-eighteenth century on, the Swiss cantons witnessed a high influx of new clergy; as a result, entry into office was blocked for candidates from the lower ranks. In the Old Reich, this development began a full generation later, and did not achieve comparable results until the first decades of the nineteenth century.[29]

---

[26]   Cf. the tables in Schorn-Schütte, *Evangelische Geistlichkeit in der Frühneuzeit*, and Luise Schorn-Schütte and Scott Dixon, 'Introduction', in Luise Schorn-Schütte and Scott Dixon (eds), *The Protestant Clergy of Early Modern Europe* (Basingstoke, 2003), tables on pp. 7–10. See also Jonathan Strom, *Orthodoxy and Reform: The Clergy in 17th Century Rostock*. (Tübingen 1999), pp. 32–7 and table A.2; Ernst Riegg, *Konfliktbereitschaft und Mobilität. Die protestantischen Geistlichen zwölf süddeutscher Reichsstätte* (Leinfelden-Echterdingen, 2002), pp. 75–110.

[27]   Cf. Wahl, *Lebensplanung und Alltagserfahrung*, and Riegg, *Konfliktbereitschaft und Mobilität*.

[28]   Cf., among others, Luise Schorn-Schütte, 'Matrimony as Profession: The Clergyman's Wife', in Silvana Seidel Menchi, Thomas Kuehn and Anne Jacobson Schutte (eds), *Time, Space, and Women's Lives in Early Modern Europe* (Sixteenth Century Essays & Studies, 57) (Kirksville, MO, 2001), pp. 255–77; Riegg, *Konfliktbereitschaft und Mobilität*, pp. 84–91; Strom, *Orthodoxy and Reform*, pp. 32–4.

[29]   Luise Schorn-Schütte, 'Zwischen "Amt" und "Beruf": Der Prediger als Wächter, "Seelenhirt" oder Volkslehrer. Evangelische Geistlichkeit im Alten Reich und in der schweizerischen Eidgenossenschaft im 18. Jahrhundert', in Luise Schorn-Schütte and Walter Sparn (eds), *Protestantische Pfarrer. Zur sozialen und*

A glance at England confirms the observations concerning the social integration of the Protestant clergy on the Continent. In the late sixteenth and early seventeenth centuries, following a period of insecurity and instability, the new Anglican and Puritan clergy succeeded in getting socially established. Their new social status meant that now the gentry sought entrance to clerical office as well, so that the opportunities for upward mobility for yeomen's sons, which had existed since the mid-sixteenth century, began to dwindle.[30] This does not mean, however, that a new aristocratic Church was established within English Protestantism. Instead, the close connection between gentry and urban bourgeoisie helped create a new middle social group in England as well, from which, as on the Continent, academically trained office holders were recruited. The Protestant clergy was part of this group. Both in England and on the Continent, the clerical elite belonged to this 'middle class'. Anglican bishops, for example, were 'sons of merchants, clothiers, tailors, yeomen, and small gentry. They succeeded in becoming the equals of the lower gentry and of urban middle classes but never of the nobility, which they could not enter even by marriage.'[31] In this respect, there remained a significant difference between the Protestant and the Roman Catholic Church.

A glance at regional and academic mobility in the Old Reich confirms these remarks on social mobility. To be sure, a discernible change took place between the late sixteenth and the early eighteenth century. While the first two generations of Protestant clergy experienced steady recruitment from outside, after the confessional borders were consolidated an increasing number of clerical office holders came from within the territories themselves. This was, on the one hand, the result of the recently introduced scholarship system that required theology students to study at a university in their home territory. On the other hand, it was a result of the patronage system which remained unchallenged in the Protestant territories and which made clerical employment conditional upon the candidate's personal client-like relationship with their aristocratic, urban or parish patrons. In the larger territories, however, foreign theologians still made up a significant segment of clergy, even in rural areas. Throughout

---

politischen Rolle einer bürgerlichen Gruppe in der deutschen Gesellschaft des 18. bis 20. Jahrhunderts (Stuttgart, 1997), pp. 7–9; David Gugerli, Zwischen 'Pfrund' und Predigt. Die protestantische Pfarrfamilie auf der Zürcher Landschaft im ausgehenden 18. Jahrhundert (Zürich, 1988). On the problem of shortages and surpluses, see Hartmut Titze, 'Überfüllung und Mangel im evangelischen Pfarramt seit dem ausgehenden 18. Jahrhundert', in Luise Schorn-Schütte and Walter Sparn (eds), Protestantische Pfarrer. Zur sozialen und politischen Rolle einer bürgerlichen Gruppe in der deutschen Gesellschaft des 18. bis 20. Jahrhunderts.

[30] Viviane Barrie-Curien, 'The English Clergy 1560–1620: Recruitment and Social Status', History of European Ideas, 9 (1988): 453–4.

[31] Ibid. p. 454.

the entire early modern era, regional mobility remained most discernible among the ecclesiastical leadership (such as superintendents [*Oberpfarrer*], deans and theology professors).[32]

While similar developments can be observed in England,[33] in Switzerland a certain regional containment (*begrenzte Kleinräumigkeit*) was predominant from the late sixteenth century on.[34] At least two thirds of future pastors had studied either at the University of Basel or the academic gymnasium (*Scola Tigurina*) in Zurich. If there were any cross-regional contacts in the area of education at all, these remained within clearly defined confessional limits. At least among the Protestant rural clergy, such regional ties certainly contributed to a positive relationship with the parish; after all, local traditions of piety were much more accessible to those who had experienced them firsthand.

Training and Educational Levels of Clergy, Access to Clerical Office, and Economic Provisions

With the onset of the Reformation, existing criticism of the Church turned into demands for well-trained pastors. Therefore, even contemporaries understood the Reformation as an educational movement. Over the course of the early modern period, the ideal of the clerical office was being realized within all three Christian confessions in similar ways, however long it took to achieve this goal.[35] A look at the educational levels and the criticism of the conduct of both the Protestant and the Catholic clergy in the Old Reich at the end of the sixteenth century reveals striking similarities between the two 'camps'. This shows that the Catholic norms that evolved in response to the Tridentine reforms coincided largely with the Protestant ideal of a pastor in the last third of the sixteenth century. At the time, academically trained pastors constituted only a negligible number of parish clergy in both Catholic and Protestant regions of Europe.[36] Each side displayed a colourful mixture of theological positions, rooted in both Catholicism and Protestantism and founded on a combination of pastoral care and parish piety. The reforms, or

---

[32]   Schorn-Schütte, 'Priest, Preacher, Pastor'; Strom, *Orthodoxy and Reform*; Thomas Kaufmann, *Universität und lutherische Konfessionalisierung. Die Rostocker Theologieprofessoren und ihr Beitrag zur theologischen Bildung und kirchlichen Gestaltung im Herzogtum Mecklenburg zwischen 1550 und 1675* (Gütersloh, 1997).

[33]   Barrie-Curien, 'The English Clergy 1560–1620': 455–7.

[34]   Gugerli, *Zwischen 'Pfrund' und Predigt*.

[35]   Cf. the stimulating research by Rosemary O'Day, *The English Clergy*, and the important work by Bernhard Vogler, *Le clergé protestant rhénan au siècle de la réforme (1555–1619)* (Paris, 1976).

[36]   On developments in Protestantism, see Schorn-Schütte, *Evangelische Geistlichkeit in der Frühneuzeit*; Holzem, *Religion und Lebensformen*, pp. 46–7.

rather the institutionalization of the educational system – which had started originally in the Protestant regions but in the seventeenth century began taking hold in the Catholic territories as well – were aimed at enhancing theological knowledge and the 'preservation of clerical dignity' within each confession. On both sides, educational goals were tied to an ethos of clerical office that prescribed a certain way of life. The particulars of these prescribed lifestyles, however, differed from one confession to the other. The formal differences between the respective educational systems were significant, but did not necessarily translate into lower educational levels for Catholics.

Since the secular authorities had for the most part failed to implement the reform decrees of the Council of Trent, the importance of the activities of the Catholic orders (such as the Franciscans, the Capuchins[37] and above all the Jesuits) can hardly be overemphasized. Where initiatives by the territorial rulers had fallen short, the Jesuits often succeeded in establishing seminaries for preachers (*Predigerseminare*) to help redress the lack of clerical and sacral schooling for the aspiring pastoral clergy. However, their goal was only partly achieved.[38] Therefore, the period until approximately 1650 must be considered a transitional phase for the Catholic clergy in the Old Reich, characterized by lingering shortcomings in educational levels, in perceptions of office, and in the official and private conduct of clergy members. With the ideal of the *pastor bonus* (which corresponded to the Church fathers' ideal of the bishop), the Tridentine reform movement developed a new approach under which the pastor became the 'leader of the parish, proclaimer of God's word, and dispenser of sacraments'.[39] These criteria became the basis of the Jesuits' educational concept, and correct execution of the duties of office and moral integrity became the central focus of Jesuit 'education'.[40] This went hand in hand with the institutionalization of education, suitably referred to as 'churchification'.[41] In accordance with the provisions of the Order's *ratio studiorum*, all

---

[37] For the activities of the Capuchins in the Swiss Confederation, see Wendland, 'Träger der Konfessionalisierung und spiritueller Habitus'.

[38] Cf. Holzem, *Religion und Lebensformen*; Alois Hahn, *Die Rezeption des tridentinischen Pfarrerideals im westtrierischen Pfarrklerus des 16. und 17. Jahrhunderts*; Fischer, *Reformatio und Restitutio*.

[39] Holzem, *Religion und Lebensformen*, pp. 238–9; Freitag, *Pfarrer, Kirche und ländliche Gesellschaft*; Renate Dürr, 'Images of the Priesthood: An Analysis of Catholic Sermons from the Late Seventeenth Century', *Central European History*, 22 (2000): 87–107.

[40] Holzem, *Religion und Lebensformen*, pp. 239–40; Jedin, 'Das Leitbild des Priesters nach dem Tridentinum und dem Vaticanum II': 102–24.

[41] Anton Schindling, 'Schulen und Universitäten im 16. und 17. Jahrhundert: 10 Thesen zur Bildungsexpansion, Laienbildung und Konfessionalisierung nach der Reformation', in Wolfgang Brandmüller (ed.), *Ecclesia militans. Studien zur Konzilien- und Reformationsgeschichte. Remigius Bäumer zum 70. Geburtstag gewidmet* (vol 1: *Zur Konziliengeschichte*; vol 2: *Zur Reformationsgeschichte*;

Jesuit *gymnasia* taught in their five grades the *studia inferioria*, along with Catholic doctrine and confessionally specific forms of piety. In most cases, the *gymnasia* were attached to philosophical-theological institutes that provided further education for aspiring priests. There students were taught the *studia superioria* – that is, the basic knowledge of theology, the Old and the New Testaments and the Church fathers.[42] Graduates could choose to attend either a nearby faculty of arts or a theological seminary. Students at the seminary often had to practise the delivery of sermons, in order that they master the practical application of their knowledge. After four years, the candidates were ordained to higher orders. Following ordination, they would often sit in on the catechetic exercises the Jesuits offered in the city parishes.

A glance at the reality of pastoral training in some of the prince-bishoprics in the north of the Old Reich and Switzerland shows that the qualifications of the aspiring pastoral clergy increased slowly but steadily from the first third of the seventeenth century on.[43] Thus, in the early seventeenth century more than half of the clergy in a north German deanery had indeed attended the local Tridentine *gymnasium*, and there is evidence that a great majority also attended a local Jesuit college. Yet only a few of the aspiring clergymen earned academic degrees; as a rule they spent four years studying at a Jesuit college. Thus, they received a uniform specialized training, while for them – in contrast to their Protestant contemporaries – a university degree remained the exception to the rule.[44]

Professional training and ordination did not, however, guarantee entrance into office. After all, only the patron could grant a benefice – that is, appoint a candidate to a parish that would generate a liveable income. These patronage rights remained widespread among secular and ecclesiastical rulers in the Old Reich. Ultimately, since the Tridentine seminary system was not established to the same extent in all parts of the Old Reich, no common standard of clerical training emerged. Therefore, it is not possible to refer to the pastoral office as a 'profession', as the term would be understood in the nineteenth and twentieth centuries. Rather, professional qualifications were handled very differently across the various

Paderborn, 1988), pp. 561–570; Freitag, *Pfarrer, Kirche und ländliche Gesellschaft*, p. 163.

[42]   For the Jesuit course of studies, see Karl Hengst, *Jesuiten an Universitäten und Jesuitenuniversitäten* (Munich, 1981), pp. 70-71. For the Catholic schools, see Harald Dickerhof, 'Die katholischen Gelehrtenschulen des konfessionellen Zeitalters im Heiligen Römischen Reich', in Wolfgang Reinhard and Heinz Schilling (eds), *Die katholische Konfessionalisierung* (Gütersloh, 1995), pp. 348–70.

[43]   The following is based on Freitag, *Pfarrer, Kirche und ländliche Gesellschaft*; Holzem, *Religion und Lebensformen*; Fischer, *Reformatio und Restitutio*.

[44]   Freitag, *Pfarrer, Kirche und ländliche Gesellschaft*, p. 189.

regions of the Old Reich.[45] The combination of formal qualifications with client-like and/or familial connections remained the basis for employment throughout the existence of the Old Reich.

As late as the sixteenth century, it was not uncommon for Catholic pastors to seek an income for their own sons. This use of family connections faded away with the gradual implementation of the Tridentine clerical reform. Instead of trying to arrange positions for immediate kin (a habit referred to as *Pfarrfamiliensinn*), the pastor was now taking care of nephews and grandnephews.[46] While the ensuing change amongst the elites took off in the first half of the seventeenth century, it was only during the eighteenth century that these transformed family networks were consolidated.

The implementation of the clerical reform introduced by the Council of Trent turned out to be very problematic in France, Italy and Spain as well. Just as in the Old Reich, these difficulties were due to the persistence of traditional institutions such as the patronage system on the one hand, and the lack of funds for the proposed episcopal seminaries on the other. In the southwest of France and in some parts of Italy and Spain, clergy members were appointed not by the bishop or the curia, but rather by local holders of patronage rights and administrators of benefices. Therefore, it was extraordinarily difficult for reform-minded bishops to ensure that the criteria for appointment of pastoral clergy were met, both in form and in content.[47] According to the decrees of the Council of Trent, the main requirement was graduation from a preacher seminary. As a rule, however, dioceses in both the Old Reich and other European regions lacked the financial resources to establish episcopal seminaries of adequate quality. Seminaries founded in the late sixteenth century in France, for example, had to be closed down during the religious wars, and even as late as the eighteenth century such institutes failed to develop educational standards that would exceed those of the academic *gymnasia*.[48] Moreover, strong competition between these seminaries and the educational institutions of the reform orders developed; instead of co-operating in a useful manner, they hindered each other in their work.

The results in France, to begin with, were very similar to those in the Old Reich. Since the schools and seminaries led by the orders (Jesuits, Franciscans, Capuchins) were so dominant in the education of future pastoral clergy, their curricula remained largely free from episcopal

[45]   Cf. the various case studies by Holzem, *Religion und Lebensformen*; Freitag, *Pfarrer, Kirche und ländliche Gesellschaft*; Albert Fischer, *Reformatio und Restitutio*.

[46]   Freitag, *Pfarrer, Kirche und ländliche Gesellschaft*, table 11, clerical family, on p. 198.

[47]   Julia, 'Il prête', pp. 410–12.

[48]   Bergin, 'Between Estate and Profession', pp. 82–3. For more on France, Italy and Poland, see also Hsia, *Social Discipline in the Reformation*, pp. 144–64.

influence. Only when the interests of Church and royal authorities collided at the end of the seventeenth century did French bishops get the chance to exercise more power over the allocation of benefices, with the result that the Church gained greater influence over the qualification requirements for aspiring clergy.[49] Over the course of the seventeenth century, appointments to clerical office finally became contingent upon the fulfilment of certain minimal requirements. It was not the dismantling of the clientele and benefice system – so characteristic of the early modern period[50] – that led to increased educational levels of the clergy. Rather, this was achieved through combining that system with new forms of control on the part of the bishops, who relied in no small measure on the capacity of clerical candidates to provide a minimum of economic self-sufficiency. Just as in the Old Reich, the 'ordination title' proved to be an instrument with a positive long-term impact on the quality of clerical office.

Unlike in France, the training seminaries of the various orders in Italy as well as in Spain were firmly integrated into the dioceses. As a result, the bishops had much greater influence on the clerical and spiritual content of the curricula. In Italy, the large increase in the number of candidates for clerical office led to an expansion of the episcopal seminary system from the mid-seventeenth century on. The financial situation of these seminaries, however, remained highly precarious. In Spain the bishops had implemented the Tridentine reforms right from the beginning. Supported by the Spanish king, they succeeded in their efforts even against the will of reluctant patrons. Similar developments occurred in Portugal.[51]

Due to the great importance Protestantism placed on preaching the Word, the increase of theological knowledge among aspiring pastors went to the heart of all educational plans in the Protestant parts of Europe. In the German imperial cities as well as in the territories that had become Protestant, it was hoped that qualifications could be improved through the creation of an integrated system of Latin schools, cloister or chapter schools, and universities (as in Württemberg and Hesse). The Latin schools taught elementary Latin, church hymns and Luther's catechism. In some territories, the Church funded a system of scholarships to support talented but underprivileged students, who were expected to meet the additional need for junior clergy. North Germany provides a typical outline of the various steps in this process: as early as the late sixteenth century, 80 per cent of the pastors whose education can be traced through the records had studied

---

[49]   Ibid., p. 78.
[50]   Birgit Emich, Nicole Reinhardt, Hillard von Thiessen and Christian Wieland, 'Stand und Perspektiven der Patronageforschung. Zugleich eine Antwort auf Heiko Droste', *Zeitschrift für Historische Forschung*, 32 (2005): 233–65.
[51]   Cf. Paiva, 'The Portuguese Secular Clergy in the Sixteenth and Seventeenth Centuries'.

at one of the regional universities.[52] This did not mean, however, that all aspiring pastors enjoyed a more profound theological education than had the first generation of Protestant clergy. After all, despite the stipulations of Braunschweig's Church ordinance of 1569, proof of an academic degree, even if only from a faculty of arts, was not mandatory for appointment to a parish position. Studies of the educational levels of second- and third-generation Protestant theologians suggest a clear discrepancy between those in Church leadership positions and regular clergymen.[53] Duration of studies and academic degrees are useful indicators. According to these, up until the mid-seventeenth century the great majority of the regular Protestant pastors had attended university, but had not necessarily been required to attend lectures in the theological faculty, or even to provide any certification of their studies at the faculty of arts.[54]

Despite this latitude regarding university qualifications, by the mid-seventeenth century clear requirements for appointment to a parish position had been established: the Church ordinances of the late sixteenth century had had normative effects in this respect. The typical clergyman began his training – assuming he had already spent about seven years in school – at the age of 20 at a faculty of arts, from which he would graduate three or four years later. During the first half of the seventeenth century, it was customary for the graduates to go on to a non-ecclesiastical post (such as private tutor), before assuming an entry-level Church position such as adjunct pastor or school rector. Therefore, the average age of a newly appointed pastor in the late sixteenth and the early seventeenth centuries reached 33.4 years.[55] Detailed studies of the late seventeenth and early eighteenth centuries have shown that there must have been alternating periods of over- and undersupply of Protestant clergy, leading to ongoing changes in these age specifications.[56] Applicants for parish office were examined by the consistory only after having been presented by the patron. As a result, this exam was essentially reduced to a formality, a trend which in some places only changed with the Pietist reform initiatives of the late seventeenth century. After having been presented and examined, the candidate would be inaugurated into office at a church service.

---

[52] For more details, see Schorn-Schütte, *Evangelische Geistlichkeit in der Frühneuzeit*.

[53] Cf. Strom, *Orthodoxy and Reform*, pp. 77–9, and Kaufmann, *Universität und lutherische Konfessionalisierung*, pp. 145–51.

[54] For variations in length of studies, see Schorn-Schütte, *Evangelische Geistlichkeit in der Frühneuzeit*.

[55] Ibid., pp. 199–210; Wahl, *Lebensplanung und Alltagserfahrung*, pp. 88–90.

[56] Titze, 'Überfüllung und Mangel im evangelischen Pfarramt seit dem ausgehenden 18. Jahrhundert'.

Thus, in Protestantism as well, the typical early-modern fusion of traditional factors with new developments remained a key feature of clerical office. Assignment to a clerical post still generally depended on clientele or family connections, so that here, just as in Catholicism, these positions continued to be seen as sources of income (in other words, as prebends). Since in numerous territories of the Old Reich patronage rights lay in the hands of noble families, city councils or the parish itself, no centralized employment policy emerged before the late eighteenth century.[57] Thus, access to a parish office was affected as much by the applicants' personal career strategies as by local political decisions, which remained largely unaffected by the preferences of territorial rulers. Thus, there can be no talk of a 'professionalization' of the clerical office (in the sense of modernization theory) until the end of the eighteenth century. At the same time, however, the nature of the office did gain a good measure of constancy.[58]

These mechanisms were based on the integration of the clergy into certain groups through marriage and education. After all, even though the thesis of exclusive self-recruitment has been proven untenable, the social networks clerical candidates established through their families or alma maters played a decisive role in the bestowal of office and benefice. On average, newly appointed clergymen got married within three months.[59] The prospective pastors were apparently well aware of how indispensable a wife was for the practical management of the parsonage, and how important the choice of a spouse was for the social recognition of the new office holder. Then again, the search for a position was not always linked to a favourable marital connection; access to office was often facilitated by contacts the candidate had made at school, university or during educational travels.[60]

In England as well, the Anglican and Puritan clergy experienced a remarkable increase in educational standards from the late sixteenth century on, a pattern reflected, for example, in the great number of academic degrees held by pastors.[61] 'The policy of educating the clergy thus bore its fruits on the eve of the Civil War in practically the whole of England.'[62] This rise in educational levels did not, however, result in higher remuneration for pastors: at the end of the sixteenth century, 40 per cent of pastoral offices failed to provide adequate support for the pastor's entire

---

[57] See Wahl, *Lebensplanung und Alltagserfahrung*, pp. 97–132; he portrays Württemberg as an exceptional case.

[58] Cf. Riegg, *Konfliktbereitschaft und Mobilität*, pp. 119–21.

[59] Wahl, *Lebensplanung und Alltagserfahrung*, pp. 97–132, and Schorn-Schütte, *Evangelische Geistlichkeit in der Frühneuzeit*, pp. 295–304.

[60] Ibid., pp. 162ff; Riegg, *Konfliktbereitschaft und Mobilität*, pp. 75–110.

[61] Barrie-Curien, 'The English Clergy 1560–1620': 452.

[62] Ibid., p. 452.

family. This situation – along with a rising number of highly qualified university graduates – heightened the competition for well-endowed prebends, a phenomenon that grew ever more intense from the first decades of the seventeenth century on. Hence, patronage and personal connections continued to play a dominant role in the allocation of clerical positions. Here, too, the meaning of clerical office as a vocation continued to co-exist with its major traditional function as a source of income – again, there can be no talk of professionalization.[63] This dynamic is confirmed by the consolidation of the English system of patronage rights after the Reformation. The gentry had profited considerably from the dissolution of the monasteries; centralization of power by way of a 'Reformation from above' did not occur. Here is another reason why the long-term process of raising clerical qualifications cannot primarily be regarded as the expression of a 'disciplinary urge' on the part of the authorities. The predominantly aristocratic patrons remained strictly concerned with their own regions, usually installing only such clergymen into pastoral office as were residents there and/or were willing to conform to the patron's theological and political expectations. The conflict between Puritans and Anglicans was an extension of the wider conflict between gentry and Crown, and patronage rights remained an instrument of Church politics – a development that could also be observed on the Continent.

A comparison of the clergy of all three Christian confessions in Europe with regard to their material circumstances shows that even after the Reformation, clerical office remained integrated into early modern agricultural structures. The Council of Trent explicitly required that a pastor reside in his parish, which meant – as the accumulation of several benefices was expressly prohibited – that it had to be feasible for him to actually earn a liveable income. Despite all difficulties, most pastors in the seventeenth century apparently managed to make a living. Those city pastors and, to an even larger degree, rural pastors who were responsible for cultivating their own land, with or without the help of servants, shared their daily agricultural returns with their parishioners. But those leasing out their property remained firmly tied to the cycles of an agricultural economy as well. The pastors' income in the early modern pastoral system remained anchored in medieval structures – in the Protestant as well as in the Catholic Church. The problems inherent in this system could only partially be solved since the complexity of the parish revenue structure made it difficult for the pastor to secure a steady income on the one hand, and led to conflicts between parishioners and pastor on the other. After all, the pastor's different roles were constantly at odds with each other, as he had to fulfil his duty as spiritual role model and handle the challenges of

---

[63]   Patrick Collinson, *The Religion of Protestants* (Oxford, 1982), pp. 98–9, 114–15 and passim.

agricultural self-sufficiency at the same time.[64] This remained a constant source of conflict within both Protestantism and Catholicism.

The local revenues of both the Catholic and Protestant clergy derived from the crops of the land that had always, by tradition, belonged to the parsonage, the tithe and from the taxes and fees charged for clerical services. In addition, the parsonage itself with its gardens and/or surrounding meadows and fields (which made up what can be referred to as a pastor's farmstead) provided an economic foundation.[65] These basic features varied considerably from region to region. Even within each individual confession differences existed, and one could find 'poor' and 'prosperous' parishes everywhere. In the big cities (just as in the imperial cities of the Old Reich), cash income played an additional role. In general, however, it can be stated that the monetarization of clerical income only began to develop during the eighteenth century, and in many places was not completed before the nineteenth. Thus, the income of both Catholic and Protestant pastors remained highly dependent upon the cycles of agricultural economy, upon the parishioners' ability and willingness to contribute their share, and upon demographic developments, since payments for clerical services rose and fell with the population. Fluctuations in income were the rule; a standardized system of remuneration based on education and experience scarcely existed before the end of the eighteenth century.[66]

'Truly poor pastors were therefore the exception.' This statement characterizes the material conditions within all Christian confessions from the early seventeenth century on – a period when the situation even of Protestant pastors, who had to provide for legitimate families, gradually stabilized. Within the Catholic Church, differences in income were most pronounced between the higher and the lower clergy. But even among the pastoral clergy incomes varied, as they did, for example, between chaplains or vicars on the one hand and pastors on the other.[67] In the Protestant realm,

---

[64]   This problem recurs through contemporary literature under the headings 'Verbauerung des Klerus' or 'Vom Sinken des geistlichen Standes'. Cf. Holzem, *Religion und Lebensformen*, pp. 249–50; Schorn-Schütte, 'Zwischen "Amt" und "Beruf"'.

[65]   For more details (which have been studied on a regional basis, but have not yet been combined in a comprehensive overview for the whole of Europe), see Hahn, *Die Rezeption des tridentinischen Pfarrerideals im westtrierischen Pfarrklerus des 16. und 17. Jahrhunderts*, pp. 134–253; Freitag, *Pfarrer, Kirche und ländliche Gesellschaft*, pp. 202–11; Holzem, *Religion und Lebensformen*, pp. 249–59; Schorn-Schütte, *Evangelische Geistlichkeit in der Frühneuzeit*, pp. 49–83; Wahl, *Lebensplanung und Alltagserfahrung*, pp. 39–43; Strom, *Orthodoxy and Reform*, pp. 45–63; Riegg, *Konfliktbereitschaft und Mobilität*, pp. 155–7.

[66]   This conclusion is not shared by all researchers. For a different interpretation, see Freitag, *Pfarrer, Kirche und ländliche Gesellschaft*, p. 206.

[67]   Ibid., pp. 215–20; see also Holzem, *Religion und Lebensformen*, pp. 259–63.

these differences were particularly discernible between urban and rural clergy.[68] Compared to the financial situation of the parishioners, clergy in rural areas were generally well provided for. The income of urban clergy in the Old Reich, for example, was often equivalent to that of councilmen or jurists employed by the city magistrate.[69] Protestant clergy in leadership positions could always negotiate increases in salary with their respective patrons. More and more, they also received payments in cash and benefited from the introduction of a widows' pension plan. Yet existing differences in income did not generally reflect the clergy member's position in the Church hierarchy. Rather, they resulted from the varying endowments of individual parishes, a tradition that, in most cases, continued to exist even after the Reformation.

Pastor and Parishioners

The laity's expectation that the clergy lead an exemplary life – described as 'clerical conduct' – was not new. It is generally known that such demands, hopes, and expectations stood in an old tradition of criticism of the clergy, long pre-dating the reform movements of the sixteenth century. The criteria used to measure such model behaviour remained essentially unchanged since the Middle Ages, based as they were on the norms of the Old and New Testaments: pastoral care, intercession and propagation of the Word, which included the clergy's admonitory and warning functions. However, since Protestantism denied the necessity and legitimacy of a clerical estate, stressing instead the value of all human activity as worship, the clergy was gradually integrated into the daily world of the faithful; thus, the clerical estate was robbed of its sacral character.[70] In contrast, the Council of Trent had actually reinforced the dogmatic foundations of the priesthood: the sacral character bestowed on the office through ordination on the one hand, and the sacrificial nature of the mass – which could only be celebrated by an ordained priest – on the other.[71] A notable consequence of this difference was that the two confessions had completely opposite concepts of model clergy conduct. While Protestants expected the ideal pastor to be a living

---

[68]   Schorn-Schütte, *Evangelische Geistlichkeit in der Frühneuzeit*, pp. 227–86.

[69]   With regard to the purchasing power of clerical income in the sixteenth and seventeenth centuries, Hahn points out that a pastor earned as much money by reading a mass as a labourer for a whole day's work; Hahn, *Die Rezeption des tridentinischen Pfarrerideals im westtrierischen Pfarrklerus des 16. und 17. Jahrhunderts*, pp. 200–201.

[70]   For more details, see Holsten Fagerberg, 'Reformationszeit', in Gerhard Krause and Gerhard Müller (eds), *Theologische Realenzyklopädie*, vol. 2 (Berlin and New York, 1978), p. 574.

[71]   Hubert Jedin, 'Das Leitbild des Priesters nach dem Tridentinum und dem Vaticanum II': 110, 115; Holzem, *Religion und Lebensformen*, pp. 238–40.

example for all other family fathers and mothers, Catholics envisioned the ideal lifestyle as one that situated the pastor above the everyday life of the parish. Celibacy was supposed to make the priest stand out from daily life, to make him a model by virtue of his removal from secular matters. In contrast, the Protestant pastor was expected to be not only the 'father of the congregation', but the best 'father of the family' as well. He was not removed from the daily world of the parishioners, but rather was part of it in a distinctive way, expected as he was to be perfect at all times.

Accordingly, the perception of self and office on the part of the Catholic clergy 'concentrated on their sacramental powers',[72] while from the mid-sixteenth century on the Protestant clergy developed its own unique self-awareness (*Sonderbewußtsein*), drawing upon the early Christian practices of exceptional erudition and model behaviour of the 'bishops' in their everyday conduct.[73] It is therefore remarkable that with the image of the 'good shepherd', Catholicism also re-adopted a pastoral ideal that was characterized by the humanist-inspired return to the Church fathers and their ideal of a bishop.[74] The realization of this ideal began, as mentioned above, over the course of the Catholic reform of the early seventeenth century.

The relationship between pastor and parishioners was not as deeply affected by these theological divergences as one might expect. Although the confessional differences maintained and embodied by the pastor – the fact that the Protestant pastor could have a legitimate family, while the Catholic priest was at least theoretically committed to celibacy – were ever-apparent to parishioners in the sixteenth and seventeenth centuries, relations between the pastor and his congregation did not change. The reason for this could be found in the continuing interconnectedness of economic dependence and spiritual duty that marked daily life in Protestant as in Catholic parishes and which could (but did not necessarily have to) render the pastor a supplicant to a congregation more inclined to refuse than to fulfil its obligations. 'All spiritual contact between the clergy and the congregation remained caught in an interpretative network of give and take'[75] – this applied to Protestantism and Catholicism alike. The pastor's office created distance and demanded respect, since he was seen as the representative of both ecclesiastical and secular authorities. At the same time, he was part of the parish, and as such was no less tied to the

---

[72] Ibid., p. 239, and Dürr, 'Images of the Priesthood'.

[73] On the development of the perception of clerical office in Protestantism, see Jörg Baur, 'Das kirchliche Amt im Protestantismus', in Jörg Baur (ed.), *Das Amt im ökumenischen Kontext* (Stuttgart, 1980), pp. 103–38; for the term *Sonderbewußtsein*, see Schorn-Schütte, *Evangelische Geistlichkeit in der Frühneuzeit*.

[74] Jedin, 'Das Leitbild des Priesters nach dem Tridentinum und dem Vaticanum II': 110, 115.

[75] Holzem, *Religion und Lebensformen*, p. 266.

traditional subsistence economy of the early modern period than anyone else. The demand for improved execution of office, on the rise since the late sixteenth century, did not bring about any change. Conflict usually arose when the clergy's 'otherworldly' duties had to be compensated by the congregation's secular services, mostly of an economic nature. What the pastor considered a requisite for his pastoral-admonitory work could be viewed by his parishioners as a burdensome obligation, especially when they were already confronted with material shortages. In such cases, the clergy's demand for economic support could be construed by the congregation as a sign of greed, and as indifference towards the poor.

In the late sixteenth century, such demands increased in those parishes that had become Protestant, as most pastors there were now married and thus had greater material needs. Conflicts arose from opposing legal claims as well as from divergent conceptions of the relationship between pastor and parish. While the parishes repeatedly invoked their established traditions, the Protestant pastors emphasized their own rights, derived from territorial Church ordinances. Moreover, the old dispute over the equivalence of clerical service and material contributions remained seemingly unsolvable. A good example of these structural problems is the parishioners' assumption that model behaviour had to involve a diffidence regarding material status. In contrast, the pastors themselves considered it a Christian duty on the part of the parish to meet their economic needs; in their opinion, such support showed appropriate respect for the clerical office as commanded in the Bible.[76]

The social distance between pastor and parishes, particularly in rural areas, could aggravate these conflicts even more. Thus, in the first decades of the seventeenth century, pastors' calls for full payment of the tithe were repeatedly met with disgruntlement and at times outright refusal on the part of the parishioners – this was a European reality. The parishioners justified their behaviour on the grounds that the pastor acted superior to them; in their eyes, his demands showed that he was ignorant about agricultural crops and the difficulties involved in producing them. Similar conflicts were recorded in Catholic parishes as well. In the seventeenth century these conflicts were regularly the topic of printed sermons, used to offer possible solutions to the problem.[77]

The credibility of clerical office, and hence its ability to advance the political interests of the authorities, depended largely on the credibility of the office holders. Their spiritual and moral education therefore became a central concern of secular and ecclesiastical authorities. But not all of the

---

[76] For examples, see Schorn-Schütte, *Evangelische Geistlichkeit in der Frühneuzeit*, pp. 272–3.

[77] Elisabeth Moser-Rath, *Dem Kirchenvolk die Leviten gelesen: Alltag im Spiegel süddeutscher Barockpredigten* (Stuttgart, 1991), pp. 187–89.

structural problems arising between pastor and parish could be addressed through thorough training. In the end, the differences in the educational goals of Catholics and Protestants may have been few, but these remained significant. Catholicism did not aspire to 'establish a general state of subservience designed to level out the differences between the clergy and the laity'.[78] Rather, the 'prominence' of clerical office holders was to be emphasized as a way to accentuate both religious barriers and boundaries between the estates, the existence of which was justified with reference to biblical sources. This attitude was at times directed against secular authorities themselves, showing the pastor to be a less than reliable mediator in the process of social disciplining.

The same is true for the Protestant Church as well, except that here the clergy did not invoke the sacrality of office. The model conduct of the pastor did not involve his acting as a particularly obedient subject; rather, the clergy developed a special perception of itself and office that could be referred to as a unique self-awareness. As a result, the Protestant pastor became more immune to the demands of both the authorities and the parish.[79] This unique self-awareness found justification in the traditions of the New Testament as well as in the continuing validity of the doctrine of the three estates. As it turned out, this clerical self-perception could become either a source of conflict between the pastor and the parish, or an integrative force – the latter when directed against claims by authorities that were regarded as inappropriate by pastor and congregation alike. Therefore, the image of the Protestant pastor as an 'agent of the state' fails to reflect the reality.

---

[78]   Holzem, *Religion und Lebensformen*, p. 277.
[79]   For parallel development in England, see Collinson, *The Religion of Protestants*.

CHAPTER 6

The Clergy and Parish Discipline in England, 1570–1640

Christopher Haigh

What was the relationship between anticlericalism and the Reformation? Was anticlericalism a cause of Reformation, as A.G. Dickens suggested? Was it a result, as I once thought? Or was it neither? In 1983, I argued that the rising social and educational status of the post-Reformation clergy, the expansion of tithe litigation, predestinarian doctrine and harsher discipline provoked the laity into hostility towards ministers. Now I think that those things did bring tensions, but only sometimes and in some places, depending on local circumstances and the personalities and pastoral strategies of particular clergy. I suspect that, in aggregate, anticlericalism was a constant, and that what varied was clerical sensitivity to criticism. It was clericalism that created the illusion of more anticlericalism. The first generation of educated post-Reformation preachers demanded more attention and respect, and complained if they did not get them – so it can appear that there was more anticlericalism in the 1580s. The Laudian generation of gentrified priests demanded more recognition and deference, and complained if they did not get them – so it may seem that there was more anticlericalism in the 1630s. No doubt there were always anticlericals, laypeople who moaned about the privileges of the clergy, and there were always individuals who did not like their own minister or did not want to pay their tithe. But only clerical pretensions and status-consciousness turned low-level grumbling into political and social problems.[1]

For the most part, ministers and parishioners muddled along as best they could. True, there were fired-up Calvinist disciplinarians who threw their

---

[1]   C. Haigh, 'Anticlericalism and the English Reformation', *History*, 68 (1983): 391–407, reprinted in Haigh, *The English Reformation Revised* (Cambridge, 1987), pp. 56–74; A.G. Dickens, *The English Reformation* (London, 1989 edn), pp. 316–25; P. Collinson, 'Shepherds, Sheepdogs and Hirelings: the Pastoral Ministry in Post-Reformation England', in W.J. Shiels and D. Wood (eds), *The Ministry: Clerical and Lay* (Studies in Church History, 26) (Oxford and Cambridge, MA, 1989), pp. 185–220; C. Haigh, 'Anticlericalism and Clericalism, 1580–1640', in N. Aston and M. Cragoe (eds), *Anticlericalism in Britain, c.1500–1914* (Stroud, 2000), pp. 18–41.

weight around and fell out with many of their parishioners, such as William Seredge of East Hanningfield in Essex in the 1580s. And there were fired-up Laudian disciplinarians who did the same, such as Thomas Newcomen at Colchester in the 1630s. But few clergy deliberately chose the path of confrontation with the parish elite or with any substantial section of their congregation. The realities of parish life meant that a minister, Calvinist, anti-Calvinist or whatever, usually tried to get along with as many of his people as he could. Whether he wanted to save souls or have a quiet life, a clergyman would surely try to meet local expectations – and he had a hard time if he did not meet them, or not enough of them. Among those expectations was that a minister should play a part in parish discipline, and seek to sustain peace and order among his people.[2] So this chapter is not about confrontation and conflict, it is about engagement – how ministers tried to sort out parish problems at parish level. It becomes clear that much disciplinary activity took place outside the ecclesiastical courts: clergy themselves provided informal justice, arbitration and conciliation.

Ministers often tackled disciplinary problems personally, sometimes privately and sometimes publicly. In 1585, Thomas Toleman, a wheelwright of Ilminster, Somerset, was accused of adultery by the vicar and made to clear himself by swearing an oath to his innocence. That settled the matter for a while, until the two fell out over the vicar's order for more wheels, and he brought up the accusation again.[3] In 1604, the curate of Piddington, Oxfordshire, was asked by the village constable to investigate a rumour that the constable's wife had committed adultery, which the curate 'promised to do if matters might be handled quietly'. He worked out who had been spreading the story, ordered the women to keep silent, and got them to apologize at a private meeting in the fields. The vicar of Burford questioned Ann Clark when she was suspected of fornication in 1606, and she was 'found by tears so penitent and earnest protestings of amendment of life, hoping that God would never give her over to be so void of grace that s[he] should during life fall into the like', so he hoped the diocesan court would be lenient.[4] After Thomas Old had abused the rector of Collingtree, Northamptonshire, in 1612, the rector got him to apologize – but the wardens presented the offence, and the rector had to explain that it had been sorted out already. In 1623, Dr Robert Sibthorpe, vicar of Brackley, tried to stamp on an improper relationship between John

---

[2]   For Seredge and Newcomen, see C. Haigh, *The Plain Man's Pathways to Heaven: Kinds of Christianity in Post-Reformation England* (Oxford, 2007). For peacemaking, see J. Bossy, *Peace in the Post-Reformation* (Cambridge, 1998), pp. 73–82, 91–6. At his ordination, a priest promised to seek to achieve 'quietness, peace and love' among Christians, and especially among his own parishioners.

[3]   Somerset Record Office (hereafter SRO), D/D/Ca. 73, Ilminster.

[4]   Oxfordshire Record Office (hereafter ORO), Oxford diocesan papers, c. 24, fols 215r–221v; d. 9, fol. 104r.

Hillier and Gabriel Percival's wife. The two were twice forbidden to meet, but they continued their secret assignations and the affair finally went to court. In 1624, the vicar of Braunston summoned William and Elizabeth Edmunds 'to confer with him concerning crimes commonly bruited to be by them committed, that he might accordingly admit or refuse them to or from the communion as he saw cause' – but they refused to see him.[5] The curate of Nuneham Courtenay in Oxfordshire had more success in 1633: he got John Shakespeare to promise that he would never again allow drinking in his house on a Sunday. But when in the same year the rector of South Ockendon, Essex, privately pressed Thomas Lincoln to marry the servant he had got pregnant, 'as being the honestest and safest course', he was abused: 'he would take a whore's part before an honest man's,' said Lincoln's brother.[6]

A minister might choose to rebuke an offender publicly, and that could lead to argument and abuse. In 1588, the minister of Ibsley in Hampshire criticized some parishioners who were away drinking instead of attending his service, so some of the congregation walked out of the service in sympathy.[7] When Thomas Summings of Aveley, Essex, was reproved by the vicar for drunken blasphemy in 1606, he retorted: 'God's blood, vicar, you are out of your text!' The minister of St Botolph's, Colchester, told William Garrett in 1608 he should attend church more diligently, and was called '"snotty-nose knave" and other vile words'.[8] Richard Estgate of Nuthurst in Sussex told the minister 'I will learn no wit at thy hands, go hang thyself!' when reproached for brawling in the churchyard in 1610. In 1614, Elizabeth Tabor of Widford, Essex, was rebuked in church for her conduct: she told the minister than he should hold his tongue, and later complained that he preached forgiveness and ought to have forgiven her.[9] Nicholas Browse, vicar of Minehead, Somerset, reported Grace Trott in 1622 for drunkenness and railing against him and explained:

[H]er malice towards me was because I rebuked her for her drunkenness, which is my part to do unless I will partake with other men's sins. As I detest in malice to trouble any, poor or rich, so would I not that the minister should be made a jesting stock by their parishioners, but that they should be respectfully used for their office and function sake.[10]

---

[5]   Northamptonshire Record Office (hereafter NRO), X615/42, p. 134; X618/56a, pp. 227, 340.

[6]   ORO, Oxford archdeaconry papers, c. 12, fol. 63r; Essex Record Office (hereafter ERO), D/AE/A39, fol. 92r–v.

[7]   Hampshire Record Office (hereafter HRO), 21M65/C1/24, fol. 31v.

[8]   ERO, D/AE/A24, fol. 36r; D/AC/A31, fol. 17r.

[9]   West Sussex Record Office (hereafter WSRO), Ep.I/17/13, 3 Feb. 1610; ERO, D/AE/A27, fol. 281v.

[10]   SRO, D/D/Ca. 224, fol. 323r.

That was the trouble: ministers thought it was their duty to chastise sinners, but sinners thought ministers should mind their own business. During a communion service at Messing in Essex in 1627, the vicar warned Edward Matthew to be sorry for having been drunk on Michaelmas day – and Matthew stormed out of church. In 1637, the minister of Worth in Sussex rebuked Sarah Butler for causing a disturbance in the churchyard: 'Mr Whiston! I care not for our minister, what care I for Mr Whiston?', she declared.[11]

It was much better if a minister could secure a public acknowledgement and apology from an offender, but this too might not work. In 1585, Nicholas Newman of St Peter's, Bedford, was rebuked by Mr Ludford 'for his sins of contention, quarrelling and open malice', and when asked at communion to retract his harsh words, he and his wife refused to receive the sacrament. Thomas Squeere of Coggeshall, Essex, was reported in 1594 because he would not make a public apology 'for refusing to satisfy the congregation, which he offended by a wicked fart committed'.[12] John Packman of Warnham, Sussex, was presented as a non-communicant in 1614, 'being put back for refusing to acknowledge himself penitent for some misdemeanours which our minister charged him with', and in 1619, Henry Harwood of North Shoebury, Essex, refused to apologize for insults to his neighbours, 'being exhorted thereunto by our minister'.[13] When John Howlett of Rayleigh objected to Hugh Peter's sermon in 1625, 'the said Mr Peter did of his own charity cause the said Howlett to acknowledge his fault in the church before the congregation'. In these cases, the churchwardens seem to have backed their minister's action, but it was not always so. When the rector of Doddinghurst rebuked a parishioner in 1625 for mistreating the poor of the parish, the churchwardens reported him as 'a quarreller, chider and brawler'.[14] And in 1633, the vicar of Olney, Buckinghamshire, made John Lynn and his wife make public apology in church after questioning his sermon, but the wardens were unhappy, and reported the business.[15]

These are just a few examples of clergy seeking to deal with disciplinary matters in their own way and at parish level – sorting out contentions, warning sinners to mend their ways, rebuking misconduct and seeking public promises of amendment. These ministers were engaged with their people, and tried to keep them in line and at peace with one another: sometimes they did it sensitively, sometimes clumsily. There are many more

---

11   ERO, D/AC/A46, fol. 16r; WSRO, Ep.II/15/1, p. 5.
12   Lincolnshire Archives (hereafter LA), Vj. 16, fols 114r, 115r; ERO, D/AC/A22, fol. 73v.
13   WSRO, Ep.I/17/15, 23 July 1614; ERO, D/AE/A31, fol. 69r.
14   Ibid., A36, fol. 26v; A34, fo. 213r.
15   Buckinghamshire Record Office, D/A/V/2, fol. 105v.

such cases in court act books, and there were surely many, many more still that were not so recorded. We know about these examples only because they were reported, and they were usually reported just because things went wrong – because an attempt at arbitration failed or an agreement broke down, because an offender responded angrily to a rebuke or would not apologize, or because a churchwarden did not know a minister had sorted out a problem or did not approve of his solution. If conciliation worked, if a sinner repented, if minister and wardens co-operated, it is unlikely we would see such parish discipline in action. We do see cases of clergy and churchwardens working together – sometimes, again, because things went wrong. Anne Harris of Burnham in Essex was a scold, and when reproved by a warden, 'she brake out into most vehement and unwomanlike speeches against the said churchwarden'. The minister was brought in, and he attempted to get her to admit her fault and promise amendment, but she refused, and the case went to court in 1613.[16] In the same year, the vicar of East Haddon complained to the Northampton archdeaconry court that the wardens and sidesmen would not help him get the youth into church for catechism, but he later reported, 'my neighbours the churchwardens and sidesmen are sorry for their fault and do promise to be more diligent,' and the case was dismissed on payment of court costs. At Aldwinckle All Saints in 1621, the minister and wardens together investigated a suspicion of adultery, and the woman involved confessed before the minister, the wardens and her husband. It was a serious matter, and the case then went to court.[17]

There are also many examples of churchwardens themselves acting in an investigatory or disciplinary capacity. At Terwick in Sussex in 1579, there was a rumour that Elizabeth Wackford had committed adultery. The wardens investigated: they concluded that the story had been started by Edmund Colden and Elizabeth Walter, and was false. But there was disagreement in the parish – 'great unquietness which we cannot pacify' – so they reported the allegation.[18] In 1612, the churchwardens of Maxey in Northamptonshire even tried to impose a public penance on Alice Smith, using a formula drawn up for them by a gentleman of the parish and a neighbouring parson: this unofficial punishment was only prevented when their own minister bundled Alice out of the church. The wardens of Stansted Mountfitchet, Essex, were cited by the minister in 1620 for not reporting a game of stoolball during a Sunday service. They told the court, '[T]here were certain young maids of the parish whose parents and masters they have admonished thereof, and promised a reformation,' and

16   ERO, D/AE/A27, fol. 83r.
17   NRO, X615/42, p. 556, and loose letter at pp. 556–7; X618/55, fol. 32.
18   WSRO, Ep.I/23/5, fol. 29r.

they had supposed that resolution was the end of the matter.[19] In 1621, the wardens of Abington, Northamptonshire, did not believe Agnes Johnson's claim that John Wheatley had committed adultery with her, probably because she was dying of a sexually transmitted disease but Wheatley did not have it. They sent some of the older women of the parish to try to persuade Agnes not to slander Wheatley, but she stood her ground and described what had happened, so the churchwardens reported Wheatley to the archdeacon's court.[20] When in 1628 Andrew Hedges of Beckington, Somerset, was accused by a neighbour of incontinence with a servant, the wardens wrote to the chancellor of the diocese on his behalf: Hedges was an honest man, they said, and the allegation was malicious – the case was dropped.[21] Two former churchwardens of Glaston in Rutland were presented in 1639 for not disclosing a suspicion of pre-marital fornication between Brian and Elizabeth Falkland. The couple's first child had died within a few hours, and the wardens considered this was a miscarriage rather than a pre-marital conception, because Elizabeth had lost two other babies in a previous marriage. There was no offence to report, they thought.[22]

These wardens wanted to sort questions out locally, just as many ministers tried to do the same. For some clergy and churchwardens, discipline was first a parish matter, and formal presentment to a court was a last resort. Henry Sharrock, vicar of Long Bennington, Lincolnshire, wrote to his bishop in despair in 1606: 'I live in a town so disordered and the persons so headstrong in their disorder that if I reprove publicly I am cavilled at afterwards; if privately, scorned and reviled to my face.' He had tried dealing with indiscipline himself and had failed: he now reported the chief offenders, and would name the rest later.[23] Churchwardens, too, turned to higher authority when they found they could not cope. The wardens of Romford, Essex, reported a married couple living apart in 1613, after the wife had accused her husband of adultery: 'the contention is greater than by private exhortation can be quieted, therefore the authority of the ecclesiastical court is in this case to be implored'. If we could have sorted it out informally, they were saying, we would have – but we cannot, so we need formal process. In 1622, the minister and wardens of Great Bardfield told the Colchester archdeaconry court:

> [T]here are some of the poorer sort for absence from church on the Sabbath days, and others for going out of the church before sermon is ended, and some

---

[19] NRO, X615/43, fols 68v–9r; ERO, D/AC/A42, fol. 104r.

[20] NRO, X617/54, 12 July 1621.

[21] SRO, D/D/Ca. 261, fols 218r, 224v, 233v, 242r, and loose letter at fol. 242r.

[22] NRO, X621/69, fol. 11r, and sheet pinned to fol. 13r.

[23] LA, Ch.P/9/11.

others for being drinking in the alehouse not only on the working days but on the Sabbath days, sometimes in divine service time, as liable to be presented, but we have given them sufficient warning of these abuses.

If they reform themselves, you will hear no more – if they do not, then we will present them.[24] William Hoare of Pattishall, Northamptonshire, was cited by the vicar in 1623 for disorderly behaviour in church, 'to the great disturbance of attentive hearers'. The vicar had admonished him 'for his offence in not sitting reverently to hear God's word and cannot be reformed'.[25] The usual informal procedure had not worked. In these examples, a presentment was a confession of local failure.

In many of these cases, the local priority was peace in the parish. In a case of minor misconduct such as one-off drunkenness or loose words or breach of the Sabbath, then the issue might be dealt with by private warning or public reproof, or sometimes by apology before the congregation – rather than by prosecution, conviction, court fees and formal penance, which would surely cause more resentment against accuser, wardens and minister. If there was an allegation of sexual immorality, minister and wardens wanted to know whether it was a serious possibility or a case of malicious trouble-making – and if the latter, whether accuser and accused could be reconciled without a contentious court case. The alternatives to a local settlement were presentment and penance, or an expensive and divisive defamation suit. It is sometimes suggested that the hierarchical and legalistic system of English Church discipline meant that accusations and disputes went to court instead of being dealt with by arbitration at parish level.[26] But this can be an illusion created by the nature of the record. Where the court books simply record presentments and formal court procedures, then local arbitration will not be detailed – but in some jurisdictions the act books also contain follow-up proceedings and the statements of accusers and accused, and where there are depositions books, they can tell a fuller story. Often we can know what happened outside the court, and see informal procedures in action.

In 1592, Richard Griffin and his wife of Theydon Garnon in Essex were presented for not taking communion at Easter. Griffin appeared in court in July, and explained that they had been absent because they were not in charity with one of their neighbours, but the argument was now settled: 'there was some controversy between him and Harry Archer of the same town, the which now he saith is ended and arbitrated by Mr Dr Dunn and

---

24   ERO, D/AE/A27, fol. 108v; AC/A42, loose sheet in packet.
25   NRO, X618/56a, p. 226.
26   See M. Todd, *The Culture of Protestantism in Early Modern Scotland* (New Haven, CT and London, 2002), pp. 261–4, where the detailed record of parish-level kirk sessions in Scotland is contrasted with two laconic act books from English archdeaconry courts.

the churchwardens'[27] (Dunn was an ecclesiastical lawyer who happened to live in the parish). English Church courts were not simply interested in guilt and punishment: judges cared about peace and reconciliation. In 1596, the Gloucester consistory dealt with the nonconformity of the curate of Ashchurch, John Ashby, and the breakdown in relations between him and some of the parishioners. Ashby was ordered to 'preach a sermon of love and charity to be holden amongst neighbours', and then in the following week to go with two 'honest men' of the parish:

> to three or four of his greatest adversaries, vizt to Mr Cole, Mr Collet and Richard Guy, and shall desire their goodwill and their friendships and shall promise by God's grace he will give them no just cause of offence hereafter ... If he shall find (as God defend) any of his parishioners unreconcilable, the said Ashby shall forbear to requite ill word for ill word or malice for malice, but he shall denounce him to his ordinary that the offender may be reformed to the good laws of the realm.[28]

This was not the grinding and punitive process of an impersonal, legalistic system, but a serious attempt to solve a pastoral problem – and to have it solved face-to-face at parish level.

Reconciling minister and people was crucial, because it was the minister above all others who was supposed to keep peace in his parish. That is what people expected. At the 1576 visitation of the diocese of Gloucester, the curate of Morton Valence, the vicar of Prestbury and the rector of Swinden were each reported by churchwardens as 'no peacemaker', and the curate of Great Rissington was 'no peacemaker but rather a sower of discord'.[29] The rector of Little Casterton, Rutland, was presented in 1600 'for not living quietly amongst his neighbours and not persuading them to peace and charitable agreement', and in the same year Mary Bradley of Welford, Northamptonshire, told her minister: 'Thou shouldest make peace, but thou settest their neighbours together by the ears.'[30] Of course there were clerical troublemakers, but ministers were supposed to resolve disputes. In 1606, William Quench of Standlake told the Oxford consistory that he had been in controversy with one of his neighbours, and 'Mr Dr Inckforby willed him to come unto him to end the matter between them.' There was an expectation that persons in contention should seek arbitration by their minister. Christopher Foot of Broomfield in Essex was cited for missing communion in 1617: 'being known to be very uncharitable and malicious to some of his neighbours, neither came he to our minister in any convenient time that he might be reconciled to his neighbours.'[31] It

---

27   ERO, D/AE/A16, fol. 85v.
28   Gloucestershire Record Office (hereafter GRO), GDR 76, fol. 31r–v.
29   GRO, GDR 40, fols 9, 36v, 40v, 87r.
30   NRO, X612/32, fol. 132; 613/34, fol. 139r.
31   ORO, Oxford diocesan papers d. 9, fol. 103r; ERO, D/AE/A30, fol. 42r.

was an additional offence that he had not used the ordinary means for settling quarrels.

The Church's rule that no one should take communion who was not in charity with others imposed a double obligation – on the disputants to seek reconciliation, and on the minister to facilitate it – and this made Lent the season for pastoral peacemaking. On 2 April 1568, Anne Warton of Lingfield in Surrey told the curate, William Auden, that 'because it was towards the good time of Easter she came to declare her mind unto him that she might receive the holy communion in perfect love and charity, which she could not do because Mistress Anne Gainsford had spoken slanderous words against her'. Auden summoned the two Annes to see him in church, and tried to mediate between them, but without success: 'in the end, after long and uncharitable talk between the said parties, this deponent [Auden] said that neither of them should receive the communion at Easter for that they were out of charity.' Indeed they were: as they went from the church, Gainsford cried, 'Go, whore, go to the knave thy man and carry stewed broth to thy chamber and make whole his head!', and Warton replied, 'Go, Mistress Gainsford, go and take your fetter-lock gentleman to you.'[32] If Auden's effort had succeeded, the women could have taken communion, and there would have been no costly defamation case between them. Similarly, at Whitsun in 1569, the vicar of Swalcliffe in Oxfordshire encouraged the Soden brothers to make up a family quarrel, so they could receive communion in charity with each other and their mother. He showed them the rubric in the Prayer Book that authorized him to refuse them communion, 'but the said William and Geoffrey regarded it not but still continued their obstinacies'. The vicar tried reconciliation again before Easter 1570, but once more without success, and the Sodens sued him for refusing them communion.[33]

The obligation of charity and exclusion from communion gave the clergy a powerful sanction in parish peacemaking. There was much dissension at Brimpsfield in Gloucestershire in 1575, so the rector delayed the communion in the hope of reconciliation and 'used due exhortations and sermons' to try to quell the discord.[34] Probably most parishioners recognized the necessity to be in charity before receiving, though in 1581 Richard Jackman of Wellow in Hampshire thought he had found a way out: 'he being demanded how he could receive the communion with a safe conscience, being so at variance, he said that when time did serve he could

---

[32]   HRO, 21M65/B1/9, fols 116v–18r. For the rules on exclusion, see C. Haigh, 'Communion and Community: Exclusion from Communion in Post-Reformation England', *Journal of Ecclesiastical History*, 51 (2000): 722–4.

[33]   ORO, Oxford diocesan papers c. 21, fols 23r–v, 75r–6v.

[34]   GRO, GDR 31, pp. 415–17, 440.

receive it and spew it up again'.[35] If the bread was not swallowed, it did not count – and perhaps others did not care if it did count. In 1582, the wife of William Robbyn of Great Holland, Essex, was charged 'that she, being perceived to be a contentious person, did without reconciliation first made, being by the curate admonished so to do, did presume to come to the communion at Christmas'.[36] But the sanction of exclusion could work. Before Easter 1590, Agnes Long of Towersey in Oxfordshire told the curate that Margaret Adams refused to make up a quarrel between them, and the curate said he would do what he could. When the two women went to take communion, Agnes complained that there had still been no reconciliation, and Margaret was refused communion, but then she agreed to apologize to Agnes.[37] In 1594, three people from a Somerset parish did not receive at Easter: 'But cause is that there is controversy between them, which the vicar and other honest neighbours have sought and persuaded them to leave off and be reconciled to each other.' No more was heard of them, and presumably they settled their differences.[38] Things were more complicated when a minister himself was involved in a dispute, but even then the risk of exclusion could restore harmony. In 1600, Christopher Gates had an argument with the quarrelsome vicar of Ellington, Huntingdonshire, but as Easter approached, he asked two gentlemen 'to make them friends again, because else he feared that Mr Armitage would not admit him to the communion'.[39]

There are many cases of attempted peacemaking at the communion itself, though this was rather too public for likely success. In 1607, the minister of Milton Malzor, Northamptonshire, asked two men to make up their differences as they came to communion, but one of them walked out.[40] When Edmund Cotton of Long Burton in Dorset went up to the communion table in 1608, the vicar 'did advise and persuade him to reconcile himself to such as he had misused' and to ask God's forgiveness for his swearing: 'By God, thou dost lie!', he cried, striking the table with his fist. But usually it was before the communion that reconciliation was tried. Alexander Knight and Richard Ambrose of Boynton, Wiltshire, fell out when Ambrose spread a story that Knight was guilty of adultery, but on Easter Saturday 1615, Knight went to make up their quarrel.[41] It is not known whether Knight succeeded, but usually we only know about attempted reconciliation if it failed. William Drakeford, minister of Little

---

[35]   HRO, 21M65/C1/21, fol. 46v.
[36]   ERO, D/AC/A10, fol. 52r.
[37]   ORO, Oxford diocesan papers c. 18, fol. 61r–v.
[38]   SRO, D/D/Ca. 98, p. 56.
[39]   LA, CP69/2/15, fol. 2r.
[40]   NRO, X614/40. fol. 17r.
[41]   Wiltshire Record Office (hereafter WRO), D5/28/10/37; D1/42/30, fols 124v–25r.

Houghton, Northamptonshire, warned Anne Battison in 1624 that he would refuse her communion unless she made peace with his own wife. Anne sent a message that she would go to communion and see if he dared to refuse her. She did, he did, the case went to court, and we can read it.[42] But if a minister managed to arbitrate a quarrel before Easter, then the parties would receive communion and we would know nothing about it.

The Prayer Book, the royal injunctions and the canons also required ministers to refuse communion to known sinners – fornicators, drunkards, swearers and the like. This, too, gave the clergy a disciplinary sanction, and any who refused to reform themselves could be excluded from the sacrament. Exclusion was used to force notorious sinners into public repentance. John Odell of Ashdon in Essex was refused communion in 1587–88 because he was suspected of perjury, 'to the great offence of the congregation until he acknowledged his fault with repentance to the satisfaction of the congregation'.[43] Margery Wycher of Buriton, Hampshire, was rejected by the rector in 1588 'because she hath not satisfied the congregation for her offence'. The threat of exclusion could certainly work. William Smith of Winscombe, Somerset, was 'a common disturber of his neighbours', but in 1588 he 'promised he would live quietly and in charity with his neighbours, whereupon the vicar received him to the communion'.[44] However, as with restoration of charity, reform was better achieved before the communion rather than at the service and in front of the parish. Thomas Creake of Yardley Hastings, Northamptonshire, got so drunk about midsummer 1612 that he could not find his own way home. The following Sunday, he went up to receive communion:

> where the minister (having heard of his misdemeans) persuaded him not to approach to the Lord's table without some inward sorrow and outward show of repentance for his late and lewd drunkenness. Then he rose up and, without any show of penitency, put on his hat saucily in the chancel and so departed with all irreverence, to the dishonour of God, the contempt of the sacrament and the offence of the congregation.[45]

It is in the nature of our records that we usually know of the cases where efforts to secure reformation did not succeed. Simon Long of Coombe Bissett in Wiltshire was a notorious swearer and could not recite the Lord's Prayer or the Creed, but before Easter 1620 he promised the minister he would mend his ways and he was allowed communion. A little later, however, he was reported for sexual harassment, and the minister had to admit that his reform attempt had failed.[46] John Cary of Weston-super-

---

42   NR0, X618/56a, pp. 268, 311, 317, 322.
43   ERO, D/AC/A15, fol. 69r.
44   HRO, 21M65/C1/24, fol. 41v; SRO, D/D/Ca. 85, 18 September 1588.
45   NRO, X615/42, p. 376.
46   WRO, D5/28/20/28.

Mare, Somerset, was presented 'for a notorious and common slanderer of his neighbours' at the archdeacon's visitation in 1625. No action was taken, and he continued his abuse, though he was refused communion 'until he hath made satisfaction'.[47] William Crickett was rejected from communion at Winterborne Kingston, Wiltshire, in 1626 'for his ignorance and rudeness'. But he received in 1627, and bragged to his friends that he had deceived the minister:

> for that he had promised him to become a new man, but he had no such purpose, and we present that he is a common swearer, curser, sleeper at church, a railer, and was seen to come in railing for over-drinking himself into our church, and being a very saucy and stubborn fellow to and with his elders and betters.[48]

Thomas Winter of Upminster, Essex, abused his neighbours, railed at the minister and spent too much time in the alehouse. The minister warned him in 1637 that he should not go to the communion unless he acknowledged his faults and gave signs of repentance, but he turned up anyway, and was rejected.[49]

Exclusion – or the threat of it – was also used to press the young to learn the catechism, essentially the Commandments, the Creed and the Lord's Prayer. Joan Edwards went to receive communion at Rogate in Sussex at Easter 1579, 'but the curate would not admit her because she had not learned the Ten Commandments, although often admonished thereto'.[50] When Jane Carter knelt to receive the sacrament at East Horndon, Essex, in 1595, the parson demanded that she first recite the Creed – 'If you will not say your Belief, I pray you avoid the place' – so she left the church.[51] In 1606, the rector of Rollright in Oxfordshire was required to explain in the consistory court why he had rejected some of his parishioners from communion: 'he refused to receive them to communion because they were unfit upon his examination', he declared.[52] The vicar of Boxgrove, Sussex, excluded a girl from communion in 1622, 'being a very ignorant and simple maid and unfit for it'. The objective was to exclude the unworthy from communion, but the consequence was forcing the young to become worthy.[53] In 1633, the churchwardens of Donnington in Sussex reported that all the parishioners had communicated except three, put back by the minister as 'somewhat ignorant in their catechism' until

---

[47]   SRO, D/D/Ca. 260, fol. 145r.
[48]   WRO, D5/28/27/26.
[49]   ERO, D/AE/A41, fol. 159r.
[50]   WSRO, Ep.I/23/5, fol. 29r.
[51]   ERO, D/AE/A17, fol. 31v.
[52]   ORO, Oxford diocesan papers d. 9, fol. 74v.
[53]   *Churchwardens' Presentments (17th Century): Part 1. Archdeaconry of Chichester*, ed. H. Johnstone (Sussex Record Society, 49, 1948), p. 39.

the next communion, 'that they may be better learned and taught for the communion'.[54]

We know when the threat of exclusion had not worked – but surely it usually did, because the sacrament really mattered. Parishioners knew who should and should not be admitted to communion, and they expected the standard to be maintained. The churchwardens of St Ives, Huntingdonshire, complained in 1585 that 'their vicar doth minister the communion to offensive persons not reconciled' – offenders who had not acknowledged their wrongdoing and made peace with their neighbours.[55] Similarly, in 1594, the wardens of Kingswood, Gloucestershire, protested that the curate 'hath admitted persons suspected of lewd life to the holy communion'.[56] The well-behaved wanted sinners rejected, but the sinners wanted communion like everyone else. The vicar of Godmanchester, Huntingdonshire, reported Anne Hearne to the bishop of Lincoln about 1603: she had been warned not to go to the communion, but she presented herself, and when refused, 'she defied them or him and all that take their part or his part, or words to the like effect, to the disturbance of divine service and the congregation and evil example of others'.[57] John Hyde of Graffham in Sussex was suspected of adultery, and before the Easter communion in 1615, he sent his son and a neighbour 'to go to Mr English [the minister] and to certify him that he did intend and would receive the communion if he, the said Mr English, would accept of him, but the said Mr English replied that his hand should never give him the communion more'.[58] Hyde wanted the sacrament, but he wanted to avoid the shame of a public rejection. Rejection was a serious matter, and in 1619 the churchwardens of Pensford, Somerset, reported that Elizabeth Richards had been refused communion 'two or three times, to the great grief and discomfort of the said Elizabeth Richards'.[59] Drunkards, fornicators, backbiters and the ignorant – all wanted to communicate along with their neighbours. Richard Stevenson of Thornton Curtis, Lincolnshire was warned by the minister not to seek communion in 1638, as a drunkard and a disruptive person, but he tried to receive the sacrament and swore at the wardens when they held him back.[60] So the sanction of exclusion was a powerful tool, and not only because rejection could lead to presentment, excommunication and signification, bringing in the secular authorities and the threat of arrest. Customary observance and real religion were also at work.

---

[54] WSRO, Ep.I/17/25, fol. 12v.
[55] LA, Vj. 16, fol. 134r.
[56] GRO, GDR 76, fol. 285v.
[57] LA, CP69/1/44.
[58] WSRO, Ep.I/17/17, 8 June 1616.
[59] SRO, D/D/Ca. 215, fol. 183r.
[60] LA, Vj. 30, fol. 64r.

But parish discipline – discipline exercised at parish level – often failed. Indeed, to judge from the court books, it seems that it almost always failed, but that is because only the failures got to court. Where possible – and when the issues were not too serious – disputes and offences were dealt with at parish level. If this failed, then minister or wardens (and often both together) would make a formal presentment to a court. However, a court case was not the end of parish discipline, of sensitive local involvement in disciplinary cases. Clergy and churchwardens did not simply hand issues over to the bureaucratic procedures of ecclesiastical justice and forget about them. Ministers certainly remained engaged in cases, and sought to influence the courts' treatment of offenders. Judicial proceedings could be made sensitive to particular situations, and it is a mistake to think of ecclesiastical justice as distant, impersonal courts motivated primarily by fee income and processing cases by the mindless application of rigid rules.[61]

Ministers often interceded with the courts on behalf of parishioners. The vicar of Flitwick in Bedfordshire wrote to the chancellor of Lincoln about 1599 to ask for absolution for Margaret Pink so she could share in the consolations of God's word, 'wherefore I heartily desire your worship to weigh her beggar's estate for to remit the charges due for such malefactors, and because she should not be swallowed up of sorrow, she being penitent'. Robert Chaloner of Amersham wrote three times between November 1599 and January 1600 to ask that old and poor parishioners excommunicated for not appearing in court at Godmanchester should be absolved locally to avoid the difficulty and expense of travel.[62] In 1620, Edward Warren of Ashby-de-la-Zouche, Leicestershire, was ordered to purge himself with six compurgators when he denied the wardens' presentment for adultery, but the vicar, Thomas Pestell, investigated, found that Warren was not guilty, and that the rumour of adultery had been started by Alice Oving. The case was dismissed. Also in 1620, Pestell intervened in the case of William Bodell and his wife, presented for pre-nuptial fornication. Pestell told the commissary of Leicester that the Bodells' child had been born only two or three weeks short of a normal term, and asked that Bodell should not be shamed, 'the matter being not very heinous'. The prosecution was dropped. And Pestell wrote once more to the commissary in 1621 and asked him to delay the excommunication of Mrs Burrows, whom he hoped to dissuade from her nonconformity: the commissary allowed another month.[63]

---

[61] For the case against Church courts, see C. Hill, *Society and Puritanism in Pre-Revolutionary England* (London, 1969 edn), pp. 288–332, 343–69; and for a more positive assessment, see M. Ingram, *Church Courts, Sex and Marriage in England, 1570–1640* (Cambridge, 1987), pp. 323–63.

[62] LA, Ch.P/5/22, 27–9.

[63] Leicestershire Record Office, 1D41/13/50, fols 138v–39v, 146v, 149v; 1D41/13/51, fols 3v–4a, 40a r–v.

In 1622, the minister of Crixeth in Essex asked the official of Colchester archdeaconry to absolve without costs Mary Gray, who had been excommunicate for seven years and was now 'very poor and very old and diseased': 'Which favour, if you shall vouchsafe her, not only shall the party have cause to thank you for your charity, but she shall have like occasion with more contentment to dispose herself towards God.'[64] Three wives of Fareham, Hampshire, were cited in 1623 for 'contention and striving betwixt them about a seat', a common enough occurrence. The vicar appeared in the Winchester consistory and pointed out that it would be a great inconvenience to the parish to have lots of witnesses go to court. He asked 'for the settling thereof accordingly, and also for avoiding of further trouble in this behalf, [it] might be made over and referred to him being vicar there and to Emmanuel Badd Esq. and to Robert Riggs gent., parishioners there.' At the same session, the vicar also asked for a dispute over the church rate at Alverstoke 'to be referred to some indifferent persons'. The court agreed in both cases: this was arbitration in action, to get local resolutions and to save parishioners trouble and cost.[65] Clergy could be sensitive, and courts could be responsive. In 1626, the curate of Irthlingborough enlisted the help of Sir Rowland St John to intercede with the chancellor of Peterborough diocese so that Elizabeth Bryan would be absolved without fees, 'she being a poor man's wife'.[66] Similarly, in 1638, when the vicar and wardens of Long Bennington in Lincolnshire presented two couples for nonconformity and standing excommunicate, they added: 'all the said parties are exceeding poor and have not means to procure money to pay for their absolutions'.[67] Ministers were as concerned for their parishioners' penitence as their poverty. The minister of Little Horkesley, Essex, asked in 1640 that Elizabeth Culpeck should be absolved, 'and although she hath done amiss yet we hope she will reform her life and become penitent for her misdoings'. And also in 1640, the vicar of West Ham requested that Florence Taylor should be allowed to do her penance quietly on Ash Wednesday, when there would be a smaller congregation, rather than a Sunday, 'in regard the fact for which she is accused was committed is nine or ten years since done, and out of this jurisdiction, being also but a single fornication and she very penitent for the same'. The court agreed.[68]

So ecclesiastical discipline in England was not exercised solely through impersonal, legalistic procedures in the Church's courts: it was also exercised

---

[64] ERO, D/AC/A42, loose sheet in packet.

[65] HRO, 21M65/C1/35, fols 17r–v.

[66] NRO, X619/58, 17 April 1626, and mutilated sheet there.

[67] LA, Vj. 30, fol. 202v. There was a recognized procedure for absolution *in forma pauperis*, and ministers helped parishioners achieve this end.

[68] ERO, D/AC/A54, fol. 204r, and loose sheet in packet; D/AE/A42, fol. 168v.

at local level by clergy and churchwardens, who knew their people and wanted peace in their parish – and even the courts might be persuaded to be sensitive and flexible. Ministers investigated allegations and sought to obtain admissions of guilt and promises of reform. They admonished the wicked in public, and obtained public apologies – offenders were expected to 'satisfy the congregation'. Clergy and wardens tried arbitration and conciliation, especially to ensure parishioners could receive communion in good conscience. And the threat of exclusion was used to enforce concord among neighbours and reformation of sinners. If all this failed, then cases went to court – but even then, local influences mediated and moderated the bureaucratic process. Ecclesiastical discipline could be local, personalized, conciliatory and flexible.

Local knowledge, personal contact, conciliation and flexibility: these were identified by Margo Todd as the characteristics of parish discipline in Scotland, applied by kirk sessions in each parish. She explained the success of Reformation in Scotland, the extent of Reformation in Scotland, by the work of the kirk sessions. The Kirk's provision of social discipline, and the involvement of the minister and lay elders in local disciplinary processes and arbitrations, made a Calvinist Reformation acceptable. Scotland became 'a puritan nation', she declared; England did not, because 'Quite simply, England lacked kirk sessions.'[69]

True, England did not have kirk sessions – but it had clergy, churchwardens and sidesmen who worked in concert, and it had parish communities that, by and large, wanted to live in peace and avoid inflaming quarrels. The features of Scottish discipline identified by Margo Todd were often there in England, too – lay involvement, local knowledge, personal admonition, local arbitration, graded penalties and flexible responses.[70] True, offenders were dealt with informally in English parishes, but often in quite formal situations. Suspects were called before minister and wardens in church, and often asked to account for themselves on oath. Rebukes were issued in church, and apologies were made in church before the congregation. England was not the same as Scotland, certainly, but England was not so different from Scotland that we can explain success or failure of Reformation by the presence or absence of parish discipline. Many disciplinary matters were settled at parish level in England, and

---

[69]   Todd, *Culture of Protestantism*, pp. 22–3, 403, 408.

[70]   For similar arguments on the use of local arbitration and other informal arrangements in secular matters, see T.C. Curtis, 'Quarter Sessions Appearances and their Background', in J.S. Cockburn (ed.), *Crime in England, 1550–1800* (London, 1977), pp. 138–43; J.A. Sharpe, 'Enforcing the Law in the Seventeenth-century English Village', in V.A.C. Gatrell, B. Lenman and G. Parker (eds), *Crime and the Law: The Social History of Crime in Western Europe since 1500* (London, 1980), pp. 103–17; S. Hindle, *The State and Social Change in Early Modern England, c.1550–1640* (Basingstoke, 2000), pp. 106–9, 114–15.

settled swiftly. Disputes did not have to wait for annual presentments and the slow procedures of courts: ministers and wardens responded instantly, and if they could not settle an issue, many jurisdictions had 'quarterly bills' or apparitors to get cases to court quickly. It was common for offences to be dealt with a couple of weeks after they had been committed. Professor Todd contrasted a hierarchical and impersonal English court system with local and flexible kirk sessions in Scotland. It was not as simple as that – and if historians of Scotland want an explanation for their Reformation, they will have to find another one.

CHAPTER 7

The Virgin Mary and the Publican: Lutheranism and Social Order in Transylvania

Christine Peters

In the closing decades of the fifteenth century, as Turkish attacks increased, the Saxons of eastern Transylvania fortified their churches, and in the larger towns built defensive earthworks, obliging all inhabitants, Saxon and non-Saxon, to take their part in the building works or in transporting stone from the surrounding villages. In this, the village of Honigberg, not far from the important trading city of Kronstadt (see Map 7.1), was typical, but its building project required one further decision, whether or not to incorporate the churchyard chapel into the fortifications. In the end, but with drastic modifications to the eastern apse, it was decided to do so. The damage was made good with a new scheme of wall paintings with complex iconography, including unusual depictions of the Virgin Mary, the Publican and the three orders of society, which capture the essence of pre-Reformation catholic piety in this region, and also do much to explain the nature of Saxon Lutheranism, instituted in the 1540s, and its development in terms of a rigorous concern for social discipline, but a fairly relaxed attitude towards variations in ritual.

Ritual diversity, as Susan Karant-Nunn has reminded us, was, of course, a common feature of Lutheranism: there was no uniform 'reformation of ritual'.[1] Luther had to be prevailed upon to produce detailed liturgical solutions and Church orders, and even then these were not perceived as universally binding. Instead, they could be responsive in details to the existing customs and requirements of particular places. This was the case even with the mass itself, as shown by the Wittenberg Order of 1523. Luther saw his task as one of purification, a stripping away of the human additions and abuses which had crept into the Church as a result of priestly greed and pride; but he did not wish to impose such decisions on all other congregations, modestly recognizing that a better solution could be revealed to others. In the Wittenberg Order and in the Order for Public

---

[1]   Susan Karant-Nunn, *Reformation of Ritual: An Interpretation of Early Modern Germany* (London, 1997).

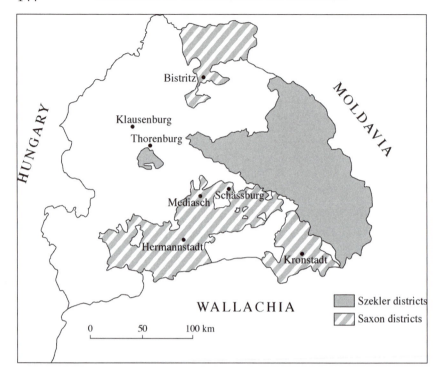

Map 7.1   Map of Transylvania showing Saxon and Szekler districts.

Worship significant details were left to the discretion of individuals and communities, ranging from the frequency of services to optional ceremonial aspects such as the wearing of vestments. This flexibility characterized his whole approach. Luther's *Traubüchlein*, for example, responded to the plethora of local marriage customs by accepting proverbial wisdom and permitting as many customs as regions.[2]

The result could be confusion for the unwary traveller, as Pierre Lescalopier found in 1574, when he attended a church service in the Saxon village of Neustadt. By this time the Saxon Reformation in Transylvania was already thirty years old, but the Latin songs, stained glass and wall paintings of religious scenes, as well as the officiating priest dressed in Catholic vestments, all led him to think that the church was Catholic. It was only when he heard a prayer for the destruction of papal and Turkish tyranny that he realized it must be Lutheran.[3] For Lescalopier,

---

[2]   *Ein Traubüchlein für die einfeltigen pfarherr* (1529/1534), WA, vol. 30/3, p. 74.

[3]   P.I. Cernovodeanu, 'Călătoria lui Pierre Lescalopier în Țara Romînească și Transilvania', *Studii și Materiale de Istorie Medie*, 4 (1960): 447.

Saxon Lutheranism seemed to be simply Catholicism without the Pope. Moreover, since the people of Neustadt are unlikely to have been the first Lutherans encountered by this Parisian lawyer, the closeness of Saxon Lutheran observance to Catholicism must have been particularly striking and unusual. Lescalopier, a well-travelled Catholic, was amazed that he could have been so taken in. Looked at more closely, of course, Saxon Lutheranism was not simply Catholicism without the Pope, but it did differ significantly from the practice of Lutheranism in other areas, and Lescalopier's misunderstanding underlines the need to investigate how the Saxon inhabitants of Transylvania understood the Lutheran Reformation.

Precisely those aspects of Lutheran practice that struck Pierre Lescalopier – the outward observances of religion – are therefore a principal focus of this chapter, since such practices define religious experience, even if they can be subject to misunderstandings. The liturgy was an essential tool with which the Lutheran Reformation shaped the experience of religion; it articulated and interpreted the theological underpinnings of Saxon Lutheranism in the heart of the urban and village community. But liturgy is only one tool in defining religious identity. Another is discipline, which, as the Philippist controversy demonstrates, was becoming a particularly contentious issue within Lutheranism at precisely the time when Saxon Lutheranism was searching for its identity. The outcome was an unusual synthesis: liturgically, Saxon Lutherans could be mistaken for Catholics, but in their disciplinary intentions they were much more demanding than many Lutheran, and even Calvinist, communities elsewhere.

An obvious way of trying to understand this, particularly given the assumptions of existing denominational historiography, is to focus on the man usually assumed to be the founder of the Saxon Reformation, Johannes Honter (1498–1549), who became town preacher of his native Kronstadt. Following the interpretation of Erich Roth, he should be seen as steering a course between Wittenberg and the Swiss, with the accent on the latter in key matters such as confession and absolution.[4] There are many strengths in such an approach, especially since Roth's usage of 'Swiss' incorporates a wide range of reformation practice, including that pursued in Nuremberg, a city with strong trading contacts with Transylvania. Moreover, 'Swiss' reform in the Confederation, like that in Saxon Transylvania, was built upon a strong tradition of lay communalism,

---

[4]   Erich Roth, *Die Reformation in Siebenbürgen: Ihr Verhältnis zu Wittenberg und der Schweiz* (2 vols, Cologne, 1962, 1964). Subsequent debate includes Oskar Wittstock, 'Johannes Honterus: Der siebenbürger Humanist und Reformator', *Kirche im Osten, Monographienreihe*, 10 (Göttingen, 1970), and Ludwig Binder, 'Johannes Honterus und die Reformation im Süden Siebenbürgens mit besonderer Berücksichtigung der Schweizer und Wittenberge Einflüsse', *Zwingliana*, 13/10 (1973): 645–87.

encapsulated in the communal election of pastors, and in the case of the Saxons, in the retention of all tithes within the parish community. However, despite Honter's 'Swiss' preferences, the Saxons of Transylvania resolutely did not 'turn Swiss', most obviously in their (and probably Honter's) apparently unwavering commitment to a Lutheran understanding of real presence, but also in matters of less obvious doctrinal moment such as the abandonment of Honter's instruction that a complete Bible chapter should be read successively in services (*lectio continua*).

How far Honter's own priorities account for the nature of the Saxon synthesis of discipline and ritual flexibility thus needs more examination. As the author of the *Reformatio Barcensis*, a set of guidelines for the official adoption of reform in Kronstadt and its dependent villages in 1543, Honter was clearly influential, even if many details were altered later in the *Reformatio ecclesiarum saxonicarum* (1547). His contribution encapsulates the dilemma facing a humanist reformer exposed to the variety of Swiss and Lutheran ideas. In various places in the *Reformatio Barcensis*, he outlines his principles in elaborating a Church order. He stresses that it is desirable to follow the customs of the evangelical Churches and not to deviate from them, as there is scarcely anything which could be more damaging for Christian unity. As there is one Christ, one Holy Spirit, one baptism and one God, so there should be one way of celebrating the eucharist. Explicit in these comments is criticism of particular orders being established for particular places.[5]

Honter's view is typical of a humanist aspiration for unity, and goes with hopes for the settlement of the religious questions by a general council of the Church. But at the same time, in drawing up guidelines for the evangelical Church in Siebenbürgen, Honter was eclectic in his use of sources.[6] Thus, the section on the sacrament of baptism opens with a clear statement that his Church follows the Wittenberg Church ordinance in the use of the native tongue of the godparents for the rite, but Honter's directions follow the Swiss, rather than Luther, in the clear rejection of exorcism (Luther in his revisions of the baptismal rite progressively reduced the number of exorcisms, but still retained some).[7] Similarly, the granting of a significant

---

[5]   *Schriften des Johannes Honterus, Valentin Wagner und Markus Fronius in deutscher Uebersetzung* (Beiheft zum VIII. Band der Quellen zu Geschichte von Braşov-Kronstadt, Braşov 1927–29), p. 16.

[6]   According to the analysis of Erich Roth, the closest model for Honter's *Reformatio Barcensis* (or *Reformationsbüchlein*) is the then unpublished 'Nuremberg Ratschrift' of 1524, attributed to Lazarus Spengler. Some similarities are noted with the Church orders of Basel (1529) and Schwäbisch Hall (1526); Roth, *Die Reformation in Siebenbürgen*, vol. 1, pp. 57–79 and appendix.

[7]   *Schriften des Johannes Honterus*, p. 15; Karant-Nunn, *Reformation of Ritual*, pp. 50–53, 59–61.

role to the congregation in pronouncing verdicts of excommunication can also be seen as following the practice of some Swiss reformers.

However, although eclectic, Honter's text was not unacceptably 'Swiss': the procedures for excommunication closely follow Matthew 18:15–17, as advocated by Luther in his *To the Christian Nobility* (1520), and Luther could recognize *lectio continua* as appropriate when Christians gathered without a preacher.[8] Moreover, in general, its Swiss elements relate more to observance and methods than to the content of doctrine or discipline. The text is non-committal on eucharistic doctrine, and in discussing the practice of excommunication shows more of a lay reformer's concern about the misuse of the power by unreliable clerics than it does about the notions of discipline and repentance underpinning it. It was a reformation proposal that could be welcomed into the Lutheran fold. When Mathias Ramser of Hermannstadt was wondering whether to adopt a Kronstadt-style reformation in his own city, he sent a copy of Honter's text to Wittenberg, and received an effusive and enthusiastic reply from Luther himself: 'Everything you ask me you will find better set down in this little book than I can write. I liked it beyond measure: it is so learned, pure and truly written.' That these were no mere empty words, or a device to avoid writing a long answer to Ramser, is shown by the fact that Honter's text was published in Wittenberg in the same year with a preface by Melanchthon.[9]

Despite Luther's approval, Honter's original text was not adopted unchanged as the formal basis for the reformation of all the Saxon lands in Transylvania in 1547. Some modifications are perhaps unsurprising. More detailed consideration of some issues was necessary, and it was evidently in the clergy's interest to reduce lay influence over excommunication. However, although the new text was more comprehensive, it still left many aspects of religious practice unclear, despite the fact that the stated aim of the Nationsuniversität, the political body of the Saxon nation, in calling for a committee of learned men was to introduce uniformity, especially in ceremonies. Significantly, the committee was not formed with alacrity, but only after successive exhortations. Once assembled, its compilers, like Honter earlier, were eclectic and discriminating in their use of sources. Although the committee had access to Church orders, especially from Nuremberg, which could have served as models, it did not use them in drawing up the *Reformatio ecclesiarum saxonicarum*.

---

[8]   *An den christlichen Adel* WA, vol. 6, p. 143; *Von Ordenung gottis diensts ynn der gemeyne* (1523), WA, vol. 12, p. 36.

[9]   Adolf Schullerus, *Geschichte des Gottesdienstes in der siebenbürgisch-sächsischen Kirche*, (Archiv des Vereins für siebenbürgische Landeskunde 41) (1923), p. 435. Luther's approval of Honter's text and the letters of Melanchthon and Bugenhagen were also printed in Kronstadt under the title *Approbatio Reformationis Ecclesiae Coronensis*.

The *Agenda*, also produced in 1547, probably by the same committee, borrowed extensively from Luther's writings, the Wittenberg *Agenda* of 1540, and the Brandenburg-Nuremberg Church order of 1533. But, oddly for an Agenda, its compilers simply omitted to include sections on controversial topics, including the communion service, thus tacitly recognizing that the Wittenberg version could not be applied to the Saxon lands as a whole. For the committee, as also for Honter in 1543, detailed comprehensiveness was not the main aim. In extending the geographical scope of the Reformation, its members were prepared to accept the need to accommodate regional and local variation in such key matters as the use of vestments, the elevation and private or general confession.

This weakness might be thought to reflect that of the Nationsuniversität as a political institution. Although it had gained the right in 1469 to elect its own Königsrichter, it had, after all, only gained effective jurisdictional autonomy in 1542 as a consequence of the partition of Hungary, functioning previously mainly as one of the three 'nations' summoned to the Hungarian diet. Moreover, it can be argued that it was its role in institutionalizing the Reformation that gave this political body its strength, rather than vice versa. Certainly, the eventual acceptance in 1550 of the committee's 1547 text for the Reformation of all the Saxon lands was a watershed not only in the Reformation, but also in the Nationsuniversität's ability to claim to impose uniformity.[10] Nevertheless, in a sense the language of 'weakness' is misplaced here: it was a representative body, the bearer and defender of corporate privileges built on ideas of local and communal autonomy. Aspirations to uniformity were commonplace, but for all but the zealot, the aim was to create uniformity at a level capable of sustaining that idea.

It was also significant that for all these controversial practices Luther's preferences offered no clear lead. Thus, the 1547 text was able to cultivate flexibility and ambiguity where Honter had offered clarity. Honter had rejected elevation in 1543, perhaps following Luther's acceptance of Bugenhagen's decision to do so in 1542 as the new pastor of Wittenberg.[11] In 1547, the *Reformatio ecclesiarum saxonicarum* instructed the minister

---

[10]   Walter Daugsch, 'Die Nationsuniversität der Siebenbürger Sachsen', in Wolfgang Kessler (ed.), *Gruppenautonomie in Siebenbürgen. 500 Jahre siebenbürgisch-sächsische Nationsuniversität* (Archiv des Vereins für Siebenbürgische Landeskunde, 3rd series, vol. 24, Cologne and Vienna, 1990), pp. 179–216.

[11]   Karant-Nunn, *Reformation of Ritual,* p. 118; Bodo Nischan, 'The elevation of the host in the age of confessionalism: Adiaphoron or ritual demarcation?', in Bodo Nischan, *Lutherans and Calvinists in the Age of Confessionalism* (Aldershot, 1999), pp. 7–11, notes that Luther defined elevation as a matter of free choice or *adiaphoron* in his *Against Heavenly Prophets* (1525) and maintained this view throughout his life, as clarified in his *Brief Confession Concerning the Holy Sacrament* (1544). Changes in policy were measured against sacramentarian threat and popular support for the rite.

after the words of institution to hold the elements in his hands in turn (*per vices utrumque tenens in manibus*). As Roth noted, such a formulation allowed the possibility of elevation, and also its omission. Given Ramser's defence of elevation in 1544, it seems obvious that we are dealing here with a compromise solution aimed at accommodating the preferences of Hermannstadt and Kronstadt. The same geographical division underpinned the question of private or general confession and absolution.[12]

Accommodation of regional preferences was not simply a transitional solution. It was integral to the Saxon Reformation. Regional differences in ritual practice continued after 1547, and were apparently accepted in the next overhaul of Saxon practice ten years later, the synod of 1557. At this time, vestments and candles were specifically mentioned, and continued diversity of practice was implicitly accepted in the aspiration that vestments (apart from the alb) should be abandoned when the people were sufficiently educated to accept this.[13] Melanchthon's letter to the Saxon Church of Transylvania the following year, counselling against drives to impose ritual uniformity in such matters as baptismal exorcism because they were potentially disruptive, may have consolidated this trend, but it did not create it.[14] Moreover, when strong political pressure was brought to bear, the strength of the attachment to local diversity was also demonstrated. In 1572, the Catholic ruler Stefan Bathory attempted to standardize Saxon ritual practice and to secure recognition of the Augustana. But the demand that all parts of the Siebenbürgen should use the ornaments and vestments as in Hermannstadt and Kronstadt evoked a protest from the chapters of Mediasch and Bistritz because they had abandoned liturgical vestments and altar candles and saw such things as papistical and idolatrous abominations.[15]

Alongside this flexibility in ritual observance, there developed a rigorous concern for discipline, the details of which were often unusual, and certainly not shared by the majority of Lutheran Churches. Thus, for example, the synod of 1565 stipulated that weddings of couples who did not know the catechism were to be deferred pending improvement. Parallel provisions

---

[12] Schullerus, *Geschichte des Gottesdienstes*, pp. 415–16; Erich Roth, *Die Geschichte des Gottesdienstes der Siebenbürger Sachsen*, (Göttingen, 1954), pp. 97, 105.

[13] *Urkundenbuch der evangelischen Landeskirche A.B. in Siebenbürgen*, ed. Georg Daniel Teutsch (2 vols, Hermannstadt, 1862, 1883), vol. 2, p. 5.

[14] *Philippi Melanchthonis Opera quae supersunt omnia*, ed. G.C. Bretschneider (28 vols, Halle, 1834–60), vol. 9, pp. 430–31.

[15] Roth, *Die Reformation in Siebenbürgen*, vol. 2, pp. 111–15; *Urkundenbuch der evangelischen Landeskirche*, vol. 2, pp. 133–4. This division had also been a subject of fierce debate in 1564, but the synod of 1565, citing the authority of St Augustine, acknowledged the status quo; *Urkundenbuch der evangelischen Landeskirche*, vol. 2, pp. 77–8, 107.

can be found in Hesse the following year, and the practice appears to have become more widespread by the 1580s, when it was stipulated in Torun (1575), the Silesian principality of Troppau (1584), Hoya (1581), Kursachsen (1580) and Niedersachsen (1585).[16] However, despite the strong attachment to the catechism as a tool of instruction, this did not become general Lutheran practice. This was largely because such policies always ran the more fundamental risk of encouraging couples to cohabit without seeking the blessing of the Church. In Siebenbürgen, we can deduce this was not the case. Far from struggling to persuade parishioners of the need for a church wedding ceremony, the Church was able to use the threat of withholding marriage as a disciplinary sanction. Moreover, the Church was also able to use ritual as the sole disciplinary tool for the practice of marriage itself, reinforcing the conclusion that attachment to the wedding ceremony was unusually strong in the region.

The demand that there should be no sex or cohabitation between betrothal and marriage was a staple of Lutheran Church ordinances almost everywhere, but the penalty in Transylvania for anticipating marriage was not shared by all: at the wedding ceremony, which took place at the church door, the bride had to appear with her head covered, symbolizing that she was already a married woman, and the whole ceremony had to be performed without a procession and splendour. However, unlike in Wolfenbüttel (1569), for example, where such weddings also took place without guests and with a ritual indication that the bride was not a virgin, in Transylvania, a shaming ritual sanction was sufficient. There was no perceived need in this case for additional penalties of imprisonment on a restricted diet of bread and water, even though for other offences this could be the appropriate penalty.[17] From 1557, confinement in the *Narrenhaus* or *Feddel* was prescribed for being engaged in other activities during the Sunday service, and twenty years later this was extended to all work and ungodly activities carried out on Sundays. Most unusually, and apparently without parallel in Lutheran Church orders, it was stated in 1577 that disobedient and godless children who revile, scold and hit their own parents should not only be placed in the parish prison (*Feddel*), but also be beaten with rods and chased out of the community.[18] Less unusual,

---

[16]   *Urkundenbuch der evangelischen Landeskirche*, vol. 2, p. 106; *Die evangelischen Kirchenordnungen des xvi. Jahrhunderts*, ed. Emil Sehling, 16 vols (vols 1–5, Leipzig, 1902–13; vols 6–8, 11–14, Tübingen, 1955–1969; vol. 15, Tübingen, 1977; vol. 16, Tübingen, 2004): Hesse 1566 – vol. 8 (1965), p. 322; Torun 1575 – vol. 4 (1911), p. 241; Troppau 1584 – vol. 3 (1909), p. 480; Hoya 1581 – vol. 6, part 2 (1957), pp. 1197; Georg Reitschel and Paul Graff, *Lehrbuch der Liturgik: Die Kasualien* (Göttingen, 1952), p. 714.
[17]   *Die evangelischen Kirchenordnungen*, vol. 6 part 1 (1955), pp. 215–16.
[18]   *Urkundenbuch der evangelischen Landeskirche*, vol. 1, pp. 72–3; vol. 2, p. 212.

but again far from universal, was the provision that habitual drunkards or despisers of God's Word should be denied burial in consecrated ground, many other Lutheran Churches being prepared to offer the compromise of burial within consecrated ground, but with a reduced religious ceremony, often in the absence of the minister.[19]

The emphasis on rigorous, but occasionally idiosyncratic, discipline may seem the logical outcome in a politically cohesive Saxon nation, but in the context of the failure to standardize ritual practice, it seems that more explanation is needed. In part, the concern for discipline may be due to theological concerns. Honter, consistent with his emphasis on the law rather than grace, saw faith as empty without good works and strove to counter opposing views by printing Andreas Moldner's song book in his press in Kronstadt in 1543, which included a song by Ludwig Hätzer to strengthen the faith of weak believers. This explained in colloquial terms that it was the doctrine of the devil that individual salvation was already assured through Christ's sacrifice (*nun zech ich auf sein kreide*), and stressed the need to submit oneself entirely to God, and to behave as befits a humble Christian in society.[20] Honter's priorities appear to have been shared by the hierarchy of the Saxon Church. On the issue of discipline, no visible rift emerged, and this consensus may have been assisted by a shared humanist background, strengthened by the large number of Saxons who obtained a university education, predominantly in Vienna, and with the growth of Lutheranism, increasingly in Wittenberg.

While these are adequate explanations for the general acknowledgement of the need for discipline, they do not fully explain its nature. As we have seen in the case of marriage, existing social practices could shape the formulation of the appropriate disciplinary response. The burial of the ungodly and stubborn sinners in the field may also follow pre-

---

[19] Ibid., vol. 2, p. 210. The key biblical text justifying burial of sinners in non-consecrated ground was Jeremiah 22:19; Mary Lindemann, 'Armen- und Eselbegräbnis in der europäischen Frühneuzeit, eine Methode sozialer Kontrolle', in Paul R. Blum (ed.), *Studien zur Thematik des Todes im 16. Jahrhundert* (Wolfenbütteler Forschungen, 22, 1983), p. 130. *Die evangelischen Kirchenordnungen* gives examples of burial in unconsecrated ground including Hesse, 1566 vol. 8, part 1 (1965), p. 337, Hoya, 1581, vol. 6, part 1 (1955), p. 1172, Oldenburg, 1573, vol. 7, part 2 (1980), p. 1110, Hohenlohe, 1582, vol. 15 (1977), pp. 479–80, and of places allowing churchyard burial with reduced ceremony including Neubrandenburg, 1559, vol. 5 (1913), p. 269, Rostock, 1561, vol. 5 (1913), p. 290, Wolfenbüttel, 1569, vol. 6, part 1(1955), p. 176, Marienhafer, Ostfriesland, 1593, vol. 7, part 1 (1963), p. 721.
[20] Karl Reinerth, *Die Gründung der evangelischen Kirchen in Siebenbürgen* (Cologne and Vienna, 1979), p. 77; Philipp Wackernagel, *Das deutsche kirchenlied von den ältesten Zeit bis zu Anfang des xvii. Jahrhunderts* (5 vols, Leipzig, 1864–77), vol. 3, pp. 480–81.

Reformation practice.[21] In other instances, Old Testament fundamentalism could influence disciplinary policy. In the case of the unruly child, the sentence of being beaten and chased out of the community according to God's commandment closely echoes Deuteronomy 22:18–21. This text featured in late medieval catechesis, including the Vienna school, but although parents and secular authorities were warned that God would hold them responsible for the unpunished sins of children and subjects, there was no expectation of literal re-enactment of the Deuteronomy text as was the case in Saxon Transylvania.[22] Nevertheless, such scriptural fundamentalism was not a constant guiding principle of Saxon reform. Had it been so, the generous policy towards the retention of images, which confused Lescalopier, would not have been possible. In fact, if Honter is to be believed, such image destruction as did occur was mainly designed to answer the criticisms of the Orthodox, and thus directed particularly against the proliferation of side altars.[23]

In more general terms, discipline seems to have been shaped by the desire that there should be some separation of the community of true Christians from the rest. Thus, in 1577, the provision that gluttons, drunkards, blasphemers and despisers of God's Word should be buried in the field rather than in the churchyard was justified by the fact that light has no community with darkness. Similarly, the need for couples to know their catechism before being allowed to marry in church is said to be to ensure that there is some difference between Christians and heathens.[24] Such anxieties suggest a community under threat. Threats in fact came from various directions: from dissolute members of the Saxon community who disregarded its doctrinal and moral standards, and from the mockery of outsiders. As a defensive measure, the synod of Mediasch (1578) stipulated that the children of Gypsies and Valachs (Romanians) should not be baptized in Saxon churches for fear of mockery. Danger also came from those of higher social status: pastors were warned not to ask nobles

---

[21]   Graeme Murdock, *Calvinism on the Frontier, 1600–1660: International Calvinism and the Reformed Church in Hungary and Transylvania* (Oxford, 2000), pp. 211–12, cites the reformed Church in Zemplén county denying burial in consecrated ground to those refusing to carry out imposed penance. Although evidently a later reference, it gains significance in view of Murdock's discussion of reformed discipline in the area as highly resistant to the admixture of secular or physical penalties in stark contrast to the Saxon Lutherans.

[22]   Robert J. Bast, *Honor your Fathers: Catechisms and the Emergence of a Patriarchal Authority in Germany, 1400–1600* (Brill and Leiden, 1997), pp. 56–7, 95–6.

[23]   *Schriften des Johannes Honterus*, p. 11 (Preface to *Reformatio Barcensis*, 1543). Image destruction in Kronstadt was carried out in 1544 with official support down to the careful weighing of the silver recovered.

[24]   *Urkundenbuch der evangelischen Landeskirche*, vol. 2, pp. 209–10.

to act as witnesses or godparents, in order to avoid the embarrassment of being snubbed by them.[25]

However, ritual as well as discipline can be seen as a tool of a beleaguered Church, which brings us back to the need to solve the problem of diversity in ritual observance and attempts at disciplinary unity. One possibility is to suggest that, despite their lack of institutionalized power, it was the presence of the smaller ecclesiastical jurisdictions within Siebenbürgen which ensured the continuing strength of local liturgical preferences.[26] Surviving pre-Reformation service books show that, despite a shared close affinity with the rite of Esztergom, particular areas favoured certain saints and allocated different gospel readings to dates in the liturgical calendar, while Victor Roth's study of sacrament houses suggests that this manifestation of eucharistic devotion was centred in the area around Mediasch.[27] Precisely how such patterns affected Reformation solutions is less clear. The present state of research does not easily permit an explanation for why on certain issues Hermannstadt and Kronstadt diverged, while on others their practice could be contrasted with that of Mediasch and Bistritz. External influences cannot be discounted. It may be no coincidence that the rejection of altar candles and vestments occurred in those areas closest to Klausenburg, where the Lutherans were losing ground to the Reformed. But that things were in fact more complex is suggested by the fact that it was Bistritz, rather than Hermannstadt or Kronstadt, which attracted the attention of the ruler Sigismund Bathory in 1592 because its clerics were failing to ensure Sabbath observance and to prevent young people gathering together at night. Moreover, the apparent effectiveness of such devices as prohibiting or recalling those who had received education in Klausenburg in shielding other areas of Saxon Lutheranism from Reformed contagion supports the view that local versions of Lutheranism were deep-rooted.

It is at this point that we must return to the area around Kronstadt, the heartland of the Saxon Reformation, and to the wall paintings of the chapel in the fortified enclosure of the church of Honigberg, mentioned at the beginning of this chapter, to see how the features of Saxon Lutheranism

---

[25]   Ibid., pp. 226–27.

[26]   Oskar Wittstock, 'Die Genossenschaftskirche der siebenbürger Sachsen vor der Reformation', *Kirche in Osten*, 17 (1974): 156–162, stresses the importance of the full political and ecclesiastical autonomy of Saxon communities on royal land, and diocesan affiliations to either Weissenburg or Esztergom, and notes that, although a union of chapters emerged in the struggle against the bishops in 1469 and the appointment of a general dean (1502), such struggles were usually carried out in conjunction with the political leadership of the Saxon nation.

[27]   Victor Roth, 'Gotische Sakramentsnischen und Sakramentshäuschen in Siebenbürgen', in *Beiträge zur Kunstgeschichte Siebenbürgens* (Strasbourg, 1914), pp. 102–15.

were shaped as much, if not more, by the logic of pre-Reformation religious and social instruction as they were by pressures arising from the co-existence of religious and local identities.

A fruitful approach in exploring pre-Reformation Saxon devotion is to analyse its 'moralized universe' alongside the 'sacramental'. Particularly helpful here is the most unusual part of the iconography of the chapel at Honigberg: the depiction on the east wall, in place of the earlier Christ in Majesty, of the Crucifixion with Mary and John, flanked on the left by the three orders of society – priest, knight and peasant – and on the right by the figures of the Pharisee and Publican (Figures 7.1–3).[28]

The image of the three orders, long out of fashion in the west by the late fifteenth century, is one that needs careful contextualization. At first glance, its portrayal in a community suffering from Turkish attacks, and the burden of providing fortifications might be thought to carry subversive resonances. In the hands of Hunyadi's peasant troops, who successfully regained Belgrade from the Turks in 1456, the peasant Bund opposing the Turks in Upper Styria in 1478 and the crucifer of the Hungarian Peasant (or Dózsa) Revolt of 1514, the doctrine of the three orders enabled an ideology of trenchant criticism of the failure of magnates and nobles to carry out their military duties in crusade and battle. However, although it is possible that the limited participation of Transylvanian peasants in the revolt of 1514 was more to do with the intervention of János Zápolyai than with the revolt's lack of appeal, it is far from clear that this is the correct reading, or why such an image should be chosen to feature on the east wall of a chapel in the Burzenland.[29]

Most obviously, the Saxons of the Burzenland were a society without nobility, and in this they were distinct amongst the three nations of Transylvania: membership of the Hungarian nation was dependent on personal nobility, and could be compatible with non-Magyar ethnicity; and the Szeklers, despite corporate privileges similar to those of the Saxons, were by this time beginning to undergo a process of inner social stratification involving the emergence of a high nobility and serfs.[30] Furthermore, in Hungary and Transylvania as a whole it is clear, as Held and Borosy argue,

---

[28]   Ruxandra Balaci, 'Noi aspecte iconografice în pictura murală gotică din Transilvania Hărman și Sînpetru', *Studii și Cercetării de Istoria Artei (Artă Plastică)*, 36 (1989): 3–17.

[29]   Norman Housley, 'Crusading as social revolt: The Hungarian peasant uprising of 1514', *Journal of Ecclesiastical History*, 49/1 (1998): 1–28; János M. Bak, 'Delinquent lords and forsaken serfs: Thoughts on war and society in the crisis of feudalism', in. S.B. Vardy and A.H. Vardy (eds), *Society in Change: Studies in Honour of Béla K. Kiraly* (New York, 1983), pp. 291–304.

[30]   Lajos Demény, 'Die Entwicklung der sozialen Beziehungen bei den Szeklern und ihre Rechtslage', in Kessler (ed.), *Gruppenautonomie in Siebenbürgen*, pp. 225–31.

Figure 7.1   East wall of the chapel at Honigberg.

that by the end of the fifteenth century the *militia portalis* system depended to a large extent on the recruitment of local peasants, as did Matthias Corvinus's experiment with a mercenary system.[31] In this context, the idea that peasants were merely peasants while nobles were warriors and defenders of their vassals made no sense at all.

The idea of the three orders is normally seen as combining concepts of hierarchy with those of mutual obligations, but it seems that the Honigberg example should be read differently.[32] Here, functions, especially

---

[31]   András Borosy, 'The *militia portalis* in Hungary before 1526', in János M. Bak and Béla K. Király (eds), *From Hunyadi to Rákóczi: War and Society in Late Medieval and Early Modern Hungary* (Columbia, OH, 1982), pp. 63–80; Joseph Held, 'Peasants in arms, 1437–8 and 1456', in ibid., pp. 81–101; Gyula Rázsó, 'The mercenary army of King Matthias Corvinus', in ibid., pp. 125–40.

[32]   The literature on the Three Orders in mediaeval society is extensive. Useful studies include Paul Freedman, *Images of the Medieval Peasant* (Stanford, CT, 1999); Giles Constable, *Three Studies in Medieval Religious and Social Thought: The Interpretation of Mary and Martha, the Ideal of the Imitation of Christ and the Orders of Society* (Cambridge, 1995), Otto G. Oexle, 'Tria genera hominum': Zur Geschichte eines Deutungsschemas der sozialen Wirklichkeit in Antike und Mittelalter', in Lutz Fenshke, Werner Rösener and Thomas Zotz (eds), *Institutionen, Kultur und Gesellschaft in Mittelalter: Festschrift für Josef Fleckstein* (Sigmaringen, 1984), pp. 483–500; Ruth Mohl, *The Three Estates in Medieval and Renaissance Literature* (New York, 1933).

Figure 7.2 Detail of the Three Orders (peasant, knight and priest) on the east wall at Honigberg.

Figure 7.3 Detail of the Pharisee and the Publican on the east wall at Honigberg.

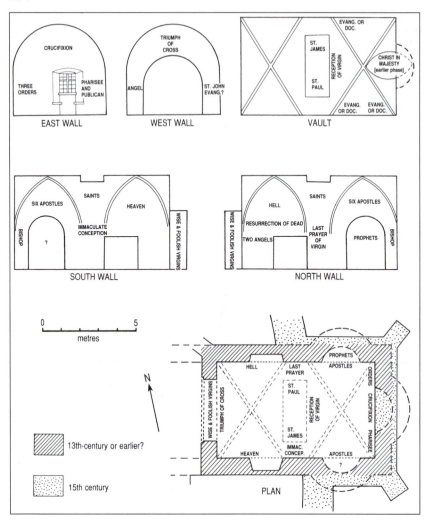

Figure 7.4 Iconographical scheme of the chapel at Honigberg.

the pressing military one of defence which had prompted the alteration and redecorating of the chapel, were not attributes of fixed social status, but intermittent obligations potentially incumbent on all. By placing those who labour, fight and pray as intercessors to the crucified Christ, notions of hierarchy, and even of mutual obligations between the orders, pale into insignificance. The principal focus is the offering of these activities in the service of Christ, a notion that incorporates both a response to the obvious threat of pagan Turkish incursions, and also a sense of appropriate individual Christian vocation. Intriguingly, such an interpretation can also be seen to share significant resonances with earlier Cistercian notions of the dignity of work and prayer, with Chelčický's radical Hussite critique of the Wycliffite stress on three separate orders adopted by other Hussites in Bohemia, and with the notion of the three orders as expounded by Luther in his *To the Christian Nobility of the German Nation*, in which all work simultaneously has the function of labour, prayer and protection in a Christian society.[33]

However, despite the presence of wall painting cycles of the life of Christ, and of fraternities and lavish processions in honour of Corpus Christi, the most striking feature of the religious culture of the Saxons was not devotion to Christ, but a heightened devotion to the Virgin Mary.[34] This can be seen in a particularly extreme form in the preaching of Johannes Zekel in Hermannstadt in 1502. In his sermon on the Nativity of the Virgin Mary, Zekel makes the remarkable claim that Mary's Assumption outdoes Christ's Ascension since Christ is met only by angels, whereas Mary is met by angels, all the righteous and even the Trinity, and led to her throne.[35] Moreover, Marian feasts were an important part of the Church calendar, including the less widespread feast of Maria de nives.

Surviving wall paintings and altarpieces also emphasize the Virgin Mary, most notably at Birthälm and the Honigberg chapel, the central area of which includes elaborate depictions of the Immaculate Conception and the Coronation (Figure 7.4). These show that there was a clear concern to relate praise of the Virgin to her role as the bearer of Christ. The Birthälm altarpiece (1483) combines episodes from the life of Mary and of Christ, and the central image of the tryptichon, added in 1515 and based on the book of Sirach, shows Mary (Wisdom) watering the vine bearing Christ and the apostles, later glossed in the text as the propagation of true doctrine. Both phases serve as a reminder not only of the complexity of the Marian cult, but also of its focus on Christ, even in an altarpiece that, in part, celebrates a largely feminine Holy Kindred.[36]

---

[33] 'Peter Chelčický: Treatises on Christianity and the social order', in Howard Kaminsky (ed.), *Studies in Medieval and Renaissance History*, vol. 1 (Lincoln, NB, 1964), pp. 106–78. *An den christlichen Adel*, WA, vol. 6, pp. 407–9, 428.

[34] Wall painting cycles of the life of Christ include Schässburg (1488), Heltau (end of fifteenth century), Rosenau (1500) and Salzburg (1522). Gustav Seiwert, 'Die Bruderschaft des heiligen Leichnams in Hermannstadt', *Archiv des Vereins für siebenbürgische Landeskunde*, 10 (1872): 314–60. There is also evidence of Corpus Christi fraternities at Kronstadt, Keisd and Weidenbach.

[35] Reinerth, *Die Gründung der Evangelischen Kirchen*, pp. 2–5. Zekel's sermon notes are in the Bruckenthal Museum, Sibiu. BBS Ms. 657, sermon on the Nativity of the Virgin Mary, fols 3r–5r.

[36] Harald Krasser, 'Untersuchungen zur mittelalterlichen Tafelmalerei in Siebenbürgen: zur Herkunft und Datierung der Birthälmer Altartafeln', *Forschungen zur Volks- und Landeskunde*, 14/2 (1971): 9–24.

Similarly, although the Honigberg painting of the Immaculate Conception focuses on the purity of Mary, it follows the more Christocentric tradition in choosing the scene of the Nativity with Mary adoring the Christ Child as its centrepiece, an image expressing reverential distance, rather than the Virgin and Child, which implies overlapping identity. That this was a deliberate choice is suggested by the fact that the opposite solution was chosen by the painter of the earlier Cologne altarpiece, which is one of the closest iconographic parallels. In both traditions, the four symbolic images of the Virgin taming the unicorn, the pelican tearing its breast to feed its chicks, the lion whose young awake on the third day, and the phoenix all carry Christocentric associations, while the four outside triangles illustrate the Old Testament prefigurations of Mary's purity.[37]

The remaining Marian iconography in the chapel consists of the scene of the Last Prayer, positioned directly opposite the scene of the Immaculate Conception and, spanning the ceiling space between these two images, an image of the Reception of the Virgin in Heaven, lavish in its use of gold. Considering these three images together produces an interesting reading. The Virgin in the Last Prayer is already crowned, suggesting her exceptional status even before the moment of her Assumption. The iconography of the Reception of the Virgin also supports this interpretation. The detail and luxuriousness of the mantle of the Trinity and of the cloak held behind them by several angels, together with the insignificant scale of Mary herself, suggest that the focus of the scene is not the act of coronation, but the enfolding of Mary into the celestial world. The choice of the Last Prayer instead of the Dormition also fits with this lack of emphasis on transition.[38] Mary's status is asserted by her purity, validated by Old

---

[37]   The Cologne altarpiece (*c.* 1420) is now in Bonn Museum, and was clearly intended as a demonstration of the Immaculate Conception. *Das Rheinische Landesmuseum* – Auswahlskatalog (Bonn, 1977), vol. 4, pp. 53–8; Carol J. Purtle, *The Marian Paintings of Jan van Eyck* (Princeton, NJ, 1982), pp. 137–8. Panel paintings similar in conception to the images at Honigberg and Cologne occur at Holy Cross, Rostock, St Lorenz, Nuremberg (Friedrich Schön epitaph), and St Sebald, Nuremberg (Elsbeth Stark epitaph). Other images with elements of this composite design can be found at Neuwerk (Mönchen Gladbach), Stettin, St Sebald, Nuremberg (Margaretha Löffelholz epitaph) and Ottobeuren; Alfred Stange, *Die Deutschen Tafelbilder vor Dürer*, (3 vols, Munich 1967–78), vol. 1, pp. 117, 189, 196, vol. 2, p. 181, vol. 3, pp. 29, 45, 49. The inscriptions on the Honigberg painting conform partly to Cologne and partly to Rostock, and a related edition of the *Biblia Pauperum* is the most likely source.

[38]   Balaci notes that the Last Prayer occurs more frequently in Byzantine iconography, where it usually precedes the Dormition. This is the context of the Last Prayer in the polyptych of St George, Prague (*c.* 1470), which depicts an uncrowned Mary; Balaci, 'Noi aspecte iconografice', 15–16. There are also similarities between the Honigberg Last Prayer and a painting at Vordernberg (*c.* 1455–60) where the Virgin is also uncrowned, but the depiction includes the

Testament prefigurations, and, particularly significantly, manifested in her veneration of her son and the devoutness of her life on earth.

These features also help to explain why in the Saxon Churches of Transylvania, Mary has very little role in the process of salvation. At Birthälm, for example, she does not appear as the Madonna of Mercy in the Last Judgement, but operates at one stage removed. At Honigberg the Marian iconography is clearly conceived as a part, and probably a subordinate part, of the general scheme, which emphasizes the importance of the Passion of Christ in the process of salvation. The prominence of the Crucifixion on the east wall of the chapel has already been noted. On the west wall, separating the resurrecting souls from the entrance to Paradise, there is no majestic Christ presiding over the judgement of the saved and the damned. Instead, the central image at Honigberg is the cross itself, garlanded with the crown of thorns and flanked by apostles and angels. In life, as the east end imagery demonstrates, it is possible to intercede with the human suffering Christ. At the Last Judgement, it is the fact of Christ's Crucifixion that makes salvation possible.

In fact, the strength of Marian devotion, and its embeddedness in Christocentric concerns, created a distinctive challenge and opportunity to Lutheran reformers in Transylvania. On the one hand, the excesses of the Marian cult, present in the belief in her Immaculate Conception and Assumption, needed to be avoided. On the other, the idea of Mary in Saxon devotion already provided a model for the godly Christian and undercut her role as the Queen of Heaven.

The Saxon Church's concern to distance Lutheran practices from the excesses of earlier Marian devotion can be seen most clearly in its treatment of saints' days, and also of churching. The specification of saints' days occurs in the *Agenda* of 1547. In general, this text borrows verbatim from Wittenberg sources, but for the list of feast days it does not, and this suggests a deliberate choice. The closest parallel is, perhaps unsurprisingly, a Nuremberg list, but there are some interesting changes in detail, especially concerning the Assumption of the Virgin Mary.

The Assumption was clearly a feast that provoked Lutheran unease and uncertainty about how to proceed. Luther himself initially permitted its retention, despite his reservations about the content of the songs used to mark the feast. In Nuremberg, a different compromise was reached: it was recognized that there was no scriptural basis for the story of Mary's Assumption, but for the sake of the country folk, the feast would be kept on the same date and the story of the Visitation substituted, since there was

---

Assumption; *Corpus der mittelalterlichen Wandmalereien Österreichs: Steiermark*, ed. Elga Lanc and Miriam Porta (Vienna, 2002), cat. 943 Vordernburg.

scriptural justification for that episode of Mary's life.[39] The compilers of the Transylvanian Agenda of 1547 rejected the Nuremberg compromise, which by this date also appeared to be advocated by Luther (*Hauspostille* 1544).[40] In Siebenbürgen, the feast of the Visitation was kept since it was supported by scripture, but not on the date of the Assumption.

Several explanations for this divergence seem possible. One may be the popularity of the feast of the Visitation itself. From at least the 1540s, protestant authors ridiculed the Papacy's association of this feast with appeals for Mary's assistance in the struggle against the Turks.[41] The offensiveness of this in their eyes consisted not only in the idea of Marian intercession, but also in its obscuring of the real importance of the Visitation as the moment at which the news of Christ's birth was first spread. Clearly, Transylvania in the 1540s had much need to fear Turkish incursions, and the dangers were seen as so pressing that Honter's reforms included modifications to service times so that parishioners would not need to go out in the hours of darkness and run the risk of Turkish attacks. However, there is no direct evidence that the association between the Visitation and Mary's protection against the Turks was made in Siebenbürgen in the 1540s, and the idea that the scriptural text describing Mary stepping over the mountain indicated that Mary might be beseeched to tread the Turks under her feet was certainly a much less obvious message of the Visitation than the Magnificat.

This difference cannot be explained by any lesser demand for the feast of the Assumption among the rural population of Siebenbürgen than in the countryside around Nuremberg. The feast had a particular significance in incorporating the blessing of the plants, partly to ensure a good crop, but especially to preserve livestock from diseases which were believed to be carried by the plants they ate. The decision not to celebrate a Marian feast on this date may therefore have been due to a desire to strip the blessing of plants of religious sanction. However, it seems likely that the religious significance of

---

[39]   Bridget Heal, 'Images of the Virgin Mary and Marian devotion in Protestant Nuremberg', in Helen Parish and William G. Naphy (eds), *Religion and Superstition in Reformation Europe* (Manchester, 2002), pp. 25–46.

[40]   The *Hauspostille*, compiled by Veit Dietrich from Luther's sermons, prefaces the text for the Assumption with the observation that it is following the usage agreed for Nuremberg. One of the advantages of transposing the Visitation to the Assumption is clear from the text: it allowed the preacher to begin with a condemnation of the Assumption and the associated practice of blessing the plants. Interestingly, the compilers of the 1547 *Reformatio ecclesiarum Saxonicarum* also stipulated that each community should have a copy of Luther's *Hauspostille* and *Kleiner Katechismus*.

[41]   Beth Kreitzer, *Reforming Mary: Changing Images of the Virgin Mary in Lutheran Sermons of the Sixteenth Century* (Oxford, 2004), pp. 61–2, cites examples from the 1570s. Ridicule of this belief can also be found in Luther's (Veit Dietrich's) *Hauspostille* (1544), which points out that the more people pray to the Virgin Mary, the more the Turks advance; WA, 52, p. 682.

Mary's Assumption was more important. In the Siebenbürgen, the problem was not simply its lack of scriptural basis or a reluctance to associate the feast of the Assumption with the Visitation.[42] Rather, it concerned the strength of Marian devotion in late medieval Catholicism in the region, and the role of the Assumption in buttressing those claims.

This extreme sensitivity to Marian devotion in Saxon Lutheranism can also be seen in the justification for churching women after childbirth. The standard Lutheran justification was the Purification of the Virgin Mary, but in the synod of 1557 this explanation is not used. Instead, the practice is explained firstly, and most unusually, by the idea that it is God's wish and command that we, unlike the giants descended from Adam and Eve, should honour our bodies and the bodies of our wives by refraining from sex for a time, and secondly by the need for public thanksgiving for deliverance from dangers of childbirth.[43] Since the Purification of Mary was retained as a feast day in the *Agenda* of 1547, and its scriptural basis was evident, it seems clear that the clergy assembled at the synod of 1557 wanted, as far as possible, to distance churching from any connection with the Virgin Mary. They chose to ground it upon general instructions from God, rather than the particular example of Mary. This was partly to avoid the excesses of Marian devotion, but to do so they buttressed, or rather grounded, an 'anglican' notion of thanksgiving with a strong sense of the ongoing validity of the divine commands of the Old Testament in which God shows man how to improve his conduct in the post-lapsarian world.

A closer look at the paintings of the Honigberg chapel suggests that such conclusions were extensions of pre-Reformation concerns (see Figure 7.4). In common with many other Saxon churches, the five wise and five foolish virgins are depicted on the intrados of the arch to underline the message that salvation depends on the use the individual makes during life of the chance offered by the Passion of Christ. However, this idea does not require fear and apprehension. The artist devotes much more space and attention to the garden of Paradise than to the torments of the damned on the opposite wall. The purpose seems to be to encourage viewers of the prospect of salvation through the sacrifice made by Christ. The possibility of reaching heaven through a virtuous and pure life on earth also refers back to the Marian imagery in the centre of the chapel. Mary's experience may not have been that of all women, but the primary purpose of this painting was not, as it was in Cologne, that viewers should

---

[42]   Saxon pre-Reformation service books provided pericopes for the vigil and feast of both the Visitation and the Assumption, and in contrast to other missals, including the rite of Esztergom, they used the key Visitation text, Luke 1:39, for the feast of the Visitation *and* for the Vigil of the Assumption; Roth, *Die Geschichte des Gottesdienstes der siebenbürgen Sachsen*, pp. 47–51.

[43]   *Urkundenbuch der evangelischen Landeskirche*, vol. 2, p. 6.

learn from it proof of the virgin birth. Instead, the inscription at the base of the Honigberg image of the Immaculate Conception emphasized Mary's kinship with ordinary humanity: '*Sicut spina rosam genuit judea mariam*'. From sinful humanity, symbolized by the thorn and Judea, the emergence of Mary, and thus of virtuous and pure individuals, is possible.

Aspects of pre-Reformation devotion therefore provided a surprising amount of material to encourage a Lutheran emphasis on proper Christian conduct and discipline, even from within what at first sight seems excessively exuberant Marian devotion. Buttressing this was the message of the depiction of the Three Orders illustrating the importance of fulfilling one's social role effectively for the cohesiveness of a Christian society and in the service of Christ. Furthermore, a sense of the need for preparedness and zeal was conveyed by depictions of the virgins in the liminal position of the chancel arch, a point picked up by Honter himself in his *Reformatio Barcensis*. In the preface, he explained the decision to advance the Reformation despite the difficulties in terms of a desire to be among the wise, rather than the foolish, virgins.

Finally, a key to the perplexing combination of this diversity of ritual observance and zeal for discipline may also be provided by one more unusual feature of the Honigberg paintings. In a unique iconographical solution, the east wall Crucifixion is flanked not only by the depiction of the Three Orders, but also by the Pharisee and the Publican. The Pharisee and the Publican offer an even more precise message, and one particularly amenable to a Lutheran interpretation. The Pharisee represents the individual self-confident in his religious status and in the strength of outward acts of religious devotion, while the Publican laments his wretched sinfulness and humbly calls on God for mercy.

In this example, the moralized universes of Catholicism and Protestantism had much in common. As Honter expressed it in 1547: 'Gott fragt mehr nach reinem Herzen denn nach geschliffenen Zungen' ('God cares more about pure hearts than glib tongues'). Similarly, his decision to append the apocryphal prayer of Manasses to the catechism served to cast all members of the congregation in the role of the Publican.[44] The image also offered a pertinent commentary on ritual and adiaphora. Ritual had an unusually strong role to play in the strategies of Saxon marriage discipline, but this was apparently accompanied by a strong concern, evident in the

---

[44]   Ibid., vol. 1, p. 48; Oskar Netoliczka, *Beiträge zur Geschichte des Johannes Honterus und seiner Schriften* (Kronstadt, 1930), p. 59. The Manasses prayer was used by Luther in his early work, *Eine kurz underweisung, wie man beichten soll* (1519), WA, vol. 2, pp. 59–65, but was usually omitted from Lutheran catechisms thereafter. The east central European context is surveyed in Krista Zach, 'Protestant vernacular catechisms and religious reform in sixteenth-century Eastern Europe', in Maria Crăciun, Ovidiu Ghitta and Graeme Murdock (eds), *Confessional Identity in East-Central Europe* (Aldershot, 2002), pp. 49–63.

pre-Reformation Church, that too much confidence should not be placed in the observance of ritual details. The Saxon Church, while aspiring to unity, was guided by the desire to avoid the error of the Pharisee. In this it broadly followed a Lutheran and Melanchthonian interpretation of adiaphora and Christian freedom, which could identify compulsion in such matters with bondage.[45] But, while it increasingly became diplomatic to claim such men as their teachers in order to foster an image of evangelical orthodoxy, such mentors had little concerted influence upon the crucial first phases of the Saxon Reformation. Moreover, in this respect the lessons they taught did not need to be learned. One unusual late fifteenth-century sequence of paintings did not, of course, make a Reformation, but it does provide a striking synthesis of the preoccupations of Saxon Lutherans in Transylvania. This understanding could justify the combination of flexibility in ritual observance and a rigorous concern for discipline, and could be compatible with Lutheran notions of Christian vocation. It encapsulates the importance of re-formation in the shaping of local Lutheran reformations.

Appendix: German, Romanian and Hungarian Forms of Place Names

German	*Romanian*	*Hungarian*
Birthälm	Biertan	Berethalom
Bistritz	Bistriţa	Beszterce
Gran	Strigoniu	Esztergom
Heltau	Cisnădie	Nagydisznód
Hermannstadt	Sibiu	Nagyszeben
Honigberg	Hărman	Szászhermány
Klausenburg	Cluj	Kolozsvár
Kronstadt	Braşov	Brassó
Mediasch	Mediaş	Medgyes
Neustadt	Cristian	Keresztényfalva
Rosenau	Rîşnov	Barca-Rozsinyó
Salzburg	Ocna Sibiului	
Schässburg	Sighişoara	Segesvár
Weidenbach	Ghimbav	
Weissenburg	Alba Iulia	Gyulafehérvár

---

[45] Clyde Manschreck, 'The role of Melanchthon in the Adiaphora controversy', *Archiv für Reformationsgeschichte* 48 (1957): 165–82, provides a useful summary and stresses the similarity between the positions of Luther and Melanchthon.

CHAPTER 8

Kirk in Danger: Presbyterian Political Divinity in Two Eras

Michael F. Graham

How did the early modern clergy react when they thought the Church was in danger? The possible responses were many, and varied depending on the setting. But the self-conscious identification of most protestant clergy with the early Christian Church meant that retreat was rarely their chosen option. Jesus had assured his followers that they were blessed when men reviled them in his name, and this could lead to the paradoxical situation in which attacks on the clergy or the position of the Church only made its adherents more confident that they were in the right. The clergy of Scotland's Reformed Kirk did not hold a monopoly on this attitude, but they certainly provide a prime example of the phenomenon.

I would like to focus on two periods in the history of the Kirk separated by a distance of a century – the 1590s and the 1690s. Both periods began with major triumphs for those activist clergy who saw themselves in the presbyterian vanguard. Both were times in which clergy would lament the apparent reluctance of magistrates to uphold the law fully (although it must be granted that such complaints occurred at other times as well). Most significantly, both periods were marked by a critical phase in which the clergy would test the extent of their influence, forcing secular authorities to demonstrate their commitment to godliness as defined by the presbyterian vanguard. In both cases there was a hostile backlash. Of course, a hundred-year time span does not represent any sort of natural historical cycle, and readers might ask why this chapter will offer no comparison with the revolutionary period 1637–51, which at times saw the presbyterian clergy exerting more influence than ever, before or since, over the political affairs of the Scottish state. The problem is that the revolutionary period was so atypical; the covenanting movement led the British kingdoms into a maelstrom of revolution and civil war through a most peculiar set of historical contingencies, not least of which was an unprecedented degree of aristocratic dissent against the Stewart Crown. While no period in history is really 'typical,' the 1590s and 1690s offer much better benchmarks of how the clergy might function with regards to political authority and the public in non-crisis circumstances.

The comparison throws into relief some of the recurring tendencies in what I would like to call 'presbyterian political divinity' – the sphere of debate in which the clerical leaders of the Kirk sought to influence the policies of the kingdom, injecting a pastoral discourse into the political arena. But it also highlights how much had changed in the century in between, as old threats passed away only to be replaced by new ones. Just as the Kirk of the 1590s saw itself as reviving the Early Church, so the Kirk of the 1690s saw itself as reviving the Kirk of the 1590s. In neither case was the idealized institution well equipped to deal with contemporary challenges. Of course, given the shrill tone of clerical complaint through much of the early modern era, we would be foolish to take ministers' laments at face value; theirs was a rhetoric which stressed danger and pollution even at times when the Kirk seemed to stand on solid footing. Thus, this is a study more of language – particularly language uttered publicly – than of the conditions that this public language claimed to describe.

In hindsight, the early-to-mid 1590s would look to some of Scotland's Reformed clergy like a golden age in their Kirk's history. It was a time of frequent co-operation between the king and leading ministers, despite the misgivings of some of the latter about James VI's alarming closeness to such Catholic courtiers as the Earl of Huntly. Introducing his narrative of 1596, the last chapter in this golden era, David Calderwood, minister of Crailing, famously proclaimed that in that year 'the Kirk of Scotland was now come to her perfectioun, and the greatest puritie that ever she atteaned unto, both in doctrine and discipline, so that her beautie was admirable to forraine kirks'.[1] One can imagine Robert Wodrow, minister of Eastwood and former librarian at the University of Glasgow, nodding in emphatic agreement as he pored over his copies of Calderwood's works just over a century later. For evidence of the brimming confidence of the Kirk's leadership in this period, one need look no further than Andrew Melville's private speech to King James VI at Falkland Palace in 1596, in which Melville, touting the 'Two Kingdoms' theory, tugged on the king's sleeve and reminded him that though he was king of Scots, he was but 'God's sillie vassall' in the divine kingdom, and thus unfit to judge ecclesiastical matters.[2] The king was not pleased, but Melville did not suffer for the comment, or at least not yet. This was a time when a faction of anti-Erastian ministers had the king's ear, and they were not shy about what they said to it.

Several of these ministers had been exiled to England after the suppression of the presbyteries in 1584. But the political tide had turned, they had

---

[1]   David Calderwood, *History of the Kirk of Scotland*, ed. Thomas Thomson (8 vols, Edinburgh, 1842–49), vol. 5, p. 387.

[2]   Ibid., pp. 439–40.

returned, and the presbyteries were revived in 1586. Their influence had grown through the late 1580s, and by the decade's end, they had clearly arrived. In 1589–90, when James sailed to Norway and Denmark to collect his bride, Anna of Denmark, he marked his comfort with the Kirk's strongly presbyterian wing with an extraordinary appointment. He placed the Edinburgh preacher Robert Bruce (a close follower of Andrew Melville but with better family connections) in a quasi-conciliar post, with considerable authority over ecclesiastical affairs and matters of state pertaining to the Kirk, although, wary of the 'Two Kingdoms' idea, Bruce was never listed formally as a privy councillor. While absent, the king wrote several letters to Bruce, and upon James's return, Bruce would serve as leading minister at the new queen's coronation, an occasion for which Melville recited a poem which the king loved so much he wanted it immediately printed. Of course, these ministers had paid for such royal closeness with compromises; the coronation was held on a Sabbath, and Bruce reluctantly agreed to anoint the new queen with oil.[3] Nevertheless, at this point, the king's own religious views seemed consonant with these ministerial connections; a Danish commentator noted that the Scots king showed himself to be 'completely a disciple of Calvin' in his theological discussions with the aged Lutheran theologian Niels Hemmingsen while on his Scandinavian travels.[4] When he returned, he flatteringly addressed the General Assembly meeting in Edinburgh in August 1590, giving thanks to God 'that he was born in such a time, as in the time of the light of Gospell, to such a place to be King, in such a Kirk, the sincerest Kirk in the world'.[5] But the Kirk's leadership could not simply bask in the sunshine of such royal favour. They were accustomed to employing a rhetoric of embattlement, with danger coming from many directions.

One of those directions was southerly. The minister James Melville, addressing the same assembly, spoke of the need to strengthen the apparatus of social discipline: 'For unlesse the Word and sacraments were keeped in Sinceritie, rightlie used and practised by directioun of the discipline, they would soone be corrupted.' But the danger was not just the innate sinfulness of humanity (in this case the Scottish version). Melville also denounced 'these Amaziahs, the bellie-god bishops in England' who (he claimed) were trying to bring the Scots Kirk into conformity with

---

[3] *Register of the Privy Council of Scotland*, 1st series (hereafter RPC), ed. David Masson (11 vols, Edinburgh, 1877–98), vol. 4, pp. 430–31, 481; Lawrence Normand and Gareth Roberts, *Witchcraft in Early Modern Scotland: James VI's Demonology and the North Berwick Witches* (Exeter, 2000), pp. 36–7.

[4] David Stevenson, *Scotland's Last Royal Wedding: The Marriage of James VI and Anne of Denmark. With a Danish Account of the Marriage Translated by Peter Graves* (Edinburgh, 1997), p. 99.

[5] *Acts and Proceedings of the General Assemblies of the Kirk of Scotland*, ed. Thomas Thomson (3 vols, Edinburgh, 1839–45), vol. 2, p. 771.

the ecclesiastical polity of England.[6] A future English bishop (he would attain that status with his elevation to the see of London in 1597), Richard Bancroft, had preached a sermon at Paul's Cross in London early in 1589, in which he had attacked what he saw as Scotland's ministerial tyranny, charging that the leaders of the Kirk had usurped the spiritual authority of the King of Scots and, 'under the pretence of their presbyteries ... trod upon his sceptre'.[7] This drew an outraged response from the Edinburgh presbytery, which commissioned several of its ministers (including Bruce) to write a reply. At the end of the year (and while James was overseas), the presbytery even wrote to Queen Elizabeth herself, asking her to 'tak ordor' with Bancroft for slandering 'the haill Discipline of ye Kirk of Scotland'. Bancroft had also cast aspersions on the king of Scots, accusing James of religious inconstancy, noting the extent to which the king's position on the polity of the Kirk had changed in the previous five years.[8] At this juncture, the leaders of the Kirk were eager to rally round their king, but this would require him to fit their model of a godly prince.

One way in which James did this was by being both a primary target for diabolical sorcery and a righteous judge of Satan's servants, and the ministry was happy to promote him in both of these roles. A series of storms which hampered the royal nuptial voyages to and from Scandinavia were, after the king's return, blamed on black magic cooked up by a group of witches who had allegedly met with the devil in North Berwick's kirk. Among those eventually accused were James's cousin Francis Stewart, earl of Bothwell (acquitted in a high-profile trial in 1593), as well as the relatively prominent Barbara Napier and Euphame Macalzean, daughter of the Laird of Cliftonhall. James participated in some of the interrogations of humbler suspects, and also intervened personally by threatening the assize which tried Napier, after which the assizors changed an acquittal to a conviction on the most serious charge. Public interest in these trials created the opportunity for media manipulation, and ministers were happy to use it in order to help shape the king's image as a godly ruler on the wider British stage.

While James's own *Demonology* was the most famous literary product of his involvement in these trials, its learned tone ensured that it was not the sort of work likely to sway a very large audience in late sixteenth-century Britain. Aimed at a much broader swath of the literate (and

---

[6]   Calderwood, *History*, vol. 5, p. 100; *The Autobiography and Diary of Mr. James Melville*, ed. Robert Pitcairn (Edinburgh, 1842), pp. 280–81.

[7]   Richard Bancroft, *A Sermon Preached at Paul's Cross the 9 of February ... 1588*, (London, 1588/89), pp. 72–4.

[8]   National Archives of Scotland (hereafter NAS) ms CH2/121/1, 29 April, 10 June and 9 December 1589; Gordon Donaldson, *Scottish Church History* (Edinburgh, 1985), p. 175; Stuart Barton Babbage, *Puritanism and Richard Bancroft* (London, 1962), pp. 31–2.

perhaps semi-literate) population was *Newes From Scotland*, a pamphlet of late 1591 which was probably the work of James Carmichael, minister of Haddington, and part of the core ultra-presbyterian party.[9] Carmichael had been among those exiled to England in 1584, but now he was happy to present his king on the side of the saints. In this pamphlet, James appears as a traditional, righteous, king participating in the interrogations of witchcraft suspects out of a concern for justice and to protect his throne and his subjects from Satan's wicked enterprises. Most significantly, he is the devil's great enemy. Carmichael, through the device of the alleged testimony of the convicted witch Agnes Sampson, claimed that the devil 'did inveigh against the king of Scotland' during a witches' sabbath in North Berwick Kirk, and when asked by the witches 'why he did bear such hatred to the king [the devil] answered, by reason the king is the greatest enemy he hath in the world'. Sampson is presented as explaining that the king would have died from the witches' various maleficia 'if his faith had not prevailed above their intentions'.[10] In concluding the pamphlet, Carmichael noted that some readers might marvel at the king's putting himself in danger through his personal involvement in the examination of 'such notorious witches', which required him to spend a lot of time in their presence:

> But to answer generally to such, let this suffice: that first, it is well known that the king is the child and servant of God, and they but servants to the Devil; he is the lord's anointed, and they but vessels of God's wrath; he is a true Christian and trusteth in God, they worse than infidels, for they only trust in the devil who daily serves them till he have brought them to utter destruction. But hereby it seemeth that his Highness carried a magnanimous and undaunted mind not feared with their enchantments but resolute in this: that so long as God is with him, he feareth not who is against him.[11]

The justiciary court records of Sampson's examinations, confession and trial have survived. Significantly for our purposes, while they mention conversations with the devil regarding whether the king would return safely to Scotland (the devil said he would) and whether he would have children (yes – boys and then girls), they offer no particular motivation for the devil wanting him dead.[12] Thus, the diabolical motives were added to the pamphlet by Carmichael. This was political spin worthy of that genre's more recent practitioners, particularly in that the pamphlet was

---

[9]   The case for Carmichael's authorship is made in Normand and Roberts, *Witchcraft*, pp. 291–3.

[10]   *Newes From Scotland*, version in Normand and Roberts, *Witchcraft*, pp. 315–17.

[11]   Ibid., pp. 323–4.

[12]   NAS mss JC2/2, fols 201–6; JC26/2/4; JC26/2/12–13; printed in Normand and Roberts, *Witchcraft*, pp. 135–49, 154–7, 231–46.

printed and sold in London, giving English readers a chance to size up their prospective future king.

But this was not cynical manipulation of public opinion; Carmichael and his colleagues saw diabolism as a serious threat and an obstacle to their efforts at godly reformation, and his subsequent penning of *Demonology* suggests that the king was equally concerned. Unlike in the 1690s, there was no perceived need to convince the public of the reality of the threat; the dangers of witchcraft were widely accepted. Both parties (king and ministers) were also seriously concerned about the centrifugal (and violent) tendencies of aristocratic insurrection, as represented by Bothwell, the archetypal loose cannon, with a pedigree dangerously close to the king's own. But Bothwell generally presented himself as protestant. To the ministers it seemed that the king practised a double standard. James was much slower to confront the threat of Catholic courtiers such as Huntly, despite what seemed obvious treason in Huntly's dealings with Philip II of Spain.

This concern about religious backsliding certainly pre-dated James's wedding voyage. Back in August 1588, fearing an imminent attack from the Spanish Armada, the General Assembly proclaimed an emergency fast and ordered the Edinburgh Presbytery to take action against Catholics and 'apostates' frequently at court, particularly Huntly, Lord Seton and Sir John Chisholm.[13] Even earlier, fear of the young king's association with his Catholic cousin Esme Stuart, duke of Lennox, had led to the drafting of the 'Negative Confession' in 1581, an anti-papal diatribe subscribed by noblemen and courtiers. But it seemed to the leading presbyterian clergy in the late 1580s and early 1590s that this battle against Catholicism would not stay won. In March 1589, preaching a sermon in the king's presence on Isaiah 38, in which the prophet told King Hezekiah to put his house in order in preparation for death (a death which, it turned out, was postponed), Robert Bruce asserted:

> praised be the living God, our king is not diseased, but surely his country is heavily diseased; for so long as Papists and Papistrie remain in it, so long as thir pestilent men remain in it, and so long as thir floods of iniquitie quhilk flows from the great men remains, there is a heavy judgement hanging over this country ....

A month earlier, Bruce had likewise attacked 'that idolatrous doctrine' of the mass, lamenting that 'our haill youth (for the maist part) are

---

13   NAS ms CH2/121/1, fol. 47r; *Acts and Proceedings of the General Assemblies*, vol. 2, pp. 730, 738; Calderwood, *History*, vol. 4, pp. 682–3, 691. The General Assembly subsequently proclaimed a fast in thanksgiving for the failure of the Armada. See ibid., p. 696.

given to it'.[14] These published sermons, like proclamations of fasts, were interventions into what passed for the public sphere in late sixteenth-century Edinburgh. Their audience was not likely to be as broad as that for Carmichael's pamphlet (these two sermons were bundled up with nine others and offered in a 384-page collection in 1591), but they were a ministerial effort to influence public (and court) opinion nevertheless.[15]

The ministers also worked through more traditional channels. A July 1591 petition to the king from the General Assembly called for stricter enforcement of laws against Jesuits, idolaters and participants in pilgrimages (a vestigial Catholic practice), as well as excommunicants and Sabbath-breakers.[16] Interestingly, it made no mention of the sexual sins which previously seem to have been such an obsession of the Kirk. The parliament of 1592, meeting in the aftermath of the slaughter of the 'Bonnie' earl of Moray by Huntly and his retainers, brought a legislative victory for the ministers, with statutory recognition for the Kirk's presbyterian structure, and the reconfirmation of earlier laws against Jesuits and missionary priests. The king, seeking treason proceedings against Bothwell while at the same time trying to mollify Huntly's enemies, was again conciliatory, and support for the Kirk among the assembled members of parliament appears to have been strong.[17] A convention of ministers held in Edinburgh late in 1592 concluded that the Kirk faced four major threats, headed by domestic and foreign conspiracies to 'execut that blodie decrie of the Counsall of Trent against all that trewlie profes the Relligioun of Chryst'. The other three dangers were a lack of ministers and money to pay them, 'a fearfull defection' to Catholicism, particularly among the nobility, and a general disorder in society.[18] The General Assembly of April 1593 threatened to excommunicate Scots who travelled to Spain for any reason, until the king could get a guarantee from the Spanish monarchy that his subjects would not be troubled for their religious beliefs.[19] Traffic with Spain was particularly suspect in the Kirk's eyes, not only because of the failed Armada, but also because of the Spanish intrigues of the earls of Huntly and Errol.

---

[14]   *Sermons of Robert Bruce*, ed. William Cunningham (Edinburgh, 1843), pp. 113, 171.

[15]   Robert Bruce, *Sermons preached in the Kirk of Edinburgh, by M. Robert Bruce, minister of Christs evangel there* (Edinburgh, 1591), STC 3923.

[16]   *Acts and Proceedings of the General Assemblies*, vol. 2, p. 784; Calderwood, *History*, vol. 5, pp. 134–5.

[17]   Alan R. MacDonald, 'The Parliament of 1592: A Crisis Averted?', in *Parliament and Politics in Scotland, 1567–70*, ed. Keith Brown and Alastair Mann (Edinburgh, 2005), pp. 57–81.

[18]   *Autobiography and Diary of Mr. James Melville*, pp. 299–300.

[19]   *Acts and Proceedings of the General Assemblies*, vol. 3, pp. 799–800.

The language of purity the Kirk had previously invoked to condemn sexual sins was now employed in the service of religious orthodoxy. The very Melvillian Synod of Fife in September 1593 lamented that, along with suffering from the actions of rebellious Catholic noblemen, 'the land [was] defiled in diverse places with the devilish and blasphemous masse'.[20] The nature of ministerial rhetoric was to offer repeated jeremiads on those issues where the Kirk was meeting resistance. Since the English attack from critics like Bancroft had been blunted, and the king became an enthusiastic partner in the witch-hunt, those topics became less prominent in presbyterian political divinity, and could be put in the victory column. But James's general hesitancy to go after Huntly et al., save for a brief (and inconclusive) military foray to Aberdeen (on which Andrew and James Melville accompanied the king) in 1594, followed by a very brief period in exile for Huntly and his allies, caused the ministers no end of public frustration, and made Catholicism their leading public concern in the mid-1590s.[21] This put them on a collision course with the king, who felt that excommunications of leading courtiers (and friends) were an effort to prevent him from freely choosing his own companions. A rhetoric which castigated courtly Catholicism could at times sound like a general critique of nobility, and criticism of seeming royal connivance in apostasy could, in the right (or wrong) hands, turn into a general attack on monarchy. That particular gauntlet was tossed in Holy Trinity Kirk, St Andrews, by the minister, David Black.

Black had been appointed to the post at Holy Trinity in 1590, and can be regarded as a poster child for the more extreme brand of presbyterian political divinity. He had already distinguished himself by going on strike in 1592, claiming his congregation was disrespectful of his ministry and was refusing to hire a fellow minister (it eventually came through on that score), and by admitting to his own presbytery that he had called some of his ministerial colleagues 'pynt aill ministeris, bellie fallowis, cycophantis, gentillmenis ministereis, leiders of the pepill to hell, and that a gritt pert of them war worthie to be hangit'.[22] One of his presbyterial enemies began taking notes on Black's sermons, so that by late in 1596, reports had reached the privy council of his highly politicized pastoral rhetoric. It touched upon several hot-button issues, not just in Scottish politics, but in the wider British polity as well. In so doing, it set off the chain of events that brought the Melvillian golden age of the early 1590s to an end.

---

[20]   Calderwood, *History*, vol. 5, pp. 263–8.

[21]   For the military campaign of 1594, see Keith Brown, *Bloodfeud in Scotland 1573–1625: Violence, Justice and Politics in an Early Modern Society* (Edinburgh, 1986), pp. 168–9; Calderwood, *History*, vol. 5, pp. 354–5; *Autobiography and Diary of Mr. James Melville*, pp. 318–22.

[22]   St Andrews University Muniments (hereafter StAUM) ms deposit 23, 9 October 1595.

Black had apparently started with the issue of the Catholic earls that so vexed the presbyterian vanguard. He charged that they had returned home with the king's 'knaulege and consent ... quhairby ... the treachery of the Kingis harte was detected'. This may have been sedition enough, but Black did not stop there. He also allegedly opined 'that all Kingis wer the devillis childrene, the devill wes in the courte, in the gudaris of the courte and in the heid of the courte'. This was far removed from Carmichael, in 1591, labelling James as Satan's greatest enemy. Black attacked the Scots nobility as 'degenerate, godles, dissemblaris, enemeyis to the Kirk' and branded members of the privy council as 'atheists'. Even more controversially, he applied the same label to the queen of England. This threatened an international incident, particularly since the matter came before the privy council the same week that James's daughter was baptized as Elizabeth, with the English ambassador Sir Robert Bowes standing in as proxy for Queen Elizabeth, the child's godmother. With his eye on the English succession, James could not allow this to pass. Black's case would test the balance of power within Scots ecclesiastical politics – specifically the question of whether ministerial speech from the pulpit was protected from state interference. How freely could presbyterian political divinity operate?[23]

Leading clergymen (including the Melvilles and Carmichael) convened in Edinburgh to support Black's claims, and were consequently banished from the capital by royal decree on 24 November, ostensibly because they were neglecting their parishes. Appearing before the privy council six days later, Black (assisted in his defence by the ministers Robert Bruce and Robert Pont) insisted that only his fellow ministers from the St Andrews presbytery could judge statements he had made from the pulpit. The council disagreed, ruling that it was competent to judge the matter, and banished Black north of the Tay. But the ministers of Edinburgh, including Bruce and Walter Balcanquhall, 'with manie uther impatient choleric preachers', according to one observer, used their pulpits to attack the judgment against Black and its authors. Balcanquhall had angered the king while the 1592 parliament had been sitting with his defence of Old Testament-style prophetic preaching and its criticism of rulers, although the matter had been smoothed over at the time, with minimal damage to the alliance between Kirk and Crown which then prevailed.[24] But attitudes had hardened in the mean time, and now Balcanquhall, Bruce and Black's other defenders found aristocratic allies in a political faction which opposed

---

[23]   Details of Black's case and its repercussions can be found in *RPC*, vol. 5, pp. 334–6, 344–9, 362–3; *The Warrender Papers*, ed. Annie I. Cameron (2 vols, Edinburgh, 1931–32), vol. 2, pp. 418–26; Calderwood, *History*, vol. 5, pp. 466–526; *Autobiography and Diary of Mr. James Melville*, pp. 374, 384–5.

[24]   MacDonald, 'The Parliament of 1592', pp. 69–71.

the influence of the Octavians – a group of privy councillors who had taken over the administration of royal finance. One of the Octavians was Thomas Hamilton (later earl of Haddington), the king's advocate, who had prosecuted the case against Black before the privy council. Matters came to a head on Friday 17 December after a sermon by Balcanquhall, in which he allegedly 'adminat[ed] the barrons to follow the futsteppis of thair fathers'. While accounts differ on the particulars of what happened immediately afterward, and the extent to which Balcanquhall and Bruce were actually trying to stir up the populace, all sources agree that this clerical discontent led to a riot which spilled out of St Giles Kirk and into Edinburgh's High Street, with the mob seeking to lay hands on Hamilton and three of his colleagues, while the king and several privy councillors were forced to hole up in the tolbooth for fear of the tumult outside. Order was restored by the provost and bailies, and King James and his councillors were eventually able to walk down to Holyrood Palace, but the king was now more determined than ever to rein in the independent-minded clergy. He had had quite enough of presbyterian political divinity. The ministers of Edinburgh were ordered into ward, but fled the town instead. They would later be reinstated, but their party's influence within the Kirk was gradually marginalized as James began to assert ecclesiastical control, starting with the imposition of an oath on all clergy that he was the supreme judge in all matters of sedition or treason, including speeches from the pulpit, and continuing with the General Assembly at Perth in February/March 1597. The ecclesiastical policies of the Stewart crown in Scotland would be increasingly Erastian and Episcopalian from this point until 1637.

Obviously, this policy shift was not the result of one riot, but rather a response to a number of issues which had been building over the previous decade or more. The Black case and the related riot merely determined the timing. Nor was the Kirk the united institution implied by the rhetoric of ministers like Bruce and the Melvilles (and echoed by Calderwood). But one important way its more politicized leaders had sought to impose unity in both Kirk and state was through an early version of covenanting.

In James's own recollections of the 17 December riot, he claimed that its ringleaders 'provokit and steirit up the commoun peoplill to tak armes, eftir joyning of handis to mantene thair caus aganis all sortis and degreis of personis without exceptioun'.[25] This language echoes the Scots tradition of the band, first introduced in the Reformation context by the Lords of the Congregation in 1557 and reiterated with the 'Negative Confession' sworn by leading courtiers in 1581. The Negative Confession was also attached to a general band to maintain religion sworn by noblemen in 1590, and one of the features of the fully mature presbyterianism that James Melville

---

[25]　*RPC*, vol. 5, p. 363.

saw as coming of age in 1596 was the swearing of a covenant that summer, in theory by all landholders. It was solemnized in St Andrews by a special Communion celebration on the first Sunday in September.[26] These social contracts, originally the preserve of noblemen and their clients, had become spiritualized, and were now becoming popularized in what Arthur Williamson has called 'a species of revivalism,' arguing that from 1596 onward, 'a national covenant was ... firmly fixed in Scottish thinking as a feature of popular piety', although David Mullan has recently downplayed any political aspects of the covenant of 1596.[27] Nevertheless, the promotion of covenants by ministers like the Melvilles, Carmichael and Bruce have to be regarded as another important form of presbyterian political divinity. A covenant, binding its adherents to God and to each other, could be a rallying tool as well as a loyalty test.

Covenanting marked the Scottish contribution to what Alan MacInnes has labelled the 'British Revolution' of 1638–60, and it would be a consistent feature of opposition to Stewart religious policies in the Restoration era. As MacInnes has observed: 'the religious covenant was a tripartite compact between the king, the people and God to uphold religious purity in which the Israelites were replaced by the Scots in the role of chosen people'.[28] And while the heavy noble participation in the National Covenant of 1638 might seem to undermine some of MacInnes's claims for its revolutionary nature, there is no mistaking who saw themselves in the role of Hebrew prophets – the Reformed clergy, through the practice of presbyterian political divinity.

One could say that after all the turmoil and bloodshed of the seventeenth century, the covenanted vision of Scotland won out with the Williamite revolution of 1688–89, since, among other things, the settlement following William's acceptance of the Scottish crown abolished episcopacy, a system of Church government which the Stewart Crown had been promoting since 1596. Thus, in large measure, the Reformed polity of the Melvilles, Bruce, Carmichael, Calderwood and the covenants had been vindicated. Viewed that way, the 1690s should have been a golden era in the eyes of ministers who saw themselves as part of that particular godly heritage. Nevertheless, in the grand tradition of presbyterian political divinity, they found plenty to be grumpy about. But the nature of that discontent had changed fundamentally, due to the political and intellectual upheavals of the seventeenth century. Try as they would have liked, the Scots Reformed

---

[26]   StAUM ms deposit 23, 22 July 1596; *Autobiography and Diary of Mr. James Melville*, pp. 353–7.

[27]   Arthur Williamson, *Scottish National Consciousness in the Age of James VI* (Edinburgh, 1979), p. 74; David Mullan, *Scottish Puritanism 1590–1638* (Oxford, 2000), pp. 191–3.

[28]   Allan MacInnes, *The British Revolution, 1629–1660* (New York, 2005), pp. 115–16.

clergy of the 1690s could not turn the clock back to the glorious summer of 1596. While their spiritual forbears had worried about religious contamination coming from England, the British nature of the Revolution Settlement meant that certain English voices now had to be attended to, and the continuing integration of the British book trade increased the audience some of those voices might reach.

Those who now comprised the political nation, having thrown off the yoke of Restoration Episcopacy, faced several related questions. First and foremost, how far should they push their victory? At what point (if ever) should those who had been involved in the now-reviled Restoration governments be brought back into any positions of authority? A parallel and inextricably linked debate was going on within the Presbyterian Kirk, which now once again dominated national religious life, but which would face a serious manpower shortage if, as many of its leaders insisted it should, it were to refuse the services of parish ministers who had conformed under Episcopacy. The issue of the Episcopal clergy was complicated by relations with England, whose Anglican religious establishment viewed the Scots Episcopal clergy as co-religionists who ought at least to be tolerated, and preferably employed as well, north of the border. The ongoing hard-core Presbyterian refusal to make concessions to Episcopalians was answered by Englishmen of High Church inclinations with a refusal to countenance protestant dissent in England (as English protestant dissenters included Presbyterians).[29] Once again, presbyterian political divinity imperilled relations with England. For most Scots Presbyterian clergy, Episcopacy was danger enough. But there were other threats: vestigial Catholicism, the new scourge of Quakerism, and even more dangerously, a new philosophical threat from Scotland's southern neighbour, Deism.

At the beginning of 1695, the management of Scottish affairs was in the hands of a group centred around John Hay, marquis of Tweeddale, a religious and political moderate who was well connected with leading political figures in England.[30] Tweeddale was Lord High Chancellor, giving him an important voice on the privy council and the critical ceremonial position of representing the king at the Scottish Parliament, which William never attended. The firmly presbyterian earl of Melville was Lord Privy Seal, while the key legal positions of Lord Justice Clerk and Lord Advocate were filled by Adam Cockburn of Ormiston and Sir James Stewart of Goodtrees respectively. Both had strong presbyterian credentials. In Whitehall, Scottish affairs were nominally under the direction of Willem de Bentinck, earl of Portland, but he, like the king, was hampered by the

---

[29]   Craig Rose, *England in the 1690s: Revolution, Religion and War* (Oxford, 1999), pp. 214–15.
[30]   P.W.J. Riley, *King William and the Scottish Politicians* (Edinburgh, 1979), p. 54.

fact that he was Dutch. So the king's (and Portland's) real advisers on Scotland were William Carstares, the king's Scottish chaplain, and the two Scottish secretaries, James Johnston and Sir John Dalrymple, master of Stair. Carstares was a minister of covenanting heritage – his father had been forfeited after the Pentland Rising of 1666, and Carstares himself had been tortured with thumbscrews in 1684 for his suspected knowledge of the Rye House Plot.[31] Johnston was the son of Archibald Johnston of Wariston, and had grown up in exile in Holland, giving him impeccable presbyterian/revolutionary credentials.[32] Dalrymple of Stair's commitment was a bit tarnished – he had served in the government of James VII while his own father was in exile in Holland – but he would be forced out of office early in 1696, ostensibly due to his bureaucratic role in the slaughter of the MacDonalds of Glencoe in 1692.[33]

Since the General Assembly of the Kirk was not a source of revenue, the king did not allow it to meet as often, or for as long, as Parliament. William was frustrated (and the bishops of England offended) by the assembly's reluctance to make peace with clergy who had conformed under episcopacy, and if the presbyterian ministry were not going to co-operate on that point, he preferred that their meetings be brief and infrequent. An assembly in early 1692 had been cut short, and a subsequent assembly had been postponed twice before it was finally allowed to convene at the end of March 1694.[34] This assembly at least appointed a committee to review applications from former episcopal clergy north of the Tay, but the king would have preferred much more. It also passed an act 'against Profaneness' which lamented the dishonouring of God 'by the impiety and profaneness that aboundeth in this nation'. As manifestations of these, the ministers listed many of the ills that had been denounced in General Assembly pronouncements dating back to the sixteenth century: swearing, cursing, Sabbath breach, fornication, adultery and drunkenness. But there were some new elements as well, such as the 'mocking of piety and religious exercises' and 'blasphemy'. The act urged ministers to 'preach plainly and faithfully against these vices' and warn listeners of the judgements threatened by God against their practitioners. Church courts were told to take action against offenders and urge magistrates to enforce relevant acts of Parliament.[35]

This was far from being the first mention of blasphemy, either in the records of the General Assembly or, for that matter, in parliamentary

---

[31] A. Ian Dunlop, *William Carstares and the Kirk By Law Established* (Edinburgh, 1967), pp. 18–21, 35–6, 42–7, 59–60.

[32] Riley, *King William*, pp. 60–61.

[33] Ibid., pp. 75, 94–7.

[34] *Acts of the General Assembly of the Church of Scotland, 1638–1842*, ed. Thomas Pitcairn (Edinburgh, 1843), vol. 1, p. 235.

[35] Ibid., p. 241.

legislation. It had occasionally come up, in the sense of 'swearing' or 'cursing', in both, dating back to the sixteenth century, and parliamentary statutes had mandated fines for the offence.[36] But in the later seventeenth century, the word had taken on a more specific – and more sinister – meaning. Rather than indicating a looseness of speech which might suggest an overly casual or disrespectful attitude toward the sacred, it now meant a conscious attack on fundamental tenets of Christianity. This was clear in an Act of Parliament passed in 1661, which stated:

> Considering that hitherto ther hath been no law in this Kingdom against the horrible cryme of blasphemy ... whosoever heirafter not being distracted in his wits shall raill upon or curse God or any of the persones of the blessed Trinity, shall be processed befor the Chieff Justice; and being fund guilty shall be punished with death.

The same was to hold for anyone who 'shall deny God or any of the persons of the blessed Trinity and obstinately continew therin'.[37] This law was made retroactive to February 1649 (and indeed was a restatement of an Act passed by the parliament which had met that year, but which was not regarded as legitimate after the Restoration). It was little used, however. A woman in Dumfries who reportedly drank to the devil's health was acquitted of blasphemy (although fined 500 merks) in 1671.[38] Ten years later, Francis Borthwick, a laird's son who converted to Judaism and underwent circumcision while abroad, was outlawed after fleeing rather than appearing for trial on a blasphemy charge.[39] The law then fell into disuse. So when the General Assembly of 1694 called for ministers and magistrates to take action against blasphemy, this was presumably the sort of blasphemy, and the parliamentary statute, that members had in mind.

King William was not unsympathetic. While he had a reputation for tolerance, neither he nor any other ruler, then or now, really wanted to appear to be a *defender* of blasphemy. It also seems likely that a minister like Carstares would have suggested to him that the General Assembly would be more sympathetic to his goals regarding the displaced episcopal ministers if the king seemed willing to take a more aggressive line with other ills perceived by the 'high presbyterians'. Even Johnston, though he later was to claim that the 1695 blasphemy statute was 'obtained by trick and surprise', wanted to get concessions from the presbyterian ministry,

---

[36] For example, in 1551 (*Acts of the Parliaments of Scotland*, vol. 2, p. 485), 1581 (under which a fourth-time utterer of 'abhominabill aithis' might be warded for a year, *APS*, vol. 3, p. 212), 1645 (*APS*, vol. 6, part i, p. 458).

[37] *APS*, vol. 7, pp. 202–3.

[38] George MacKenzie, *The Laws and Customs of Scotland in Matters Criminal* (Edinburgh, 1678), p. 28.

[39] NAS mss JC 2/15, fols 339v–340r, JC 6/10, fol. 314r; Hugo Arnot, *A Collection and Abridgement of Celebrated Criminal Trials in Scotland, 1536–1784* (Glasgow, 1812), pp. 363–4.

since he had promised Thomas Tenison, the archbishop of Canterbury, that he would do something to ease the lot of the unemployed episcopalians.[40] These considerations were incorporated into the instructions sent from the king, via Johnston, to Tweeddale on what was wanted from the parliament scheduled to convene in May 1695.[41] First and foremost, Tweeddale was to obtain all necessary supplies for standing forces, and get additional money to buy and maintain frigates for as long as the war against France lasted. After this, he could turn to the issue of the displaced episcopalians, 'to get such Acts past, as shall tend to the composing [of] differences about Church matters and amongst Church men', setting a new deadline for the ousted ministers to take oaths of allegiance. After these three top items came a long list of acts the king wanted passed – 25 in all – presumably in descending order of importance. Twenty-first on the list was the instruction 'to pass an Act for Reviving old lawes and to consent to new ones for Punishing and discouraging all Prophaneness and irreligion'. Certainly, 'prophaneness and irreligion' could run the gamut from dancing or playing golf on the Sabbath to apostasy or philosophical atheism. Johnston may have envisioned a legislative crackdown on items at the former end of the scale. Tweeddale was given additional 'secret instructions', and these, perhaps better reflecting the king's true priorities, did not mention any legislation relating to religious issues at all.[42] Meanwhile, rumours were circulating in Edinburgh that parliament would gather and then swiftly be dissolved to allow new elections which might yield a majority in favour of episcopacy. While there is no evidence in official correspondence of such a plan, the rumour, which the devout presbyterian laird George Home noted in his diary, suggests the extent to which those who remained committed to the covenanting legacy still felt embattled.[43]

As the parliament began to meet, the presbyterian ministers did their best to organize a lobbying campaign. The first sitting of the parliament was on 9 May. Johnston himself had come from Whitehall to assist Tweeddale with parliamentary management.[44] Meanwhile, a small group of ministers from all over the kingdom, but dominated by those from Edinburgh, began meeting, sending delegations to visit Tweeddale, Johnston, the

---

[40]   James Johnston to John Locke, 27 February 1697, *The Correspondence of John Locke*, ed. E.S. De Beer (8 vols, Oxford, 1976–89), vol. 6, pp. 17–19; Riley, *King William and the Scottish Politicians*, p. 82.

[41]   NAS ms SP 4/18, fols 11–14.

[42]   Ibid., fols 15–16.

[43]   *An Album of Scottish Families 1694–96, Being the First Installment of George Home's Diary*, ed. Helen and Keith Kelsall (Aberdeen, 1990) p. 56.

[44]   Tweeddale to James Johnston, 7 May 1695, National Library of Scotland (hereafter NLS) ms 7029, fols 27v–28r; Tweeddale to Alexander Johnston, 11 May 1695, NLS ms 7029, fol. 30v.

Lord Advocate and the Justice Clerk.[45] The ministers were also preparing their own address to Parliament, and apparently sharing drafts of this document with the officials they met. Johnston for one thought the ministers' list of concerns was too long. They tried several times to get him to comment and he put them off; he finally told the ministers George Meldrum, William Crichton and George Hamilton on 27 May that the list 'should be contracted as much as possible, y[ai]r being laws already for many of yese things in ye paper'.[46] The grievances were distilled into seven items during the next three days and then published.[47] All but one of the items warned of the dangers posed by episcopal clergy, seen as a threat to doctrine, discipline and the patrimony of the Kirk. Only the first item seems independent of this fixation on the dangers of incorporating the outed ministers. It warned that:

> notwithstanding of many good and excellent laws made against Prophanity of all sorts, yet all kind of Wickedness doth exceedingly abound, especially cursing, and swearing, Sabbath breaking, Drunkenness, Uncleaness, &c. And in all appearance will more and more encrease, unless some method be fallen on for a vigorous Execution of those Laws.

Given what we know of Johnston's goals, it is not hard to see why he had been unimpressed with this address. More significantly for our purposes, 'blasphemy' seems to have dropped out of the catalogue of dangers since the General Assembly of 1694. Perhaps it had been taken out in response to Johnston's concern for brevity; there was, after all, already a law against it on the books. But some time in the next few weeks it would return to the catalogue. The ministers' address was referred to the parliament's Security Committee.

The ministers also employed sermons in their campaign. Published sermons would often note the audience, so as to inform future readers who did, and who did not, pay attention. David Williamson, minister of Edinburgh's West Kirk, preached one on 9 June before Tweeddale and other high officials, using the text Isaiah 38:3, in which Hezekiah wept in fear of his impending death (the same text Bruce had used for the sermon of March 1589 cited earlier).[48] Williamson warned that all people, even powerful men such as those in his audience, would eventually face death, and they must prepare themselves by glorifying God, studying scripture, taking account of their own behaviour, and carrying out their public

---

[45]   NAS ms CH1/2/2a, fols 1–5; NLS ms 9251, fol. 107.
[46]   NAS ms CH1/2/2a, fol. 2v.
[47]   *The Humble Representation of the Ministers from the Synods and Presbytries of this Church, Met at Edinburgh, May 30 1695 Years* (Edinburgh, 1695).
[48]   David Williamson, *A Sermon Preached in the High Church of Edinburgh, June 9th 1695* (Edinburgh, 1696).

responsibilities. In a passage which offers a milder echo of David Black's prophetic preaching in 1596, he asked (and warned):

> How many of all Ranks, walks in Drunkenness, Lying, Swearing, whordom [sic], sabbath-breaking, Living a Prayerless Life bringing forth the Fruits of Atheism, which excludes People out of Heaven and brings on the Wrath of GOD ... I am afraid there is a storm of Wrath and Vengeance coming on the land, if matters mend not.[49]

Later, Williamson seemed to reinforce the address of the ministers and their fears of the episcopal clergy, but linked those with the old Covenanter scourge of innovation and the new fear of atheism. Here perhaps we see a fuller, unedited version of the address:

> Many of them [episcopal clergy] who refuse to own the Government of Kirk and State, take on them[selves] to preach Irregularly, Baptize Children, and even of scandalous persons, without regard to the removing of the Scandal; and marry persons clandestinely without Knowledge or consent of Parents. Who are secure of their Children at this rate? ... Some of them have likeways brought in *innovations* in Worship, never used under any Government of Protestants in Scotland ... from all which flows and abounds Prophaness, Irreligion and Atheism, notwithstanding of all the excellent Laws made against them.[50]

Admittedly, 'atheism' was a term used rather indiscriminately in the seventeenth century.[51] Like 'blasphemy', it could cover a multitude of sins or unacceptable beliefs or declarations. But the two (as well as the relatively new term 'deism') would be linked in the case of Thomas Aikenhead, the sometime student at Edinburgh's town college who was hanged for blasphemy in January 1697.[52] Whether or not Johnston's concerns led to the omission of any of these terms from the ministers' address, they were now creeping back onto the agenda. But in the mean time, the interests of the political nation would be distracted by the Glencoe inquiry, and a new blasphemy statute was passed in late June 1695 with, it would appear, little debate or comment – hence Johnston's claim that it passed by 'trick and surprise'.

The passage of that statute, and increasingly shrill cries for its enforcement (although Aikenhead would actually be convicted under the 1661 statute), reflect the growing sense of insecurity felt by this strongly presbyterian nexus of ministers and magistrates. Some of that was probably

---

[49]   Ibid., p. 35.
[50]   Ibid., pp. 50–51.
[51]   Michael Hunter, 'The Problem of "Atheism" in Early Modern England', *Transactions of the Royal Historical Society*, 5th series, 35 (1985): 135–57, at p. 142; David Wooton, 'New Histories of Atheism', in Michael Hunter and David Wooton (eds), *Atheism from the Reformation to the Enlightenment* (Oxford, 1992), pp. 13–53, at pp. 24–6.
[52]   While Hunter has traced the first use of the word 'deist' to the 1590s, it was not much in use until the late seventeenth century. See Hunter, 'Problem of Atheism', p. 156.

due to the obvious signs of God's displeasure seen in the long famine Scotland was experiencing, and the recurrent fears of a French invasion in 1696. Williamson's dire prophecies seemed to be coming true. But there was also a strong sense that a tide of religious scepticism was flowing north from Scotland's more powerful partner in the Union of Crowns. In January 1696, another General Assembly would pass an Act 'against the Atheistical Opinions of the Deists', claiming that 'in many places, not a few, of Atheistical principles, who go under the name of Deists, and for the time refuse the odious character of Atheist, maintain and disseminate pernicious principles tending to Scepticism and Atheism'.[53] These ministers wanted the law enforced, and sensed in magistrates a reluctance to do so.

A poorly attended parliament in October 1696, meeting under the shadow of a serious harvest failure, passed another Act against 'profaneness,' which lamented the 'mocking [of] and reproaching Religion and the exercises therof', and urged the privy council specifically to enforce the laws against such things.[54] This resulted almost immediately in the questioning before the council of the bookkeeper John Fraser, who made indiscreet references to the *Oracles of Reason* by the English deist Charles Blount in discussing a sermon with his landlord and landlady. While charged with blasphemy, Fraser was spared the harsher penalties under the law. He was imprisoned for several months and trotted out to perform public repentance in various kirks for his fault. But his case reminded the authorities in Kirk and state that deist books were circulating in Edinburgh (England's licensing Act, which had helped police the print trade, had lapsed the year before).[55] After ruling on the Fraser case, the privy council appointed a three-man committee, including the high presbyterian ministers James Webster and Gilbert Rule, to search local bookshops for heterodox books, and ordered booksellers to turn in catalogues of books they were offering for sale. News of this dragnet even reached London newspapers.[56] None of these inventories has survived, but there is certainly evidence for the existence of such books in Edinburgh's libraries. For example, the library at Edinburgh's town college in 1695 bought copies of Blount's *The First Two Books of Philostratus, Concerning the Life of Apollonius Tyaneus* (1680), which offered in its account of Apollonius of Tyana (c. 3–97 AD) an alternative to Jesus as saviour, and John Toland's *Christianity Not Mysterious*, which

---

[53]   *Acts of the General Assembly*, vol. 1, p. 253.
[54]   *APS*, vol. 10, pp. 14, 47, 65–6.
[55]   Michael Treadwell, 'The Stationers and the Printing Acts at the End of the Seventeenth Century', in *The Cambridge History of the Book in England*, ed. John Barnard and D.F. McKenzie (4 vols, Cambridge, 1998–2002), vol. 4, pp. 755–76.
[56]   NAS mss PC 1/50, fols 473v–474r; PC 1/51, fols 13r–14v, 16r; PC 4/2, fols 18r, 29r; *Protestant Mercury* 101 (26 October 1696).

had just been published with great controversy.[57] Ministers were worried, and not without reason, about the availability of unorthodox ideas in God's most covenanted kingdom. Thomas Aikenhead would feel the hangman's noose after accusations from his fellow students that he scoffed at scripture, called Jesus and Moses magicians, and ridiculed the concept of the Trinity brought him before the privy council and then the High Court of Justiciary in the wake of the Fraser case.

The problem was not just that adventurous readers were soaking up (and discussing) heterodox ideas. Ministers now lamented a general scepticism, and it was not confined to the fashionable wits of town and gown. Alexander Telfair, a minister from Kirkcudbrightshire aimed for a less sophisticated audience with his *True Relation of an Apparition*, a cheap pamphlet published in 1696, which detailed the haunting of a house in his parish. Writing his preface in December 1695, perhaps shortly before heading off to the General Assembly which would warn of the dangers of deism, Telfair noted the need for:

> the conviction and confutation of that prevailing spirit of Atheism and Infidelity in our time, denying both in Opinion and Practice the Existence of Spirits, either of God or Devils; and consequently a Heaven and Hell; and imputing the voices, Apparitions and Actings of Good, or Evil Spirits, to the Melancholick Disturbance or Distemper of the Brains and Fancies of those who pretend to hear, see or feel them.[58]

Thomas Aikenhead would die so that magistrates and ministers could prove they still meant business when it came to upholding the covenanted vision of Scottish society. A similar fate, for a similar reason, would befall the three men and four women convicted of witchcraft in connection with the bewitching of Kristen Shaw in Bargarran, Renfrewshire, in the spring of 1697, in one of the last witch-hunts in the English-speaking world.[59] The dangers here were much different than those of the 1590s. It was not the spectre of Catholicism, either Spanish or courtly, or even the devil, really, that now haunted the practitioners of presbyterian political divinity. Rather, it was the political and intellectual pressures emanating from England. They feared that the religious laxity they associated with Episcopalianism was fuelling a general tendency towards scepticism. The ultra-presbyterians were determined to stop the rot, but this would prove impossible; the genie of genteel toleration and scepticism which would

---

[57] Edinburgh University Library mss Da.1.32, fol. 134; Da.1.34, fols 1r, 7r, 9r.

[58] Alexander Telfair, *A True Relation of an Apparition, Expressions and Actings of a Spirit, which Infested the House of Andrew Mackie ...* (Edinburgh, 1696), p. 3.

[59] Michael Wasser, 'The Western Witch-hunt of 1697–1700: The Last Major Witch-hunt in Scotland', in *The Scottish Witch-hunt in Context*, ed. Julian Goodare (Manchester, 2002), pp. 146–65.

mark eighteenth-century British intellectual life was already out of the bottle. The executions of Aikenhead and the Renfrewshire witches would be ridiculed by Britain's 'fashionable wits' (including, as it turned out, the former Scottish Secretary James Johnston), and presbyterian political divinity would henceforth have to console itself with projects like the Society for the Reformation of Manners and maintaining the inner purity of the Reformed Kirk – a battle which would lead to many schisms in the future.

PART III
People

Fairies, Egyptians and Elders: Multiple Cosmologies in Post-Reformation Scotland

Margo Todd

Once upon a time, by a sparkling, spring-fed stream, in the shadow of a great hill where, 'twas said, a dragon once had its lair, there lived an old woman. This particular old woman, however, was no fictional fairy-tale heroine. She was a real, early-modern historical actor whose record confronts historians with the inadequacy of our usual categories. To understand her story requires that we examine her world on its own terms – complete with fairies and dragons, second sight and natural magic. The tale that she told to her clerical inquisitors in 1623 illumines a time when, while Protestantism and Catholicism vied with each other, both co-existed with older and quite divergent structures of meaning. Hers is a fairy tale in which historical realities are firmly embedded.

The name of the old woman in our tale is Isobel Haldane. She was born in the latter half of the sixteenth century, and her story is set in the busy burgh of Perth on the River Tay in the Scottish Uplands, beneath Kinnoull Hill. Isobel was not a countrywoman, but like all town dwellers of her day, she lived close to the natural environment around her. We know that the burghers of Perth were given to wandering in the country for recreation, visiting local springs or holy wells, golfing in the inches north and south of the town walls.[1] They kept kye and sheep outside the walls, swine and chickens in their yards. They travelled upland to trade with Highland cattlemen for their leather and meat, and to secure their timber. The town

[1]   M. Todd, 'Profane Pastimes and the Reformed Community: The Persistence of Popular Festivities in Early Modern Scotland', *Journal of British Studies*, 39 (2000): 123–56. I am grateful for suggestions and comments on this chapter from the audience at the St Andrews University Institute for Reformation Studies workshop on 'High and Low Culture' in May of 2005, especially Jane Pettegree, and from Derek Hirst on an earlier and shorter version. Research was aided by a grant from the John Simon Guggenheim Memorial Foundation, and by Visiting Fellowship in New College, University of Edinburgh. In all quotations from manuscript sources, except titles of published works and poetry, spelling and punctuation are modernized and the Scots is Anglicized for the convenience of modern readers.

was intimately tied to its 'landwart' or rural surroundings. Isobel, however, spent rather more time outside the walls than most. She was a gatherer of herbs, a concocter of herbal remedies – a healer, and some said, a charmer. Townspeople resorted to her in great numbers; indeed, they had done for many years. This was doubtless in large measure because her remedies seemed to work more often than not. In the early modern period, survival rates with herbal healers must have been greater than with physicians, whose black bags contained leeches, bloodletting bowls and quicksilver. But people also flocked to Isobel because they knew the source of her healing recipes. She got them from the fairies.

Isobel told her neighbours a story familiar to early modern people and entirely credible, even to Scots who, three generations past the Calvinist Reformation, had heard hundreds of sermons against 'superstition'. By Isobel's day, Perth's citizens were required to attend five sermons a week.[2] All the preaching in the world, however, could not dispel their belief in the fairies. The minutes of the parochial court, or kirk session, for May of 1623 report:

> Being asked if she had any conversation with the fairy folk, [she] answered that ten years since, lying in her bed, [she] was taken forth, ... [and] carried to a hillside. The hill opened, and she entered. There she stayed three days, *viz* from Thursday til Sunday at twelve hours. She met a man with a grey beard who brought her forth again.

The fairies sent her home with gifts – a combination of healing ability and second sight, enabling her to predict whether her neighbours would live or die. She foretold the death of Margaret Buchanan, then 'in health at her ordinary work', and that of John Roch's unborn child, even as the expectant father was busy ordering a cradle from the local wright.[3]

Other neighbours, she healed: Andro Duncan's bairn recovered when she washed him in water from the Tay in the name of the Trinity, then cast the water and the child's shirt back into the river; John Gow's and John Power's bairns she healed with water taken from a spring, again depositing the children's shirts in the water. The session clerk made a point

---

[2]   Perth kirk session minutes, NAS mss CH2/521/6, fols 68v, 218v, and CH2/521/7, p. 438; Perth presbytery minutes, NAS ms CH2/299/2, pp. 43, 50, 54.
[3]   NAS ms CH2/521/7, p. 531 (1623). Hearing John Roch ask the wright to make the cradle, his wife being 'near the down-lying', Isobel 'desired him not to be so hasty, for he needed not. His wife should not be light til that time five weeks, and then the bairn should never lie in the cradle, but be born, baptized, and never suck but die, and be taken away. And as the said Isobel spake, so it came to pass in every point. Isobel being demanded how she knew that, answered that the man with the gray beard told her.' She told Margaret Buchanan, 'Make you ready for death, for before Fastren's Even you shall be taken away', and again, 'as Isobel spake, so it happened, for before that term the woman died. The said Isobel being asked how she knew the term of the woman's life, she answered that she had asked the same man with the grey beard and he had told her.'

of remarking that the water used for healing was from south-running streams. We know from a variety of sources that south-running water was reputed to have magical properties; fortunately for Isobel, the Tay when it passes Perth has taken a bend and runs for a time from north to south. Isobel healed the skinner Patrick Ruthven rather more provocatively by coming 'in to [his] bed and stretch[ing] herself above him, her head to his head, her hands over him, and so forth, mumbling some words'. She also provided a protecting ritual for newly married women facing the terrors of pregnancy and childbirth. But the fairies gave power to her curses as well as her charms: when Stephan Ray caught her in the act of stealing grain from his hall, she slapped him on the shoulder, 'saying, "Go thy way, thou shall not win thyself an bannock of beer the year and day", and as she threatened, so it came to pass' – he made no profit from his baking, and 'dwindled heavily diseased'. Isobel explained that the fairy greybeard had brought about her revenge.[4]

Isobel's healing career lasted more than a decade with no objections from the authorities. In the spring of 1623, however, it came to an abrupt end when Donald More's wife asked her to heal her ailing child. Isobel mixed a drink of what she called 'fairy leaves' and 'gave the bairn a drink, after the receipt whereof the bairn shortly died'. Only at this point did the popular healer find herself before the kirk session, charged with not just consorting with fairies, but also witchcraft.[5]

Isobel's case was heard at the same time as that of her close friend Jonat Trall, also a well-known healer of children and adults by means of potions, charms, massage (with black wool and butter) and water. The water was always brought in silently from a south-running stream, in exchange for the sick persons' shirts, which she gave back to the stream. Jonat told a similar story about the source of her healing knowledge. She admitted 'conversation with the fairie folk' since a day when:

> lying in childbedlair, she was drawn forth of her bed to a dyke near her house door ... by the fairie folks who appeared some red, some grey, riding upon horses, whereof the principal that spoke to her was like a bonny white man riding upon a grey horse. He desired [her] as she says to speak of God and to do good to poor sick folks, and shewed her the means how, namely by washing, bathing, speaking words, ... and the like.

When the respectable burgess Gilbert Hyd consulted her, she prescribed 'white bread, wine and good cheer' along with washing in south-running water and putting him through a circle of green yarn. When Duncan Tallis came (along with Isobel Haldane) to seek Jonat's help for his child, whom

---

4   NAS ms CH2/521/7, pp. 531–3. For other examples of south-running water used for magical healing, see below; and for secondary literature on holy wells, see note 20 below.
5   NAS ms CH2/521/7, pp. 531–3.

he thought already 'taken away, stiff as an oak and unable to move', she 'took the bairn upon her knee before the fire [and] drew every finger of the hands and every toe of the feet, mumbling some words that could not be heard, and immediately the bairn was cured'. (The warmth and massage doubtless helped.) In some cases, people noticed a wind strong enough to shake the house when the healing occurred.[6]

The 'fairie folks came back to her' later: one day as she was shearing with her neighbours, they appeared suddenly, 'the principal ... clad in green'. This time, though, they instructed her not to heal, but 'do ill by casting on sickness upon people'. When she objected to effecting *maleficium*, they 'dung [cast] her down, and after she was beside herself'. Distraught, she took refuge with Isobel Haldane – an association that would do her no good in the eyes of the session.[7] Yet this event occurred in 1611 – twelve years before her 1623 inquisition by the parish elders. Jonat was a popular fairy healer for a very long time before the Kirk finally decided to investigate her.

Another of Isobel's friends, 'a woman stricken in age' named Margaret Hormscleuch, also suffered by association, and by her admission that she, too, had gone with the fairy folk. Margaret's fairy contact was 'a man all clad in gold' who 'many years since ... [had] put his thumb in her hand, willing her to ask what she would, and it should be granted to her'. He gave her healing recipes for people and cattle, again using 'south-running water from the Tay, the bringer to be dumb both in going and coming, holding the mouth of the pig [pitcher] to the north', along with herbs like agrimony, and sheep's grease or butter for massage. She also received 'fairy pennies' to 'cause men thrive and become rich', and a capacity for cursing men, cattle and the brewing of ale.[8] When Marjorie Lamb's sister was ill, 'she prescribed ... washing her with south-running water and rubbing her arms with fresh butter. Her direction was ... that after the washing, they should carry the water aback again to the Tay', and when the elders asked her why, 'she answered, "Lest being strawit [strewn on the ground] either beast or body shall go over it and so get ill by it".' The water had presumably absorbed the illness. She could cure blindness with a bath of agrimony, and two years earlier, she had healed William Graham, 'being cripple and impotent', by 'rub[bing] him with a little milk and pepper to comfort his heart'. Quite full accounts of all three women's activities are written on ten pages inserted at the end of the seventh extant volume of

---

[6]   Ibid., pp. 535–6.
[7]   Ibid.
[8]   Ibid., pp. 327–30.

the Perth session minutes – probably copied out to be sent as preliminary evidence for a commission to try them in the criminal courts.[9]

Men as well as women in Perth claimed to have 'gone with the fairies', generally in May, midsummer or harvest time, and to have acquired skill from them. John Gothray, who wound up before the Perth presbytery in 1640, reported being 'taken away by the fairies in a harvest evening and among them got kindness of a little lad who called himself his brother and showed him how he himself was taken away by them, being but a month old'. Gothray stayed in fairyland for some time, but was finally released with the usual gift of healing power, periodically renewed by 'that little lad who comes to him once in a month and shows him such and such herbs and tells him for what use they serve' when mixed with water from a local spring, taken while 'distracted of his wits and speechless'. Session and presbytery had left him alone until one day when he boasted 'to the lads' that in addition to healing the sick, he 'could charm a woman from childbearing'.[10] Birth control, or perhaps abortion, was obviously beyond the pale. Yet Gothray's case was allowed to lapse, 'wakened' briefly in 1642, then dropped.[11] One could multiply examples from Perthshire: in the same summer when Haldane, Trall and Hormscleuch got into trouble with the session, the presbytery received a delegate from the neighbouring presbytery of Muthill warning them that 'a chapman [a wandering peddlar] called John Clerk haunts in their bounds and abuses the people saying that he gangis [goes about] with the fairie'.[12] The presbytery took no action beyond recording the warning.

Perth and its environs were by no means the only sites of fairy activity in Scotland. We find very similar accounts from the parishes of Falkirk, Menmuir in Angus, Stow (in the south, near the Tweed), North Berwick and Haddington (in East Lothian), Dysart (in Fife), and in the southwest, in several Ayrshire parishes – among many examples just from kirk session minutes.[13] South-running water is a recurring theme: Catie Watson of Stow, for instance, had the mother of an ailing ('fairy-blasted') child fetch

---

[9] The session determined on 12 May 1623 'that a post be directed to go to my Lord Chancellor with the clerk's letter to purchase a commission for holding of an inquest and assize upon Margaret Hormscleuch indicted for witchcraft'. Copies of the 'dittays' or depositions would be required by the chancery.

[10] NAS ms CH2/299/1, pp. 377–8, 380–82. Haldane, Trall and Hormscleuch were executed as witches; Gothray's fate is unknown.

[11] Ibid., p. 422, 19 October 1642: 'The process of Gothray is appointed to be wakened and he to be cited', but with no outcome ever recorded. To be fair, the presbytery had other things on its collective mind during the war years.

[12] Ibid., pp. 88–9. Muthill parish was later included within Auchterarder presbytery, and is now within Perth presbytery.

[13] NAS mss CH2/400/1 (Falkirk session minutes), p. 91; CH2/264/1 (Menmuir session minutes), fol. 6v; CH2/338/1 (Stow session minutes), fols 16, 25; CH2/285/1 (North Berwick session minutes), pp. 5, 12–15; CH2/185/1

it 'and speak no word, afore the sunrise'.[14] In the west, Dundonald may have held the record for fairy contacts: among many others, Marion Or in 1602 went 'through the parish professing herself to ride with the fair folk and to have skill', as did Jonat Hunter, who received from the fairies not only recipes for healing potions, but also the ability to 'tell many things', including the identity of a thief. It may be worth noting that her healing recipes contained enough 'wine and *aqua vita*' to put the recipient into a thoroughly painless state.[15] Quite a lot of information survives about Dundonald fairy contacts, in part because those who had 'gang with the fair folk' were apparently perceived as competing with other healers and charmers, who regularly ratted them out to the session: economic competition here redounds to the benefit of historians.[16]

Now one thinks of post-Reformation Scotland as a haven of Calvinist orthodoxy, its uniformity of belief and practice strictly enforced by kirk sessions – the lay elders and ministers who comprised the ecclesiastical court in each parish. There is good reason for this assumption, as recent work has shown.[17] How, then, can we understand the persistence through the seventeenth century and beyond of a set of beliefs quite diametrically opposed to a Christian (let alone protestant) understanding of the world? What exactly comprised fairy belief, why did people cling to it, and how was its survival enabled in an otherwise strictly disciplined Calvinist society?

It is necessary first to examine closely the beliefs themselves. Fortunately, surviving sources for this examination abound. They include the manuscript minute books of the ecclesiastical courts (kirk sessions and presbyteries), ballads and folklore, records of the central justiciary courts and ministers' observations – especially those of Robert Kirk of Aberfoyle, who interviewed his Perthshire parishioners and then composed a treatise on fairies in 1691.[18] The sources reveal a common ground of fairy beliefs

---

(Haddington presbytery minutes), fols 23v–24v, 27v (1597); CH2/390/1 (Dysart session minutes), fols 34v–35.

[14]   CH2/338/1, fol. 25, 9 May 1630; cf. fols 32v–34v, William Henrison, the child's father, prosecuted for fishing and labour on the Sabbath in 1632–33.

[15]   The Gaelic for 'water of life' gives us the modern English 'whisky'.

[16]   *Dundonald Parish Records: The Session Book of Dundonald 1602–1731*, ed. Henry Paton (n.p., 1936), pp. 15, 51, 64, 66, 111.

[17]   M. Todd, *The Culture of Protestantism in Early Modern Scotland* (New Haven, CT, 2002).

[18]   Robert Kirk (1644–92), *The Secret Common-Wealth of Elves, Fauns, and Fairies* (1691), ed. S. Sanderson (Cambridge, 1976; 1st pub. 1893). Kirk was minister of Aberfoyle, Perthshire, as his father was before him. For his life, see D. Maclean, 'The Life and Literary Labours of the Rev Robert Kirk of Aberfoyle', *Transactions of the Gaelic Society of Inverness*, 31 (1927): 328–66. A good summary of Scots fairy folklore is Lizanne Henderson and Edward Cowan, *Scottish Fairy Belief* (East Linton, 2001). Much of their material comes, however, from printed excerpts from

across the country, and a view of the world that was emphatically not Christian.

Nor was it J.M. Barrie's. Early modern Scottish fairies were nothing like Tinker Bell. They were not particularly small, and they had neither wings nor pixie dust. They were exotic in appearance, though, and festive in behaviour. They dressed colourfully and often extravagantly, and they spent their free time in drinking, feasting and dancing – activities on which the Kirk of Scotland emphatically frowned.[19]

They lived under hills, as Thomas Rhymer's thirteenth-century ballad tells us; Kirk calls them 'subterranean'. They lingered in springs and by streams, as readers of the ballad *Tam Lin* know well. And they rode horses through meadows and woodlands (where fair Jonet rescued Tam Lin in the ballad, and where Isobel Haldane gathered her herbs).[20] Even their

---

criminal trials, so their conclusions about association of fairy belief with diabolism may be overdone, and they do not examine the degree to which people resorted to fairy healers or the local context of fairy lore, lacking the full parochial sources.

[19] The colourful garb of fairies was remarked by Jonet Trall, above; Isobel Gowdie found them dressed 'some in grass-green, some in sea-green, and some in yellow' (R. Pitcairn, *Ancient Criminal Trials in Scotland*, Edinburgh, 1833, vol. 3, pp. 604–7); and Bessie Dunlop commented on their 'gentlemen's clothes' and plaids (ibid., vol. 1, pp. 51, 55–7). The thirteenth-century ballad-maker Thomas Rhymer described the fairy queen riding 'o'er the fernie brae' in 'grass-green silk, / Her mantel of the velvet fine, / At ilka tett of her horse's mane/Hung fifty silver bells and nine.' In another version, 'her mantle was o' velvet green, / And a' set round wi' jewels fine; / Her hawk and hounds were at her side, / And her bugle-horn wi' gowd [gold] did shine': Helen Child Sargent and G.L. Kittredge (eds), *The English and Scottish Popular Ballads* (hereafter ESPB) (Boston, MA, 1904), pp. 64–6, quote at 64. Alison Peirson remarked on the piping and good cheer of the fairy court, Donald McIlmichall on the 'many candles' (Pitcairn, *Ancient Criminal Trials*, vol. 1, p. 163; J.N.R. MacPhail, *Highland Papers* 3, Edinburgh, 1928, p. 37); Kirk, *The Secret Common-Wealth*, p. 54, described it as 'large and fair'. Andro Man confessed in 1598 to having sung, danced and feasted in fairy land on All Hallow's Eve; the fairies he knew 'have playing and dancing when they please'. He was also welcomed into the bed of the fairy queen: *Miscellany of the Spalding Club* (Aberdeen, 1841), vol. 1, part 3, pp. 120–21.

[20] NAS mss CH2/521/7, pp. 527–36; CH2/338/1, fol. 25; CH2/185/1, fol. 27v; CH2/390/1, fols 34v–35; *Dundonald Parish Records*, pp. 9, 15, 53. Kirk discusses fairy hills and describes fairies as 'subterranean', *The Secret Common-Wealth*, pp. 50, 53, 61–2. Katherine Ross 'would go in hills' to talk with the fairies, and John Stewart of Irvine met them atop Lanark Hill: Pitcairn, *Ancient Criminal Trials*, vol. 1, p. 196 (Ross, 1590); *The Trial, Confession and Execution of Isobel Inch, John Stewart, ... at Irvine anno 1618* (henceforth *Irvine*) (n.p., 1855), p. 9. Donald McIlmichall, tried at Inveray in 1677, followed fairy lights into a hill: MacPhail, *Highland Papers*, p. 37; *The Justiciary Records of Argyll and the Isles 1664–1705*, ed. John Cameron (Edinburgh, 1949), vol. 1, pp. 80–82. The thirteenth-century ballads of Thomas Rhymer recount his meeting the queen of fairies in the Eildon Hills (Borders); in her abode, 'he saw neither sun nor moon'. Tam Lin (whose ballad dates from the sixteenth century or earlier) also found

clothing reflected the natural environment: Isobel Gowdie of Auldearn, Nairn, in 1662 described her fairy contacts wearing 'grass-green' and 'sea green'.[21] Fairies came up from their underground abode at Beltane – the beginning of one of the four 'raiths' that comprised the Gaelic year, in May. They returned after harvest season, at All Hallow's Eve. Marion Or rode with the fair folk at Beltane in 1602, Catie Watson did her healing then, and John Stewart admitted to the Irvine presbytery in 1618 that he encountered the fairies every Hallowe'en.[22] Fairy intervention in human medicine is often accompanied by wind. We have seen this with Jonat Trall; likewise, when Jonet Boyman of Canongate parish in 1572 sought skill to heal a particularly difficult case, she went to a spring on the south side of Arthur's seat, called up 'a great blast' of wind, received the fairies' directions, and found that the wind shook the house when she followed them – on Hallowe'en.[23]

---

fairyland 'in yon green hill'; he first appeared to Jonet by a forest spring, and Jonet met the fairy procession on horseback on Hallowe'en: ESPB, pp. 64, 67–69. Fairies ride through forests in, among others, Elspeth Reoch's 1616 account (*Miscellany of the Maitland Club*, Edinburgh, 1833, pp. 187–191) and Bessie Dunlop's 1576 trial (Pitcairn, *Ancient Criminal Trials*, vol. 1, pp. 52–3, 58. For springs or holy wells and streams as places inhabited by spirits, see Todd, *Culture of Protestantism*, pp. 202, 204–09); Alexandra Walsham, 'Reforming the Waters: Holy Wells and Healing Springs in Protestant England', *Life and Thought in the Northern Church c 1100–c. 1700*, ed. Diana Wood (Woodbridge, 1999), pp. 227–56; and J. Wood, 'Lakes and Wells: Mediation between the Real World and the Otherworld in Scottish Folklore', *Scottish Language and Literature*, ed. D. Strauss and H. Drescher (Scottish Studies, 4) (Frankfurt, 1986), p. 526.

[21]   Pitcairn, *Ancient Criminal Trials*, vol. 3, p. 606.

[22]   NAS ms CH2/722/5, n.f. (Isobel Sinclair reporting in February 1633 before the Stirling presbytery that 'at the raiths of the year she hath been controlled with the fairies and that by them she hath the second sight'); *Dundonald Parish Records*, pp. 15 (Or's riding, 1602), 34–5, 38, 51, 55–7, 59 (Pet Lowrie, Beltane 1603 and 1604; Jonat Hunter, Beltane 1604). Kirk (p. 51) reported that fairies 'remove to other lodgings at the beginning of each quarter of the year', when they are spotted by 'men of the second sight'. For Watson's Beltane healing of people 'blasted with the breath of the fairy' at Beltane in Stow, see NAS ms CH2/338/1, fol. 25. Fictional Hallowe'en fairy sightings include Jonet's in *Tam Lin* (ESPB, 68); those mentioned in real trial records include the 1572 case of Jonat Boyman of the Canongate (NAS ms JC 26/1/67); Alison Peirson's 'on horseback, on Hallow even'. The latter is recorded in verse by Robert Sempill, 'Heir Followis the Legend of the Bischop of St Androis Lyfe', *Satirical Poems of the Time of the Reformation*, ed. James Cranstoun (Edinburgh, 1891) vol. 1, p. 365; and in Pitcairn, *Ancient Criminal Trials*, vol. 1, p. 164. For John Stewart's report, see *Irvine*, p. 9. Scots in both Lowlands and Highlands lit bonfires at All Hallow's Eve, in part as a protection against fairy mischief: Todd, 'Profane Pastimes'. For liminal seasons and times, see Diana Purkiss, *Troublesome Things: A History of Fairies and Fairy Stories* (London, 2000), p. 86, and K.M. Briggs, *The Vanishing People: A Study of Traditional Fairy Belief* (London, 1978).

[23]   NAS ms JC26/1/67.

Hill and wind, flowing water and herbs, Spring and Fall: Fairies are surely best identified as nature spirits, associated with places in the natural environment around towns like Perth or Dundonald, their activities co-ordinated with the seasons of the agrarian year and with weather. They cavorted not in heaven or hell, but in or just beneath the realm of humans – in Middle Earth, as both ballads and trial depositions tell us.[24] However many presbyterian divines might try to demonize them (and not all did), they appear from their adherents' reports to be more natural than supernatural. Healers and seers attributed their powerful gifts neither to an invisible Creator of nature nor to a supernatural demonic force, but to the visible emanations of nature itself. As the reverend Mr Kirk noted in his defence of fairy belief, 'these invisible people are more sagacious to understand by the Book of *Nature* things to come, than we', since they are more like 'birds and beasts' in their close relationship to the natural world. He likened them to the ancients' 'fountain, river and sea nymphs; wood, hill and mountain inhabitants', and posed his readers the question, 'Hell is inhabited at the centre, and heaven in the circumference; can we then think the middle cavities of the earth empty?'[25]

Fairies were neither good nor evil. They had 'no discernible religion', as Kirk opined, serving both as 'guardians over and careful of men' and as mischief-makers, though in the latter case they 'acted not maliciously, like devils, but in sport, like buffoons and drolls'. They gave good gifts – healing, and perception of even invisible truths. Kirk attributed second sight to 'the courteous endeavours of our fellow creatures in the invisible world'.[26] They gave fairy pennies to make people rich, and fairy leaves to cure the sick.[27] But they also did harm. They sometimes stole people away, took babies from their cradles, disabled their adherents (as in John Gothray's temporary witlessness), and charged them to do ill. Their favoured agent one minute could be their victim the next, as in Jonat Trall's case, and there was no rhyme or reason to their choices. They were, above all else,

---

[24]   *Maitland Miscellany*, pp. 187–91; Pitcairn, *Ancient Criminal Trials*, vol. 1, pp. 52–3, 58 (Bessie Dunlop, 1576), 164 (Alison Peirson, 1588). Kirk, *Secret Commonwealth*, p. 64, has them living above and under ground, moving among humans 'as thick as atoms in the air', and moral as humans are. He identifies people and fairies as 'two kinds of rational inhabitants of the same Earth' (pp. 82, 90, 95).

[25]   Ibid., pp. 60, 85.

[26]   Ibid., pp. 82–3, 85. He insists that they are neither devils nor evil spirits. On second sight, see Hilda Davidson (ed.), *The Seer in Celtic and Other Traditions* (Edinburgh, 1989), esp. ch. 1–3, 6, though the Lowlands kirk session minute books indicate that second sight was not an exclusively Gaelic phenomenon.

[27]   For an example of fairy pennies, see NAS ms CH2/521/7, p. 530, Margaret Hormscleuch admitting she gave 'fairy pennies to cause men thrive and become rich'; for leaves, in addition to the Perth examples above, see NAS ms CH2/390/1, fol. 21v, 1625 interrogation of the healer Richard Cosie in Dysart.

capricious – amoral and indiscriminate – not like devils, but like nature itself. Contemporary authorities who tried to demonize them did so without grounds other than their own agenda to subsume an older cosmology into the Christian one. The fairies themselves represented a view of the universe that has nothing to do with sin or redemption, rewarding good or punishing evil, and everything to do with unpredictability, unreason, caprice. It was the cosmology of a people chronically vulnerable to the arbitrary forces of nature – storm, disease, and in seventeenth-century Perth, earthquake.[28] It recognized the amorality of the natural world, interpreted misfortune as a fluke of nature rather than the result of evil. The very whimsicality of this cosmology was its problem for Christian orthodoxy, which sought meaning in the events of a providential universe. The witchcraft charges that were brought in particular cases represent the victory of Christian dogma over this alternative cosmology of amoral nature spirits.

In England, Kirk's contemporary John Aubrey perceptively described fairy belief under the heading of the *Remaines of Gentilism* and found its origins in pre-Christian times: 'The Britons imbibed their gentilism from the Romans, and as the British [Celtic] language is [now] crept into corners, as Wales and Cornwall, so the remains of gentilism are still kept there', as also in 'the most northward' parts of the island. His fear, and the reason he wrote in the 1680s, was that 'the divine art of printing ... has frightened away Robin-good-fellow and the fairies', and in the absence of what he granted was 'superstition', 'atheism and consequently libertinism will certainly come into its room'. He accordingly commended the early Church's good sense 'in the infancy of Christian religion ... to plough (as they say) with the heifer of the gentiles' (as in adaptation of pagan festivities like Yule to the Christian year).[29] He argued that it is better to tolerate and, where possible, incorporate aspects of paganism, animism, gentilism – call it what you will – than open a vacuum for atheism to fill. Aubrey's use of 'gentilism' was insightful, but no innovation: however inclined the presbyters of Perth had been nearer the beginning of the century to follow their monarch's prescription and call fairy belief diabolical, when they complained about popular resort to a magic well at Trinity Gask, they put it under the heading of 'gentilism'.[30]

Even in a rigorously disciplined and catechized protestant Scotland, people of all sorts believed in fairies. Both the educated and ignorant claimed to have seen them and gone with them, and well-off as well as poor folk sought out those who had access to the fairies' power. Clearly,

---

[28]   Todd, *Culture of Protestantism*, pp. 180–81, 349–51.
[29]   John Aubrey, *The Remaines of Gentilisme and Judaisme*, ed James Britten (London, 1881) for the Folklore Society from British Library ms Landsdowne 231, written 1686–87, pp. 55, 58, 6.
[30]   NAS ms CH2/299/1, p. 243.

looking only at the prosecutions of people like Isobel Haldane as witches fails to recount the whole story. Isobel was in fact executed as a witch after her child patient died from the effects of her 'leaf brew'. But the kirk session minutes indicate that for at least a decade before that unfortunate event, she had operated with impunity and with a great following in Perth, parents of cured children spreading the word about her gift. Jonat Trall went untroubled for more than twelve years. Jonet Drever in Orkney conversed with the fair folk for twenty-six years before she was called to account by her elders in 1614.[31] Those Perth healers had joined their neighbours in communion examinations and received their tokens, and they were never reported on the absentee list from Sunday sermons.[32] John Gothray never got more than a verbal reprimand from the Perth presbytery, nor did the presbyters pursue the fairy-inspired Muthill charmer. As long as nothing untoward happened to any of their clients, they could use fairy cures and second sight in peace, with a clientele that included the propertied.

After all, it was by definition people with possessions who sought them out to find their lost goods or identify thieves. In a multitude of Scots burghs, even councillors and members of the session resorted to such heterodox means to find lost goods or guide decisions. Among other examples, the wealthy laird and erstwhile elder Alexander Peblis of Chapelhill, Perth parish, in 1619 objected strongly to a sermon against superstitious fortune-telling, including turning the riddle on a sieve, as an attack *ad hominem,* since the whole town knew the riddle was turned in his house with some regularity. It is worth noting that turning the riddle is a fortune-telling method first found in Virgil's *Ecologues,* which surely lends remarkable credence to Aubrey's argument.[33]

Neither was education a bar to belief in fairies. Jean Weir of Dalkeith, who received from 'the queen of fairy' a remarkable spinning talent, was not only literate; she was a teacher.[34] John Carswell, superintendent of

---

[31] *Court Books of Orkney and Shetland 1614–15,* ed. Robert Barclay (Edinburgh, 1967), pp. 18–20.

[32] The bailie must have failed to note her name down on that Sunday when the fairies did not release her until noon, after the morning sermon. Perhaps she made it to the afternoon preaching.

[33] Aubrey, *The Remaines of Gentilisme and Judaisme,* p. 25; NAS ms CH2/521/7, p. 65, the case of Alexander Peblis of Chapelhill, Perth parish, probably the son of the elder Oliver Peblis, objecting to a sermon of John Guthry against 'sorcery and consulting therewith by turning the riddle' (turning a sieve on the point of a shears). The rest of the session upheld his complaint. Peblis would serve as an elder, and would be provost several times between 1628 and 1638. For similar cases, see NAS mss CH2/1142/1, fol. 103 (a Fraserburgh merchant, Alexander Fraser); CH2/521/2, fol. 34; CH2/390/1, fol. 9 (riddle-turning in Dysart); *Dundonald Parish Records* p. 34, and James VI, *Daemonologie* (1597), ed. G.B. Harrison (Edinburgh, 1966), p. 12.

[34] Reported in Henderson and Cowan, *Scottish Fairy Belief,* p. 135.

Argyll and translator into Gaelic of the *Book of Common Order* (1567), seems to have believed in the fairy folk.[35] Archbishop Patrick Adamson of St Andrews, among the sponsors of the *Second Book of Discipline* before his elevation, was said to be among the clients of Alison Peirson in 1588, when he sought healing of his 'trembling, fever and flux' with a cure that Alison had learned from the fairies.[36] Among those who consulted Bessie Dunlop, the Ayrshire charmer who claimed healing power and second sight from an agent of the fairy queen, were Lady Johnstone, Lady Blackhalls, Lady Kilbowie, Lady Blair and the chamberlain of Kilwinning.[37] The celebrated and thoroughly orthodox Calvinist preacher Robert Rollock used imagery from fairy tales in his sermons, and Robert Kirk, that great clerical defender of fairy belief, was an Edinburgh University MA and translator of the first complete Gaelic metrical Psalter.[38] Fairy belief in early modern Scotland was not merely a 'weapon of the weak'.[39]

Both Kirk and parliament did regularly issue injunctions to eschew 'superstition', however.[40] Why, then, did fairy beliefs persist? Some of the reasons are obvious. First, fairies offered tangible benefits, foremost among them the hope of healing at a time when epidemic disease was rampant and the medical profession unable to offer much. They provided the possibility of 'second sight' and fortune-telling, either to aid decisions at a times of uncertainty or to provide detective services in cases of lost or stolen goods.[41] It is worth noting that many cases of consultation with

---

[35] *Transactions of the Gaelic Society of Inverness*, 22 (1897–98), p. 293, also noted by Henderson and Cowan, *Scottish Fairy Belief*, p. 19. Carswell identified fairies with deities from Irish mythology condemned by their human conquerors to dwell beneath the earth.

[36] Sempill, 'Legend of the Bischop of St Androis Lyfe', *Satirical Poems*, vol. 1, p. 365.

[37] Pitcairn, *Ancient Criminal Trials*, vol. 1, pp. 54–5.

[38] Rollock, *Certaine Sermons* (Edinburgh, 1599), p. 51. Kirk produced the *Psalma Dhaibhidh An Meadrachd* (Edinburgh, 1684); in 1689, he travelled to London to oversee the printing of William Bedell's Irish Bible. Learned Scots believers in fairies had their English counterparts: The puritan preacher Richard Greenham, *Workes*, ed. H.H. (London, 3rd edn, 1601), identified fairies with good spirits, according to his editor. And the notorious prognosticator William Lilly tried to contact the queen of fairies in the 1640s: *Autobiography*, pp. 229–32.

[39] James Scott, *Weapons of the Weak: Everyday Forms of Peasant Resistance* (New Haven, CT, 1985).

[40] For example, parliaments in 1574 and 1579 forbade the use of 'prophesy, charming or other abused sciences' to tell people's futures or fates, the first offence requiring loss of an ear, the second, hanging: *Acts of the Parliaments of Scotland 1127–1707* [APS], ed. T. Thomson and Cosmo Innes, 12 vols (Edinburgh, 1814–75), vol. 3, p. 140.

[41] Among countless examples, in 1604 Jonat Hunter of Dundonald, having 'professed that she went to the fair folk and that she could tell many things', Robert Garven of Arathill asked her who had broken into John Fulton's barn and stolen his grain, 'to the which she answered if she saw the hole that was broken,

charmers to identify thieves occurred in parishes divided by slander of theft and plagued by unsolved crimes.[42] The benefits were presumably enough to insure that local Kirk authorities, session elders, would not in fact prosecute fairy belief very rigorously unless some serious untoward event like a death were associated. Again, we should beware deducing too much from the cases that would wind up as witchcraft charges: many more cases of consorters with fairies were either dismissed lightly or allowed to lapse, making the elders quietly complicit. Marion Or's claim to 'ride with the fair folk', for instance, was simply remarked in the Dundonald session minutes; no charge was ever brought. Similar cases were allowed to lapse quietly in the parishes of Menmuir, North Berwick, and Dysart. And while those who consulted the fairy-gifted were sometimes admonished and occasionally made to perform public repentance or lightly fined, seldom were they more seriously disciplined or heavily fined.[43]

A second reason for its survival is that fairy belief was explanatory. The loss of a child (fairy-taken) or a mysterious illness (fairy-blasted) – the usual array of early modern disasters – need not be attributed to human error or sin, as Christian orthodoxy demanded; it could instead be the result of fairy mischief. And there is some comfort to be found in knowing the reason for loss. The functionalists, then, are right as far as they go. But the evidence allows us to venture a little further in an effort

---

she then could tell who it was'. Jonat Wilson, Fulton's wife, then sought her out to identify the culprit: *Dundonald Parish Records*, pp. 64, 66. A few weeks later, Jonat Hunter also identified a rival charmer, 'Auld Katherin Neill', as the culprit when John Muckill of Corsbie asked her why his cow had ceased to give milk. Muckill was ordered to perform public repentance for seeking her out, but not until about eighteen months later (ibid., p. 111). A similar case in Stow, 1626, is NAS ms CH2/338/1, fols 1v–3.

[42] For example, NAS ms CH2/338/1, fols 1v–3, an effort in Stow, 1626, to find the thief of James Armstown's 16s. At the same time, the community was torn by another case of slander concerning theft (fol. 3, cf. fol. 17v): it made a certain amount of sense in this case to try to avoid a slander charge by going to the local charmer (one Isabel Clughorne) in hopes of correctly identifying the culprit. Another case in point is NAS ms CH2/1142/1, fol. 103, in a parish plagued with unsolved theft cases (fols 77v–78) and slander of thievery (fols 2, 29, 96, 101v–102v, 107, 109, and so on).

[43] Jonat Hunter, who also 'went with the fair folk' and was at several points questioned by the Dundonald session, but seems to have been let off and died in her bed: *Dundonald Parish Records*, pp. 15, 51, 64. See also the lapsed cases in NAS mss CH2/264/1, fol. 6v; CH2/285/1, fol. 5 and pp. 12–15; CH2/390/1, fols 34v–35. A rare case of one who consulted with a fairy healer being punished with public repentance is that of John Muckill in Corsbie; however, it is worth noting that this occurred during plague time, when sessions were generally more draconian in their efforts to stamp out superstition and other sin: see *Dundonald Parish Records*, p. 111, 122, for evidence of the plague.

to understand why this particular view of the cosmos survived the Kirk's official opposition.

Fairy belief is a sort of environmental cosmology. It supposes a sanctity in nature itself that would have been all the more attractive in an age when people lived closer to the natural environment than modern urbanites do – closer to springs, rivers and mountains that in fact determined the viability of their communities. Fairies were associated with real places in the immediate environment that had long histories (or legends) as sources of power. There was good reason for Perth's Isobel and Jonat to find their fairy contacts in hills. Kinnoull Hill, brooding over the town from across the Tay, was long reputed to be the home not only of fairies, but also of a dragon, vanquished (one story has it) by St Serf. Young men and maids resorted to a cave called the 'Dragon Hole' on Kinnoull on May Day to find their true loves.[44] (Indeed, they still do.) It may have been known from pre-Christian times as a source of power, rooted in the earth itself. The recurring Perthshire earthquakes from 1597 to 1614 would only reinforce this identification.[45] The earth's power was intrinsic and utterly unpredictable, and all too tangible to early modern Scots.

The Tay itself and the nearby springs of Ruthven and Huntingtower were likewise loci of mysterious power. For a community whose very existence depended on the river, it was not unreasonable for Isobel Haldane and John Gothray to wash sick children in Tay water, and to repay the spirits of the waters with the shirts of their patients. Other citizens of the town regularly risked the ire of the session by skipping church on Beltane to visit the springs and leave behind hair ribbons as offerings to the spirits of running streams in exchange for pitchers of healing water.[46] They might have been perfectly good Calvinists while sitting in the kirk; indeed, they must have been, since failure at catechetical performance and examination by the elders would result in their names appearing on the disciplinary list (well kept in Perth's minutes). But when need demanded, they could resort just as easily to a nature religion whose beliefs resonated with the powerful sense of place that characterized early modern communities, and

---

[44] We know this because the kirk session prosecuted (albeit with very light admonitions) those who went to the Dragon Hole on May Day: NAS mss CH2/521/1, fols 37v–38, 56, 57v ; CH2/521/4, pp. 2, 44–5; CH2/521/7, pp. 330, 441 – cases dating from the 1570s through the 1620s. *The Book of Perth*, ed. J.P. Lawson (Edinburgh, 1847), p. 95, recounts May Day costumed processions gathering garlands of flowers and celebrating a legendary dragon slaughter on Kinnoull Hill.

[45] There were major earthquakes recorded by contemporaries in 1597, 1608 and 1614: *The Chronicle of Perth*, ed. James Maidment (Edinburgh, 1831), pp. 5, 12, 15, from National Library of Scotland, Edinburgh, ms Adv 31.4.4, entries in an early seventeenth-century hand.

[46] Todd, 'Profane Pastimes', pp. 133–4, 139–44, 150–51.

with the obvious power that resided in quaking earth and flooding river.[47] The River Tay was the foundation on which the town's trading prosperity was built, but when it flooded (as so often it did), it took homes and lives as well as fortunes. The kirk authorities responded to floods with fasts for the sins that had drawn divine wrath, but why not avoid the guilt and attribute flood to the caprice of the spirits of running water? It is at least as internally coherent a cosmology as the Christians' providentialist one.

Fairy belief could also serve as an incorporative cosmology. Consider two cases in point – the physically handicapped, and the nomadic stranger. Among the fairy-gifted to whom people resorted for healing or other aid were people called, in a multitude of session books, 'Dumbie'. Individuals who lacked the power of speech, perhaps deaf as well, seem all too often to have occupied 'outsider status' in early modern Scotland. Perhaps balancing out that less than charitable exclusion, the community effectively re-incorporated the ostracized by explaining their handicap as a result of fairy contact and then elevating them to a higher status – the gifted healer or second-sighted. Haddington presbytery, for instance, was in the 1590s troubled by people in a variety of parishes 'consulting the dumb boy', a 'diviner or soothsayer', for the health of their relatives. Helen Porteous admitted that she had sent to the dumb boy 'and inquired for some gear she wanted'. In the 1630s, Trinity College kirk in Edinburgh also dealt with 'divers persons using of an unlawful means in consulting with a dumb man for seeking of stolen goods back again by Dumbie's revelations'.[48] What is interesting about such examples (and they could be multiplied) is that 'to be struck dumb' was often called 'the fairy'.[49] We have seen that John Gothray was struck dumb when he got spring water for his healing potions; John Stewart, who met the fairies while travelling in Ireland on a Hallowe'en in the 1610s, lost his speech and the sight of one eye. Elspeth Reoch got from the fairies a ritual that brought her second sight, but it cost her the 'power of her tongue'. Robert Kirk also reported that fairies might blind the people they stole away, 'or they strike them dumb'. He told of a woman taken from childbed, missing for two days, and returning from fairyland sightless in one eye.[50] For those who vary from the physical norm thus to be both explained and given a paid occupation – healer or

---

[47] Robert Kirk makes the interesting observation that people gifted by the fairies with second sight actually lost it when they were transported to other countries: 'every country and kingdom having their topical spirits or powers assisting and governing them, the Scottish seer banished to America, ... wanting the familiarity of his former correspondents, could not have the favour and warnings that he gets in his own familiar place'; *Secret Commonwealth*, p. 83.

[48] NAS mss CH2/185/1, fol. 24v; CH2/141/1, fols 48, 53.

[49] *Records of Orkney*, pp. 57, 261.

[50] NAS ms CH2/299/1, pp. 377–8, 380–82; *Irvine*, p. 9; *Maitland Miscellany* (Edinburgh, 1833), pp. 112–13; Kirk, *Secret Commonwealth*, pp. 54, 69.

detective – suggests both the uneasiness that early modern people had with disabilities and with their own uncharitableness, on the one hand, and on the other hand their willingness to create space for individuals who do not fit within social norms by resorting to fairy belief. An added bonus for the disabled was that they were almost never prosecuted for their charming; as a general rule, only those who resorted to them seem to have been brought before the sessions.

Occasional mentions of other wandering outsiders in the same session books where 'dumbies' are reported are tantalizing. Helen Porteous, having failed to get what she needed from the dumb boy in Haddington, then consulted a healer named Jonet Steil, who claimed to have gotten her recipes for potions (mixed with south-running water) from 'a poor man that said he used to go with the Jews'.[51] Together with itinerant Highlandmen (called 'Irish' in the extant records), these wandering Jews, also never prosecuted themselves, provided access to natural remedies much like those associated with fairies, and thereby achieved some standing in a community from which they were otherwise excluded. It may be significant that the fairy-frequenting chapman who troubled the Muthill presbytery was also by definition a wanderer, peddling his wares as he travelled. Modern observers tend to think of early modern British communities as xenophobic, intent on a strict definition of Insider and Outsider. It is time to amend our judgement.

Another, larger nomadic group that first appeared in Scotland in the sixteenth century reinforces this message, and suggests another reason for survival of fairy belief. From the 1570s, we find at all levels of Scottish government, secular and ecclesiastical alike, increasing concern with 'Egyptians', or Gypsies. Parliamentary legislation threatened them with death if they remained in the realm. The statutes make quite clear the association in lawmakers' minds between 'the idle people calling themselves Egyptians' and claims to esoteric 'knowledge in physionomy, palmestry, or other abused sciences whereby they persuade the people that they can tell their ... fortunes and such other fantastical imaginations'. They forbade householders to give 'money, herbry or lodging, set house or show any other relief to' Gypsies.[52] Parishes and presbyteries followed suit, passing

---

51   NAS ms CH2/185/1, fol. 27v.
52   *APS*, vol. 3, pp. 86 (1574), 576 (1592); vol. 4, pp. 140 (1597, allowing kirk sessions to 'punish' Egyptians and strong and idle beggars), 440 (1609 'Act anent the Egyptians' ordering 'vagabonds, sorners and common thieves commonly called Egyptians to pass forth of this kingdom and remain perpetually forth thereof and never to return within the same under the pain of death ... as well woman as men', and ordering people who 'receives them or entertains' them to be dispossessed and warded at the judges' will). Sheriffs and magistrates in bounds where Gypsies remained were to be called before the Secret Council and 'severely censured and punished for their negligence in execution of this Act'. A notorious trial in Banff

– and repeating – their own 'acts anent [concerning] Egyptians' from the 1590s, aimed mainly at those who 'entertained' or offered hospitality to the wanderers.[53]

Now, generally speaking, governments do not go to the trouble of forbidding activities that no one is participating in anyway. But prosecutions of people 'entertaining Egyptians' are *very* numerous, in parishes from Glasgow to the Fife village of Burntisland, from the Borders to the far north. Since the punishments meted out were nothing like so severe as the law required, the same names recur in subsequent prosecutions. (Typically, Stow parish levied a 6s. 8d. penalty, rather than the parliamentary £5.) What is striking is that the same parishes where people 'went with the fairies' were also ones where gypsies were entertained – Stow and Dundonald being cases in point.[54]

Why would householders risk a fine to lodge and feed a people known for theft and disorder – as Gypsies certainly were?[55] In part, simply because the traditional virtue of hospitality had not died out in post-Reformation Scotland. Margaret Houson told the Dundonald elders she could not turn away 'an old woman, an Egyptian' who came to her for help; Thomas Davie explained that he sent away most Gypsies, but had kept 'one wife, whom he alleged was not able to go away for sickness, and one man with

---

in 1700 suggests the negligence of some Scots lairds in actually carrying through the harassment of the Gypsies, though: 'Process: Procurator Phiscall against the Egyptians', *Miscellany of the Spalding Club*, 3 (Aberdeen, 1846), pp. 175–91.

[53] Mitchell Library, Glasgow, ms CH2/171/1 (Glasgow presbytery ordering in 1593 that parishes 'take order with the Egyptians'); NAS ms CH2/471/1, fol. 10 (Lasswade in 1615 ordered that 'no harlots nor vagabonds namely such as are called Egyptians, sturdy idle persons, wandering from place to place, be received and entertained in the parish under pain of 40s for the receiver ... and present banishment of the person who is kept'). See also NAS mss CH2/1/1 (Aberdeen presbytery, 1608); CH2/448/3 (Aberdeen session, 1619); CH2/400/2 (Falkirk session, 1639); CH2/1142/1, fol. 92 (Fraserburgh session, 1619); CH2/84/28, fol. 70 (Dalkeith, St Nicholas East session, 1617), and CH2/523/1, unfoliated pages at beginning of volume (Burntisland, 1602, forbidding entertainment of 'all persons using subtle crafty and unlaw[ful ways] such [as] plays fast and loose with such others, all jugglers, all Egyptians, all that fain them to have the knowledge of charming, prophecy, and other abused science', and all 'songsters').

[54] Among many examples, in Stow, a 1630 case involving fairy potions for healing is shortly followed by a series of prosecutions for entertaining Egyptians (NAS ms CH2/338, fols 25–37v); see also NAS ms CH2/185/1, fols 24v, 40, and *Dundonald Parish Records*, pp. 15, 51, 55, 64, 111, 255–7, 259, 276–8, 280, 283–4, 300, 306, 363, 510–11.

[55] 'Process', p. 178, for example; p. 179 finds 'these commonly called Egyptians ... to be idle beggars, blacking their faces, fortune-tellers, cheating of the people by vain superstitions, by professing knowledge of charming, tellers of words, which is clearly explained to be the inseparable attributes of those called Egyptians, ... James 6, cap. 74 ...'. For theft, see pp. 186–7, for example.

her'.[56] These were kindly Scots – though poorer for their pains, thanks to the elders. In part, though, it was because Scots were actually rather more multi-cultural than we generally credit, even intermarrying with Gypsies and Highlandmen: John Wilson, burgess of Futtie in 1593 lodged 'an Egyptian woman and a Scottishman with her who had married her', and Perth's citizens were regularly in trouble for drinking on the Sabbath with Gypsies or 'Irish'. There, of course, a factor was proximity to the Gaelic Highlands and regular business dealings with semi-nomadic cattle-drovers for the hides needed by the leather craftsmen of the burgh.[57] But there was no such factor in play for James Sinclair, Lord of Roslyn, when in 1599 he released a Gypsy from the gibbet. Perhaps the medieval myth, recounted by Boece in the *Scotorum Historiae* (1523), that Scotland was founded by descendants of Egyptians and named for Scota, the daughter of a Pharoah, inclined many Scots to receive the Gypsies, whom they seem really to have thought came from Egypt.[58]

The Gypsies also offered many of the same benefits as the fairies, and indeed may have helped to sustain fairy belief. Gypsies looked like fairies. By all accounts, they dressed colourfully and flamboyantly. Like fairies, they travelled, often on horseback, and they revelled – with pipers and fiddlers, dancing and feasting.[59] Bessie Scot of Stow was in 1634 censured by her session for having joined them in guising and song.[60] And like fairies, Gypsies offered healing and told fortunes. Patrick Bodie, an Aberdeen tailor, readily admitted in 1619 that he had 'made inquiry at the Egyptians for a gentlewoman's gown which was stolen out of his booth'. In Dundonald, Robert Fulton housed Gypsies when his wife was ill, and received in return a cure (involving water and knots of straw); and a goodwife there 'baked bread and roasted flesh to [an] Egyptian woman' and then invited her other guests to 'ask fortunes of her'.[61] The session did nothing in either case. Sometimes the connection with fairies was more

---

[56]   *Dundonald Parish Records*, pp. 255–6, 283.

[57]   Mitchell Library, Glasgow, ms CH2/171/1, fol. 9v.

[58]   Hector Boece, *The Chronicles of Scotland*, trans. 1531 by John Bellenden (Edinburgh, 1936 and 1941), vol. 1, pp. 21–23; Alexander Sinclair, *Sketch of the History of Roslin & Its Possessors* (Irvine, 1856). James Sinclair inherited the title in 1582; the story reported by his descendant is that the whole of the Gypsy tribe adopted him as its patron after the release from the gibbet.

[59]   For example, NAS ms CH2/338/1, Bessie Scot 'granted she was at the Egyptians, ... guising [and] singing' in 1633; see 'Process', p. 184, on Gypsy music, feasting and drinking, and 'dancing all night'.

[60]   CH2/338/1, fol. 37v. Another Stow citizen reportedly gave clothes to visiting Gypsies in 1633 (ibid., fol. 37).

[61]   NAS mss CH2/448/3, n.f., 31 January 1619, and CH2/338/1, fol. 37, John Scot in 1633 confessing 'he went to the Egyptians and gave them their clothes hoping to be the better of them'. See also *Dundonald Parish Records*, pp. 278, 280, 284.

direct: Alison Peirson said in 1588 that her uncle, William Simpson, once 'taken by a man of Egypt' and returned only after twelve years away, then got himself stolen again by fairies; he became her own connection to the fairy world.[62]

We know too little of sixteenth-century Gypsies, but it is clear from anthropological studies that they were nothing if not generously syncretistic in their adoption of the religions and cosmologies of the larger cultures in which they found themselves.[63] Whether they brought healing and fortune-telling with them to Scotland or picked it up from local traditions, or both, it does not seem too much of a stretch to suppose that they fostered a continuity of many of the beliefs associated with fairies. Can it be a coincidence that a ballad called *The Fairies Fegaries, or, Singing and dancing being all their pleasure*, published in 1635, was set to a tune called *The Spanish Gypsie*?[64]

Fairy belief was a cultural construct that served psychological and social needs and allowed a sense of control over fortune and the forces of nature. But it also expressed a fundamentally different conception of the cosmos from the one the Kirk taught, making its persistence problematic, especially in so thoroughly Reformed a realm as Scotland. Its embodiment of the connections between human well-being and the natural environment helped. So did its balancing of incorporation with separation of the Other, whether those with disabilities or nomadic Outsiders. Fairy belief achieved a balance of hospitality over against order, of charity against discipline, that was surely necessary in a culture both as diverse as Scots/Gaelic Scotland and as rigorously overseen as presbyterian Scotland. If parochial authorities generally punished lightly or even ignored those who went with the fairies, it was because of their *de facto* recognition that cosmological pluralism worked, however the theologians might object. If the fairies help us hedge our bets in risky times, why not set them alongside the more orthodox resort to prayers and fasting? They do not blend very well, but they can and did co-exist.

---

[62] Pitcairn, *Ancient Criminal Trials*, vol. 1, p. 164.

[63] On Gypsy syncretism, see E.B. Trigg, *Gypsy Demons and Divinities* (Seacaucus, NJ, 1973), ch. 3–4, 10; C.G. Leland, *Gypsy Sorcery and Fortune Telling* (London, 1891); T.W. Thompson, 'Two Tales of Experience', *Journal of the Gypsy Lore Society*, series III, 22: 47–8; David Mayall, 'The Making of British Gypsy Identities, c. 1500–1980', *Immigrants and Minorities* (1992), vol. 11, pp. 21–41. More generally, see Angus Fraser, *The Gypsies* (Cambridge, MA, 1992); Jim MacLaughlin, 'European Gypsies and the Historical Geography of Loathing', *Review* (Fernand Braudel Center) (1999), 22: 31–59.

[64] In R.B., *A Description Of the King and Queene of Fayries, their habit, fare, their abode, pompe, and state, Beeing very delightfull to the sense, and full of mirth* (London, 1635).

None of this should be taken to suggest that early modern Scots were not thoroughly instructed in not just Christianity, but rigorously Reformed theology. They were. But one message seems not to have gotten through – the exclusivity of the Christian creed. It was possible, in practice, for multiple and mutually contradictory cosmologies to exist simultaneously in a world of uncertainty and subjection to the arbitrary forces of nature.

CHAPTER 10

Sacred Spas? Healing Springs and Religion in Post-Reformation Britain

Alexandra Walsham

Research conducted over the last decade has greatly enriched and complicated our understanding of the relationship between religion and medicine in early modern Europe. It is no longer possible to identify the Reformation as an unequivocal ally of the so-called Scientific Revolution in the secularization of the eclectic culture of healing that had characterized the medieval period – to fit it into a narrative that charts the progressive 'disenchantment of the world' and celebrates the progressive triumph of rationalism over 'superstition'. Old certainties about Protestantism's role in these processes of desacralization have been eroded in the face of increasingly complex and nuanced accounts of the intimate interconnections between religious ideology and medical knowledge and practice in the sixteenth and seventeenth centuries. The work of Andrew Cunningham, Ole Grell, David Harley and Andrew Wear, among others, has highlighted how far developments such as the rise of Paracelsian and Helmontian medicine were both stimulated by and implicated in the confessional upheavals of this era. It has also underlined the extent to which the diagnosis, explanation and treatment of illness remained governed by moral and theological assumptions. Patients and doctors continued to regard disease as a spiritual as well as physical condition, and to approach its prevention and relief in the context of deep-seated convictions about providential intervention. By repudiating many traditional magical and ecclesiastical remedies and condemning unlearned practitioners, the Reformation did play a part in demarcating sharper boundaries between the care of the soul and the cure of the body and in facilitating the emergence of the latter as a secular profession. But many points of overlap and intersection remained. Physicians were often imbued with a belief in the heavenly origin and nature of their vocation; ministers frequently combined the practice of divinity with that of medicine; and, albeit sometimes grudgingly, Protestantism found ways of meeting the ongoing lay desire and need for supernatural healing.[1]

---

[1]   Some key contributions include Charles Webster, *The Great Instauration: Science, Medicine and Reform 1626–1660* (London, 1975); W.J. Sheils (ed.), *The Church and Healing*, Studies in Church History, 19 (Oxford, 1982); Andrew Wear,

This chapter seeks to add a further dimension to this intricate and ambivalent picture by exploring the impact the Reformation had upon the beliefs and practices associated with healing springs in early modern Britain. Close study of these sites further questions any suggestion that the transformations that followed in the wake of the advent of Protestantism decisively severed the ties between the cultures of religion and healing. Rejecting any simple link between the demise of medieval holy wells and the apotheosis of fashionable resorts renowned for their sanative waters, I shall draw attention instead to the more subtle processes of adaptation and modification that accompanied the entrenchment of the Reformation between 1550 and 1700.[2] The hallmark of this story is a triangular interaction between the priorities of religious reform, the pretensions of learned medicine, and the unruly medical pluralism that marked the outlook of the English people at large. Its central contention is that healing springs and spas were still regarded by contemporaries as in some sense sacred.

Holy Wells and the Early Reformation

We must begin by briefly reviewing the place that wells and springs occupied in the late medieval culture of healing. In a context in which sickness was widely believed to be a trial or punishment sent by the Almighty, many instinctively turned to the Church in search of relief from their physical and mental afflictions. On the eve of the Reformation, it had

---

'Puritan Perceptions of Illness in Seventeenth-century England', in Roy Porter (ed.), *Patients and Practitioners: Lay Perceptions of Medicine in Pre-industrial Society* (Cambridge, 1985), pp. 55–99; David Harley, 'Spiritual Physic, Providence and English Medicine, 1560–1640', in Ole Peter Grell and Andrew Cunningham (eds), *Medicine and the Reformation* (London, 1993), pp. 101–17; David Harley, 'Medical Metaphors in English Moral Theology, 1560–1660', *Journal of the History of Medicine*, 48 (1993): 396–43; Andrew Wear, 'Religious Beliefs and Medicine in Early Modern England', in Hilary Marland and Margaret Pelling (eds), *The Task of Healing: Medicine, Religion and Gender in England and the Netherlands, 1450–1800* (Rotterdam, 1996), pp. 145–69; Ole Peter Grell and Andrew Cunningham (eds), *Religio Medici: Medicine and Religion in Seventeenth-century England* (Aldershot, 1996); Andrew Wear, *Knowledge and Practice in English Medicine, 1550–1680* (Cambridge, 2000); Ole Peter Grell, 'Medicine and Religion in Sixteenth-century Europe', in Peter Elmer (ed.), *The Healing Arts: Health, Disease and Society in Europe 1500–1800* (Manchester, 2004), pp. 84–107.

[2]   This chapter builds on my 'Reforming the Waters: Holy Wells and Healing Springs in Protestant England', in Diana Wood (ed.), *Life and Thought in the Northern Church, c.1100–1700: Essays in Honour of Claire Cross*, Studies in Church History 12 (Woodbridge, 1999), pp. 227–55, and draws on material gathered for a chapter in *The Reformation of the Landscape: Religion, Identity and Memory in Early Modern Britain and Ireland* (Oxford, forthcoming, 2009).

a flourishing department of health. When conventional human remedies failed, the laity invoked a vast hierarchy of celestial doctors – specialist saints renowned for healing particular diseases and complaints. Their relics and images, together with the consecrated host and a proliferating body of sacramentals, were supposed to be potent sources of therapeutic power and appropriated in ways that constantly tested the boundaries between religious supplication and magical coercion and between prayer and spell. Many undertook pious and penitential pilgrimages to shrines and holy places associated with Christ, the Virgin Mary and other heavenly helpers in anticipation of miraculous cures, engaging in ritual perambulations around them, reciting specified prayers, and often leaving behind *ex voto* gifts in fervent thanks for thaumaturgic services rendered. It is hardly surprising that so many charitable hospitals grew up in the vicinity of and on the routes to them.[3]

Hallowed wells were an integral part of this late medieval geography of the sacred. Some such sites built upon a continuous tradition of visitation dating from before the arrival of Christianity in these islands. While some early Christian missionaries had sought to combat heathen worship of water by destroying venerated fountains, others re-dedicated them to the new faith they preached, ingeniously converting them into baptisteries, absorbing them into ecclesiastical precincts, and disseminating fresh legends about their supernatural origin as testimonies of divine approbation of the martyrs and saints who had struggled to vanquish paganism.[4] Other holy wells were later discoveries or rediscoveries. Although known to the Romans as Aquae Arnemetae, Christian pilgrimage to St Anne's Well at Buxton, for instance, seems to date from around the mid-fifteenth century, after an image of the saint was allegedly found immersed in it. Some of these springs, like St Winifred's Well in North Wales, which was said to have burst forth where the severed head of this seventh-century Celtic virgin fell, enjoyed royal patronage and papal support in the form of the grant of special indulgences. As a consequence, they were covered by elaborate architectural structures, served by designated priests, and surrounded by buildings erected for the accommodation of devout and

---

[3]   See Ronald C. Finucane, *Miracles and Pilgrims: Popular Beliefs in Medieval England* (London, 1977), ch. 4–5; on the medieval culture of healing more generally, see Nancy G. Siraisi, *Medieval and Early Renaissance Medicine: An Introduction to Knowledge and Practice* (Chicago, IL, 1990), esp. ch. 5, and Carol Rawcliffe, *Medicine and Society in Later Medieval England* (Stroud, 1995), esp. ch. 1.

[4]   See Valerie I.J. Flint, *The Rise of Magic in Early Medieval Europe* (Oxford, 1991), ch. 8–9, esp. pp. 256–7, 262–8; James Rattue, *The Living Stream: Holy Wells in Historical Context* (Woodbridge, 1995), ch. 3–5; John Blair, *The Church in Anglo-Saxon Society* (Oxford, 2005), esp. pp. 221–8, 471–89.

poorly visitors.[5] But many more operated on or beyond the edges of the ecclesiastical establishment. Occupying marginal locations in the natural landscape, these numinous places often evoked clerical unease and anxiety. Bishops like Oliver Sutton of Lincoln and Robert Mascall of Hereford frowned upon spontaneous lay cults which sprang up around wells which had worked medical miracles, and did their best to suppress them, ever conscious of the danger that orthodox piety could spill over into 'superstition'.[6] This was especially true of those sites associated with saintly figures revered by the populace who had not yet been formally canonized. In the eyes of senior churchmen, too often the laity seemed to treat such springs as if they possessed intrinsic holiness, as if the water itself was an infallible remedy rather than dependent on the grace of God and the intercession of the company of heaven. Such concerns were powerfully re-articulated by humanists like Erasmus, who ruthlessly satirized the vulgar credulity of visitors to the well associated with Our Lady of Walsingham, who hoped it would relieve them from migraines and digestive troubles, among other ailments.[7] The contempt of such divines for holy wells was frequently reinforced by the scorn of learned physicians sceptical of treatments somewhat at odds with the rigid conventions of Galenism and intent upon preserving their own monopoly on healing. This is not to say that drinking from and bathing in water had no place in university medicine, as the role doctors played in promoting Bath and the renowned spas of Continental Europe reveals.[8] But it remains true that many wells hovered on the fringes of both religious and medical respectability. They symptomized the therapeutic eclecticism of the late medieval period and the vitality and vulnerability of pre-Reformation piety.

---

[5]   For St Anne's Well, see John Jones, *The benefit of the auncient bathes of Buckstones* (London, 1572), fo. 1v. It is mentioned by William Worcestre *c.* 1460: *Itineraries*, ed. John H. Harvey (Oxford, 1969), p. 69. For Holywell, see my 'Holywell: Contesting Sacred Space in Early Modern Wales', in Will Coster and Andrew Spicer (eds), *Sacred Space in Early Modern Europe* (Cambridge, 2005), pp. 211–36, esp. 213–14.

[6]   Rosalind M.T. Hill (ed.), *The Rolls and Register of Bishop Oliver Sutton 1280–1299*, vol. 6, Lincoln Record Society, 64 (1969), pp. 186–7; E.N. Dew (ed. and trans.), *Diocese of Hereford. Extracts from the Cathedral Registers A.D. 1275–1535* (Hereford, 1932), p. 97.

[7]   Desiderius Erasmus, *The Whole Familiar Colloquies*, trans. and ed. Nathan Bailey (London, 1877), pp. 238–57.

[8]   Richard Palmer, '"In this our Lightye and Learned Tyme": Italian Baths in the Era of the Renaissance', in Roy Porter (ed.), *The Medical History of Waters and Spas*, *Medical History*, Supplement 10 (1990), pp. 14–22, and other chapters in this volume; Katharine Park, 'Natural Particulars: Medical Epistemology, Practice and the Literature of Healing', in Anthony Grafton and Nancy Siraisi (eds), *Natural Particulars: Nature and the Disciplines in Renaissance Europe* (Cambridge, MA, 1999), pp. 347–67.

The emergence of Protestantism in England, as elsewhere, was accompanied by a sustained assault on the assumptions that underpinned the practice of pilgrimage to sacred healing springs. Reformed theologians vehemently rejected the idea that particular places and material objects had any kind of implanted sanctity, and condemned the cult of saints and its many manifestations as a species of idolatry that would draw down the consuming wrath of the Almighty. Those who undertook ritual journeys to wells in search of medical assistance were guilty of placing an almost animistic trust in created nature which such writers compared with pagan worship of old. In the context of a growing chorus of claims that miracles had ceased, they insisted that many celebrated cures associated with these sites were evidence of diabolical guile or human fraud, denouncing them as the stratagems Satan used to seduce human beings to sin and as deceitful stories spread by corrupt and greedy clerics intent upon lining their own pockets or filling the coffers of churches and monasteries. Such suggestions were echoed by the Elizabethan rector of Radwinter in Essex, William Harrison, in the 1570s, who declared that the alleged virtues of many such holy wells were 'now found to be but baits to draw men and women unto them, either for gain unto the places where they were or satisfaction of the lewd disposition of such as hunted after other game'.[9]

Not a few wells were the targets of iconoclasm. Thus in 1538 the Henrician authorities 'lokkyd upp and sealyd the bathys' at Buxton and took away the crutches, shirts and sheets left behind by grateful pilgrims, 'being thynges thatt dyd alure and intyse the ygnorant pepull'.[10] Sadler's Well at Islington, the therapeutic properties of which were said to derive from the prayers of the priests of the priory of Clerkenwell, was likewise defaced and filled in during the early phases of the Reformation.[11] The suppression of such sites was an ongoing process. A spring in Pembrokeshire dedicated to St Meigan was only destroyed in 1592, the workman being told not to leave a single stone of the associated chapel still standing;[12] in Scotland, the presbytery of Dunbarton was ordering a well at Lochlongshead to be 'ditt up and demolish[ed]' as late as 1643, to the end that 'it be no more a stumbling block'. St Mary's Well at Seggat was twice 'stopt up with

---

[9]   William Harrison, *The Description of England*, ed. George Edelen (Ithaca, NY, 1968), p. 274. For an earlier denunciation, see Hugh Latimer, *Sermons and Remains*, ed. G.E. Corrie, Parker Society (Cambridge, 1845), pp. 363–4.

[10]   Thomas Wright (ed.), *Three Chapters of Letters Relating to the Suppression of the Monasteries*, Camden Society, OS 26 (1843), pp. 143–4.

[11]   R.C. Hope, *The Legendary Lore of the Holy Wells of England: Including Rivers, Lakes, Fountains, and Springs* (London, 1893), p. 89.

[12]   Francis Jones, *The Holy Wells of Wales* (Cardiff, 1992; 1st pub. 1954), pp. 59–60.

stones' on the instruction of the Synod of Aberdeen in the mid-seventeenth century.[13]

The protracted character of the crusade against consecrated wells reflects the fact that the Church and state lacked both the bureaucratic capacity and the mechanical resources to tackle all the watery 'idols' that were scattered across the varied landscape of the British Isles. Consequently, many outlying springs which lay beyond the gaze of overworked justices survived the upheavals of 1540s, 1550s and 1560s or fell outside their jurisdiction, having been absorbed into the estates of gentlemen who purchased monastic and ecclesiastical lands after the Dissolution. Some eventually fell into abeyance, but numerous others seem to have remained the destination of a steady stream of sick patients. The Council of the Marches took repeated steps to prevent 'superstitious flocking' to Holywell, and elsewhere in England and Wales people continued to frequent less conspicuous hallowed wells and springs hoping to be cured of their ills, sometimes attracting the negative attention of diocesan officials.[14] In Scotland, the Calvinist Church made more systematic and determined efforts to stamp out such practices. A parliamentary Act imposing draconian penalties upon offenders was passed in 1581, and the records of the kirk sessions provide telling evidence of the difficulty elders had in persuading the laity that such visits were wicked. In 1630, for example, it was declared that any inhabitants of Nigg found visiting St Fittack's well 'in an superstitious maner for seeking health for thameselves or their bairnes' would be punished as 'fornicatouris'. Despite repeated admonitions, many stubbornly persisted in circumambulating such sites, depositing pins and leaving behind sacrificial scraps of clothing as symbols of the diseases from which they had been or hoped to be relieved by washing or drinking. Christ's Well at Mentieth, for instance, was described as 'all tapestried about with old rags' in 1618.[15] The tendency for such visits to take place on the Sabbath, and the disorderly sociability for which wells acted as a magnet, further fuelled the determination of the authorities to eradicate these lingering traces of popish error and idolatry. Against the

---

[13]   Ruth and Frank Morris, *Scottish Healing Wells* (Sandy, 1982), pp. 189, 190.

[14]   British Library, London, MS Cotton Vitellius C. I, fos 81v–82r; MS Royal 18B, VII, fo. 1v. For examples of such practices attracting ecclesiastical attention, see W.P.M. Kennedy (ed.), *Elizabethan Episopal Administration*, Alcuin Club Collections 25–7 (London, 1924), vol. 3, p. 142; J.S. Purvis (ed.), *Tudor Parish Documents of the Diocese of York* (Cambridge, 1948), pp. 169, 179.

[15]   T. Thompson and C. Innes (eds), *The Acts of the Parliaments of Scotland 1124–1707* (1814–75), vol. 3, pp. 212–13; Morris and Morris, *Scottish Healing Wells*, pp. 38–9; Jones, *Holy Wells*, p. 95. See also Margo Todd, *The Culture of Protestantism in Early Modern Scotland* (New Haven, CT, 2002), pp. 202–8, 219.

backdrop of a wider attack on the therapeutic use of amulets, charms and Catholic sacramentals and on the illicit astrological remedies peddled by local sorcerers and wizards, the Protestant campaign against thaumaturgic springs may be seen as one strand of a vigorous drive to curtail and reform a vibrant popular tradition of magical and mystical healing.

Healing Springs and Protestant Piety

Yet it would be wrong to imply that the Reformation created a climate of opinion that was inherently hostile to the watering places to which men and women from all sections of the social spectrum had long resorted when other sources of help had proved of no avail. In this regard, it is striking to find that the period from the 1570s onwards saw the revival of a number of springs that had enjoyed a notable reputation for cures in the medieval period, but which had withered in the face of the iconoclastic fury of the previous three decades. Within less than a generation of the Elizabethan Settlement, the physician John Jones was lauding the remarkable medical benefits of 'the auncient [thermal] Bathes' of Buxton in a tract dedicated to the earl of Shrewsbury, through whose generosity new facilities had recently been erected for the convenience of visitors and patients.[16] The so-called Bristol Hotwells at Clifton had hitherto been known as St Vincent's Spring, and a 'new found well' at Utkinton in Cheshire whose therapeutic powers were advertised in a pamphlet of 1600 appears to have been the reincarnation of an earlier fountain dedicated to St Stephen.[17] Bath, the Christianized shrine of Aquae Sulis Minerva, likewise grew to new prominence as a centre for hydrotherapy in this period, the virtues of this 'verye excellent treasure' being celebrated in a book written by the former Edwardian dean of Wells and Protestant exile Dr William Turner.[18]

The ability of such wells successfully to re-invent themselves was usually dependent upon demonstrating that their waters possessed mineral content. The sulphurous qualities of several springs in the vicinity of Knaresborough and Harrogate helped to secure their future as the pre-eminent northern 'spaw' before the end of the sixteenth century, promoted first by a local minister Timothy Bright, a former physician at St Bartholomew's Hospital in London, and later by the York practitioners Edmund Deane, Michael Stanhope and John French. But despite its long-standing reputation for healing lameness and for curing the debilitating condition of rickets in infants, St Mungo's well, just six miles away at Copgrove, was dismissed as

---

[16]   Jones, *Benefit*, sigs ±2r–3r.

[17]   British Library, London, MS Sloane 640, fo. 341v; G.W., *Newes out of Cheshire of the New Found Well* (London, 1600); Rattue, *Living Stream*, p. 111.

[18]   William Turner, *A booke of the natures and properties as well of the bathes in England as of other bathes in Germany and Italy* (Cologne, 1562), at sig. A2r.

'an ineffectual superstitious relique of popery' because no such properties were detected upon experiment. Tales of its efficacy were denounced as 'feigned' and 'imaginary'.[19] The same fate befell St Winifred's Well in North Wales: in 1579, the Privy Council ordered its deputies in the West Midlands to assess its freezing waters to see if they were 'medicinable', and if so, to facilitate the admission of 'dyseased persons' to the same.[20] But it, too, failed the test and was relegated beyond the clinical pale.

The emphasis that Elizabethan writers placed on the natural causes of the cures wrought by healing springs was driven by a fervent distaste for the cult of saints and underpinned by a conviction that in the modern age, miracles had, for the most part, ceased. It reflected the distinctly anti-Catholic agenda that lay behind of the early promotion of English spas. Phyllis Hembrey has argued that the Church, state and medical profession collaborated in propagating new watering places like Wellingborough and Newnham Regis in order to counteract the attractions of medieval holy wells and foreign baths which were becoming focal points not merely for conservative resistance to the new religion, but increasingly for militant recusancy and conspiratorial activity.[21] This took place against the backdrop of attempts by Tridentine missionaries trained in Rome and the Low Countries to harness the repudiated thaumaturgic tradition at Holywell for polemical and proselytizing purposes. The decaying shrine became the centrepiece of the evangelical endeavours of Jesuit and seminarians in the region, and authenticated post-Reformation miracles wrought by the spring were recorded in a register and circulated in manuscript, not a few of them involving the conversion of hardened Protestants to the Catholic faith and detailing the divine judgements that befell heretics who mocked its therapeutic properties.[22] At the same time, new well cults were emerging in connection with martyred priests such as George Napper: a spring near the spot where his mangled quarters were displayed in Oxford in 1611 attracted crowds of miracle-seeking pilgrims until it was stopped up by order of the vice-chancellor of the university.[23] And Michael Stanhope expressed his relief that Knaresborough had not fallen into the hands of

---

[19]   Edmund Deane, *Spadacrene Anglica. Or, the English spa fountain* (1626), ed. James Rutherford (Bristol, 1922); M[ichael] S[tanhope], *Newes out of Yorkshire* (London, 1627); M[ichael] S[tanhope], *Cures without care, or a summons to all such who find little or no helpe by the use of ordinary physicke to repaire to the northerne spaw* (London, 1631); John French, *The York-shire spaw* (London, 1652). Quotations from ibid., p. 1 and Deane, *Spadacrene Anglica*, pp. 72–4.

[20]   British Library, MS Cotton Vitellius C. I, fos 81v–82r.

[21]   Phyllis Hembrey, *The English Spa 1560–1815: A Social History* (London, 1990), ch. 1.

[22]   See Walsham, 'Holywell', pp. 221–30.

[23]   Michael Questier (ed.), *Newsletters from the Archpresbyterate of George Birkhead*, Camden Society, 5th series, 12 (1998), p. 99.

'our jugling [and] imposturing' 'Romish locusts': otherwise, by means of 'Mountebank trickes' they would surely have used it as propaganda to uphold the erroneous doctrines of the resurgent Catholic Church.[24] Such commentators saw mineral springs which cured through natural causes as a means of counteracting clerical efforts to restore the nation to obedience to Rome.

Over time, anti-popery may have receded as a motive for promoting mineral springs, but the process of reclaiming former holy wells which bore traces of vitriol, alum, bitumen, chalybeate and nitre gathered momentum and pace in the seventeenth century. A brackish spring at Witherslack in the Barony of Kendal, once reputed sacred and still known locally as 'Holy Well', was found 'by accident' in 1656 by a girl collecting strawberries who drank from it to quench her thirst.[25] Writing in 1677, Robert Plot believed that an ancient Staffordshire well dedicated to St Erasmus, though now 'overgrown with weeds', might still be of considerable benefit to the sick because its oily waters were infused with sulphur.[26]

The rehabilitation of older sites occurred alongside the development of 'new' ones, though often it may be suspected that earlier Catholic – not to say pagan – associations of these places had simply passed out of living memory. This may have been influenced by the growing vogue for iatrochemical medicine as espoused by Paracelsus and Van Helmont and by the evolving interest of erudite gentlemen in natural history.[27] The scientific trial of springs became the learned pastime of men like John Aubrey, who were also eager to make money from their discoveries.[28] Physicians, clergy and lay people co-operated in bringing such springs to public attention and in presenting them as serious rivals to Continental watering places such as Sauvenieu and Spa. Detailing the amenities of these sites and making inflated claims about their curative potential, the technical treatises advertising them embodied a blatant attempt to attract new clients and to discredit competitors. The origins of the renowned Georgian spas Tunbridge Wells, Epsom and Scarborough can all be traced back to the early or later Stuart period, while in presbyterian Scotland, doctors such as William Barclay and Patrick Anderson joined forces with

---

[24]   Stanhope, *Newes*, pp. 28–9.
[25]   Jane M. Ewbank (ed.), *Antiquary on Horseback: The Collections of the Rev. Thomas Machell, Chaplain to King Charles II , towards a History of the Barony of Kendal*, Cumberland and Westmorland Archaeological and Antiquarian Society, extra series, 19 (Kendal, 1963), p. 80.
[26]   Robert Plot, *The natural history of Staffordshire* (Oxford, 1686), p. 99.
[27]   See Noel G. Coley, '"Cures without Care": "Chymical Physicians" and Mineral Waters in Seventeenth-century English Medicine', *Medical History*, 23 (1979), pp. 191–214.
[28]   Michael Hunter, *John Aubrey and the Realm of Learning* (London, 1975), esp. pp. 109, 110n, 196.

wealthy lairds in advertising the virtues of healing springs at Aberdeen, Kinghorne Craig and Peterhead.[29] While some such sites thrived, becoming highly fashionable resorts of the rich and refined, others, like one identified near Sherburn in Yorkshire in 1613, were rather more short-lived, their fame evaporating after a few short years or months.[30]

As the heated theological battles of the sixteenth century abated and the influence of the chemical physicians waned, even springs that lacked notable mineral properties began to acquire the imprimatur of health professionals. Sir John Floyer's influential *Essay* on cold bathing of 1702 is indicative of the way in which the frigid waters of once disparaged wells like St Mungo and St Winifred came to be re-embraced as an efficacious natural cure for a veritable A to Z of painful and incapacitating conditions. Its principal aim was to encourage public resort to a bath lately constructed around a plentiful spring a mile from Lichfield, which Floyer, a high Church enthusiast, christened St Chad's in respectful memory of the medieval bishop of the city who was 'one of the first converters of our nation'.[31] A similar long-term shift from total rejection to partial resurrection and eventual acceptance has been traced in Lutheran Denmark, though here healing springs were never commercialized to the same degree that they were in Britain.[32]

We should pause before seeing the medicalization of wells as a symptom of the onward march of secularization and the triumph of a scientific rationalism for which Protestantism acted as an enthusiastic midwife. It is important to stress that contemporary perception of such sites remained firmly locked within a framework of religious assumptions. The physicians who wrote such tracts may have stressed that God now rarely chose to

---

[29]   See Hembrey, *English Spa*, pp. 44–9, 74–5; Lodowick Rowzee, *The Queenes welles. That is a treatise of the nature and vertues of Tunbridge water* (London, 1632); Robert Wittie, *Scarborough spaw, or a description of the nature and vertues of the spaw at Scarborough* (London, 1660). William Barclay, *Callirhoe, the nymph of Aberdene, resuscitat* ([Edinburgh], 1615); William Barclay, *The nature and effects of the new-found well at Kinghorne* (Edinburgh, 1618); Patrick Anderson, *The colde spring of Kinghorne Craig* (Edinburgh, 1618); A[ndrew] M[ure], *Pegiama: or the vertues of, and way how to use the minerall and medicinall-water at Peterhead in Scotland* ([Aberdeen, 1636?]).

[30]   *The Life and Times of Anthony Wood*, ed. Andrew Clark, Oxford Historical Society, 19, 21, 26, 30, 40 (1891–1900), vol. 2, p. 302.

[31]   John Floyer, *The ancient psychrolusia revived, or, an essay to prove cold bathing both safe and useful in four letters* (London, 1702), p. 17 and passim. See also Mark Jenner, 'Bathing and baptism: Sir John Floyer and the politics of cold bathing', in Kevin Sharpe and Steven N. Zwicker (eds), *Refiguring Revolutions: Aesthetics and Politics from the English Revolution to the Romantic Revolution* (Berkeley, CA, 1998), pp. 197–216.

[32]   Jens C.V. Johansen, 'Holy Springs and Protestantism in Early Modern Denmark: A Medical Rationale for a Religious Practice', *Medical History*, 41 (1997), pp. 59–69.

work by interrupting or overriding the order established at Creation and devoted increasing attention to secondary and subordinate causes, but this did not mean that they lacked reverence for the supreme and first. If they dismissed 'monkish' legends about the intercession of the saints, they did not deny the intervention of the omnipotent hand of Almighty, the only true physician of bodies and souls. Their search for a deeper comprehension of the mysterious workings of nature in these marvellous waters was by no means incompatible with providential piety.

Tract writers drew frequent parallels between the spas and springs they sought to promote and the thaumaturgic waters described in the Old and New Testaments: the River Jordan which had cured Naaman the Syrian of his leprosy, and the Pool of Bethesda, around which the lame and impotent lay, waiting for the angel to ripple its surface. Quoting Ecclesiastes 38:4 ('The Lord hath created Medicines out of the Earth, and he that is wise will not despise them'), Protestant physicians described health-giving baths and springs as the 'precious gifts' and 'great blessings' bestowed upon the British nations by a benevolent deity. Discussing the healing wells near Newnham Regis in the late 1570s, Walter Bailey, Regius Professor of Physic at Oxford, patriotically insisted that they were evident tokens that God approved of the English Reformation itself – 'plaine arguments, to bring other princes to imbrace the Gospell' and root out all superstition and idolatry from their kingdoms and 'to induce all men to forsake such puddle pits which mans devise hath digged and drinke onely of the cleere fountaines of his word'.[33] Later writers intent on attracting patients to Latham Spa in Lancashire, to the vitrioline spring at Durham and the Lewisham wells in Kent continued to trace out the 'disposing and digitating hand of Providence' in a similar vein, detecting the Lord's finger and 'signature' in the emergence of sites that supplemented the acknowledged deficiencies of the human art of physic.[34] Sometimes the serendipitous discovery or rediscovery of sanative springs was described as providential or even 'miraculous' itself. With regard to Tunbridge Wells, Thomas Fuller commented that it was 'usual for Providence when intending Benefit to Mankind to send some signal chance on the Errand to bring the first Tidings thereof', and as late as the 1750s the healing properties of a well

---

[33]   See Stanhope, *Newes*, title page; Turner, *Booke*, sig. A2r; Edward Jorden, *A discourse of naturally bathes, and minerall waters* (London, 1631), p. 139; Walter Bailey, *A briefe discours of certain bathes or medicinall waters in the countie of Warwick nere unto a village called Newnham Regis* (London, 1587), sigs A2v–3r.

[34]   Edmund Borlase, *Latham Spaw in Lancashire* (London, 1670), p. 8 and passim; E[dward] W[ilson], *Spadacrene Dunelmensis* (London, 1675); John Peter, *A treatise of Lewisham (but vulgarly called Dullwich) wells* (London, 1680), p. 73.

at Glastonbury were supposed to have been revealed through the preter- or supernatural medium of a dream.[35]

In keeping with the conviction that medicine was a godly calling, some doctors even presented themselves as instruments of divine will. Having been settled by the 'disposing hand of Providence' in Lewisham, which the Lord 'out of his liberal bounty hath blest with this Medicinal water', the later seventeenth-century London practitioner John Peter regarded it as his duty to use his 'utmost endeavour to investigate its virtues for the general good' and to offer his professional assistance at no cost to those who came to drink it.[36] It is not always easy to gauge the depth of this pious rhetoric and assess how far it was merely a deceptive veneer masking self-interest. The stress that the authors of these tracts placed on the necessity of following the directions and seeking the advice of learned and licensed physicians was at one level a fairly transparent bid to establish their hegemony in a crowded medical marketplace. It was an attempt to undermine the credibility and appeal of a heterogenous body of quacks, astrological doctors, cunning men and women, and in the words of Tobias Venner of Bath, 'pil-boasting Surgeons' and 'sottish Empirickes'.[37] According to Edward Wilson of Durham, such fraudsters were adept at 'cunningly pick[ing] men's purses with applause and satisfaction'.[38] Only after rigorously preparing the body by purgation and by adhering to the strict rules regarding diet, the timing of bathing and drinking, and a pattern of gentle but bracing exercise under professional supervision, would healing springs prove efficacious to ailing laypeople. There was a certain irony in this: the very detail they went into in print supplied patients with sufficient instruction to render their personal services redundant and unscrupulous practitioners with the smattering of practical knowledge they needed to set themselves up in business. In his pamphlet about the healing well at Aberdeen published in 1615, William Barclay refrained from prescribing precise forms of bodily preparation for this exact reason, lest they 'minister occasion to ignorant leeches to the abuse of men's health'.[39]

The authors of the spa literature went on to warn that the 'voluntarie wilfulness' of those who neglected all counsel and glutted themselves with ridiculous quantities of liquid was not merely foolhardy; it could also be

---

[35]   Thomas Fuller, *The history of the worthies of England* (London, 1662), 2nd pagination, p. 62; Hembrey, *English Spa*, p. 170, and Rattue, *Living Stream*, p. 122.

[36]   Peter, *Treatise of Lewisham*, 87–8 (*vere* 107–8).

[37]   Tobias Venner, *The baths of Bathe* (London, 1628), pp. 15–16.

[38]   Wilson, *Spadacrene Dunelmensis*, sig. B4v.

[39]   Barclay, *Callirhoe*, sig. B2r. On this theme, see also David Harley, 'A Sword in a Madman's Hand: Professional Opposition to Popular Consumption in the Waters Literature of Southern England and the Midlands, 1570–1870', in Porter (ed.), *Medical History of Waters and Spas*, pp. 48–55.

fatal. It was a 'vulgar and unpardonable errour' to partake of them in a rash and unadvised manner: healing springs used without proper guidance might well prove rather 'Messengers of death' than 'Angels of God'.[40] According to Patrick Madan's short work on Tunbridge Wells, they were like 'a Sword in a Mad-mans hand' – 'not at all Auxiliary, but [instead] pernicious and hurtful'.[41] These warnings were linked with an insistence that healing springs, like other natural medicines, were not absolute or infallible, nor could they cure every condition known to man -- to echo Lodowick Rowzee's remark about the premier Kentish spa, contrary to common opinion, it was not a 'direct Panpharmacon'.[42] Other Stuart physicians such as Michael Stanhope and Edward Jordan also sharply reproved those who took a 'preposterous course', 'expecting a miracle', and then rebuked or blasphemed against God when they went home without any benefit.[43]

The temptation to dismiss all such claims as a cloak for more mercenary motives should be resisted. Precise separation of the 'secular' and 'spiritual' strands of this discourse is as difficult as it is anachronistic. It should not be forgotten that a number of the early spa doctors were also the incumbents of ecclesiastical livings. They saw their efforts to publicise therapeutic wells as an extension of their pastoral endeavours. Elizabethan pioneers in this field, like John Jones (who was presented to the rectory of Treeton in the West Riding of Yorkshire in 1581), envisaged a close partnership between the established Church and the gentlemen proprietors of medicinal baths and springs. Jones called for graduates of physic to be appointed to benefices in Salisbury, Worcester, Bristol, Exeter and other towns within a day's journey of Bath and to prebends in the region's cathedral churches so that they could counsel the ill and prepare them for the waters 'to the better setting forth of Gods glorie, and the magnificence of [his] Maiestie'.[44]

Such writers also continued to underline the necessity of patient prayer and humble repentance. Before one sought the advice of a worldly physician or ventured to travel to a healing spring, wrote William Turner, it was vital to acknowledge that all sickness and affliction was a divine trial of faith or a punishment for iniquity and sin. Jones encouraged bathers at Bath and Buxton to make contrite supplications on their knees

---

[40] Venner, *Baths of Bathe*, p. 5; Wilson, *Spadacrene Dunelmensis*, p. 78; Stanhope, *Newes*, sig. A4v.

[41] Patrick Madan, *A phylosophical, and medicinal essay on the waters of Tunbridge* (London, 1687), p. 5.

[42] Rowzee, *The Queenes welles*, p. 48.

[43] Stanhope, *Newes*, sigs B2v–3r; Edward Jorden, *A discourse of naturall bathes, and mineral waters* (London, 1631), p. 139.

[44] John Jones, *The bathes of bathes ayde*, bound with *A briefe, excellent, and profitable discourse, of the naturall beginning of all growing and living things* (London, 1574), fo. 22v.

in their chambers or by the edge of the waters, and incorporated into his tracts an appropriate prayer for the use of diseased persons, which dwelt on human wickedness and implored the Lord that 'these thyne Elementes of water and mineralles' might 'thorowe thy mighty operacion, clense awaye the lothesomeness of our feeble bodyes'.[45] Writing in 1628, Tobias Venner was no less insistent that prospective patients 'make peace betwixt God and their consciences' before they undertook a journey to a mineral spring or thermal bath.[46] In 1692, Bishop Thomas Ken set forth a fresh compendium of prayers for visitors to Bath, urging bathers to defer to the instruction of their physician, 'for the Lord hath created him', and to begin their cure by reading edifying devotional books.[47] Lutheran clergymen sought to establish a similarly pious atmosphere at German spas dating from this period, such as the cluster of wholesome fountains discovered in the village of Hornhausen near Halberstadt in 1646. Here a wooden chapel was erected by the wells and prayers of thanksgiving held twice a day to acknowledge this great blessing sent by the Almighty. Private forms of meditation were also encouraged by the ministers who served Protestant pilgrims anxious for lasting relief from conditions that had proved to be beyond the feeble reach of human medicine.[48]

Nor were the cures for which such sites became renowned discussed in purely natural terms. The language used to describe the remarkable recovery of patients forsaken by the medical establishment as hopeless cases was often suffused with references to the magnanimous dispensations of Providence, though here, too, it is hard to distinguish between frilly formulae and real fervour. Thus, in the 1630s Mr William Tompson, a postmaster from Wetherby who was desperately sick of a hectic fever, was said to have been restored to perfect health by the waters of Knaresborough '(within a small time, through God's blessings)'.[49] Ten years later, it 'pleased the Lord' to cure three lame children by means of bathing and drinking in the Bristol Hotwells such that they recovered the complete use of their once crippled limbs, and the Essex vicar Ralph Josselin wrote in his diary in 1675 that many glasses of the famous Tunbridge waters had 'passed well

---

[45]   Turner, *Booke*, fos 14v–15r, 17r–v; Jones, *Bathes of Bathes ayde*, fos 27v, 34v–35r; Jones, *Benefit*, fos 13r, 21r–v.

[46]   Venner, *Baths of Bathe*, preface 'To the Reader'.

[47]   Bishop Ken, *Prayers for the use of all persons who come to the baths for cure* (London, 1692), pp. 18–21.

[48]   *A full relation concerning the wonderfull and wholsome fountain. At first discovered in Germany, two miles from the city of Halberstadt* (London, 1646), pp. 1–9. I have also benefited from discussions with Ute Lotz-Heumann, who delivered a paper entitled 'Holy wells and *Wundergeläuf*: Wonders and water in sixteenth- and seventeenth-century Germany' at the Sixteenth Century Studies Conference, San Antonio, Texas, in October 2002.

[49]   Stanhope, *Cures without care*, pp. 10–11.

through him' 'through God's mercy', relieving him (temporarily) of his chronic physical afflictions.[50]

Sometimes ministers, doctors and patients even slipped into speaking of cures as miracles, notwithstanding the fact that this class of events had reputedly stopped occurring when the Primitive Church came of age. This was partly rhetorical, but it also reflected a degree of theological ambiguity on this issue within reformed circles which historians have not always adequately recognized.[51] In the late 1580s, Walter Bailey may have dismissed as superstitious those who 'supposed some secret vertue to be imparted from God to these wels, whence such rare cures were miraculously performed farre beside and beyond the ordinary course of nature', but other writers implied otherwise.[52] Thomas Fuller said that the waters of Buxton were 'little less than miraculous in the effects' they wrought upon numbed joints, frozen nerves and infertile wombs. John Thorp, a sixteen-year-old boy from Chester cured of the scrofula he had been afflicted with since birth after six weeks at the Latham Spa, stood, according to Edmund Borlase, as 'a Miracle of Restoration'.[53] Apparently, not all Protestants were prepared to rule out the possibility that extraordinary remedies of individuals suffering from chronic illnesses and terminal diseases wrought by healing springs might indeed be supernatural in character. Some even believed that they had received divine premonitions that particular springs would be efficacious in healing them of their diseases. In an account of the providences vouchsafed to his family, Sir William Wentworth recalled how his father had been visited by the apparition of an angel clothed as a middle-aged lady during a critical illness in 1561. She anointed his private parts (this made him somewhat 'bashful'), and told him to go to St Anne's Well at Buxton and bathe there. He duly went and thanked God for his happy delivery. It may be suspected that the younger Wentworth had edited the memory of an event rooted in a lingering Catholic belief in the intercession of the saints and glossed it for Protestant consumption, but the story is nevertheless suggestive of the capacity of reformed piety to accommodate older assumptions about the divine origins of healing.[54] Even more revealing is an incident linked with St Madron's Well in Cornwall, a

---

[50]   British Library, MS Sloane 640, fos 343v–344r, and see other examples on fos 340r–350r; *The Diary of Ralph Josselin, 1616–1683*, ed. Alan Macfarlane (Oxford, 1976), p. 586.

[51]   See my 'Miracles in Post-Reformation England', in Kate Cooper and Jeremy Gregory (eds), *Signs, Wonders, Miracles: Representations of Divine Power in the Life of the Church*, Studies in Church History, 41 (Woodbridge, 2005), pp. 273–306.

[52]   Bailey, *Breife discours*, p. 4.

[53]   Fuller, *Worthies*, 1st pagination, p. 231; Borlase, *Latham Spaw*, p. 60.

[54]   J.P. Cooper (ed.), *Wentworth Papers 1597–1628*, Camden Society, 4th ser. 12 (1973), pp. 28–9.

spring that was never formally reclaimed by medical science. Bishop Joseph Hall of Exeter personally investigated the case of the Cornish cripple John Trelille, cured around 1640 after being admonished in a dream to wash in it, concluding that this was 'no lesse then miraculous' and 'the Author [of it] invisible'. In this case, Protestantism can be seen effectively condoning a popular tradition of healing.[55]

The recipients of such blessings continued to leave behind tokens and testimonies of their gratitude in the form of the crutches, sticks and carts that mineral springs and spas had rendered redundant. Notable cures were recorded in registers for the edification of posterity in much the same way as the therapeutic wonders performed by the saints of the Middle Ages, and patients who were fortunate enough to have enjoyed relief were encouraged to bestow alms and offerings on the image of Christ in the poor and needy, many of whom continued to gather promiscuously at such sites just as they had at fourteenth- and fifteenth-century shrines. Michael Stanhope urged readers of his *Cures without care* to look charitably upon the 'poore desolate Parishes' that bordered on Knaresborough, 'which save the ordinary service scarce once a yeare know what the comfortable reflection of a teaching minister meaneth' and to consider the 'starved soules there' who wanted adequate means to have 'the word [of the Lord] dispensed to them'. By 'supplying that defect' by their beneficence, he declared, 'God shall be honoured, and a blessing will be the readier to attend the waters'.[56] Here was an approved alternative to 'popish' good works which Protestant ministers disdained as a means of earning merit or securing salvation, but which some readers may have inferred might still help to speed their recovery.

It was, moreover, widely supposed that medicinal fountains were resources supplied by Providence especially for the sake of those unable to pay the high fees charged by contemporary doctors. Not infrequently articulated by the medics who wrote vernacular tracts about them, this was often in tension with a fear that these 'moyst Physicians' would take away their livelihoods.[57] Describing springs as 'Surgeons to heale sores' and 'Physicians to cure diseases', Thomas Fuller, for instance, saw them as 'the Largesse of heaven to poor people who cannot go to the price of a costly cure'. The idea that such sites constituted a kind of divine NHS also helps to explain the emphasis which many writers placed on the need to dispense the waters *gratis*: it was quite wrong 'to set them to sale and

---

[55]   Joseph Hall, *The great mysterie of godliness* (London, 1652), bk I, pp. 169–70.
[56]   Stanhope, *Cures without care*, pp. 29–30. See also Turner, *Booke*, fo. 17r.
[57]   Quotation from Richard Banister, *A treatise of one hundred and thirteene diseases of the eyes, and eye-liddes* (London, 1622), sig. d1v.

make gain of Gods free gift therein'.[58] The same assumption underlay the stories that were sometimes told about the consequences of unscrupulous attempts to exploit them for personal financial benefit or their profanation or misuse by rowdy visitors. The cures wrought by the wells at Newnham Regis had only occurred for a limited space in the 1570s, suggested Walter Bailey, because of 'the great abuse of them' by people who superstitiously believed they would be automatically efficacious, thereby making them into dangerous idols.[59] According to 'a credible but somewhat unaccountable report', the Lewisham wells lost their taste, odour and salutary effects after an entrepreneurial gentlemen living in the vicinity set about implementing 'a design to inclose and monopolize the Water'. This put a rapid end to 'that specious Project', 'from which undeniable matter of fact', wrote the physician John Peter in 1680, 'give me leave to draw this observation, that in behalf of the Poor (incapacitated to right themselves) God oftentimes immediately steps in for their assistance'.[60] Although she thought it a 'fable', the late seventeenth-century traveller Celia Fiennes similarly recounted the tale of how the owners of the land upon which St Mungo's well was situated 'forbad people coming and stopped [it] up' to prevent inconvenience, only to find themselves overtaken by 'severall Judgements'.[61]

Other forms of abuse might also lead the Lord to take away the singular benefit of these waters. As one Georgian writer lamented, such spas were increasingly becoming less the 'hospitals of invalids' than the 'rendezvous of Wantonness', magnets for pleasure-seeking tourists whose taste for luxury and lack of decorum had long worried moralists. Such anxieties probably contributed to puritanical calls from the late sixteenth century onwards for the abolition of the 'heathenish custom' of mixed bathing, on the grounds that it was an occasion for 'begetting lustfull fires', and to the Sheffield doctor Thomas Short's diatribe in 1734 against this 'beastly filthiness', which revealed a far too flippant regard to the 'high and excellent Gifts of Almighty God'.[62]

Such examples arguably attest to the emergence of a distinctively Protestant version of the concept of sacrilege. It is somewhat ironic that in shifting attention away from the intervention of saints towards the mineral

---

[58] Fuller, *Worthies*, 1st pagination, pp. 3–4.
[59] Bailey, *Briefe discours*, sig. A3r.
[60] Peter, *Treatise*, pp. 75–7.
[61] Christopher Morris (ed.), *The Journeys of Celia Fiennes* (London, 1947), p. 81.
[62] Stanhope, *Newes out of York-shire*, p. 21; Thomas Short, *The natural, experimental, and medicinal history of the mineral waters of Derbyshire, Lincolnshire, and Yorkshire, particularly those of Scarborough* (London, 1734), pp. 244–6, 51, respectively.

and other properties that God had instilled in these waters, the Reformation may inadvertently have encouraged some to a near-idolatry of nature itself. As well as carving out a place for healing springs and spas which had no link with the tainted Catholic and pagan past, Protestantism proved willing and able to embrace, rehabilitate and integrate ancient holy wells into its world in a way that did not inevitably entail their desacralization. In this, as in other respects, it did not effect as decisive a break with the concept of a sacramental universe and magical landscape as we have sometimes been led to believe. Especially as it moved into its second generation, it developed ways of meeting (if not entirely controlling) the continuing lay desire for access to supernatural forces that could alleviate distress and disease. There is perhaps some justification for speaking of a distinctly Protestant tradition of sacred healing.

Popular Medicine on the Margins

Finally, we must turn our attention briefly to the many holy wells and healing springs that failed to become fashionable spas. Eclipsed by their more glittering and commercialized cousins, these more marginal sites largely lay outside the control of learned physicians and profit-seeking gentlemen and of godly magistrates and ministers. They represent an important part of an eclectic lay culture of medical self-help that remains hidden in the shadows. Some of these emerged spontaneously in the course of the early modern period and then as suddenly disappeared, one minute the focus of crowds of health-seeking visitors, the next the victims of the whims of popular fashion and the determination of the representatives of the Tudor and Stuart state to put down such manifestations of disorderly mobility. William Harrison grumbled about the unsubstantiated rumours 'now spread of every spring', and the Cornish topographer Richard Carew recorded in his survey of the county the ephemeral phenomenon of Scarlet's Well near Bodmin: following reports of its efficacy for curing many diseases, 'folke ranne flocking thither in huge numbers, from all quarters'.[63] Edmund Deane and Michael Stanhope of York, bemoaned the credulity and 'giddy precipitation' of the common and meaner sort, who 'no sooner heare' of a medicinal spring 'but (all fit circumstances set apart) they violently rush upon it, perswading themselves ... a sudden laying hold upon any novelty, to be the most advantagious course'.[64]

Others were places where a tradition of healing seems to have been virtually uninterrupted by the Reformation and where, as we have seen, ecclesiastical authorities initially struggled to suppress the residues of the

---

[63] Harrison, *Description of England*, p. 287; Richard Carew, *The survey of Cornwall* (London, 1602), fo. 126v.
[64] Deane, *Spadacrene Anglica*, p. 72; Stanhope, *Newes*, sigs A4v–B1r.

popish religion in the form of old-fashioned rituals of circumambulation, dipping and the depositing of pins, rags, ribbons and coins. The persistence of the practice of visiting such sites in search of remedies is also well documented by seventeenth- and eighteenth-century topographers and local historians. In his collections of 'parochialia', the distinguished scholar Edward Lhwyd, for instance, listed many examples of Welsh people resorting to springs at specified times of the year such as Ascensiontide, washing themselves in them, and then keeping vigil or sleeping in rocky hollows or under ancient megaliths located in the vicinity.[65] Martin Martin, whose celebrated description of the Western Isles of Scotland published in 1703 was even more anthropological in character, recorded evidence of similar ceremonies at wells involving offerings and sunwise perambulation during the ancient season of Beltane in various parts of this barren region.[66] A study of William Borlase's exhaustive research papers on Cornwall compiled in the 1740s and 1750s likewise yields frequent reference to individuals who bathed the bodies of themselves and their children in once-hallowed springs on successive Wednesdays in May and reclined on the cold floor of the ruined chapels situated nearby them.[67] Such examples can be replicated from many other counties of England in the Victorian period, where it is clear that numerous wells had acquired or retained a reputation for dealing with particular complaints, rheumatism, epilepsy, cancer, sterility, headaches and poor eyesight among them.[68]

The learned lay and clerical amateurs who recorded these visitations and practices tended to dismiss them as lamentable relics of popery and paganism, traces of a Catholic and heathen past that seemed an affront to the dignity of a Protestant country but which were simultaneously a source of a certain nostalgia and fascination. No doubt there was a sliver of truth in such claims, especially in the first fifty years after the Reformation. As mentioned above, wells were often places to which Catholics instinctively gravitated, the natural landscape being a repository of memories of an officially obliterated section of British religious history. But, particularly when applied to later centuries, we must be careful of taking these allegations too much at face value, filtered as they were through the distorting lenses of neo-classicism and of the successive obsessions later scholars developed

---

[65]   *Parochialia: Being a Summary of Answers to 'Parochial Queries' in Order to a Geographical Dictionary, etc. of Wales Issued by Edward Lhwyd*, 3 parts, *Archaeologia Cambrensis*, Supplements (London, 1909–11), part 1, pp. 110, 144, 156; part 2, p. 93; part 3, pp. 4, 11, 26, 29, 45, 47, 60, 65–6, 68, 75, 76, 88, 91.

[66]   Martin Martin, *A description of the western islands of Scotland* (London, 1703), pp. 7, 33, 140–41, 229–30, 242, 276–8.

[67]   British Library, London, MS Egerton 2657, fos 10r, 14v, 28v, 38r, 43r–44r.

[68]   See the many examples in Hope, *Legendary Lore*.

with the nation's druidical heritage and the theory of primitive survivals.[69] Many of the people who undertook the journeys and performed the rites in question clearly considered themselves to be upright Protestants and saw no contradiction between their conduct and Reformed theology. Nor should we regard them as telling indices of the long-term failure of the British Reformations to transform collective mentalities. On the contrary, it is possible that they survived in popular culture as much because of the advent of Protestantism as in spite of it.

Several points may be made in conclusion. The first is that visits to unreclaimed springs in fields, woods and on the edges of villages may reflect not so much resistance as adaptation to the changes wrought by the Reformation. In an intriguing essay on Denmark, Jens Johansen has contended that resort to springs in this part of Scandinavia evolved as a way of compensating for the loss of those aspects of worship proscribed from churches by the advent of Lutheranism, less as an underground alternative than as a supplement to the new faith, and one to which the clergy eventually gave a medical and indeed theological rationale.[70] Could a process of displacement from demolished chapels and shrines to numinous spots in the natural world have occurred in England, too? How many of the wells around which the 'popish' and 'pagan' rites recorded by folklorists crystallized were actually fairly recent discoveries rather than ancient holy ones – how many were new spas that had simply failed to take off, rather than timeless loci of therapeutic sanctity? Deprived of the ritual and sacramental ways of alleviating illness which had been supplied and sanctioned by the medieval Church, popular Protestantism spontaneously reproduced them in other contexts. These tentative suggestions find some resonance in Ronald Hutton's recent work on the migration of proscribed liturgical rituals linked with Candlemas, Palm Sunday, Easter and All Saints out of ecclesiastical settings into domestic ones, their transmutation into pastimes reflecting both the resilience of tradition and its capacity to reshape itself in order to survive in a new ideological environment.[71]

The second point is linked with the observation that some wells shed their explicitly Catholic overtones and acquired new associations. In the case of Mother Pugsley's Well in Bristol, for instance, fresh layers of legend were superimposed upon and supplanted older ones. Once owned by St James's Priory and dedicated by the Virgin Mary, in the early eighteenth century it regained its former reputation for healing, its powers allegedly

---

[69]   See my 'Recording Superstition in Early Modern Britain: The Origins of Folklore', in S.A. Smith and Alan Knight (eds), *The Religion of Fools? Superstition Past and Present*, Past and Present Supplement series (forthcoming, 2008).

[70]   Johansen, 'Holy Springs and Protestantism'.

[71]   Ronald Hutton, 'The English Reformation and the Evidence of Folklore', *Past and Present*, 148 (1995): 89–116.

deriving from the tears of the pious widow of a soldier who had been killed in a Civil War siege in 1645. Here, as elsewhere, the end-products of this process sat more than a little uncomfortably with strict Protestant orthodoxy.[72]

Thirdly, there is a sense in which Protestantism actively if unwittingly perpetuated the idea that some healing springs were sacred by continuing to integrate them into the official liturgy. Annual rogationtide processions around the parish bounds often paused at wells to recite a portion of the Gospel or read a prayer. In at least one case recorded by John Aubrey, some Cheshire villagers 'did believe that the water was the better' thereafter.[73] The revival of ceremonies of well dressing and blessing and the refurbishment of surviving medieval well chapels that seems to have accompanied the Laudian campaign to restore the beauty of holiness in England in the 1630s may also have contributed to reinforcing the notion that these fountains should be treated with a certain amount of awe and reverence.[74]

Finally, even where the continuity of older patterns of ritual behaviour and pilgrimage at such sites can be firmly established, these practices had so altered their original meanings that they were coming to be considered harmless, at least by a proportion of the Protestant clergy. In his *Antiquitates vulgares* of 1725, the Newcastle curate Henry Bourne considered the recreational customs associated with springs and wells to be innocent, and even 'commendable'. Even though he suspected they were a distant remnant of popish idolatry, he could see no real danger in the habit of the common people of going to them on summer evenings, 'to refresh themselves with a Walk after the Toil of the Day, to drink the Water of the Fountain, and enjoy the pleasing Prospect of Shade and Stream'.[75] The same may well have applied to the medical customs that continued to be carried out in and around them. Although educated doctors and minister may have regarded them as silly and futile, they no longer saw them as traces of a religious outlook that had to be eliminated. Such attitudes may have helped to preserve lingering traces of medieval techniques of religious healing, even as they index the repeated cycles of re-contextualization that transformed these therapeutic practices in accordance with the rhythms of the Protestant world.

The evidence presented in this chapter thus further emphasizes the ambivalence and tension that lay at the heart of the relationship between

---

[72]   Phil Quinn, *Holy Wells of Bath and Bristol Region* (Little Logaston, 1999), pp. 112–14.

[73]   John Aubrey, *Three Prose Works*, ed. John Buchanan Brown (Fontwell, Sussex, 1972), p. 189.

[74]   I intend to explore and document this phenomenon more fully elsewhere.

[75]   Henry Bourne, *Antiquitates vulgares: or the antiquities of the common people* (Newcastle, 1725), p. 66.

the Reformation and the culture of healing. Protestantism certainly sought to reform some aspects of the eclectic approach of the populace to the relief and prevention of illness, and its priorities did in some respects chime with broader trends that were encouraging a permanent and decisive split between those charged with the treating the body and those with soothing and curing the soul. But this should not be overstated. In complex and interesting ways, it simultaneously sustained other aspects of the pluralistic and inconsistent medical culture which early modern people shared with their medieval forebears. It partially integrated holy wells into a reformed, providential universe. It preserved a nexus between religion and healing, albeit one that was more tenuous and less sacramental than that upheld by either its Catholic precursor or its Tridentine counterpart.

CHAPTER 11

The Reformation of Astronomy

Adam Mosley

Revolutionizing Astronomy

Historians of early modern astronomy and mechanics have traditionally focused on a small number of individuals considered to have contributed most to the evolution and convergence of these disciplines. Tracing the emergence of a new understanding of the cosmos, one that integrated mathematical analysis with natural philosophy, and celestial with terrestrial dynamics, they have tended to move from Copernicus to Newton along two narrative paths. The first of these, passing through Tycho Brahe and Johannes Kepler, encompasses the development of technical astronomy on the basis of new and improved observations of the heavenly bodies. The second, via Galileo Galilei and René Descartes, follows the articulation of a new science of motion combining quantitative and qualitative study of falling objects, projectiles and other difficult cases. Terminating in the so-called Newtonian synthesis of the *Principia*, these two pathways take historians of science from scholastic Aristotelianism to the birth of modern 'classical' physics. They lie at the core of the grand narrative of progress dignified by the title of the Scientific Revolution.

The first of the two strands, from Copernicus to Newton via Tycho and Kepler, constitutes what historians of scientific thought have often called the astronomical or Copernican revolution. Study of the heavens in the sixteenth and seventeenth centuries encompassed a wide range of interests and practices, producing an astronomical culture that was richer by far than the story of revolution would tend to suggest.[1] Nevertheless, focusing on the emergence of the 'new astronomy' of the seventeenth century provides the best way of demonstrating the *significance* of sixteenth-century religious debate in shaping the study of the heavens. Indeed, any treatment that purported to do so without considering at least some of the better-known figures and theories would rightly be considered deficient. It would fail to persuade those most resistant to the idea that attempting to separate the history of early modern science from the history of religion results, at best, in a very partial account. This chapter will therefore concentrate

---

[1]   N. Jardine, 'The Places of Astronomy in Early-modern Culture', *Journal for the History of Astronomy*, 29 (1998): 49–62.

on setting the traditional revolutionary narrative in the context of the Protestant Reformation.

Until relatively recently, the significance of the Reformation for early modern astronomy was not well understood. That there was an important relationship between Christian belief and early modern cosmology was generally recognized in the earlier literature, but this was often represented as being malign. Thanks to nineteenth-century authors such as Andrew Dickson White, it has taken historians some time to see organized religion as anything other than an obstacle to emergence and reception of the new work in astronomy.[2] The Galileo affair, in particular, played a key role in the construction of a myth of warfare between 'science' and 'religion' that it has taken considerable effort on the part of more recent historians of science to dispel. Even now, particularly in the popular imagination, this myth has its adherents. But whereas Galileo was once seen as a rational lover of truth unjustly and irrationally persecuted by the Catholic authorities merely for holding his 'scientific' beliefs, he is now more likely to be depicted as an over-bold trespasser on ground expressly forbidden him, as a non-theologian, by the Council of Trent.[3] Equally, it has taken time and effort to repudiate nineteenth-century claims about the attitudes of the principal Reformers to heliocentrism, and to establish what Martin Luther and Jean Calvin *actually* knew and thought about the Copernican planetary hypotheses.[4] A good deal of labour has therefore been devoted simply to clearing the historical ground of some basic misconceptions about the relationship between study of the heavens and organized religion.

Difficult as it has sometimes been for historians to combat the depiction of Christian faith as an obstacle to science, the harder step has been to appreciate the full extent of the role that both organized religion and personal belief played in shaping approaches to nature. The philosophically informed tendency to see the history of science in terms of the emergence of a method or methods that would exclude the effect of 'irrational' beliefs and 'extraneous' factors has sometimes obscured the fact that the faith of certain individuals might actually have helped

[2]   A.D. White, *A History of the Warfare of Science with Theology in Christendom* (New York, 1896). See also T. Kuhn, *The Copernican Revolution: Planetary Astronomy in the Development of Western Thought* (Cambridge MA, 1957), pp. 185–228.

[3]   R. Blackwell, *Galileo, Bellarmine and the Bible* (Notre Dame, IN, 1991).

[4]   For example, W. Nørlind, 'Copernicus and Luther: A Critical Study', *Isis*, 44 (1953): 273–6; E. Rosen, 'Calvin's Attitude toward Copernicus', *Journal of the History of Ideas*, 21 (1960): 431–41; J. Dillenberger, *Protestant Thought and Natural Science: A Historical Interpretation* (London, 1961), pp. 28–41; J. Christianson, 'Copernicus and the Lutherans', *Sixteenth Century Journal*, 4/2 (1973): 1–10; R. White, 'Calvin and Copernicus: The Problem Reconsidered', *Calvin Theological Journal*, 15 (1980): 233–43; C. Kaiser, 'Calvin, Copernicus and Castellio', *Calvin Theological Journal*, 21 (1986): 5–31.

them to arrive at the 'truth'. And even historians receptive to this thesis have had to overcome the temptation to represent religious belief as a motivating factor or context wholly external to scientific cognition, even one as potent as the 'Puritanism' of Robert Merton in his account of seventeenth-century England.[5] An important historiographical step, still far from universally adopted, has been a reversion to the period language of 'natural philosophy', with all that implies, in place of an anachronistic concept of 'science'. Natural philosophy, as the study of the Created world, was an intrinsically pious activity, and God, in His various guises (first cause, unmoved mover, guarantor of natural law, and so on) was usually invoked in one way or another.[6] The key question is therefore not *whether* religious belief informed individual's perceptions and studies of nature in the early modern period, but *how* did it do so. Once this point of view is accepted, it is a very small step to see that the issue with respect to the Reformation and astronomy is not understanding *whether* some relation between them existed, but determining *what form* that relationship took and just *how far* it extended.

Copernican Astronomy: Content and Context

The Copernican Revolution cannot, of course, be subsumed within the phenomenon of the Reformation, however we choose to define it. Nor, indeed, can the Reformation be said to have been the *principal* cause of the emergence of the new astronomy of the seventeenth century. Assuming that we wish to locate the first significant intellectual shift no later than the realization of the explanatory advantages that heliocentric planetary hypotheses enjoyed over geocentric ones, then we are looking at an event at least three years prior to the indulgence controversy of 1517.[7] In any case, although far less is known about Copernicus' faith than historians might like, there seems no good reason to doubt his outward Catholic conformity. Copernicus' close associate Tiedemann Giese, bishop of Kulm, was an advocate of Erasmian religious tolerance, but not a promoter of Reform.[8]

---

[5] R. Merton, 'Science, Technology, and Society in Seventeenth Century England', *Osiris*, 4 (1938): 360–632; S. Shapin, 'Understanding the Merton Thesis', *Isis*, 79 (1988): 594–605.

[6] A. Cunningham, 'How the *Principia* Got its Name: or, Taking Natural Philosophy Seriously', *History of Science*, 29 (1991): 377–92.

[7] N. Swerdlow, 'The derivation and first draft of Copernicus' planetary theory: A translation of the Commentariolus with commentary', *Proceedings of the American Philosophical Society*, 117 (1973): 423–512, esp. 431.

[8] R. Hooykaas, *G. J. Rheticus' Treatise on Holy Scripture and the Motion of the Earth* (Amsterdam, 1984), pp. 24–7.

Were it necessary to trace the origin of the new cosmological understanding that emerged from Copernicus and his work to just one historical phenomenon, however complex and protracted, then Renaissance humanism would seem to be a far stronger candidate. Copernicus' innovation, in constructing a world-system in which the Earth was set in motion about the Sun, depended on a thorough understanding of the work of his ancient predecessor Ptolemy. Indeed, this move was motivated not by any inherent cosmological radicalism on Copernicus' part, but rather by a desire to emend Ptolemaic mathematical astronomy so as to make it compatible with the Aristotelian principle of uniform circular motion. Both Copernicus' understanding of Ptolemy and his wish to reconcile the ancient authorities in his chosen field of study can readily be interpreted in humanistic terms. Certainly, he, along with other mathematical astronomers of his generation, owed an enormous amount to the humanistic labour of Georg Peurbach and Johannes Regiomontanus, who studied and epitomized Ptolemy's *Almagest* under the patronage of the great Greek-speaking humanist Cardinal Bessarion.[9] Of course, the urgency of the task of reconciliation may well, for Copernicus, have had its roots in matters of faith.[10] He may even have been stimulated by particular Averroist challenges to orthodox Aristotelian natural philosophy that, because they concerned the nature of the soul, pertained to the issue of personal salvation as well as the question of the nature and agents of planetary motion.[11] Yet there is little evidence to suggest that his humanism led him very far even along a path of *Catholic* reform prior to the publication of *De revolutionibus* in 1543.[12]

But if the Reformation was not the wellspring from which the Copernican world-system emerged, it certainly played a substantial role in its subsequent history. The Protestant Reformation shaped the conditions under which the Copernican world-system was publicized. It moulded the circumstances of its reception, both through the creation of a substantial community of competent interpreters of Copernicus' mathematical work and by ensuring that a significant portion of their game needed to be

---

[9]   P.L. Rose, *The Italian Renaissance of Mathematics: Studies on Humanists and Mathematicians from Petrarch to Galileo* (Geneva, 1975), pp. 90–117; N. Swerdlow, 'Astronomy in the Renaissance', in C. Walker (ed.), *Astronomy Before the Telescope* (London, 1996), pp. 187–230, esp. 188–95.

[10]   See B. Wrightsman, 'The legitimation of scientific belief: theory justification by Copernicus', in T. Nickles (ed.), *Scientific Discovery: Case Studies* (Dordrecht, 1980), pp. 51–66.

[11]   P. Barker, 'Copernicus and the Critics of Ptolemy', *Journal for the History of Astronomy*, 30 (1999): 343–58.

[12]   For his use of a rhetoric of reform in 1543, however, see R. Westman, 'Proof, Poetics and Patronage: Copernicus's preface to *De revolutionibus*', in D. Lindberg and R. Westman (eds), *Reappraisals of the Scientific Revolution* (Cambridge, 1990), pp. 167–205.

played on the field of scriptural exegesis, a pitch that it queered. And it played no small part, through its effect on the intellectual development and life choices of several notable individuals, in bringing about some of the key developments in post-Copernican astronomy. Without the Protestant Reformation, therefore, and in particular without the Lutheran reformation, the astronomical revolution as traditionally understood might never have happened.

That the Reformation shaped the circumstances under which the Copernican hypothesis became known is well understood. Copernicus disseminated an outline of his world-system in his *Commentariolus*, a manuscript work that achieved a very small circulation in the mid-1510s, and then began work on a fuller exposition of his theory.[13] It was not, however, until the arrival of Georg Joachim Rheticus, a Wittenberg-trained mathematician, that publication of this fuller account was set properly in motion. Rheticus arranged the printing of *De revolutionibus* with Johannes Petreius in Nuremberg, announced the Copernican theory in his *Narratio prima*, published in 1540, and began the process of overseeing the work through the press.[14] Rheticus' departure to take up a university chair left the oversight of the publication in the hands of a leading Nuremberg reformer, the pugnacious Andreas Osiander. Osiander furnished *De revolutionibus* with an unsigned 'Address to the Reader', in which he reminded Copernicus' audience that astronomers were not in the business of making true claims about the universe. Their role was rather to produce hypotheses, in the form of geometrical devices, that would model the visible celestial phenomena; ease of comprehension and not truth was supposed to be the guiding objective. Often seen as a premeditated betrayal of Rheticus' trust and Copernicus' intentions, Osiander's behaviour has occasionally been interpreted more charitably. It has been pointed out, for example, that by not signing this *Ad lectorem* preface, Osiander protected *De revolutionibus* from the stigma and scrutiny which association with such a notorious reformer would bring.[15] The work was, after all, dedicated by Copernicus to Paul III, the first Counter-Reformation Pope. It has been suggested, therefore, that Osiander's desire, in so undermining the claim to truth of Copernicus' work, was actually to secure a favourable reception for the work and protect it from controversy. If that was so, then Osiander succeeded in his aim: Copernicus' work was studied and utilized by a number of scholars, many of whom seem to have given its cosmological content little credence or thought. Hence, it was really only with the

---

[13] Swerdlow, 'The derivation and first draft of Copernicus' planetary theory'.
[14] Hooykaas, *G. J. Rheticus' Treatise*, pp. 13–14.
[15] B. Wrightsman, 'Andreas Osiander's Contribution to the Copernican Achievement', in R. Westman (ed.), *The Copernican Achievement* (Berkeley, CA and Los Angeles, CA, 1975), pp. 213–43, esp. 233.

advocacy of Galileo in the early seventeenth century that the potential of *De revolutionibus* to excite controversy was properly realized.

Wittenberg Astronomy: Philipp Melanchthon and His Followers

Among the leaders in the utilitarian use of the Copernican hypothesis were the large number of mathematically competent Lutherans trained at Wittenberg, or at Wittenberg's satellite universities by Wittenberg men. In the 1970s, Robert Westman coined the phrase 'the Wittenberg Interpretation of the Copernican Theory' to describe the way in which these scholars made use of the Copernican astronomical models, praising certain of their technical features, but ignored or flatly denied their claim to represent cosmological reality.[16] It was even the objective of many of these scholars to convert the Copernican models once more to a system of the universe with an unmoving Earth at the centre. But as the more recent work of scholars such as Sachiko Kusukawa and Charlotte Methuen has revealed, underlying the Wittenberg Interpretation was something more fundamental and of wider significance. That something was Philipp Melanchthon's conception of the religious and philosophical role for the study of the heavens.[17] It was Melanchthon, of course, who instituted the curricular reforms that supported the study of mathematical astronomy to a significant degree, and it was therefore Melanchthon's understanding of astronomy and cosmology that, variously inflected and adapted, underlay much of the north European astronomical scholarship of the later sixteenth century. The 'Wittenberg Interpretation' of the Copernican theory was part of one inflection of this Phillippist attitude: it was, indeed, the one that Melanchthon himself would seem to have sanctioned. Other inflections were those of Rheticus, the Wittenberg-trained Copernican Christoph Rothmann, and the Tübingen-based Copernican Michael Maestlin. In the broad sense of the term recently advocated by Peter Barker, these and many other individuals, from Melanchthon onwards, can properly be considered 'Wittenberg astronomers'.[18]

Melanchthon encouraged the study of the heavens for two related reasons: because the movements of the stars and planets provided clear

---

[16]   R. Westman, 'The Melanchthon Circle, Rheticus and the Wittenberg Interpretation of the Copernican Theory', *Isis*, 66 (1975): 165–93.

[17]   S. Kusukawa, *The Transformation of Natural Philosophy: The Case of Philip Melanchthon* (Cambridge, 1995), esp. pp. 124–73; C. Methuen, 'The Role of the Heavens in the Thought of Philip Melanchthon', *Journal of the History of Ideas*, 57 (1996): 385–403. See also B. Moran, 'The Universe of Philip Melanchthon: Criticism and Use of the Copernican Theory', *Comitatus*, 4 (1973): 1–23.

[18]   P. Barker, 'The Role of Religion in the Lutheran Response to Copernicus', in M. Osler (ed.), *Rethinking the Scientific Revolution* (New York, 2000), pp. 59–88.

evidence of God's providential ordering of the cosmos, and indeed were active elements within the divine system of governance, and because signs and portents in the heavens were one of the means by which God communicated with man. For Melanchthon, therefore, study of the heavens involved both astronomy and a species of astrology, and although he affirmed the inseparability of these disciplines, the latter was arguably the more important to him of the two. That was because, in Melanchthon's conception, astrology was primarily a study of the causal relationships operating between the heavens and Earth, and such causal study not only licensed the inclusion of these traditionally mathematical subjects under the category of natural philosophy, it also led the practitioner to knowledge of the first cause, God. Astronomy was an essential prerequisite for the study of astrology, and geometry and arithmetic were prerequisites for the study of astronomy. Study of all of these branches of mathematics was therefore mandated in Melanchthon's reformed educational curriculum.

In elaborating and defending his conception of heavenly study, Melanchthon naturally drew on a wide range of sources, ancient, medieval and modern, to weld a number of arguments and authorities into a coherent whole. Among the component parts of the Philippist attitude was the view that the heavens exhibited a structure and order that was mathematically knowable. This could be further broken down into the Platonic belief that God, in creating and ordering the cosmos, 'always geometrizes', and the claim that the mind of man, created in the image of God, was endowed with the capacity to recognize these traces of the divine. The Philippist view also included the claim that the heavens, because of their greater perfection, could be more successfully analysed mathematically than the sublunary realm; the claim that, indeed, it was God's intention that men study the heavens; the claim that both the mathematical order visible in the world and the provision of celestial portents were aspects of Providence, and the claim that astrological interpretation of such portents was licit on the grounds that it was a diagnosis of hidden causes on the basis of manifest signs, in the same manner as the diagnoses and prognoses of a physician.[19] Overall, they were forged into a particular version of the view that natural philosophical study complemented the study of the Bible, that one could learn about God and His plan by reading the *two* books he had written, Nature and Scripture.

Of course, Melanchthon and his followers did not possess a monopoly on any of these doctrines or the sources from which they were derived, and Philippist works in natural philosophy and mathematics were read and assimilated by scholars of other confessions. Partly for these reasons,

---

[19]   S. Kusukawa, 'Aspectio divinorum operam: Melanchthon and astrology for Lutheran medics', in A. Cunningham and O. Grell (eds), *Medicine and the Reformation* (London, 1993), pp. 33–56, esp. 39.

and partly because – as suggested above – Philippists adopted a range of astronomical and cosmological views, this characterization of Philippist belief can only take us so far. Identification of a Philippist astronomer necessarily rests on biographical evidence as well as on the details of their natural philosophy. Once identified, however, such scholars can be studied more closely to see exactly how the Philippist tradition informed their work on the heavens. This process has been undertaken in some depth for one of the two most famous 'revolutionaries' of post-Copernican astronomy, Johannes Kepler. It can also be shown to shed some light on the work of the other, the Dane Tycho Brahe.

Johannes Kepler: Theological Cosmology

Of the two, Johannes Kepler presents the easier case, not only because of the regularity and clarity with which he referred to his astronomical work as a theological endeavour, or expressed his personal religiosity, but also because of the labour that has gone into establishing the facts of his life and the evolution of his thought. Kepler was a scholarship student at the seminary in Tübingen, the beneficiary of a scheme designed to turn bright but poor boys into well-trained Lutheran pastors who would serve the Duchy of Württemberg and surrounding territories.[20] Theology, not astronomy or philosophy, was the discipline for which he was being groomed, and theology, not astronomy or philosophy, was the discipline which he imagined his future self practising. Unsurprisingly, therefore, Kepler's theological views were both well formed and firmly held from his student days onwards. These beliefs were also, during the course of his life, to prove immensely inconvenient. Kepler suffered at the hands of both Counter-Reformers and Lutheran sectarians – the latter because he refused to subscribe to the Formula of Concord (1577), and in particular found himself unable to accept the doctrine of the ubiquity of Christ.[21] In respect of the Eucharist, at least, Kepler's theology was Philippist rather than Gnesio-Lutheran.[22]

Whether because some scent of his heterodoxy reached his tutors or, as seems more probable, because he exhibited a rare mathematical talent, Kepler was despatched to the Lutheran school in Graz, as mathematics

---

[20]   M. Caspar, *Kepler* (New York, 1993), pp. 38–44; C. Methuen, 'Securing the Reformation through Education: The Duke's Scholarship System of Sixteenth-century Württemberg', *Sixteenth Century Journal*, 25 (1994): 841–51.

[21]   M. Caspar, *Kepler*, pp. 24–7, 48–49, 188–9, 204–5, 213–20, 258–64, 304–7.

[22]   R. Kolb, 'Dynamics of Party Conflict in the Saxon Late Reformation: Gnesio-Lutherans vs. Philippists', *The Journal of Modern History*, 49 (1977): D1289–D1305; E. Cameron, *The European Reformation* (Oxford, 1991), pp. 161–6.

teacher and District Mathematician, before he was able to complete his theological studies.[23] It was in Graz that Kepler made his first significant contribution to the study of the heavens, published in the form of his *Mysterium Cosmographicum* of 1597, and hence it was in Graz that Kepler first expressed the view that astronomical achievements could substitute for theological ones. 'I wished to be a theologian,' he wrote to his astronomical mentor Michael Maestlin. 'I was distressed for a long time. But look! God is worshipped by my work, even in astronomy.'[24] Like his oft-quoted later remark, that astronomers were priests of God with respect to the book of Nature, the statement clearly testifies to Kepler's sense of vocation.[25]

To dwell on the various ways in which Kepler articulated his sense of having uncovered an element of the Divine Plan through mathematical analysis of the planetary intervals is unnecessary, but it is worth mentioning two that are otherwise likely to be overlooked. The first of these is the theological resonance of the title he chose for the book announcing his 'discovery' that the universe was patterned according to the nesting of the five regular solids. *Mysterium* was more frequently employed in theological works than philosophical or mathematical ones, often being employed to refer to the Eucharist. The second is what Kepler wrote to his patron, Duke Friedrich of Württemberg, about the 'great discovery in astronomy' that the Almighty had revealed to him. Proposing the construction of an instrument that would model his depiction of the universe, he stated that it 'would be, and might be called, a truly real image of the world, and the pattern of Creation, as far as human reason may attain it, and never before seen or heard by any man'.[26] Strange though it may seem, Kepler proposed to represent this divine design of the cosmos in the form of a drinks-dispensing machine that could be used to play an astrological joke on a courtier for the duke's entertainment.[27] Kepler's piety, though deep, was not unduly solemn.

For our purposes, the apparent absurdity of both this instrument's design and the great cosmological discovery which it was supposed to

---

[23]   See M. Caspar, *Kepler*, pp. 50–52.

[24]   M. Caspar et. al. (eds), *Johannes Kepler Gesammelte Werke* (Munich, 1938–) (hereafter KGW), vol. XIII, p. 40: 'Theologus esse volabem: diu angebar: Deus ecce mea opera etiam in astronomia celebratur.'

[25]   Ibid., vol. XIII, p.193; R. Hooykaas, *Religion and the Rise of Modern Science* (Edinburgh, 1977), p.105; P. Harrison, *The Bible, Protestantism and the Rise of Natural Science* (Cambridge, 1998), p. 198.

[26]   KGW, vol. XIII, p. 50: 'Wölliches dan ein recht eigentlich Ebenbild der Weltt, und Muster der Erschaffung, so weitt Menschliche Vernunfft reichen mag, und dergleichen zuvor nie von kheinem menschen gesehen noch gehörtt worden, sein und heissen möchte.'

[27]   Ibid., pp. 52–3.

represent are largely irrelevant. The important thing for us to realize is that, as Kepler himself affirmed, and as modern scholarship has shown, the epistemology and metaphysics underlying Kepler's mature work in astronomy and cosmology, the work for which he is fêted, were largely unchanged from those exhibited in the *Mysterium Cosmographicum*.[28] God, for Kepler, was a mathematician whose Creation instantiated archetypes: geometrical relationships and arithmetic ratios productive of harmonies that were present from before Creation in the mind of God. The mind of man, created in the image of God, was endowed with the facility to uncover these archetypes, and hence to determine the divine blueprint underlying the cosmos.[29]

Invocation of archetypes was the means by which Kepler overcame the epistemological problem that had troubled his predecessors. Explication of the observed celestial motions in terms of planetary hypotheses utilizing a combination of circles was reasoning *a posteriori* or *quia* in the sense in which these terms were understood in the period. That is to say, it demonstrated the effect from a *possible* cause, but it did not demonstrate the effect from the *actual* cause. To do so would be to reason *a priori* or *propter quid*, and would result, according to Aristotelian philosophy, in *scientia*, certain knowledge of the heavens. Normally, according to the scholastic commentators, a move from *a posteriori* to *a priori* demonstration could be accomplished through a process of elimination. Possible but not actual causes arrived at *a posteriori* could be sifted and rejected. However, many philosophers doubted the capacity of living men to discriminate between the range of available planetary hypotheses – whether one was considering the epicycles and eccentrics used to account for planetary motions, or rival world-systems – that were empirically equivalent for an earthbound observer. This, and not the 'instrumentalism' for which it has sometimes been mistaken, was the reason for the agnosticism about hypotheses expressed by Osiander's preface to *De revolutionibus* and underlying the 'Wittenberg Interpretation'.[30] It represented an obstacle to astronomical knowledge that only a few Philippist astronomers were able to overcome to their own satisfaction. Maestlin, for example, did so on the basis of his observations of the comet of 1577; failing to reconcile his observations with a cometary hypothesis compatible with the Ptolemaic

---

[28]   A.M. Duncan (trans.), *Johannes Kepler. Mysterium Cosmographicum: The Secret of the Universe* (Norwalk, CT, 1981), pp. 38–9.

[29]   R. Martens, *Kepler's Philosophy and the New Astronomy* (Princeton, NJ, 2000).

[30]   N. Jardine, 'Scepticism in Renaissance Astronomy: A Preliminary Study', in C. Schmitt and R. Popkin (eds), *Scepticism from the Renaissance to the Enlightenment* (Wiesbaden, 1987), pp. 83–102; P. Barker and B. Goldstein, 'Realism and Instrumentalism in Sixteenth Century Astronomy: A Reappraisal', *Perspectives on Science*, 6 (1998): 232–58.

arrangement of the planets, he took the path of the comet to be empirical evidence in favour of the Copernican system.[31] But this was a less than wholly satisfying proof. Kepler used the concept of archetypes to provide, in his and Maestlin's opinion, an *a priori* demonstration of the Copernican hypotheses.[32] Subsequently, he employed them in order to underwrite the work in physical astronomy and cosmology found in the *Astronomia Nova* (1609) and *Harmonice Mundi* (1619), including the famous move from circles to ellipses.

Like Melanchthon, therefore, Kepler conceived of the mathematical study of the heavens as a means of establishing causal knowledge of the cosmos; unlike him, however, what he thought was at stake was the physical causes of the arrangement and motion of the planets, not simply their causal effect on the sublunary realm and the testimony they provided of the benevolent first cause at work in the world. At the same time, Kepler did not eschew astrology. Indeed, it was as inseparable an element of his mathematical route to physical knowledge of the heavens as in the work of Melanchthon, although Kepler saw himself as a reformer of the art. 'I am', he wrote to Maestlin in 1598, 'a Lutheran astrologer, throwing away the chaff and keeping the kernel.'[33] In accordance, therefore, with Kepler's extended notion of the role of mathematics in producing causal knowledge of the heavens, Kepler utilized the analogy with the art of the physician not only in respect of astrology, but also with regard to mathematical astronomy – or rather, as it became in Kepler's work, celestial physics. 'If this art knows absolutely nothing of the causes of the heavenly motions, because you believe only what you see, what is to become of medicine in which no doctor ever perceived the inwardly hidden cause of a disease except from the external bodily signs and symptoms which impinge on the senses, just as from the visible positions of the stars the astronomer infers the form of their motion?'[34] Ultimately, Kepler's 'theological cosmology' was, like other inflections of Philippist natural philosophy, uniquely his own. Undoubtedly, however, it had its origins in the education that he received in Lutheran Tübingen in the late 1580s and early 1590s.[35]

---

[31]   R. Westman, 'The Comet and the Cosmos: Kepler, Mästlin, and the Copernican System', *Studia Copernicana*, 5 (1972): 7–30.
[32]   A.M. Duncan, *Mysterium Cosmographicum*, pp. 92–101; KGW, vol. XIII, p. 54; Martens, *Kepler's Philosophy*, pp. 39–56; P. Barker and B. Goldstein, 'Theological Foundations of Kepler's Astronomy', *Osiris*, 16 (2001): 88–113.
[33]   KGW, vol. XIII, p. 184: 'Ego sum Lutheranus astrologus, qui nugis abjectis retineo nucleum." See J. Field, 'A Lutheran Astrologer: Johannes Kepler', *Archive for the History of the Exact Sciences*, 31 (1984): 189–272, at 220.
[34]   N. Jardine, *The Birth of History and Philosophy of Science: Kepler's A Defence of Tycho against Ursus with Essays on its Provenance and Significance* (Cambridge, 1988), p. 151.
[35]   C. Methuen, *Kepler's Tübingen: Stimulus to a Theological Mathematics* (Aldershot, 1998).

Tycho Brahe: Semi-Paracelsian Philippism

Tycho Brahe's Philippism, although not quite overlooked by historians, has not yet been identified as central to his astronomical work to the same extent that recent accounts have made the notion of the divine archetypes the key to understanding Kepler's cosmology. One reason for this may be that, as a personality, Tycho simply appears rather more secular than his famous collaborator. Though nominally a Lutheran and the beneficiary of an education received, in part, at the reformed universities of Rostock, Wittenberg and Leipzig, Tycho the pious, child of the Reformation, is somewhat overshadowed by Tycho the pugnacious, high-living and hot-tempered member of the Danish nobility. Certain pieces of evidence seem, at first, to reinforce the impression of an individual who was indeed rather worldly by sixteenth-century standards. Tycho's piety was called into question during his lifetime; he failed to take communion for a number of years, and he was, at best, an indifferent custodian of Church properties assigned to his care.[36] And although he referred to scripture as evidence that the Copernican hypotheses could not be correct, his published works suggest that he was not much inclined either to theological reasoning or scriptural exegesis. Indeed, he made some effort to distance himself and his work from theology *per se* and from religious dispute. To one correspondent, in a letter that he subsequently published, he remarked: 'I do not profess to practice theology, or claim to be one of those who studies it closely and well.'[37] And in another letter, he made clear that the astronomical works he had prepared and would prepare for the press would not 'treat religious matters, now variously taught, under the guise of mathematics ... For I do not want to entangle myself in those things. We have a sufficient number of heresies and confusions; there is no need, and it is not for me, to produce new ones or support those that already exist.'[38] Admittedly, the second set of remarks was made with a view to obtaining, via Archbishop Ernst of Cologne, a printing privilege valid within the Spanish Catholic Netherlands. And the first preceded Tycho's critique of

---

[36]   V. Thoren, *The Lord of Uraniborg: A Biography of Tycho Brahe* (Cambridge, 1990), pp. 348–9, 357; J. Christianson, *On Tycho's Island: Tycho Brahe and His Assistants, 1570–1601* (Cambridge, 2000), pp. 200–204. The charge of failing to take communion, however, was levelled in relation to the prosecution of Tycho's appointee pastor on Hven for omission of exorcism from the rituals of baptism – a Philippist practice.

[37]   J. Dreyer (ed.), *Tychonis Brahe Dani Opera Omnia* (15 vols, Copenhagen, 1913–29) (hereafter TBOO), vol. VI, p. 186: 'Nec ego ... Theologiam non profitear, neque quispiam eorum qui eam solide & sincere exercent.'

[38]   Ibid., vol. VII, pp. 380–81: 'ne sub specie rerum Mathematicarum religionis negotia, quae nunc varie trahuntur, tractarem ... Ego enim me illis immiscere nolo. Satis habemus haeresium et confusionum, non opus est, nec mearum partium, aut novas condere, aut priores stabilire.'

his correspondents' exegetical defence of heliocentrism. Nevertheless, the context – not just of the rest of these letters, but of Tycho's work in general – would suggest that they were, from their author's point of view, sincerely intended.

Tycho's Philippism can be demonstrated, however, on a number of grounds. Biographical evidence forms an essential part of the argument, as suggested above, although the admissible material is not necessarily restricted to the facts of Tycho's own life. A number of Tycho's assistants on the island of Hven went on to become prominent Philippist clergymen and theologians who continued to defend Melanchthonian views even after Philippism began to lose its ascendancy in Lutheran Denmark: this group includes bishops Niels Arctander, Cort Aslakssøn and Christian Hansen Riber.[39] And the strength and duration of that earlier ascendancy should not be overlooked: Melanchthon's theology dominated both court and university opinion throughout the later sixteenth century, provided the backdrop against which Tycho's education occurred both at home and abroad, and helped to shape an environment conducive to new forms of natural philosophy. In particular, Danish Philippism fostered the introduction, by Petrus Severinus and Johannes Pratensis, of a form of Paracelsian medicine compatible with Galenism and acceptable to the political and scholarly elite.[40] Tycho was close to both of these men, and he too pursued iatrochemical work. Indeed, Tycho's empirical project was one that combined study of the heavens with what he referred to as 'terrestrial astronomy' or the *ars spagyrica*, and this conjunction of activities, far from being incidental, would appear to have been dictated by his cosmological views.

A clear picture of Tycho's cosmology and the manner of its evolution is hard to obtain. In comparison with Kepler, Tycho produced relatively little in the way of explicit metaphysical or epistemological reflection. This fact may itself be explained, in part, by paying some attention to the course of his life. Although it is tempting to see Tycho's work in terms of publications such as the *De mundi aetherei recentioribus phaenomenis* (1588), the *Astronomiae instauratae mechanica* (1598) and the posthumous *Astronomiae instauratae progymnasmata* (1602), neither these nor the observational data he bequeathed to Kepler represent the fulfilment of Tycho's project as he conceived it himself. The account Tycho gave in his 1588 work of his geoheliocentric system of the world, for example, was an abbreviated one that he intended to supplement with a

---

[39] Christianson, *On Tycho's Island*, pp. 251–3, 340–43.

[40] J. Shackelford, *Paracelsianism in Denmark and Norway in the Sixteenth and Seventeenth Centuries* (PhD thesis, Madison, WI, 1989); O. Grell, 'The Reception of Paracelsianism in early modern Lutheran Denmark: From Peter Severinus, the Dane, to Ole Worm', *Medical History*, 4 (1995): 78–94.

fuller exposition in other publications.[41] But many of the books that he projected in the late 1580s were ones that he did not live to produce. The empirical astronomical labour with which Tycho is so strongly associated was clearly fundamental to his work, to the extent of occupying the greater part of his visible effort and output. Had he succeeded in completing it, by producing a new observationally grounded astronomy, he might have proved more forthcoming with respect to his natural philosophical views. As things stand, however, it can be difficult not only to determine Tycho's thought on certain key topics at particular moments in his life, but also to determine whether his position on them changed significantly during the course of his career. And the situation is hardly improved by Tycho's self-conscious reticence about the more occult components of his natural philosophy.

Astrological analysis, for example, was prominent within Tycho's earliest publication, on the so-called nova of 1572.[42] Indeed, there is reason to believe that astrology played a crucial role in motivating Tycho's entire observational programme: in the *Mechanica*, he stated that it was observing the great conjunction of Saturn and Jupiter in 1563 which brought the errors in existing astronomical tables to his attention.[43] This was a phenomenon of primarily astrological interest. Yet on treating the nova of 1572 again in the *Progymnasmata*, Tycho reproduced the astronomical analysis from his earlier work without the astrology.[44] Similarly, his published work on comets concentrated on the supralunar location and motion at the expense of their astrological meaning. Was this due to disillusionment with the aims and methods of astrology, or was it a strategic choice, given that the observational and mathematical work required to reform astrology had not been completed? This question is not easy to answer, since evidence exists that seems to point in both directions.[45] And yet it is precisely in relation to astrology that we most clearly see Tycho's debt to a Philippist view.

As late as 1591, Tycho published, under the name of one of his assistants, a preface to a collection of weather prognostications in which he was concerned to set out the *causal* relationship between events in the heavens and events on the Earth. In God's creation, according to this document, the air acts a medium, an *instrument*, for the transmission of the celestial

---

[41]   TBOO, vol. IV, p. 159, lines 1–10.
[42]   Ibid., vol. I, pp. 30–44, 58–64.
[43]   Ibid., vol. V, pp. 106–7.
[44]   Ibid., vol. III, pp. 93–107.
[45]   For example, ibid., vol. VI, pp. 142, 171. See also G. Oestmann, 'Tycho Brahe's Attitude towards Astrology and his Relations to Heinrich Rantzau', in J. Christianson et. al. (eds), *Tycho Brahe and Prague: Crossroads of European Science* (Frankfurt am Main, 2002), pp. 84–94.

influences to the created beings of the terrestrial realm.[46] Tycho was also concerned with astrology in his unpublished German tract on the comet of 1577, thought to have been prepared for King Frederick II. Here Tycho was keen to emphasize the limits to human knowledge of the true nature of the heavens, and to identify comets as supernatural phenomena, the product of acts of special creation, whose natural *causal* effects on the Earth were nevertheless amenable to some sort of analysis.[47] These and other sources suggest that Tycho's study of the heavens was, and remained, Philippist, in its concern with causation and Providence. It was, however, a Philippism inflected by Tycho's semi-Paracelsian understanding of the relationship between different parts of cosmos. Thus, in his debate with Christoph Rothmann over whether the substance of the heavens was elemental air or quintessential aether, Tycho showed himself keen to maintain a distinction between sub- and supra-lunary regions conducive to the notion of a causal relationship, while at the same time finding empirical evidence for the existence of celestial aether in terrestrial matter. Distillation could be used, he argued, in order to produce indisputable proof of an aethereal substance.[48]

Tycho's clearest evocation of Philippist themes can be found in an early defence of astrology delivered as the introduction to a course of lectures he gave by invitation at the university of Copenhagen in 1574. This address, subsequently published as the *Oratio de disciplinis mathematicis*, has recently been analysed as a key document for understanding Tycho's technique for interpreting the bible.[49] Scriptural exegesis was clearly important in the reaction to, and defence of, Copernican cosmology in the later sixteenth and early seventeenth centuries. It was significant enough to have been anticipated as a potential source of objections by Copernicus in his dedicatory letter to Pope Paul III; to have been the subject of a treatise by Rheticus, lost for many years, reconciling scripture and the Copernican world-system; to have formed a component of the unpublished handbook on astronomy by Christoph Rothmann, in defence of his view that the (Copernican) heavens were fluid and airy; and of course, to have taken

---

[46]   J. Christianson, 'Tycho Brahe's Cosmology from the Astrologia of 1591', *Isis*, 59 (1968): 312–18.
[47]   J. Christianson, 'Tycho Brahe's German Treatise on the Comet of 1577: A Study in Science and Politics', *Isis*, 70 (1979): 110–40.
[48]   TBOO, vol. VI, pp. 195–6 and 359, note to p. 145, line 42. See also J. Shackelford, 'Providence, Power, and Cosmic Causality in Early Modern Astronomy: The Case of Tycho Brahe and Petrus Severinus', in Christianson et. al. (eds), *Tycho Brahe and Prague*, pp. 46–69.
[49]   K. Howell, *God's Two Books: Copernican Cosmology and Biblical Interpretation in Early Modern Science* (Notre Dame, IN, 2002), pp. 78–83.

centre stage in the Galileo affair of the early seventeenth century.[50] It has therefore merited the historical attention it has increasingly tended to receive. But this focus on exegesis can also mislead. In the case of Copernicans, the central argument was always of the same form, namely an appeal to the principle of 'accommodation': the idea that the Bible was written for, or accommodated to, the understanding of the common man and could not therefore be used as a means of discriminating between competing natural philosophical theories.[51] In the case of a non-Copernican, such as Tycho Brahe, it does not suffice to say he resisted Copernicanism because of its perceived conflict with scripture, since it is not clear whether we are identifying a symptom, a cause or a concomitant cause of his resistance to heliocentricism.[52] Tycho, though happy to abandon what he perceived to be Aristotelian cosmology and meteorology, proved unwilling to depart from the received terrestrial physics, and his natural philosophical commitments probably played a greater part in the shaping of his cosmological thought than his reading of the Bible. Tycho, it is true, occasionally made use of scriptural exegesis when promoting and defending his cosmological views. He attacked Rothmann's accommodationist defence of heliocentrism in correspondence that he published.[53] And he employed a form of accommodation himself in order to reject Caspar Peucer's view that sound reading of the Bible would lead one to believe in the existence of 'supra-celestial' waters, doing so in letters that he did not print, but probably intended to, and certainly circulated in manuscript.[54] In both cases, however, he reacted to, rather than initiated, the recourse to exegesis. The *Oratio* seems to be one of the few occasions when Tycho expressed his views on particular biblical passages without any prompting, and it is highly likely that, even then, his choice and mode of readings were at least partially borrowed.

As an epideictic oration in praise of mathematics, the *Oratio* displays many conventional elements, including a justification of the study of mathematics on the basis of its practical utility, and a lineage of

---

[50]   N. Copernicus, *De revolutionibus orbium coelestium* (Nuremberg, 1543), sig. iiii verso; R. Hooykaas, *Rheticus' Treatise*; M. Granada, J. Hamel and L. von Mackensen (eds), *Christoph Rothmanns Handbuch der Astronomie von 1589* (Frankfurt am Main, 2003), pp. 198–205; Blackwell, *Galileo, Bellarmine*.

[51]   A. Williams, *The Common Expositor: An Account of the Commentaries on Genesis, 1527–1633* (Chapel Hill, NC, 1948), pp. 176–7; R. Hooykaas, *Rheticus' Treatise*, pp. 30–31; P. Harrison, *The Bible*, pp. 129–38.

[52]   B. Moran has made a similar point with respect to Melanchthon; see 'The Universe of Philip Melanchthon', p. 13.

[53]   TBOO, vol. VI, pp. 177–8, 185–6.

[54]   Ibid., vol. VII, pp. 133–4, 231–5; K. Howell, *God's Two Books*, pp. 97–106.

practitioners or founders of the art going back to the biblical patriarchs.[55] The bulk of it, however, is devoted to a defence of astrology against what Tycho labelled as the arguments of theologians and physicists. Tycho built up to astrology, and related it to the other mathematical arts, through the traditional genealogy. From geometry and arithmetic, another sublime science, far removed from the dross of the Earth, was born: this was astronomy. And astronomy, Tycho asserted, would be worthy of study even if had no uses at all:

> For it affects and sharpens, the intellect of man with an incredible and joyful delight, and his thoughts, in which his life consists, from these terrestrial, trivial and transitory things, to celestial, serious, and permanent contemplations, and it affects the man himself with with true pleasure and recreates him in the likeness of the residents of the heavens, raising him beyond the mortal sort.[56]

It is clear, he claimed, that God wanted mankind to study this art:

> But would that wise and foreseeing author of all things, have established laws of celestial motion so admirable and perpetual, with such great diversity, and such elegant harmonies, if he had wanted them, the causes of which he also made visible for the most part, to be ignored by men? Nay, he wanted this indefatigable labour to be investigated and examined, so that his majesty and his wisdom also, could hence be perceived and celebrated by mortals.[57]

Study of the natural world taught mortals God's wisdom and majesty, but study of the heavens taught it best of all. Tycho's first arguments for the validity of astrology were also harnessed to a conception of Providence. Alluding to a passage of scripture, Genesis I.14, that Melanchthon also deployed to justify astrological study, Tycho pointed out that the fact that 'we measure the differences of years and months and days is through the sky as if it were a perpetual and unwearying clock' was insufficient to explain the complexity of the celestial apparatus.[58] God, though a free agent in theory, had in fact providentially ordered the world in such a

---

[55] Ibid., vol. I, pp. 145–70; N. Jardine, *The Birth of History and Philosophy of Science*, pp. 262–4.

[56] TBOO, vol. I, p. 151: 'Nam ingenium hominis incredibili et jucunda delectatione afficit et acuit, cogitationesque, in quibus vita illius consistit, a terrenis his, ridiculis et caducis rebus, ad coelestes, serias et fixas contemplationes avocat, hominemque ipsum vera voluptate, simili quodammodo coelestium incolarum, eum ultra mortalem sortem evehens, afficit et recreat.'

[57] Ibid., p. 152: 'Quorsum vero sapiens ille et providus rerum universitatis autor, tam admirandas et perpetuas motuum coelestium leges, tanta diversitate, et tam concinna harmonia effinxisset, si eas ab hominibus, quorum etiam caussa magna ex parte visibilia condidit, ignorari voluisset? Imo potius haec indefesso labore perscrutari ac inquiri voluit, ut ipsius majestas et sapientia quoque, hinc a mortalibus perspici et celebrari possit.'

[58] Ibid., p. 153: 'annorum et mensium, dierumque discrimina, per coelum tanquam perpetuum et indefessum horologium metiamur'; S. Kusukawa, *The transformation of natural philosophy*, p. 127.

way that the celestial motions were instruments, second causes, for events on the Earth. And hence the art of astrology was born. As signalled by its concern with Providence and with the causal explication of astrological effects, Tycho's *Oratio* was clearly Philippist in its overall thesis and arguments. But this was not simply a case of Tycho telling his audience what he thought they wanted to hear. It is evident that Tycho believed he was challenging his listeners, not least perhaps because Paracelsian ideas were also brought into play. Thus, Tycho drew the familiar analogy between astrology and medicine:

> Astrology therefore, *a posteriori*, that is from experience, draws its principles, and from many particular observations, rarely faulty, constructs universal conclusions: no differently than is customarily done in the art of medicine, which from experience inquires into the virtues of herbs and minerals, and from many particular observations thence produces a universal judgment concerning their nature and effects.[59]

But he also made much of the more specific relationships between heavenly bodies, terrestrial substances and bodily organs which, for him at least, were part of an alchemical philosophy.[60] And for Tycho, the relationship between man and the universe that underwrites claims to knowledge about the heavens was not so much that God made man in his own image, enabling him to glimpse the divine plan through the exercise of his intellect, but that physically, man is an image of cosmos. Thus, one of his later arguments against the Copernican system was that it lacked the proportionality with which, as study of Albrecht Dürer's work makes clear, God invested the human body and therefore the universe.[61]

Unlike Kepler, Tycho was not accommodating enough to state that the *Oratio*, one of the earliest public expressions of his views on the study of the heavens, set an agenda that he pursued for another twenty-five years. Increasingly, however, consideration of the evidence regarding Tycho's natural philosophy suggests that this was the case. A Philippist outlook inflected by alchemical philosophy shaped his empirical programme, informed his rejection of the Copernican world-system and elaboration of his own system of the world, and underlay his understanding of the causal relationships operating between God and the heavens, and the heavens and Earth. The 'new astronomy' of the early seventeenth century was doubly indebted, therefore, to Melanchthon's legacy: it helped to stimulate Tycho's

---

[59]   TBOO, vol. I, p. 160: 'Astrologia igitur a posteriori, hoc est ab ipsa experientia, sua sortitur principia, et a multis particularibus rarius fallentibus observationibus universales constituit conclusiones: non aliter quam in arte medica fieri assolet, quae ab ipsa experientia herbarum et mineralium virtutes inquirit, et ex multis particularibus observationibus, deinde de eorum naturis et efficacia universale promit judicium.'

[60]   Ibid., pp. 157–8; ibid., vol. VI, pp. 144–6.

[61]   Ibid., p. 222.

systematic collection of the data necessary to reform astronomy, and it underpinned Kepler's use of that data in elaborating a new understanding of the mathematical order underlying the cosmos.

Conclusion

The history of the 'Copernican Revolution' of the sixteenth and seventeenth centuries cannot be reduced to a history of Lutherans. Other confessional groups must also be explored in order to show how the changing contours of faith supported and resisted innovations in astronomical theory and method.[62] Similarly, the history of sixteenth- and seventeenth-century study of the heavens ought not to reduced to the elaboration and gradual acceptance of a new understanding of the arrangement of the planets, and the emergence of a new conception of the relationship between mathematical astronomy and celestial physics. The story that runs from Copernicus to Newton via Tycho Brahe and Kepler no longer satisfies as an account of early modern astronomy in its entirety. Nevertheless, that revolutionary narrative, and its protagonists, retain much of their interest and importance as a means of understanding the processes of change leading to later developments. As we have seen, it was a story strongly shaped by the Lutheran Reformation, and in particular by the educational reforms and natural philosophy of Philipp Melanchthon.

In his study of the relationship between religion and science over the centuries, John Hedley Brooke, in a chapter entitled 'The Parallel between Scientific Religious Reform', has explored 'Reformed Astronomy' and reformed religion with a view to establishing whether Protestantism was particularly conducive to the development of the scientific enterprise.[63] Brooke rightly concludes that the role of religious belief in shaping receptiveness to Copernicanism was far too complex for this test to prove or disprove so simple a thesis. Nevertheless, I have aimed to show here why the 'reformation of astronomy' is an apt term for the developments that occurred after 1540. Both Tycho and Kepler sought to reform the study of the heavens, and both of them pursued this goal for reasons that were intimately related to their particular species of Lutheran faith.

---

[62] R. Vermijj, *The Calvinist Copernicans: The Reception of the New Astronomy in the Dutch republic, 1575–1750* (Amsterdam, 2002).

[63] J.H. Brooke, *Science and Religion: Some Historical Perspectives* (Cambridge, 1991), pp. 82–116.

CHAPTER 12

French Books at the Frankfurt Fair

Andrew Pettegree

Almost from the first days of the invention of moveable type, the creation of an international book market was essential to the economics of the industry. Of course, even in the manuscript age, owners of books were used to sending abroad for precious items to borrow, copy or purchase. But the invention of moveable type necessarily carried this European market to a new level. Providers of books now had to think in multiples of hundreds, rather than single items. With the exception of the simplest school books, it was impossible to dispose of the major part of a print run locally. Rather – and this was especially true of those Latin books that dominated the output of most major printing houses – to turn a profit, books would have to be dispersed across a market that was essentially pan-European.

This simple basic principle would result in a drastic restructuring of the European world of print a bare thirty years after Gutenberg's invention was recognized as an irreversible technological breakthrough. The first, exuberant age of experimentation witnessed a huge proliferation of new centres of printing, as news of the new technology spread around the European intellectual community. This first wave of expansion was fuelled by the interest and underwritten by the investment of rich local patrons, princes, bishops and city dignitaries, all determined to see that the new art was established in their jurisdictions. But these smaller presses were never commercially viable, and by the 1490s many of the more ephemeral had fallen away.[1] Now the industry was consolidated around a far smaller number of large centres of production, dominated by merchant publishers with the capital to sustain a major venture.

The production of a large book required the investment of considerable capital before any return could be expected. Aside from the fixed costs of setting up the press, paper had to purchased, and wages paid over the weeks and months before a large folio volume was complete. The completed books then had to be stored until the edition, sometimes 1200 copies or more,

---

[1]   For the phenomenon of press failure in the fifteenth century, see Martha Tedeschi, 'Publish and Perish: The Career of Lienhart Holle in Ulm', in Sandra Hindman (ed.), *Printing the Written Word: The Social History of Books, circa 1450–1520* (Ithaca, NY, 1991), pp. 41–67. Susan Noakes, 'The development of the book market in Late Quatrocento Italy: Printers' failures and the role of the middleman', *Journal of Mediaeval and Renaissance Studies* (1981): 23–55.

could be disposed of. This latter process, by which books were brought to their potential purchasers, often widely scattered around Europe, was the most vital part of the whole operation, even though it is now in many respects the least studied. When contemplating the publication of a book, it was vital not to underestimate potential demand, since it was no simple matter to print off a second run of a folio volume of many leaves, not least because the type would have to be completely reset. But to print too many copies was also potentially ruinous. It is well known that in the sixteenth century, the price of paper represented the main part of the cost of a book; but it is equally the case that few businesses could afford the capital tied up by accumulating huge stocks of unsold books, piled up and steadily deteriorating in expensive warehouse space.[2]

It is therefore hardly surprising that a sophisticated mechanism for the exchange and distribution of books in a pan-European market developed within a few years of the invention of printing. At the heart of this international book market was the Frankfurt book fair. Frankfurt was established as the home of a major book fair as early as 1475, and it would retain unchallenged pre-eminence as the centre of the international book trade for more than two centuries.[3] Frankfurt's effortless domination of the international book market rested on three main pillars. Firstly, as the seat of a major medieval fair, Frankfurt was used to the demands and rhythms of seasonal commerce. The city was blessed by an excellent situation, astride the Main, the main tributary of the Rhine. Hence the city neatly bisected the two main arties of trade linking the major commercial markets of Italy and the Netherlands, to north and south, and France and the Empire, to east and west. These lands were the major engines of the medieval economy, and they would become, not surprisingly, the major centres of the Latin book trade, along with the Swiss Confederation – also conveniently situated for trade with Frankfurt. The Frankfurt fair, confirmed by imperial charter in 1240, already attracted large numbers of merchants to its twice yearly gatherings, the Lenten fair and the autumn fair, which took place at Michaelmas. Many towns promoted such fairs, not least as a logical response to the notorious danger of travel in the era. Merchants could travel together, and between them pay for the necessary protection for their valuable merchandise. But few trade centres could

---

[2]   Printer/publishers could accumulate a stock of astonishing size; Graham A. Runnalls, 'La vie, la mort et les livres d'imprimeur-libraire parisien Jean Janot d'après son inventaire après décès (17 février 1522 [n.s.])', *Revue Belge de philologie et d'histoire*, 78 (2000): 797–850.

[3]   On the Frankfurt fair, see especially Alexander Dietz, *Frankfurter Handelsgeschichte* (Frankfurt, 1921), vol. III, pp. 1–178. Bruno Recke, *Die Frankfurter Büchermesse* (Frankfurt, 1951). A valuable account in English is the introduction to James Westphal Thompson (ed.), *The Frankfort Book Fair: The Francofordiense Emporium of Henri Estienne* (Chicago, IL, 1911).

rival Frankfurt for the opulence and international esteem of its fairs. In 1374, the merchants of Nuremberg travelled to Frankfurt in a party 500 strong, with 250 laden wagons and 300 horses.[4] Visitors from other lands, especially France, Italy and the Low Countries, were a familiar sight.

Even in the manuscript age, merchants would certainly have brought books, along with other merchandise, to Frankfurt's fairs. Frankfurt merchants were closely involved in the earliest ventures in book production; here, its proximity to Mainz, the scene of Gutenberg's triumphant experiments, was an undoubted factor.[5] Yet curiously, Frankfurt did not develop as an especially important centre of book production in the incunabula age; perhaps the close experience of Gutenberg's financial travails proved a sufficiently cautionary experience.[6] Rather, it was Frankfurt's experience of the mechanics of international trade – especially the credit and barter transactions that became the mainstay of the international book trade – that allowed it quickly to attach a large part of the trade in Latin books to its established fairs. Frankfurt was also exceptionally well placed to act as a nodal point for the trade in vernacular books within the German-speaking territories of the Holy Roman Empire. In this respect at least, Frankfurt did face serious competition, from Strasburg on the Rhine, and Leipzig in Saxony. But Frankfurt would always have the advantage, not least because of the large number of foreign merchants gathered to view the Latin books on offer. The trade in German books developed as a subsidiary, though very important, aspect of this larger international trade. Statistics gathered by Friedrich Kapp for his classic study of German book trade indicate that for the last four decades of the sixteenth century, Latin titles made up on average 65 per cent of the books traded in Frankfurt, and German books around 30 per cent. Of the Latin books, by far the largest part were published outside Germany; the largest proportion of the German books came from Frankfurt itself, or other south German cities.[7] In this respect, Frankfurt thrived by offering a simultaneous location for two largely distinct, though interlocking markets: an international Latin trade, and a trans-German market in vernacular books.

The quantities of books traded in Frankfurt could be very large. The leading figures in the European book world became accustomed to

---

[4]   Ibid., p. 52.

[5]   On the economic relationship between Frankfurt and Mainz, see Stephan Füssel, *Gutenberg and the Impact of Printing* (Aldershot, 2003), p. 10. Albert Kapr, *Johann Gutenberg, the Man and His Invention* (Aldershot, 1996).

[6]   The first printer settled in Frankfurt was Beatus Meurer, active for the short period 1511–12; there was no permanent press in the city before the arrival of Egenolph in 1530.

[7]   Friedrich Kapp, *Geschichte des deutschen Buchhandels bis in das 17e Jahrhundert* (Leipzig, 1886), pp. 791–2.

organizing the rhythms of production around the impending market.[8] This was not only the case with publishers with wares to sell: authors also became accustomed to shaping their writing plans around the rhythms of the fair.[9] Publishers would hope to dispose of a substantial part of their print run at the first fair after publication, either by direct retail sale, or more usually, by placing consignments with other publishers or booksellers. Many of these trades took place by exchange, with publishers accepting packets of books from other printing centres in return for their own recent publications. In 1534, the Zurich printer Christopher Froschauer took with him 2000 copies of one work, in octavo and folio, and sold 1000 of them.[10] This would recoup the large part of the initial investment, and even turn a profit; to sell less would mean returning home with a large and potentially expensive unsold stock. Worst of all was to miscalculate the time needed for an edition, and miss the fair altogether. Many print workers found themselves working exceptionally long hours as the fair drew near to get the necessary books ready.[11]

The best established publishers could make more elaborate arrangements. Christophe Plantin of Antwerp kept a shop and a warehouse in Frankfurt, in which books remaining unsold at the end of the fair could be stored. This had the obvious advantage that purchasers could not wait until the last days of the sale in the hope that he would offload stock at reduced prices. After the Lenten fair of 1579, Plantin had 11,617 copies of some 240 titles in this storehouse. In Plantin's case, this probably represented a steady accumulation of unsold stock, since he still brought vast quantities of new books to each fair: in 1579, his new stock amounted to 5212 copies, of 67 titles, with the most recently published obviously most strongly represented.[12]

In order to ensure the best possible sales, it was obviously advantageous to give potential visitors to the fair advance notice of what might be available. This was often done by correspondence. Surviving letters between publishers, authors and scholars make frequent mention of books they hoped to find available, or sell, at the next Frankfurt fair. But from an

[8]   Although Jean Calvin finished his commentary on Romans by October 1539, publication was held back until March 1540 to coincide with the next available fair. For this and several other examples, see Jean François Gilmont, *John Calvin and the Printed Book*, trans. Karin Maag (Kirksville, MO, 2005), pp. 46, 54, 220–22.

[9]   Contemplating a polemical reply to a work by Albert Pighius in 1542, Calvin decided he had time only to reply to the first six books if his tract was to be ready for the fair. The end of the book contained the announcement, 'I will leave this topic [predestination] to the next fair'; Gilmont, *Calvin and the Printed Book*, p. 221.

[10]   Thompson, *Frankfort Book Fair*, p. 77.

[11]   Gilmont, *Calvin and the Printed Book*, pp. 221–2.

[12]   Colin Clair, *Christopher Plantin* (London, 1960), pp. 204–5.

early date, publishers also began to issue catalogues of their stock.[13] These were usually single printed sheets giving a simple list of titles, though it was also not unknown for such a catalogue to be printed in the back of another book, or as a separate publication.[14] It would be almost one hundred years, however, before an enterprising German publisher, Georg Willer of Augsburg, conceived the idea of a consolidated catalogue of all the new titles to be offered at the fair. Willer's first catalogue was published in 1564, and seems to have been an instant success. It would be published regularly at each successive fair to the end of the century.[15]

Willer's catalogue may be taken to be an accurate reflection of the business of the fair. About two-thirds of the books offered for sale were in Latin, ordered according to a conventional range of thematic categories. Books of theology were followed by works of jurisprudence, medicine, philosophy, history, poetry and music. The subsequent section of German books followed much the same order, though with a small miscellaneous section of works that has no Latin equivalent: books of proverbs, cookbooks and the like.

A striking feature of the catalogues is that the fair offered a lively trade in both Catholic and Protestant books. In Willer's catalogue, these were carefully differentiated into separate sections, but despite Frankfurt's status as a thoroughly Protestant town, Catholic books were well represented. On average, Protestant theological texts outsold Catholic texts by a margin of around two to one. This may partly have been a reflection of Frankfurt's own ideological preference, but was almost certainly also a consequence of the city's physical proximity to the major centres of production of Protestant learned editions in the Swiss Confederation.[16]

Willer's catalogue also, however, directs our attention to a previously neglected aspect of the Frankfurt trade. From 1568, along with the steadily expanding range of Latin and German titles, Willer included a small number of books in other vernaculars, mostly in French or Italian. At first, these were only a handful of titles, and the section variously described as 'Bücher in frembden Sprachen' or, more portentously, 'Libri peregrine idiomate conscripti' never grew beyond a couple of pages. Nevertheless it

---

[13] Plantin issued catalogues of his own titles in 1566, 1567, 1568, 1575 and 1584. Clair, *Plantin*, p. 203.

[14] A fine survey, including facsimiles of some of the earliest examples, is Graham Pollard and Albert Ehrman, *The Distribution of Books by Catalogue from the Invention of Printing to AD 1800* (Cambridge, 1965).

[15] The whole sequence of catalogues for the period 1564–1600 is available as a facsimile reprint: Bernhard Fabian, *Die Messkataloge des sechzehnten Jahrhunderts* (5 vols, Hildesheim, 1972–2001).

[16] Paul Chaix, *Recherches sur l'imprimerie à Genève de 1500 à 1564* (Geneva, 1954), pp. 56ff. Hans Joachim Bremme, *Buchdrucker und Buchhändler zur Zeit der Glaubenskämpfe* (Geneva, 1969), pp. 48–51.

is clear that over the course of the second half of the century, a significant quantity of books in French were offered for sale in Frankfurt.

These French books on sale at the Frankfurt fair have never been the subject of systematic analysis. It is interesting to ask why Willer included them in his catalogues, and indeed why these particularly books were chosen to take to Frankfurt. Who were likely to be their purchasers? The information provided in Willer's individual catalogues is helpfully summarized in a three-part composite catalogue that listed all the books offered for sale at the fair between 1568 and 1592.[17] This catalogue seems to have been the response to a long-felt need for a composite work of reference from which scholars could discover when and by whom particular books had been published. Foreign vernaculars are listed in the third volume of this work, after the much longer lists of Latin and German books. And in contrast to Willer's small miscellaneous list of foreign items in each individual catalogue, here the French, Italian and Spanish works are classified according to subject matter – using, it must be said, a detailed but extremely idiosyncratic system of classification (see Appendix 2). This allows us to survey at a glance the relative importance attached to the market in different categories of literature, as well as the relative demand for books in French and Italian. To see how the market evolved over the more than three decades covered by this summary, it is necessary to return to the individual catalogues issued by Willer.

The production of Willer's catalogues was a co-operative venture. Printers intending to come to the fair sent Willer title pages of their forthcoming works, so that he could arrange them in subject order.[18] The catalogues could then be distributed to printers around Europe, and be passed by them to prospective customers. Their principal usefulness was therefore for the reading public and publishers who could not attend the fair, but bought their stock from printers who did. But it also helped publishers coming to the fair to have a sense of what would be available, and to be able to gauge from their customers how many copies they would be able to dispose of. Since the major part of the economy of the fair was based on barter between publishers (who were thus able to carry away from Frankfurt a vastly more varied stock), Willer's catalogues played a vital role in ensuring that the leading figures of the European book world approached the fair with the best possible information.

---

[17]   *Collectio in unum corpus, librorum italicae, hispanice et gallice in lucem editorum a nundinis Francofurtensibus anni 68. usque ad nundinas Autumnales anni 92. &c. C'est a dire, recueil en un cours des libres italiens, espagnols et francois, qui ont este exposez en vente en la boutique des imprimeurs frequentans les foires de Francfort depuis l'an 1568 jusques à la foire de Septembre 1592. Extraict des catalogues desdictes foires, & reduict en methode convenable, et tresutile* (Frankfurt, 1592).

[18]   Polland and Ehrman, *Distribution of Books by Catalogue*, p. 75.

As has been stated, Willer issued his first catalogue in 1564; it comprised some 202 works, exclusively in Latin and German. By the following year he had refined his method of description to include fuller details of the publisher and place of publication of each item. The Latin books are drawn from a variety of international presses, among which Paris publishers are well represented. In this respect, the catalogue was already highly international in character. The first mention of other foreign vernaculars occurs in the Lenten catalogue of 1568, with a list of four titles: three in French, and one in Italian. Perhaps this represented no very large innovation, since three were texts printed by Plantin in Antwerp, and no doubt included in his regular consignment of books to the fair.[19] The remaining title was a French Plutarch by the Paris publisher Vascosan.[20] The following year, 1569, the two catalogues issued for the Lent and autumn fairs included a number of Italian books published in Venice, a single Genevan edition (Calvin's sermons on Job)[21] and a first book in Spanish: a quarto Bible.

These early lists set the tone for the foreign-language books on sale in Frankfurt for some years to come: predominantly in Italian and French, with a smattering in Spanish. It is nevertheless interesting to see what books it was thought likely that customers would wish to purchase in these languages. In the first years, books of history vie for attention with popular works of literature and philosophy and modern theological works. From 1570 onwards, however, turbulent contemporary politics impact increasingly on the works offered for sale. The Lenten catalogue of 1570 offers the recently published Protestant account of the third civil war; the following year visitors may purchase Louis Le Roy's influential *Exhortation aux françois pour vivre en concorde*.[22] At the autumn fair of 1571, the selection of French books on offer is both broad and topical, including editions of Machiavelli, du Bellay and, more ominously, the first military manuals to be included on this list.[23] The effect of the French troubles has been to crowd out the Italian books that previously dominated the list: significantly, the books by Machiavelli and Bernardo Rocco on the art of war are both offered in French translations, rather than in their original languages.

The choice of titles hints at the influence in the international book world of members of the French Huguenot elite, many of whom at some point attended the fair in person. The French statesman theologian Philippes du Plessis Mornay visited the fair in 1569, where he met and conferred with Hubert Languet, another influential writer and strategist in the Huguenot

---

19   Appendix 2, nos 1, 3, 86.
20   Appendix 2, no. 150.
21   Appendix 2, no. 35.
22   Appendix 2, nos 90, 152.
23   Appendix 2, nos 137, 138, 157.

cause; Mornay returned to Frankfurt again two years later, in 1571. In this unsettled period, the Huguenot leadership could still hope for a political solution to the French troubles even while they planned for military action; a year later, with the Massacre of St Bartholomew's Day, the political context would change for ever. The slaughter in Paris produced considerable disruption in the French printing industry, and a temporary hiatus in the supply of French books to the Frankfurt Fair. But by 1574, interest in the Huguenot cause, and the French Crown's stumbling efforts to eliminate resistance, had revived, with a flurry of titles documenting Huguenot defiance, political and military. Books on sale included the *Histoire memorable de la ville de Sanserre*, an account of one of the most notable sieges of the war, where Huguenots successfully fought off their Catholic assailants, and reflecting the unhappier face of these turbulent times, the *Discours du massacre de ceux de la religion reformee, fait à Lyon*.[24] More ominously for those who continued to hope for a negotiated settlement, the Frankfurt fair also offered for sale a French version of the *Francogallia* of François Hotman, one of the group of French political writings that postulated a radical reconfiguration of the relationship between Crown and subjects.[25]

The principles of resistance and Huguenot strategy for an eventual settlement continued to feature strongly among the books offered for sale at the fair during the rest of this troubled decade. In 1577, those sympathetic to the French Huguenot cause could purchase both the *Resolution Claire et facile sur la question tant de fois faicte de la prise des armes par les inferieurs* and the incendiary *Tocsain contre les massacreurs*.[26] A second edition of this work was on sale in 1579, along with the magisterial *Droit du magistrate* of Theodore de Bèze.[27] The fair also offered two editions of hostile satirical history of the house of Guise by Pierre de La Planche, *La legende de Charles, Cardinal de Lorraine*, and an edition of Simmler's *Republique des Suisses*, a highly suggestive account of the state of government in the Confederation since it had thrown off the Habsburg yoke.[28]

These years also witnessed a quickening of interest in events in the Netherlands. The period between the Pacification of Ghent in 1576 and the fracturing of the opposition to Spain in 1579 were the years that offered the best prospect of a successful resolution of the rebellion from the perspective of William of Orange and his allies. These hopeful prospects were evident in a number of works on sale at the fair: the *Discours sommaire des justes*

---

[24]   Appendix 2, nos 166, 168.
[25]   Appendix 2, no. 102.
[26]   Appendix 2, nos 142, 143.
[27]   Appendix 2, no. 120.
[28]   Appendix 2, nos 118, 172.

causes et raisons qui on contrainct les Estats generaulx de pourveoir à leur defence and the *Discours veritables des choses passées*, both in 1578; the *Sommaire annotation des choses plus memorales* and the *Discours sur la permission de liberté de religion* in 1579, and the *Vraye narration de ce qu' est traicté avec ceux de Malines* and *Lettres interceptes de quelques patriots masqués* in 1580.[29] These overtly political works were put on sale alongside a range of Protestant theological and religious works, including both contemporary volumes such as Philip du Plessis Mornay's *Traité de l'Eglise* and revivals of publications from the 1560s, including Pierre Viret's *Le monde à l'Empire* and the anonymous *Glaive du geant Goliath.*[30]

These were years when contemporary French and Netherlandish events gave a very particular colour to the vernacular works available for purchase. More recreational literature was also brought to the fair; but the sale catalogues suggest that on the whole, buyers of French books in these years had more earnest preoccupations than to supply themselves with the sort of book that would normally have whiled away the leisure hours in an aristocratic household or a bourgeois drawing room. So although the books on sale did include works of poetry, literature, musical part books and philosophical texts, the largest categories by far were works of theology, history and books on contemporary politics. These three categories alone make up 60 per cent of the 302 French books offered for sale between 1568 and 1592.

With these remarks, we are close to discerning the profile of the likely purchasers of these French books offered for sale in Frankfurt. Certainly, one category of purchasers would have been members of the French Huguenot movement who found themselves obliged to travel abroad during periods of particular turbulence and danger at home. The Frankfurt fair also undoubtedly served the needs of French nationals settled in Germany on a longer-term basis, such as the congregations of the French exile churches along the Rhine.[31] Through Frankfurt, the more learned members of these churches would have been able to supply themselves with the latest editions of important works of theology by Protestant writers such as Mornay, Lambert Daneau or Jean de L'Espine.[32] Frankfurt may also have acted as a midway point for the exchange of Protestant theological works published in Geneva or the Netherlands. A central figure in this network was the émigré French printer André Wechel, who had moved to Frankfurt in the wake of the St Bartholomew's Day massacre.[33] Wechel was closely

---

[29]   Appendix 2, nos 115, 144, 182, 191.
[30]   Appendix 2, nos 45, 46, 47.
[31]   Philippe Denis, *Les églises d'étrangers en pays rhénan (1538–1564)* (Liège, 1984).
[32]   Appendix 2, nos 41, 63, 70, 77.
[33]   Ian Maclean, 'André Wechel at Frankfurt, 1572–1581', *Gutenberg Jahrbuch*, (1988): 146–76.

connected to Hugues Languet, who had been instrumental in assisting his flight from Paris in 1572; in Frankfurt, the two men remained closely allied, and Wechel profited in particular from the vast network of contacts developed by Languet in the course of his activities as political agent of the duke of Saxony. Languet's correspondents feature prominently among the authors of the books published by Wechel in Frankfurt, a list that was almost exclusively scholarly and Latinate. His authors also include men like Hugues Sureau, a notorious figure in the French Calvinist movement for his double abjuration after St Bartholomew, who eventually settled in Frankfurt, where he translated a number of French texts into Latin and German for the international market.

While André Wechel's output was almost exclusively Latinate, the choice of texts very much reflects the scholarly and philosophical preoccupations of many of those who bought the vernacular titles offered for sale in Frankfurt. This does not seem, by and large, to have been a market serving mercantile buyers (witness the relatively insignificant numbers of books of arithmetic),[34] nor were books offered for sale to be carried back for retail sale in France. We can note here the relative absence of medical texts, a far greater presence in both the German and Latin lists, the small number of dictionaries and grammars, and the almost total absence of classic school texts.[35] This is a market, it seems clear, that responded to the interests of engaged laymen, rather than the professional needs of men of business.

The French Wars of Religion inspired a considerable diaspora as members of the Huguenot churches took refuge from the bloody vengeance of their hostile Catholic neighbours. This flight is much more frequently studied from the point of view of the ministers and Church leaders forced to flee than the members of the Huguenot aristocracy who either went abroad themselves or sent their families and children. The young comte de Laval was one who spent his formative years abroad under the care of Protestant tutors; another was Jacques Bongar, later Henry IV's ambassador to the German Empire. For men of this stamp, often bustling here and there on the affairs of Condé, and later Henry of Navarre, the Frankfurt fair offered an important place of exchange – a chance for conversation and consultation as well as the purchase of books. One might imagine that they also took the opportunity to exchange copies of the latest pamphlet accounts of French events, and the edicts and proclamations with which the Crown sought, usually in vain, to put an end to the hostilities. This is a class of book that scarcely features in the booksellers' catalogues at all, presumably because individual items were too inexpensive to be worthy of listing. But one can well imagine that they would have been eagerly passed around by men starved of news at home.

---

[34]   Appendix 2, nos 230, 231, 232.
[35]   Appendix 2, nos 86–9, 264–70.

It would be wrong, however, to assume that all the purchasers of French books sold at the Frankfurt fair were themselves French. On the contrary, the evidence presented here points to an important market for French vernacular literature among important categories of other foreign readers. This is a phenomenon that has not much been commented upon up to this point. It is well known, for instance, that German readers avidly consumed French literature in the age of the Enlightenment; their taste for French literature in the earlier period is much less fully documented. Similarly, the amount of French literature that found its way to England in the sixteenth century is only gradually becoming evident.[36] In both of these emerging Protestant literary cultures there was considerable demand for the sober works of theology and governance that would allow members of the political classes to keep abreast of French events. But this interest in modern French politics built on a healthy pre-existing interest in French literary culture. This is one of the most striking emerging findings of the work of the St Andrews French book project group, which has conducted in the last ten years a comprehensive survey of French vernacular print in the sixteenth century. These investigations have involved, for the first time, an extensive survey of French-language literature in libraries outside France, a survey that reveals for the first time the importance of contemporary collecting of French vernacular literature in sixteenth-century Germany.

Even in this era, Germans seem to have been great readers of French literature. The great cycle of Amadis de Gaule, which in the French translation of Nicolas de Herberay became a bestseller throughout Europe, was eagerly sought by purchasers in England and Germany, and considerable numbers survive in collections in those countries (and also now in the United States).[37] Sometimes these books survive only in these libraries – as is the case with a number of volumes in the Longis imprint of the popular Paris octavo edition of 1555. The copies that survive in Gotha and Tübingen were clearly contemporary purchases, judging by contemporary marks of ownership, and in the case of the Tübingen copy, copious annotations.[38] The Tübingen set was the treasured possession of the Tübingen University professor Martin Crucius, a distinguished Humanist whose fine collection of scholarly books is an important part of the Tübingen collection. But he also valued his Amadis, noting carefully where he purchased each volume (as soon after it became available as possible) and when he finished reading it. It is no surprise that this highly

---

[36]   See, from diverse perspectives, John J. O'Connor, *Amadis de Gaule and its influence on English Literature* (New Brunswick, NJ, 1970); Francis Higman, 'Calvin's Works in Translation', in Andrew Pettegree et al. (eds), *Calvinism in Europe, 1540–1620* (Cambridge, 1994), pp. 82–99.

[37]   Andrew Pettegree, 'Translation and the Migration of Text', in Tom Betteridge (ed.), *Borders and Travellers in Early Modern Europe* (Aldershot, 2007).

[38]   Tübingen UB: Dk IV 32–5.

portable octavo was popular with readers abroad, rather than the stately folio favoured by many wealthy French purchasers. It may also have been with the export market in mind that Jean Longis in 1557 published a fine, serviceable edition in an even smaller size, 16mo: though at the cost of forgoing the woodcut illustrations.[39]

The Amadis craze pre-dates the Frankfurt catalogues, but the demand for recreational literature certainly made its impact. The Frankfurt catalogues carry a significant quantity of lighter literary works, and the ever-popular musical part books.[40] If the catalogues suggest that by the second half of the century purchasers of French books in England and Germany had their minds on more serious subjects, this is certainly not exclusively the case.

The trade in French books was probably not on the same scale as the trade in German vernacular books. We do not, of course, know how many copies printers sent to the fair of most of the titles listed here, but they were unlikely to be the vast quantities shifted of some sorts of books. It is interesting to compare these observations on the French trade with the books sold by the Zwickau bookseller Michael Harder at the Lenten fair of 1569.[41] Harder sold 5918 items, at this fair. This is an astonishing total, particularly if one considers that he was one of 87 dealers represented at the fair. If he was only averagely successful, then this would imply a total trade of something in the region of half a million books.

Harder's most successful books were of a type that have only a secondary place in the French lists. Chivalric romances feature strongly among books of which he sold more than 100 copies; the most successful of all were two collections of didactic narratives and droll stories, and a household medicine book, *Das handbüchlein Apollinaris*, which sold 227 copies. Herder sold 69 copies of Aesop at this fair, and 77 of Eulenspiegel. These were books of a type that sold extremely well in France in normal circumstances; the French, in particular, had an almost inexhaustible appetite for chivalric romances, which sold in large quantities and in all formats throughout the century. But none of the publishers from Paris, Lyon or Antwerp who published these books thought it worth their while to bring them to Frankfurt. For these were books for more leisured times, and more settled households. This seems also to have been the case for the books of popular morality which must have been a speciality for Herder, since he sold almost four hundred copies of works devoted to denunciations of the sins of pride, drunkenness, gambling and profanity. But these were the sins of prosperity. For the French abroad, far from home and often short of cash, the purchase of admonitory literature would itself have been a form of frivolity. Instead, precious husbanded resources were invested

---

[39]   Mannheim UB: Sch 077/163a–d.
[40]   Appendix 2, nos 233–57, 282–91.
[41]   Thompson, *Frankfort Book Fair*, pp. 34–8.

in more substantial works that offered solace, or proposed solutions to the pressing problems facing the dispossessed victims of France's current troubles.

The French books sold at the Frankfurt fair were, by and large, books that would represent a significant investment; a considered purchase of a book intended to be carefully studied, or valued for its perspective on pressing contemporary events. Bearing this in mind, it is striking how many of the books listed leave little trace in contemporary collections. For the purpose of this study, the attempt was made to identify actual editions of the three hundred or so French books listed in Willer's catalogues and recapitulated in Baker's summary catalogue of 1592. The amount of detail given in of the catalogue entries (clearly transcribed direct from the title page) often made this a relatively simple matter, not least because we have at our disposal the information compiled for the bibliography prepared by the St Andrews French book project. This data provided surviving copy information for some 50,000 editions of French vernacular books, representing over 175,000 copies presently located in around 1620 libraries, worldwide.

This investigation reveals that of the 304 books listed, around 10 per cent cannot be traced to a surviving copy. This is not as surprising as it might seem. Many sixteenth-century books had disappeared altogether, and not only the mundane everyday print of broadsheets and cheap pamphlets. Many other far more prized, and sometimes expensive, books were often simply used to destruction.[42]

Of course, the danger exists that in accepting catalogue entries as proof of publication, one creates books that never actually existed – either because the catalogue misrepresents a crucial piece of data (such as the date of publication) or because a publisher failed to publish the work promised. But the sheer wealth of detail in the Frankfurt lists leads us to believe that the catalogue entries may, by and large, be trusted. That so many of the books listed survive only in one, two or three copies also makes it inherently plausible that others are completely lost – though presumably they may continue to turn up as other libraries continue the work of cataloguing their rare books.[43]

The 'lost' books of the Frankfurt catalogue bear further scrutiny, not least because they demonstrate the point that some classes and categories

---

[42]   This is notably true of musical part books, which despite their high cost and sophisticated clientele, often survive in only one of the four or five parts printed; see F. Lesure and G. Thibault, *Bibliographie des editions d'Adrian Le Roy and Robert Ballard (1551–1598)* (Paris, 1955); Henri Vanhulst, *Catalogue des editions de musique publiées à Louvain par Pierre Phalèse et ses fils 1545–1578* (Brussels, 1984).

[43]   For instance, Appendix 2, no. 224 (only surviving copy in Wolfenbüttel HAB), 229 (Ghent UB).

of sixteenth-century books were far more likely to survive than others. The works of Protestant theology listed, for instance, can almost all still be traced to surviving copies, and some survive in large numbers; the Catholic books rather less so. This may seem a perverse conclusion, given that Protestant collections within France itself suffered sustained attrition in the sixteenth and seventeenth centuries, culminating in wholesale destructions at the time of the Revocation of the Edict of Nantes. So it is not surprising that sometimes these Protestant works survive only in libraries in Britain, Germany and Switzerland, where they had often made their way, via Frankfurt, very soon after publication. The same phenomenon is even more pronounced in the case of the literary works listed here. These suffered a far higher rate of attrition than the works of theology listed in Willer's catalogue. These were sometimes relatively ephemeral books published in a handy 16mo. Some, like Guicciardini's *Heures de recreation*, were works translated from the Italian; others, such as the popular *Comptes du monde adventureux*, were original compositions in French.[44] The undisputed master of such small-format literary compositions was Benoist Rigaud of Lyon, and his books are extremely well represented in German collections: indeed, any study of his output based only on copies surviving in Paris, or even in all French libraries, would seriously underestimate his contemporary impact. Many of his books survive only in Germany, where the appetite for his particular form of recreational literature seems to have been particularly keen. Despite this, a number of his works are among those listed in the Frankfurt catalogues that have proved impossible to trace.

The study of the lost books from the Frankfurt catalogues offers some important lessons about the phenomenon of loss and survival. The rate of survival has often been assumed to have been largely a factor of size: that is, large and expensive books usually survive, and smaller, more ephemeral books are frequently lost. This is certainly true up to a point. But the most influential factor seems to be whether books were systematically collected at, or close to, the time of production. Such considerations explain why rates of survival are spectacularly good for pamphlet literature of Luther's day, because though essentially ephemeral, the *Flugschriften* were gathered up and collected assiduously at the time of publication. Against this, countless school books, Latin and vernacular, often leave little trace. In other cases, books do not survive because care was taken that they should not. This probably explains the complete disappearance of the three books listed here by Hendrik Niclaes, the leader of the Family of Love, none of which have been traced in a contemporary collection.[45]

---

[44]   Appendix 2, nos 283, 285.

[45]   Appendix 2, nos 83, 84, 85. The standard bibliography of the works of Henrik Niclaes lists only one sixteenth-century French translation: an edition of

The twists and turns of political events in France continue to leave their imprint on the books on sale in Frankfurt throughout the 1580s, and into the last decade of the century. Genevan imprints feature strongly among the relatively small number of books offered for sale in 1586: in this and subsequent years, Philippes du Plessis Mornay and Jean de l'Espine were among the most popular authors on sale.[46] Visitors to the fair would also have been able to furnish themselves with successive volumes of Simon Goulart's compendious collection of contemporary tracts.[47] Otherwise, the furious pamphlet literature of the League revolt of 1588–93 makes little impact on the Frankfurt sale catalogue. During these years, Leaguer presses in Paris and Lyon turned out literally thousands of editions lauding the martyred Guise, and denouncing first the treachery of Henry III then the perjured usurper Henry of Navarre.[48] But these short, cheaply produced and often highly ephemeral works were not offered for sale in Frankfurt. Visitors to the spring fair of 1590 could read an account of Henry IV's crucial victory over the forces of the League at Ivry, near Evreux in Normandy, on 14 March. This was an edition published not in France, but dashed off the press by the local Frankfurt printer Joannes Wechel.[49] But this pamphlet, however heartening its contents would have been to many of Frankfurt's French visitors, was a rare instance of the polemical literature of the last decade of the French wars impacting on the Frankfurt book market. Otherwise, the shifting spirit of the times is evident more in an increased equilibrium between Catholic and Protestant theological works available at the fair. It is possible that some of the fair's visitors had some premonition of Henry of Navarre's impending spiritual journey, and sought to anticipate it.

The imminence of peace does bring a subtle change in the French books offered at the Frankfurt fair. The last five years of the century see an increase in the number of bilingual and multilingual works on offer: products both

---

the *Vrai tesmoignage de la terre spirituelle*, published by Niclaes Bohmbargen in Cologne in 1580. *Bibliotheca dissidentium. Répertoire des non-conformistes religieux des seizième et dix-septième siècles, 22: The family of Love. I: Henrik Niclaes by Alastair Hamilton* (Baden-Baden, 2003), no. 1 ac. These three other French editions may well also have been Cologne imprints.

[46] Appendix 2, nos 59, 63.

[47] Appendix 2, nos 204, 205.

[48] Denis Pallier, *Recherches sur l'imprimerie à Paris pendant le Ligue (1585–1594)* (Geneva, 1975). The French book project now lists several hundred editions not known to Pallier or Baudrier.

[49] Appendix 2, no. 206. There remains uncertainty whether Joannes Wechel was the son or nephew of André Wechel, or even whether they were related at all. When Joannes Wechel came to Frankfurt in 1581, he gave Cologne as his place of origin, but a connection with the Paris family seems likely. R.W.J. Evans, *The Wechel Presses: Humanism and Calvinism in Central Europe, 1572–1627* (Past and Present, Supplement 2, Oxford, 1975), p. 3n.

of the Antwerp presses, which built quite a specialism in such literature, and German publications. It is possible that the fair is responding both to a change in the character of their French visitors and a reduction in their overall number. In several of the catalogues at the very end of the century, there is no section of foreign books at all.

It is clear that trade in French, Italian and Spanish books occupied only a tiny fraction of the turnover of the Frankfurt fair. Nevertheless, the market was significant enough for publishers from Paris, Antwerp and Geneva to ensure that a selection of their latest books were available for purchase. The French trade at Frankfurt may be set alongside other small, distinct markets that can be identified in Europe's shifting kaleidoscope of trade. The movement of books around the European book world was never in perfect equilibrium, and frequently shifting. The supply of Latin and Italian books from southern Europe seems, for instance, never to have been balanced by an equivalent movement of texts in the opposite direction. Investigations of these specialized micro-markets will no doubt shed further light on how the trade managed to satisfy particular demands: for instance the trans-European trade in scientific books.[50] The trade in foreign vernacular books at the Frankfurt fair may appear at first sight quite general, but it turns out on further inspection to be very different from the market for vernacular books within France itself. It reflects the particular needs of an educated group of often unwilling travellers, and of interested foreign observers, for news and spiritual solace, but most particularly for guidance through the difficult political choices facing France's warring parties in the second half of the sixteenth century.

Appendix 1: Foreign Vernacular Books at the Frankfurt Fair

	French	Italian	Spanish	Totals
Catholic theology	34	35	7	76
Protestant theology	48	0	0	48
Unclassified theology	3	0	0	3
Medicine	4	5	0	9
Philosophy	8	4	0	12
Politics	35	19	0	54
Rhetoric	0	5	0	5
Dialectic	1	0	0	1
Apologetics	4	1	0	5

[50]   Alexander Marr (ed.), *The Worlds of Oronce Fine: Mathematics, Instruments, and the Book in Renaissance France* (forthcoming, 2008).

Polemics	11	5	3	19
Architecture and Military	2	6	0	8
History	62	48	2	112
Poetry	18	9	1	28
Arithmetic	3	0	0	3
Music	25	37	0	62
Cosmography	2	5	2	9
Topography	4	4	0	8
Astronomy	0	3	0	3
Grammars and Dictionaries	7	8	1	16
Voyages	2	1	0	3
Dueling	1	0	0	1
Agriculture	1	2	0	3
Equestrianism	1	4	1	6
Nobility	2	2	1	5
Funerals	2	2	0	4
Games	2	1	0	3
Culinary	0	2	0	2
Love	10	4	0	14
Earthquakes	1	0	0	1
Varia erudite	12	11	0	23
Totals	304	223	18	545
Percentages	55.8	40.9	3.3	

Appendix 2: French Vernacular Books at the Frankfurt Fair[51]

Collectio in unum corpus, librorum italicae, hispanice et gallice in lucem editorum a nundinis Francofurtensibus anni 68. usque ad nundinas Autumnales anni 92. &c.

C'est a dire, recueil en un cours des libres italiens, espagnols et francois, qui ont este exposez en vente en la boutique des imprimeurs frequentans les

---

[51]   The French items in this appendix are transcribed from the composite list published in 1592; the original contains French, Italian and Spanish items. The section headings are as given in the original published list; the sequential numbering of items has been added for convenience of reference. The date and identification of the Fair (V = *vernus*, spring; A = *autumnus*, autumn) represents the fair at which the book was offered for sale; particularly in the case of the Lenten fair, this may be the year after publication.

foires de Francfort depuis l'an 1568 jusques à la foire de Septembre 1592. Extraict des catalogues desdictes foires, & reduict en methode convenable, et tresutile.

I. Pontificiorum Theologorum

1. Le manuel de devotion. Antverpiae apud Platinum 12. 1568. A

2. Heures de nostre dame à l'usage de Rome en latin en francoys. Antverpiae, apud Plantinum 16.

3. L'histoire de l'ancien Tobie, & de son fils le jeune Tobie. Item, L'histoire de la noble vefue Judith. Le vertueux faict de la noble dame Susanne, &c. Antwerpiae apud Plantinum in 4. 1568. A

4. Le prompuaire des exemples des vertus & vices, recueilli de l'ancien & nouveau Testament. par Nicolas Hapae en Anvers 1569. V

5. La defence de la foy de nos ancestres par F. Christophle cheffontaines. 8. A Paris 1571 A

6. La theologie naturelle de Raymond Sebon. A Paris 1571. A

7. L'art et maniere de parfaictement ensuivre Jesus Christ & mespriser de toutes les vanitez de ce monde, autrement dite L'eternelle Consolation jadis compose en latin par Thomas des Champs, & puis n'agueres fidelement traduite selon le sens de l'Autheur. 12. à Anvers 1572. V

8. Six sermons sur l'explication de l'oraison Dominicale, & autres quadres sur l'incarnation de nostre redempteur Jesus Christ. Tous faicts par Messire Françoys Richardot Evesque d'Arras. 8. à Anvers 1572. A

9. Le nouveau Testament de nostre Seigneur Jesus Christ traduit de latin en françoys par les theologiens de Louvain. 16. à Anvers. 1573. A

10. Exposition avec exhortations sur les leçons; Epistres & Evangiles du Quatresme: divisees en huict tomes et le huictiesme tome en huict parties: par F. Gabriel Dupuyherbault. à Paris par Jean de Roigny. &c 1574 & 1576 V

11. L'Imitation de Christ. Comment il faut mespriser toutes les vanitez de ce monde, faite il a fort long temps, par un home craignant Dieu, nouvellement translate en françoys 16. 1576. A

12. Manuel general, & instruction des Curez & Vicaires contenant sommairement le devoir de leur charge soit à faire prosnes, adminstrer les Saincts sacremens & enseigner leurs paroissiens, par exhortations propres adaptées à iceux. Le tout tire des escriptures Sainctes, & anciens docteurs de l'Eglise. Avec plusieurs sermons pour la declaration des ceremonies de l'Eglise de Dieu. par F. Denys Peronet docteur en Theologie. 8. à Paris 1577. V

13. La sainct Bible contenant le viel & nouveau Testament traduicts de latin en françoys. fol. à Anvers de l'Imprimerie de Christofle Plantin. 1578. V

14. Decoration de la fameuse Abbaye des freres de Morges. 8. 1578 V

15. La saincte Bible in folio. Lugduni par Barthelemi Honorat. 1578 A

Ex Patribus.

16. Dix livres de Theodoret Evesque de Cyr ancient docteur de l'Eglise touchant la providence de Dieu contre les Epicuriens & Atheistes. 8 à Lyon 1578. A

17. La leçon Chrestienne, ou les offices & debuoirs familiers & convenables à tous disciples de Christ tirez des precepts & institutions du souverain Maistre, & colligez en un brief sommaire pour l'instruction du petit troupeau. par Benoit Arias Montan, traduict du latin en francoys. à Anvers 1579. A

18. Bref traité de l'institution des pecheurs, par M. Claude de Vieymont. 16. à Anvers par Jean Bellere 1582. A

19. Heures de nostre dame à l'usage de Rome selon la reformation de nostre S. Pere le Pape Pie V. 4. à Paris 1583. & 1584. V

20. Sept dialogues auquels sont examinez cent soixante et quatorze erreurs des Calvinistes. par Françoys Feuardent. à Paris. Sebastien Nivelle. 8. 1585. V

21. Pratique spirituelle d'une servante de Dieu à l'exemple de laquelle se peut exercer toute religieuse personne spirituelle. à Louvain. 12. 1585. A

22. La somme des pechez, & le remede d'iceux, premierement recuillie, & puis nouvellement reveue, corrigée, augmentée, & amplifiée, par Reverend P. F. I. Benedicti, professeur en Theologie, de l'ordre des freres mineurs de l'observance & Pere Provincial de la province de Touraine Pictavienne. à Paris chez Arnold Sittart. in fol. 1586. & 1587. V

23. Rescriptions faictes entre M. Gilles de la Cousture Lillois depuis son retour du Calvinisme au giron de l'Eglise Romaine & M. Antoine L'Escaillet encores ministre Vallon en la ville de Cantorberi pays d'Angleterre. 8. Antverpiae. Plantinus 1588. V

24. Le livre de la compagnie, C'est a dire les cinq livres des institutions Chrestiennes, dressees pour l'usage de la confrererie de la tresheureuse vierge Marie, mis en François du latin de R. P. Françoys Coster Docteur en Theologie de la compagnie du nom de Jesus. 8. Antverpiae apud Christoph. Platinum. 1588. V

25. Cinquante meditations de toute l'histoire de nostre Seigneur, par R.P. Françoys Costerus docteur en Theologie de la societé & compagnie de Jesus, & mises en François de la traduction de Gabriel Chappuis Tourangeau, Annaliste & translateur de la Majesté treschrestienne, & tresreligieuse. 8 Antverpiae apud Plantinum. 1588. V

26. La practique spirituelle de la devote & religieuse princes de Parme, utile à tous pour vivre chrestiennement, Auec les Letavies de la sacrée

vierge Marie, comme les disent ceux, qui sont de la congregation de ladite vierge. Et un Catalogue de livres spirituals: tant pour se converter à Dieu, que pour faire progrez aux sainctes vertus. 24. Antverpiae excudebat Christophorus Plantinus 1588. V

27. L'Antechrist demasqué, par Claude Caron docteur medecin d'Annonay en Vivarois. à Tournon par Guillaume Linocier. 8. 1589 A

28. Le manuel des Catholiques contenant la vraye maniere de prier Dieu, du R. pere P. Canisius mis en François par Gabriel Chappuis. Antverpiae apud Plantinum 16. 1589. A

29. L'Adieu de l'ame devote laissant le corps, avec les moyens de combatre la mort par la mort, & l'appareil pour heureusement se partir de ceste vie mortelle. Composé par R.P.M Loys Richeome de la compagnie de Jesus. A Tournon par Guillaume Linocier. 8. 1590 A

30. Response aux blasphemes d'un ministre de Calvin sacramentaire semez dans les escris, contre le S. Sacrifice de l'Autel par Claude Caron docteur medecin d'Annonay en Vivaroys. A Tournon 8. 1590 & 1591. V

31. Guidon & pratique spirituelle du soldat Chrestien par le R.P. Thomas Sailly prestre de la compagnie de Jesus. A Anvers 8. 1590 & 1591. V

32. Traité du S. sacrement de Baptesme, & ceremonies d'iceluy, par Claude Caron docteur medecin d'Annonay en Vivaroys. A Tournon 8. 1591. V

33. De la saincte philosophie livrée A Lyon pour Jaques Faure 24. 1591. V

34. Guidon & Practique spiritual du soldat Chrestien, recueillie pour l'armee de sa majesté Catholique, par le R.P. Thomas Sailly prestre de la compagnie de Jesus. à Anvers, en l'Imprimerie Plautiniene, chez la vefue de Jean Mourentorff. 1592. V

II. Protestantium Theolog.

35. Sermons de M. Jean Calvin sur les livres de Job. A Geneve. fol. 1569. A

36. Les pseaumes de David, mis en rime françoise par Clement Marot, & Theodore de Beze. Avec la prose en marge, & une oraison a la fin d'un chacun pseaume par M. Augustin Marlorat. 16. A Geneve par Abel Rivery. 1577. V

37. L'Excellence de la justice chrestienne compose par Jean de L'Espine ministre de la parole de Dieu, & nouvellement mise en lumiere, pour l'instruction & consolation des enfans de Dieu. 8. 1577. V

38. Exhortation chrestienne à Heildelberg sur le trespass du treshaut & tresdebonnaire Prince Monseigneur Frideric Conte Palatin du Rhin, Electeur du S. Empire. Pere de la patrie & protecteur des fideles affligez, faicte & preschée par Daniel Toussain. 8. A Heidelberg 1577. V

39. Le nouveau Testament, c'est a dire la nouvelle alliance de nostre seigneur Jesus Christ. Reveu & corrigé de nouveau sur le grec par l'advis des ministres de l'Eglise de Geneve. Avec annotations revues & augmentées par M. Augustin Marlorat. 16. A Geneve. pour Jacob Chouet. 1577. V

40. Traité de l'Eglise, contenant un vray discours pour cognoistre la vraye Eglise, & la discerner d'avec l'Eglise Romaine, & toutes fausses assemblees. 8 A Geneva. par Eustache Vignon 1577. A

41. Traité de l'Antechrist revue & augmenté en plusieurs endroits en ceste traduction françoise par l'advis de l'Autheur compose premierement en latin par l'Ambert Daneau, & tranduit nouvellement en françoys par I.F.S.M. 8. A Geneve chez Eustache Vignon 1577. A

42. L'Alcoran des Cordeliers, tant en latin qu'en françoys, c'est a dire recueil des plus notables bourdes, & blasphemes impudens de ceux qui ont osé comparer sainct Françoys à Jesus Christ, tire du grand livre des Conformitez, jadis compose par frere Barthelemi de Pise, Cordelier en son vivant. Parti en deux livres. 8. A Geneve par Guillaume de Laimarie 1578. V

43. Traicté de l'Eglise auquel sont disputes les principales questions qui ont esté meues sur ce point en nostre temps. Par Philippe du Mornay Seig. du Plessis Marlyn. 8. Imprimé à Londres, par Thomas Vautrollier 1578. A

44. Response Chrestienne au premier livre des calumnies & nouvelles faussetez des deux Apostats, Matthieu de Launoy Prestre, & Henry Pannetier n'agueres ministres & maintenant retournez à leur vomissement. 8. 1578. A

45. Le monde a l'Empire, & le monde demoniacle faict par dialogues. reueue & augmenté par Pierre Viret. A Geneve. 1579. A

46. Le glaive du gean Goliath Philistin, & ennemi de l'Eglise de Dieu. 8. 1579. A

47. Traité de l'Eglise auquel sont disputes les plus principales questions, qui ont esté meues sur ce point de nostre temps. Par Philippe du Mornay Seigneur du Plessis Marlyn. 16. 1579. A

48. La Bible qui est toute la saincte Escriture, contenant le viel & nouveau Testament. On a adiousté en ceste edtion entre autres choses les argumens sur chacun livre, figures, cartes, tant chorographiques que autres, avec l'Harmonie des passages correspondans des quatre derniers livres de Moyse. in fol. A Geneve de l'Imprimerie de Jacob Stoer 1580. A

49. Des Grands & redoutables jugemens & punitions de Dieu advenus au monde, principalement sur les grands, a cause de leurs meffaits, contrevenans aux commandemens de la loy de Dieu, le tout mis en deux livres, suivant la distinction des deux tables de ladicte loy &c. A Morges par Jean le Preux. 8. 1581. V

50. L'estat de la Religion, & Republique du people Judaique. par Paul Eber ministre de Vuitemberg. chez Eustache Vignon. 8. 1581. & 1582. V

51. De la verité de la Religion Chrestienne, contre les Athees Epicuriens, payens, Juifs, Mahumetistes, & autres infideles. par Philippes de Mornay, sieur de Plessis Marlyn. A Anvers de l'Imprimerie de Christophle Plantin 4. 1581 & 1582. V

52. Institution de la Religion Chrestienne, par Lucas Osiander D. Tubinge. 8. 1582. V

53. Traité de l'Eglise auquel sont disputes les principales questions qui ont esté meues sur ce point en nostre temps, Par Philippes du Mornay S. du Plessis Marlyn, gentilhomme François. A Francfort chez les heretiers d'André Wechel. 1582. A

54. L'Exercice de l'ame fidele, C'est assavoir, Prieres & meditations pour se consoler en toutes sortes d'afflictions & singulierement pour se fortifier en la foy, reueues parcidevant, & digerees par ordre selon les aricles de nostre foy, & de nouveau en ceste derniere edition enrichies & augmentees par Daniel Toussain ministre de la parole de Dieu. 16. A Francfort par les heretiers d'André Wechel. 1583. V

55. Les lamentations & saincts regrets du prophete Jeremie avec paraphrase ou exposition appropriée à ce temps en toutes sortes lamentables. Par Daniel Toussain. 8 A Spire par Bernard Dalbin 1584. V

56. Traité du mespris de la mort, distingué en huict livres. Par Christofle de Beaulieu seigneur de laugle gentil'homme François. A Anvers par Jaques Henric. 1584. & 1585. V

57. La consolation de l'ame sur l'asseurance de la remission des pechez, &c. par Jean Chassanion. 8. Excudebat Jean le Preux. 1585. V

58. Response aux cinq premieres & principales demandes de F. Jean Hay, Moyne Jesuite aux ministres Escossois. 8 par Jean le Preux 1586. A

59. Sermons sur les trios premiers chapitres du cantique des cantiques de Salomon. Par Theodore de Beze ministre de la parole de Dieu en l'Eglise de Geneve. 8. Jean le Preux 1586. A

60. Histoires memorables des grans & merveilleux jugemens & punitions de Dieu advenues au monde, principalement sur les grands a cause de leurs mesfaits, contrevenans aux commandemens de la loy de Dieu. Par Jean Chassanion de Momstrol en Vellay. 8. Imprimé par Jean le Preux. 1586. A

61. Meditations chrestiennes. A Londres par Thomas Vautrollier in 16. 1586. A

62. La religion chrestienne declare par dialogue, & distinguee en trois livres, dont la substance & liason se trouvera es pages suivantes la preface, compose par Matthieu Virelle ministre du sainct Evangile. Imprimé a Geneve chez Eustache Vignon. 8. 1587. V

63. Excellens discours de Jean de Lespine Angevin, touchant le repos & contentement de l'esprit, distinguez en sept livres nouvellement mis en

lumiere, avec sommaires & annotations qui monstrent l'ordre & la suite des discours. in 8. Imprimé à Basle 1587. A

64. Les actes du Colloque du Montbeliardt, qui s'est tenu l'an de Christ 1586. avec laide du seigneur Dieu tout puissant y presidant le tresillustre prince & seigneur Monseigneur Frideric Conte de Virtemberg & Montbeliardt, &c. Entre tresrenommez personnages le docteur Jaques André Preposé & Chancelier de l'Université de Tubinge, & le sieur Theodore de Beze professeur & ministre à Geneve. Imprimé à Montbeliardt par Jaques Foillet. 8. 1588 V

65. Response à la profession de foy publiee par les moynes de Bordeaux contre ceux de l'Eglise reformee pour leur faire abjurer la vraye religion. 8. 1588. A

66. Chrestienne & necessaire exposition du Catechisme tiree de la parole de Dieu & dressee par demandes & responces publiee en la principauté des deux ponts par le commandement de tresillustre Prince Jean Conte Palatin du Rhin, Duc de Bavieres, Conte de Veldents, Spanheim, &c. A Geneve de l'Imprimerie de Jean le Preux. 8. 1588. A

67. Le livre des marchans, ou plustost des affronteurs, & vendeurs pe hapelourdes. A Frankdal chez les heretiers de Jean Barsanges. 16. 1588. A

68. Traité de l'Eglise auquel sont disputes les questions principales qui ont esté meues sur ce point en nostre temps, par Philippe du Mornay, seigneur de Plessis Marlyn gentil'homme François. A Lausanne, de l'Imprimerie de Jean Chiquelle. in 16. 1588. A

69. L'Antimoine aux responces que T. de Beze fait à 37 demandes de deux cens & six proposees aux ministres d'escosse par M. Jean Hay de la compagnie de Jesus. A Tournon, par Claude Michel 8. 1588. A

70. Excellens discours de Jean de L'Espine Angevin, distinguez en sept livres, nouvellement mis en lumiere, avec sommaires & annotations, qui monstrent l'ordre & suite des discours. A la Rochelle par Theophile Regius 8. 1588. A

71. L'Antimartyr de frere Jaques Clement, de l'ordre des Jacopins, C'est a dire, s'il a justement tué le feu Roy de tresheureuse memoire Henry III: Et s'il doit estre mis au rang des martyrs de Jesus Christ, avec une belle remonstrace aux François. 8. 1590. A

72. Le miroir par lequel on voit les assaux que l'Eglise Chrestienne a receus depuis la mort de Jesus Christ jusques auiourdhuy, tant par les Payens, Turcs, Infideles, Sarrasins, & Juifs, que par leur successeur Romain, contenant les troubles guerres civiles, & massacres qui on esté faits en France jusques aux troubles commencez l'an 1585. in 8. Imprimé à Montauban par Jean de Tours 1590. A

73. Simple recit de la verité contenue es sainctes escritures & livres des Peres orthodoxes docteurs de l'Eglise primitive touchant l'Ascension &

Majesté, la Cene, le Baptesme, & la predestination de Christ. Par Jaques Macler ministre de l'Eglise de Montbeliard in 8. A Montbeliard 1590. A

74. La devocieuse semaine de Jean Avenaire docteur en Theologie nouvellement traduits de latin en François. in 12. à Monbeliard 1590. A

75. Brief recueil du colloque de Montbeliard tenu au mois de May 1586. Entre Jaques André D. & M. Theodore de Beze. traduit de latin en François. in 8. 1590. A

76. Les pseaumes de David mis en rithme françoise par Clement Marot, & Theodore de Beze, & en Alemand par Ambrosius Lobwasser: avec mesme chant, & oraisons le tout vis a vis l'un de l'autre. A Geneve par Jacob Stoer. 1591. V

77. Traite de la providence de Dieu, pour le repos & contentement des consciences fideles, par M. J. de Lespine. De l'Imprimerie de Jean le Preux 8. 1591. V

78. Sermon sur l'histoire de la passion & sepulture de nostre Seigneur Jesus Christ, descrite par les quatre Evangelistes par Theodore de Beze. Par Jean le Preux 8. 1591. A

79. Traité des vrayes essentielles & visibles marques de la vraye Eglise Catholique. Par Theodore de Beze. Par Jean le Preux. 8. 1591. A

80. Excellens discours de Jean de Lespine Angevin Theologien touchant le repos & contentement de l'esprit contenans infinies doctrines & fermes consolations à toutes sortes de personnes affligees en ces derniers temps. Distinguez en sept livres & mis en lumiere avec sommaires & annotations. par S.G.S. & dediez au sieur de la Noue A Geneve 16. 1591. A

81. Response de Theodore de Beze, pour la justification par l'imputation gratuite de la justice de Jesus Christ, apprehendé par la seule foy. Contre un certain escrit sans le nom de son autheur imprimé n'agueres furtivement, & semé par & la par un certain Antoine L'Escaille, traduit de latin en François. Par Jean le Preux 8. 1592. V

82. Le nouveau Testament. A Geneve par Pierre de S. André in 8. Stoer. 1592. V

III. Anonimi cuiusdam scripta a Theologica quem separatism ponendum esse duximus nec adscribendum classi Pontificiorum vel Protestantium Theologorum.

83. Declaration evidente de l'exigence du Seigneur, & des tesmoiniages salutaires du Sainct Esprit, de la charité de Jesus Christ. Produite par Fidelitas Coancien avec HN. en la famille de Charité. Traduite de bas Alleman. 8. 1579. A

84. Epistre HN. une voix d'appel du Sainct Esprit de la charité par laquelle tous peoples sont de pure grace, appellez & inuitez par HN. à la vraye

penitence de leurs pechez à l'ingression de la droite vie Chrestienne, & à la maison de charité de Jesus Christ. 8 1579. A

85. Annoncement de la paix sur la terre, & du temps propice & l'aimee agreeable du Seigneur Jesus Christ, & de son Sainct esprit de charité, est maintenant au dernier annoncé par HN. sur la terre. Traduit de bas Alleman. 8 1579 A

IV. Medici.

86. Deux livres des venins, ausquels il est amplement discoureu des bestes venimeuses, theriaques, poisons, & contrepoisons par Jaques Grevin. Item ensemble les oeuvres de Nicandre medecin & poete Grec, traduites en vers François. à Anvers apud Plantinum. 8. 1568. V

87. Cinq livres de Chirurgie. I. Des bandages. 2. Des fracteures. 3 Des luxations, avec une Apologie touchant les harquebousades. 4. des morsures & picqueures venimeuses. 5. des goutes. Par Ambroise Paxé. 8 A Paris 1572. A

88. Les oeuvres de M. Ambroise Pare conseiller, & premier chirurgien du Roy. Avec les figures & pourtraits tant de l'Anatomie que des instrumens de Chirurgie, & de plusieurs monstres. fol. à Paris. 1575. A

89. Commentaires de M. Pierre Mattiole medecin Senois sur les six livres de Ped. Dioscorid. Anazaarbeen de la matiere medicinale. fol. A Lyon par Guillaume Rouille. 1579. A

V. Philosophici & Morales.

90. Exhortation aux François pour vivre en concorde, & iouit du bien de la paix. Par Louys le Roy. A Paris. 8. 1571. V

91. Les oeuvres morales de Plutarque translatees en françois. A Basle 1574. A

92. Academie françoise en laquelle il est traité de l'institution des meurs, & de ce qui concerne le bien, & heureusement vivre en tous estats & conditions, par les precepts de la doctrine, & les exemples de la vie des anciens sages & homes illustres, par Pierre de la Primaudaye. fol A Paris 1577. A

93. L'institution de la femme Chrestienne, tant en son enfance comme en marriage, & viduité avec office de mari, traduite en François du latin. de Louys Vives. in 8. & imprimé à Anvers. 1579. A

94. Deux livres de la Constance de Juste Lipse, mis en François 4. Christoph. Plant. 1584. A

95. Le Theatre du Monde, ou il est faict un ample discours des miseres humaines, compose en latin par Pierre Boistuau surnommé Launay, natif

de Bretagne, puis traduit par le mesme Autheur en françois. Imprimé à Lyon par Jean Gazeau in 16. 1588. A

96. Les offices de M. Tulle Ciceron traitant du debuoir des homes. le tout latin & François In 16. Genevae 1589 V

VI. Politici.

97. Ordonnance edict & decret du Roy nostre Sire sur le faict de la justice criminelle es pays bas. A Anvers de l'imprimerie de Christofle Plantin 4. 1571. V

98. La harangue que fit le Roy à Messieurs de la court de parlement en son palais à Paris, estant lors en son siege Royal, le lundi douzieme jour de Mars. 8. 1571. A

99. Diete Imperiale, ou Ordonnances & resolution de l'Empereur & des Estats du S. Empire, deliberee & arrestee en la derniere journee tenue à Spire en l'an 1570. &c. 8. A Paris. 1572. A

100. Epistres des princes, lesquelles ou touchent, ou traittent les affaires des princes, ou parlent des princes 4. A Paris 1573. V

101. Harangue faicte & prononcee de la part du Roy treschrestien le 10. jour du mois d'Auril 1573. parMonseigneur Jean de Moluc, &c. A Paris 1573. A

102. La Gaule françoise de François Hotoman jurisconsulte, traduite de latin en François. 1574 V

103. Les premieres oeuvres de Philippe Desportes au Roy de France & Pologne. 8. à Annecy par Jaques Bertrand 1576, & 1577. V

104. Discours sur les moyens de bien gouverner maintenant en bonne paix un Royaume, ou autre principauté, divisez en trois parties assavoir du Conseil, de la Religion, & Police que doit tenir un Prince, contre Nicolas Machiavel Florentin, a treshaut & tresillustre Prince Françoys Duc d'Alençon fils & frere du Roy. 8 A Lyon 1576 & 1577. V

105. La France Turquie, C'est a dire conseils & moyens tenus par les ennemis de la couronne de France pour reduire le royaume en tel estat que la tyrannie Turquesque 8. A Orleans de l'Imprimerie de Thibaut des Murs 1576. & 1577. V

106. Remonstance pour la paix aux Estats. 8. Au Souget. 1576. & 1577. V

107. Remonstrance d'un bon Catholique François aux trois Estats de France, que s'assembleront à Blois, suivant les lettres de sa Majesté du 9. d'Aoust presentee l'annee 1577. 8 V

108. Remonstrance aux françois pour les induire de vivre en paix a l'advenir. 8. 1576. & 1577. V

109. Remonstrance au Roy treschrestien III. de ce nom Roy de France & de Pologne, sur le faict des deux Edicts de sa Maiesté donnees à Lyon, l'un du X de Septembre, & l'autre du xiij. d'Octobre dernier passé, presentee

l'annee 1574. touchant la necessité de paix, & moyens de la faire. 8. à Angenstein par GabrielJason 1576 & 1577. V

110. Les six livres de la Republique de Jean Bodin Angevin à M. du Faur, seigneur de Pibrac, conseiller du Roy, en son conseil privé. 8. A Lausanne 1577. V

111. Notable & sommaire discours de l'estat des affaires de France depuis l'edict de pacification faict au mois de May 1576. contenant les artifices dont les ennemis du repos de France ont usé, pour abolir le dernier Edict de pacification, & introduire plus grands troubles que jamais. 8. Imprimé à Reins par Jean Martin 1577. A

112. Readvis & abduration d'un gentil'homme françois de la Ligue contenant les causes pour lesquelles il a renoncé à ladite ligue, & s'en est departy. 1577. A

113. Vive description de la tyrannie, & des tyrans avec les moyens de se garentir de leur joug. in 16. A Reins par Jean Mouchar 1577. A

114. Harangue prononcee devant le Roy, seant en ses Estats generaux à Blois, par Reverend Pere en Dieu, Messire Pierre Despinac, Evesque, Comte de Lyon, primat des Gaules, au nom de l'Estat Ecclesiastique de France. 8. à Anvers 1577. A

115. Discours sommaire des justes causes & raison qui ont contraint les Estats generaux des pays bas de pourvoir à leur deffence contre le seigneur don Jean d'Austruce. in 4. Imprimé A Anvers par Guillaume Sylvius, imprimeur du Roy 1577. & 1578. V

116. Les six livres de la Republique de Jean Bodin Angevin A Monseigneur du Faux, seigneur de Pibrac, &c. fol & in 4. A Paris 1578. A

117. Discours de Jean Bodin sur le rehaussement & diminution des monoyes, tant d'or que d'argent, & le moyen d'y remedier & response aux paradoxes de Monsieur de Malestroit. A Paris 1578. A

118. Republique des Suisses, contenant le gouvernement d'iceux depuis l'Empereur Paoul de Haspourg jusques à Charles le Quint, &c. Descritte en latin par Josias Simler de Zurich, & nouvellement mise en françois 8. 1579

119. Discours sur la permission de liberté de Religion, dicte Religionvrede au pais bas. 8. 1579. A

120. Du droit des magistrats sur leurs subjets. 8. 1579. A

121. Exhortation amiable, & conseil salutaire pour le pays bas, monstrant la cause de la presente dissension intestine & le remede qui y pourroit estre mis. 8. 1579. A

122. Recueil de la negociation de la paix traitee à Coulogne en la presence des commissaires de la Majesté Imperiale, Entre les ambassadeurs du serenissime Roy Catholique, & de l'Archiduc Matthias, & les Estats du pays bas. 8. Anvers. 1580. A

123. Le secret des finances de France. 8. 1581. V

124. De la puissance legitime du prince sur le peuple, & du peuple sur le prince. Traité tresutile & digne de lecture en ce temps, escrit en latin par Estienne Junius Brutus, & nouvellement traduit en françois. 8. 1581. A

125. Traité de la Justice recueilli des oeuvres de ce grand philosophe & parfait orateur M. T. Ciceron & traduit en françois par Henry de Vuithem. 4. à Anvers 1582. A

126. Instruction aux Princes pour garder la foy promise, contenant un sommaire de la philosophie Chrestienne & morale, & debuoir d'un homme de bien, Par M. Cognet, Chevalier, Conseiller du Roy, 4. A Paris chez Jaques du Puys 1584. V

127. Sixiesme edition & recueil d'Arrests des Cours souveraines de France, par Jean Papon. Imprimé par Jean de Tournes, in 8. 1587. A

128. La harangue faicte par le Roy Henri III. de France & de Pologne, a l'ouverture de l'assemblee des trois estats generaux de son Royaume, en sa ville de Bloys, le 36. jour d'Oobre l'an 1588. A Bloys par Barthelemi Gomet, & Jamet Mestayer imprimeurs du Roy. 4. 1588. & 1589. V

129. Discours sur l'estat de France, avec la copie des lettres patentes du Roy depuis qu'il s'est retiré de Paris: ensemble la copie des deux lettres du Duc de Guise. 1588 & 1589. V

130. Declaration du Roy pour la remise de l'assemblee generale des princes, Cardinaux, Ducs, & pairs de France. in 4. A Tours chez Jameot Metuyer imprimeur 1590. V

131. Les lettres d'Estienne Pasquier conseilier & advocat general du Roy en la chambre des Comtes de Paris. à Avignon 16. 1590. 1591. V

VII. Rhetorici.

VIII. Organum Analysis & Dialectica.

132. L'Organe, c'est a dire l'instrument du discours, divisé en deux parties, sçavoir est l'analytique pour discourir veritablement, & la dialectique pour discourir probablement. Le tout puisé de l'organe d'Aristote. Dedié au Roy treschrestien. Par M. Philippes Canaye Sieur de Fresnes, Conseiller de sa Majesté en son grand Conseil. Imprimé par Jean de Tournes, imprimeur du Roy. fol. 1589. V

IX. Apologetici

133. Apologeme pour le grand Homere, comme la reprehension du divin Platon sur aucuns passages d'iceluy, par Guillaume Paquelin Beaunois. 4. A Lyon par Charles Pesnot 1577. V

134. Apologie on deffence pour les Chrestiens de France, qui sont de la religion Evangelique ou reformee, satisfaisant à ceux qui ne veluent vivre en paix & concorde avec eux. 8. A Geneve par Antoine Chuppin. 1578. A

135. Protestation & deffence pour le Roy de Navarre Henry III. premier prince de France, & Henry aussi prince de Condé aussi prince de mesme sang, contre l'injuste & tyrannique Bulle de Sixte cinquiesme. traduite du latin intitulé Brutum Fulmen. 8. 1587. A

136. Apologie pour les Chrestiens de France de la Religion Evangelique ou reformee, fondee sur la S. escriture & approuvee par la raison, & par les anciens canons au Roy de Navarre. Par Innocent Gentillet Jurisconsulte Dauphinois. 1588. V

X. Polemici.

137. Du maniement & conduite de l'art & faicts militaires. faict en Italien, par M. Bernard Rocque, Placentin, & mis en françois, par Françoys de Belleforest 4. A Paris. 1571. A

138. Des entreprises & ruses de guerre, & des fautes qui par fois surviennent es progrez & execution d'icelles, &c. 4. A Paris. 1571. A

139. Les discours de paix et de guerre de M. Nicolas Machiavel. A

140. Harangues militaires & concions de Princes, Capitaines, Ambassadeurs & autres manians tant la guerre que les affaires d'estat. fol. A Paris. 1573. V

141. Missive de tresillustre prince, Henry, prince de Condé, Duc de Bourbon, &c. Envoyee à tresillustre Prince Jean Casimir Conte Palatin du Rhin, Duc de Baviere, &c. Escritee de Strasbourg. 8. 1575. & 1577. V

142. Reconciliation claire & facile sur la question tant de fois faite de la prise des armes par les inferieurs. 16. Imprimé à Reins par Jean Mouchar. 1577. A

143. Le Tocsain, contre les Massacreurs & auteurs de confusions en France, addressé à tous les princes Chrestiens. 8. A Reins de l'Imprimerie de Jean Martin. 1577. A

144. Lettres interceptes de quelques Patriots masquez. 4. A Anvers 1580. A

145. Le vray but ou doivent tendre tous gens de guerre qui ayment honneur, auquel est traité du Butin, & droit usage d'icleluy. 8. 1587. A

146. Discours politiques & militaires du sieur de la Noue, recuillis & mis en lumiere par le Sieur de Fresnes. A Basle, pour François le Fevre. 16. 1591. V

147. Discours politiques & militaires du Sieur de la Noue, recuillis & mis en lumiere par le Sieur du Fresnes, & dediez au Roy treschrestien Henry IIII. Derniere edition enrichie de deux Indices, dont le premier est

des sommaires & argumens sur chacun discours. Le second des choses plus notables contenues en toute l'oeuvre. A Basle 16. 1591. A

XI. Architecturae militaris.

148. Discours sur pleusieurs points de l'Architecture de guerre concernans les fortifications tant anciennes que modernes, Ensemble le moyen de bastir & fortifier une place delaquelle les murailles ne pourront estre aucunement endommagées de lartilerie. Par M. Autelie de Pasino Ferrarois. 4. à Anvers. 1579. V

149. Discours sur le faict de fortifications du Seig. Charles Tetti. ausquels est amplement declaré, quelle doit estre l'assiete d'une forteresse, la forme, lenceinte, les fossez, bolevarts, citadelles, & autres choses concernantes ledit faict, avec les figures de chacune d'icelles, nouvellement mis en françois, reueu, corrigé, & augmenté. A Lyon par Barthelemi Vincent. 4. 1589. V

XII. Historici.

150. Les vies des hommes illustres, Grecs & Romains comparees l'une avec l'autre par Plutarque de Cheronce translatees premierement de Grec en françois par M. Jaques Aymot lors Abbé de Bellozane, & depuis en ceste troisieme edition reveues & corrigees en infinis passages, &c. à Paris par Vascosan. 8. 1568. A

151. Chronique abbregee des Rois de France, & d'autres illustres hommes. 8. Lugduni 1570. V

152. Memoire de la troisieme guerre civile, & des derniers troubles de France. 8. 1570. V

153. Les epistres dorees, & discours salutaires de don Antoine de Geuare, Evesque de Mondonedo, prescheur & Chroniqueur de l'Empereur Charles cinquiesme, traduites d'Espagnol en françoys par le Sieur de Guttery. Item, ensemble la revolte que les espagnols firent contre leur jeune prince l'an 1520. & l'issue d'icelle, avec un traité des travaux & privileges des galeres, le tout du mesme autheur. Traduit nouvellement d'Italien en françois. A Paris par Jean Reuelle. 8. 1570. A

154. Les memoires de Messire Martin du Bellay seigneur de Langey, contenans le discours de plusieurs choses advenues au Royaume de france, depuis l'an 1513. jusques au temps du Roy françois premier, ausquels l'autheur a inseré trois livres, & quelques fragmens des Ogdoades de Messire Guillaume du Bellay, &c. Parisiis fol. 1571. V

155. De l'estat & succez des affaires de France. Ensemble une histoire sommaire des seigneurs Contes, & Ducs d'Anjou. Par Bernard de Girard. 8, A Paris 1571. A

156. L'histoire des neuf roys Charles de France. par Françoys de Belleforest Commingeois. fol. A Paris 1571. A

157. Les memoires de M. Martin du Bellay seigneur de Langey. 8. A Paris 1571. A

158. Les Chroniques & annales de Flandres, contenantes les heroiques & tresvictorieux exploits des Forestiers, & Contes de Flandres, depuis l'an de nostre Seigneur Jesus Christ vj. & xx. jusques à l'an 1476. composees par M. Pierre Doudegherst. 4. à Anvers apud Christoph. Plantinum 1572. V

159. Chroniques d'Enguerran de Monstrelet gentil'homme jadis demeurant à Cambray en Cambresis in fol. à Paris 1572. V

160. La vraye & entiere histoire de ces derniers troubles advenus tant en France, qu'en Flandres, & pays circumvoisins, comprinse en dix livres. Dediee à la noblesse de France. 8. A Coulogne. 1572. V

161. Histoire de nostre temps, contenant un recueil des choses memorables passees & publiees pour le faict de la religion, & estat de la france depuis l'edict de pacification du 23. jour de Mars 1568 jusques au jour present. 8. 1572. V

162. L'Histoire universelle du monde, contenant lentiere description, & situation des quatre parties de la terre. in 4. Imprimé à Paris. 1572. V

163. Discours modernes, & facetieux des faits advenus en divers pays pendant les guerres civiles en France. 16. A Lyon 1572. A

164. L'Heptameron ou histoires des amans fortunés des nouvelles de tresillustres & tresexcellent Princesse, Marguerite de Valois Royne de Navarre. 16. A Lyon 1573. A

165. Le printemps d'yver contenant cinq histoires, discoureues par cinq journees en une noble compagnie, au chasteau du printemps par Jaques Yver. 16. A Paris. 1573. A

166. Histoire memorable de la ville de Sancerre. 8. 1574. V

167. Les vies des hommes illustres Grecs & Romains, comparees l'une avec l'autre par Plutarque de Cheronce. Translatees de Grec en François par Messire Jaques Amyot lors Abbé de Bellozane. fol. A Lausanne par Françoys le Preux 1574. V

168. Discours du massacre de ceux de la religion reformee, faict à Lyon par les Catoliques Romain, &c 8. 1574. V

169. Pourparler faict à la Rochelle par monsieur le mareschal de Cosse, &c. 16. 1574. V

170. De la vicissitude ou verité des choses en l'univers, & concurrence des armes, & des lettres, par les premiers & plus illustres natios du monde, depuis le temps ou a commencé la civilité, & memoire humaine, jusques a present. fol. A Paris chez Pierre l'hulier, rue Sainct Jaques à l'Olivier. 1575. V

171. Alliances genealogiques des Rois & princes de Gaule. Par Claude Paradin. in fol. A Lyon 1561. & 1575. A

172. La legende de Charles Cardinal de Lorraine, & de ses freres & de la maison de Guise, descritte en trois livres, par Françoys de l'Isle. 8. A Reins 1576. A

173. L'Histoire de l'estat de France, tant de la Republique que de la Religion sous le regne de François xj. 8. 1576. A

174. Memoires de l'estat de France soubz Charles neufviesme: second volume in octavo, 1576. A

175. Memoires de l'estat de France soubz Charles neufuiesme troisieme volume. 8. 1576. A

176. Memoires de l'estat de France soubz Charles neufuiesme, reduits en trois volumes chacun desquels a un indice des principales matieres y contenues, premier volume. A Meidelburg par Henry Wolf. 8. 1576. A

177. L'Histoire de l'estat de France, tant de la Republique que de la Religion. soubz le regne de Françoys xj. 8. imprimee 1576. & 1577. V

178. L'Histoire de France, par Bernard de Girard, seigneur du Haillan, historiographe de France. Tome premier & tome second. 8. par Pierre de S. André. 1577. V

179. Les diverses leçons de Pierre Messie, avec trois dialogues dudict autheur, contenans veritables & memorables histoires, mises en françois par Claude Gruget Parisien. in octavo. A Lyon 1577. A

180. Recueil des choses jour par jour advenues en l'armee conduite d'Alemagne en France, par Monsieur le prince de Condé. pour le restablissement de l'estat du Royaume, & nommeément pour la Religion, commençant au mois d'Octobre 1575. & finissant au mois de May suivant, que la paix, non paix fut faite, & publiee à Etigny pres Sens. 8. 1577. A

181. Histoire des guerres d'Italie, escritte en Italien par M. Françoys Guiciardin, gentil'homme Florentin Docteur és loix, & traduite en françois par Jerosme Chomedey, gentil'homme & conseiller de la ville de Paris. 8. A Geneve par Pierre de Sainct André. 1577. A

182. Discours veritables des choses passees és pays bas de Flandres, depuis la venue du Seigneur don Jean d'Austruce. in 8. A Lyon 1578. A

183. Histoire de Fl. Josephe sacrificateur Hebrieu, mise en françois. Reveue sur le grec, & illustree de chronologie, figures, annotations, & tables, tant des chapitres, que des principales matieres. P. D. Gil. Genebrad. in fol. A Paris. 1578. A

184. L'Histoire d'un voyage faict en la terre du Bresil autrement dit Amerique. Le tout recueilli sur les lieux par Jean de Lery natif de Margelle, terre de sainct Seneau Duché de Bourgogne. 8. A Geneve pour Antoine Chuppin. 1578. A

185. Les grandes Annales & histoire generale de France des la venue des Francs en Gaule jusques au regne du Roy treschrestien Henry III. par Françoys de Belleforest Comingeois. In fol. à Paris 1579. V

186. Sommaire Annotation des choses plus memorables advenues de jour a autre és xvij. provinces des pays bas des l'an lxvj. jusques au premier jour de l'an lxxix. 8. à Anvers 1579. V

187. Histoires, disputes & discours, des illusions & impostures des diables, des magiciens infames, sorcieres & empoisonneurs des ensorcelez & demoniaques, & de la gairison d'iceux. Item de la punition que meritent les magiciens, les empoisonneurs, & les sorcieres. Le tout comprins en six livres par Jean Wier medecin du Duc de Cleves. 8. par Jaques Chouet 1579. V

188. Histoire Ecclesiastique des Eglises reformees au Royaume de France, en laquelle est descritte au vray la renaissance & accroissment d'icelle depuis l'an 1521. jusques en l'annee 63. leur reiglement ou discipline, Synodes persecutions tant generales que particulieres, noms & labeurs de ceux qui ont heureusement travaillé, villes & lieux, ou elles ont esté dressees, avec le discours des premiere troubles ou guerres civiles, desquelles la vraye cause est aussi declaree. 8. à Anvers 1580. V

189. Recueil des Rois de France, leur Couronne & maison ensemble les rangs des grands de France, par Jean du Tillet, sieur de la Bussiere, Protenotaire & secretaire du Roy, Greffier de son Parlement. in fol. A Paris 1580. V

190. Les Genealogies & anciennes descentes des Forestiers & Contes de Flandres, avec brieves descriptions de leurs vies & pestes, le tout recuilli des plus veritables, approuvees & anciennes Chroniques, & annales qui se trouvent. par Corneille Marti Zelandois. Et ornees de pourtraits, figures & habits, selon les façons & guises de leurs temps, ainsi quelles ont esté trouvees és plus anciens tableaux, par Pierre Balthasar, & par luymesme mise en lumiere. fol. à Anvers 1580. A

191. Vraye narration de ce qui est traité avec ceux de Malines tant par escrit, que verbalement de la part de l'Archiduc Matthias gouverneur general du pais bas. Ensemble de ceux de la ville d'Anvers 1580. A

192. Histoire de Portugal, comprinse en vingt livres, dont les douze premiers sont traduits du latin de Jerosme Osorius, &c. nouvellement mise en françois par S.G.S. Avec un discours du fruit qu'on peut recuillir de la lecture de ceste histoire, & ample Indice des matieres principales & contenues. De l'imprimerie de François Estienne, pour Ant. Chuppin. fol. 1581. A

193. L'Estat de l'Eglise, avec le discours des Temps, depuis les Apostres jusques à present. chez Eustache Vignon. 8. 1581. A

194. L'Estat de la Religion, & Republique du peuple Judaique depuis le retour de lexil de Babilone jusques au dernier sacagement de Jerusalem. Par Paul Eber ministre de Witemberg. chez Eustache Vignon. 8. 1581. A

195. L'Histoire de France, enrichie des plus notables occurences survenues és provinces de l'Europe, & pays voisins, soit en paix, soit en guerre, tant

pour le fait seculier, qu'Ecclesiastique depuis l'an 1550. jusques à ces temps, de l'imprimerie de Abraham H. fol. 1581. A

196. L'Histoire de France depuis l'an 1580. jusques à ces temps. 8. 1582. V

197. Hexameron, ou six journees contenans plusieurs doctes discours sur aucuns points difficiles ou diverses sciences, avec maintes histoires notables, & non encores ouies. Faict en Espagnol par Antoine de Torquemade, & mis en françois par Gabriel Chappuis Tourangeau. A Lyon par Antoine de Hersy. 8. 1581. & 1582. V

198. Histoire de la confession d'Ausbourg recuillie par le D. David Chrytens professeur des sainctes lettres en l'université de Restoc, & nouvellement mise en françois par Luc le Cop. 4. A Anvers chez Arnauld Comux 1582. A

199. Histoire des troubles & guerres civiles du pays bas, autrement dit la Flandre, contenant l'origine & progrez d'icelle, les stratagemes de guerre, oppugnations & expugnations des villes & forteresses, aussi la barbare tyrannie, & cruauté de L'Espagnol, & des Espagnolisez. in octavo. le tout departi en quatre livres 1582. A

200. Histoire Romaine de Tite Live Padoan. Assavoir les trente-cinq livres, restans de tout l'oeuvres contenue de la fondation de Rome jusques au temps d'Auguste, nouvellement traduits en françois par Antoine de la Faye, A Geneve de l'Imprimerie de Jacob Soer 8. 1582. V

201. Histoire de la guerre civile du pays de Flandres. A Lyon par Jean Stratius 1583. A

202. Les Chroniques & Annales de France, de l'origine des François & leurs venues és Gaules. Augmentees & continuees en ceste edition depuis le Roy Charles ix. jusques au Roy treschrestien de France & de Pologne Henry III. a present reignant par G. Chappuis. à Paris chez Jean Cavellat. fol. 1585 & 1587 V

203. Histoire veritable des choses les plus signalees & memorables qui se sont passees en la ville de Bruges, & presques par toute la Flandre, soubz le gouvernement de tresillustre Prince Charles de Croy prince de Chimay. &c. 8. 1588. V

204. Le second recueil contenant les choses memorables advenues soubz la ligue. 8. 1590 V

205. Le premier recueil, contenant les choses memorables advenues soubz la ligue, tant en la France, Angleterre, qu'autres lieux. 8. 1590 V

206. Declaration veritable de la bataille faicte à Juri la chaussee le 14 de Mars, & de la victoire obtenue par sa Majesté Henry IIII. Roy de Franc & Navarre, sur ceux de la ligue. Ensemble les articles de la grace que sa Majesté à faicte aux Suisses du parti contraire. Francofurti apud Joannem Wechelum in 4. 1590 V

207. Merveilleux & estrange rapport, toutesfois fidele, des comoditez qui se trouvent en Virginia, des façons des naturels habitans d'icelle laquelle a esté nouvellement descouverte par les Anglois que Messire Richart Grinvile chevalier y mena en Colonie l'an 1585. a la charge principale de Messire Valter Raleigh Chevalier superintendant des mines d'estain, favorisé par la Royne d'Angleterre, & authorisé par ses lettres patentes. Par Thomas Hariot serviteur dudict Messire Valter l'un de ceux de ladite Colonie, & qui a esté employé a la descouvrir. chez Jean Wechel, à Francfort 1590. V

208. Discours tresveritable, des horribles meutres & massacres commis & perpetrez de sang froid par les troupes du Duc de Savoye par les pauvres paysans du balliage de Ges & mandement de Gaillart & Tervy, pres de Geneve, sans aucune exception d'aage ou sexe, tant hommes, femmes qu'enfans, masles & femelles. in octavo. Imprimé dans Langres. par Jean le Court. 1590 A

209. L'entreprise de la ligue contre l'estat & couronne de France, avec tout ce qui s'est faict & passé contre ladite ligue jusques à la bataille de Mante, & à la victoire que Dieu en a donnee à Henry de Bourbon Roy de France & de Navarre, & autres qu'il a eu contre ladite ligue depuis son advenement jusques à la Couronne, ayant renversé tous les complots d'icelle, jusques auiourdhuy. Imprimé à Montauban par Jean de Tours, le 15. de Juillet in 8. 1590 A

210. Sommaire description de la France, Allemagne, Italie, & Espagne, avec la guide des chemins pour aller & venir par les provinces, & aux villes plus renommees de ces quatre regions. Imprimé par Jacob Stoer in 16. 1591. A

211. Les Roys & Ducs d'Austrasie de Nicolas Clement traduits en François par François Guibaudet Dijonnois. Col. 4. 1592 V

XIII. Poetici.

212. Les emblemes de maistre André Alciat. 8. Parisijs 1570. V

213. D'amour furieux, Rolland furieux, composé en rithme Tuscane par Messire Loys Arioste. 8. A Paris 1572. V

214. L'Eneide de Virgile prince des poetes latins, translaté de latin en françois & nouvellement reveue & corrigee, par Louys des Masures. Avec les carmes latins correspondans verset par verset 1573. V

215. Roland Furieux, mis en françois de l'Italien de Messire Loys Arioste noble Ferrarois. 8. A Lyon par Barthelemi Honorat. 1577. A

216. Discours de la Comete apparue à Lausanne le 8. jour de Novembre 1577. à six heures du soir. fait en vers françois par J. R. de Digne en Provence. 4. A Lausanne 1578. A

217. La sepmaine ou Creation du modne de G. de Salluste Seigneur de Bartas. 4. A Paris 1578. A

218. Les oeuvres de mesdames des Roches de poetiers mere & fille. 4. A Paris 1579. V

219. Le miroir du monde, reduit premierement en rithme Brabanconne par M. P. Heyns, & maintenant tourné en prose françoise. Non moins duisant par chemin à tous voyagers curieux que le Theatre d'Abraham Ortelius. 4. A Anvers 1579. V

220. Tragedie nouvelle appellee Pompee. En laquelle se voit la mort d'un grand seigneur, faicte par une malheureuse trahison. 4. Lausannae 1579. A

221. Clement Marot. A Lyon par Jean de Tournes imprimeur du Roy. 16. 1588. A

222. La sepmaine ou creation du monde de Guillaume de Salluste seigneur du Bartas, reveue, augmentee & embellie de divers passages par l'autheur mesme. Pour Jaques Chouet. 12. 1588. A

223. Les tragedies de Robert Garnier conseiller du Roy lieutenant general criminel, au siege Presidial & seneschaussee du Maine, au Roy de France, & de Pologne. A Thoulouse par Pierre lagourt. 16. 1588. A

224. La muse guerriere en deux livres de divers Poemes sur pleusieus ingenieux & plaisans argumens avec les hymnes & Cantiques de l'hermitage. A Rouan par Joachim Bontemps. in 16. 1590. A

225. La premiere & seconde sepmaine de Guillaume de Saluste seigneur du Bartas. A Heidelberg in 8. 1591 A

226. Pour plus grand enrichissement de cest oeuuvre y ont esté adjoustez les vers françois des Evesques de Meaux, & de Cambray, & les latins de N. de Clemenges docteur en Theologie, sur la grand disparité de la vie rustique avec celle de la Cour. Par Jean de Tournes. 16. 1591. A

227. Larmes & chants funebres de Joseph du Chesne & sieur de la Violette, sur les tombeaux de deux tresillustres princes du S. Empire, & de trois rares fleurs de nostre France, & perles precieuses de nostre temps. 4. 1592. V

228. La premiere & seconde sepmaine de Guillaume de Saluste, S. du Bartas 1592. V

229. Sonnets & Epigrammes de Jean le Poli I.C. Liegeois: puis deux discours latins, l'un de la preexcellence du Royaume de France avec une deploration de son miserable estat d'aujourdhuy: l'autre sur l'excellence de la cité de Liege; ensemble une exhortation aux princes Chrestiens pour la guerre contre les infidelles. A Liege. 4. 1592. A

XIV. Arithmetici.

230. L'Arithmetique de Simon Stevin de Bruges contenant les computations des nobles Arithmetiques ou vulgaires. Aussi l'Algebre avec les equations de cinq quantitez. 8. A Leyde Chr. Plant. 1585. A

231. L'Arithmetique, & Algebre de Simon Stevin. Antwerpiae. 8. 1585. A
232. La pratique Arithmetique de Simon Stevin de Bruges. 8. A Leyde. en l'Imprimerie de Chr. Plant. 1585. A

XV. Musici.

233. Chansons & madrigales à quatre parties, composees par M. Jean de Castro. 4. Lovanij 1570. V.
234. Septiesme livre des chansons à quatre parties, plusieurs autres nouvelles chansons augmenté. 4. Lovanij 1570. A
235. Livre cinquiesme des chansons nouvelles a cinq partes avec deux dialogues: a 8. d'Orlande de Lassus. Lovanij. 4. 1572. V
236. L'excellence des chansons musicales, composees par M. Jaques Arcadet. 4. A Lyon. 1572. A
237. Livre des meslanges contenant un recueil de chansons a 4 parties, choisy de plusieurs excellens autheurs de nostre temps, par Jean Castro musicien, mis en ordre convenable, suivant leurs tons. 4. A Anvers chez Jean Bellere, &c. 1575. V
238. La fleur des chansons a trois parties, contenant un recueil produit de la divine musique de Jean Castro. imprimé à Louvain 1574. & 1575. V
239. Des chansons reduites en tablature de Lut, a deux, trois & quatre parties. 4. Lovanij. 1575 & 1576. V
240. La fleur des chansons, des deux plus excellens musiciens de nostre temps, assavoir de M. Orlande de Lassus, & de M. Claude Goudimel. Celles d'Orlande ont esté mises en lumiere. 1574 & 1576. V. 4 Lugduni
241. Sonnets de Pierre de Ronsard, mis en musique a cinq, six & sept parties par M. Philippe de Monte. 4. 1575. Louvanij & 1576. V
242. Thresor de musique d'Orlande di Lassus contenant 7. chansons a 4. 5 & 6 parties. 8. 1576. A
243. Livre septieme des chansons a quatre parties nouvellement recorrigé & augmenté de plusieurs chansons, non imprimees auparavant, accommodees tant aux instrumens, comme à la voix, toutes mises en ordre convenable selon leurs tons. 4. A Louvain. 1576. A
244. Premier livre du meslange des Pseaumes & cantiques a trois parties, recuillis de la musique d'Orlande de Lassus, & autres excellens musiciens de nostre temps. 8. 1577. V
245. Chansons, odes & sonnets de Pierre Ronsard mises en musique a quatre, cinq & huict parties. par Jean de Castro. 4. Louvain. 1576 & 1577. V
246. Livre septieme des chansons a quatre parties, nouvellement recorrigé & augmenté de plusieurs chansons non imprimees auparavant. &c. Imprimé à Anvers chez Jean de Bellere 1580. & 1582. V

247. Chansons nouvelles a trois parties de Jean Castro, 4. A Anvers, chez Jean Bellere. 1582. A

248. Cent vingt & six quatrains du sieur de Pibrac conseiller du conseil privé du Roy, & presidant à Paris de nouveau mis en musique, a deux, trois, quatre, cinq & six parties. par Paschal de L'Estocart. 4. A Lyon 1582. A

249. Livre des meslanges de C. le jeune a six parties. in 4. A Anvers. Christoph. Plant. 1585. A

250. Livre de chansons a cinq parties, convenable tant à la voix, comme à toute sorte d'instrumens, avec une pastorelle a vij. en forme de dialogue. le tout nouvellement composé par M. Jean de Castro. Superius. A Anvers chez Pierre Phalese, & chez Jean Bellere in 4. 1586. A

251. L'excellence des chansons musicales composees par M. Jaques Arcadet, tant propres à la voix qu'aux instruments, par Jean de Tournes, imprimeur du Roy à Lyon 4. 1587. A

252. Instruction methodique & fort facile pour apprendre la musique practique, reveue & corrigee en divers endroits par Corneille de Monfort, dict de Glockland, gentilhomme Escossois, excellent musicien. par Jean de Tournes. A Lyon 1587. A

253. Chansons d'André Pevernage, maistre de la chappelle de l'eglise cathedrale d'Anvers, livre premier contenant chansons spirituelles a cinq parties. A Anvers chez Christoph. Plantin. 1589. V

254. Livre second & troisieme des chansons d'André Pevernage maistre de la chappelle de l'eglise Cathedrale d'Anvers, a cinq parties. in 4. A Anvers de l'Imprimerie de Christophle Plantin 1590. A

255. Livre quatrieme des chansons d'André Pavernage, maistre de la chappelle de l'eglise Cathedrale d'Anvers. 4. 1591. V

256. Sonnets avec une chanson, contenant neuf parties, l'une suivant l'autre, le tout a deux parties convenables à la voix, comme aux instrumens, nouvellement mis en musique par M. Jean de Castro. A Anvers chez Pierre Phalese, & chez Jean Bellere. 4. 1592. V

257. Trois odes contenant chacune delles douze parties, l'une suivant l'autre, le tout mis en musique a quatre parties par Jean de Castro. A Donay, de l'Imprimerie de Jean Bogart. 4. 1592. V

XVI. Cosmographici.

258. La Cosmographie universelle de tout le monde, auteur en partie Munster, mais beaucoup plus augmentee, ornee & enrichie par Françoys de Belleforest, &c. A Paris 1575 A

259. Cosmographie ou description des quatre parties du monde de Pierre Apian & Gemma Frison. 4. A Anvers chez Jean Bellere 1582. A

XVII. Tipocosmici & topographici.

260. Miroir du Monde contenant les cartes de tour le Monde. Antwerpiae apud Christoph. Plantinum. 4. 1583. V

261. Epitome du theatre du monde d'Abraham Ortelius auquel se representent par figures & characters la vraye situation & proprieté de la terre universelle. in 4. Antwerpiae 1589. V

262. Le theatre du monde. fol. V

263. Description des pays bas reueue & augmentee plus de la moitié par l'auteur mesme avec toutes les cartes geographiques des dits pays, & plusieurs pourtraits des villes, tirees au naturel. de l'Imprimerie de Christoph. Plantin. 1582. V

XVIII. Astronomici.

XIX. Grammatici & Dictionarij.

264. Les fondemens de la langue françoise, composee en faveur des Allemans par Gerard de Vivre, maistre d'Escole. Imprimé à Coulogne, in quarto. 1574. A

265. Synonimes. C'est a dire plusieurs propos, propres tant en escrivant qu'en parlant, recueillis en François & Allemand, par Gerard de Vivre, 8. 1574. A

266. Grammaire de Pierre de la Ramee, lecteur du Roy en l'université de Paris, à la Royne mere du Roy. 8. A Paris 1572. V

267. Grammatica Italica, & Gallica, de Scioione Lentulo Neapol. conscripta. Francof. Wech. in 8. 1591 V

268. Colloques ou dialogues avec un dictionaire en six langues, Flamend, Anglois, Allemand, François, Espagnol & Italien. 16. à Anvers 1579 A.

269. Dittionario volgare & francese, & reciprocamente francese & volgare, novamente posto in luce da M. Gioantonio Felis. 8. Parigi appresso Nicolo Niuello 1584. V

270. Dictionarium cum colloquijs aliquot quatuor linguarum Latinae, Germanicae, Gallicae, & Italicae, in 16. 1591. V

XX. Miscellanei distincti.

XXI. Nauticae artis.

271. Le voyage de Messire Françoys Drak Chevalier, aux Indes Occidentales l'an 1585, auquel les villes de S. Lago S. Domingo S. Augustino, &

Cartagena, ont esté prises avec cartes Geographiques de tout. 1588. &
1589. V

272. Miroir de la navigation de la mer Occidentale & Orientale pratiqué
& assemblé par Lucas fils de Jean Chartier divisé en deux parties, & de
nouveau aufmenté d'une historiale description des proprietez & origine de
chacune province, par Richart Slotboom. in fol. à Anvers par Jean Bellere
1591. A

XXII. Monomachiae.

273. Chrestienne confutation du point d'honneur, sur lequel la noblesse
fonde aujourdnuy ses monomachies, & querelles par R.P.C. de Cheffontaine
Archevesque de Cesaree n'agueres ministre general de tout l'ordre de Sainct
François. Dediee à treshaut & puissant seigneur Pierre de Boiseon Seigneur
de Coetinisan. Reveu corrigé & augmenté, outre les precedentes editions.
octavo. imprimé à Paris en l'Imprimerie de Arnold Sittart 1586. V

XXIII. Agriculture.

274. L'Agriculture & maison rustique de H. Charles Estienne D. en
medecine, &c. 4. à Paris 1572. V

XXIV. Equestris disciplinae.

275. Traité de la maniere de bien emboucher, manier, & percer les chevaux,
avec les figures des mors de bride, tous & manimens & fers qui y sont
propres, faict en langage Italien, par le Sieur Cesar Fiaschi gentilhomme
Ferrarois, & n'agueres tourné en françois. 4. A Paris. 1578 & 1592. V

XXV. De nobilitate & vita aulica.

276. Le miroir des Courtisans, ou sont introduites deux courtisanes, par
l'une desquelles se descouvrent plusieurs tours, fraudes & trahisons qui
journellement se commettent. Fait en dialogue par Pierre Aretin. 8. A Lyon
1580. V

277. Mespris de la Cour, & louage de la vie rustique par D. Antoyne de
Guevarre en Espagnol François & Italien, par Joan de Tournes 16. 1591.
& 1592. V

XXVI. Funeralia.

278. Oraison funebre, faite & prononcee aux Exeques & funeralles de M. Madame d'Austriche douairiere de Baviere, &c. par Maistre George Tourin Chanoine & Escolatre de ladite Eglise. 4. 1591. V

279. Oraison funebre prononcee en l'Eglise Cathedrale de Liege aux obseques de feu Madame M. Anne d'Austriche douairiere des deux Bavieres, en presence de M. l'Electeur de Coulogne & Prince de Liege son filz, par M. George Thourin docteur en Theologie, chanoine theologal & escolastre en ladite Eglise. 4. A Liege 1591. A

XXVII. De ludis & choreis.

280. Briefve remonstrance sur le jeu de hazard. 8. 1574. A

281. Traité des danses, auquel est amplement resolue la question assavoir s'il est permit aux Chrestiens de danser. 8. 1579. A ·

XXVIII. De esculentis & poculentis.

XXIX. De re amatoria & lata.

282. Le labirinthe d'amour de M. Jean Boccace. à Paris, decimosexto, 1571. A

283. Les heures de recreation, & pares disnees de Louys Guiciardin citoyen & gentilhomme Florentin in decimosexto. A Paris 1571. A

284. Les facecieuses nuicts du seigneur Jean Françoys Straparole. Avec les fables & enigmes, racontees par deux jeunes gentilshommes, & dix damoiselles. 16. A Paris. 1573 A

285. Les comptes du monde adventureux. par A.D.S.D. 16. A Paris 1573. A

286. Le decameron de maistre Jean Bocace Florentin, traduit de Italien en François, par maistre Antoine Maçon, conseiller du Roy, &c. 16. A Paris A

287. Propos amoureux contenans les discours des amours & mariage du seigneur Clitophant, & damoiselle Leusippe. 16. imprimé à Lyon 1572. par Benoist Rigaud, & 1577. V

288. Lettres amoureuses de Messer Girolam Parabosque avec quelques autres adioustees de nouveau à la fin: reduites de l'Italien en vulgaire François, par Hubert Philippe de Villiers. 16. A Lyon 1574 & 1577. V

289. Comptes amoreux par Madame Jeane Flore touchant la punition de ceux qui contemnent & mesprisent le vray amour. 16. A Lyon 1574. par Benoist Rigaud, & 1577. V

290. Les nouvelles recreations & joyeux devis, de feu Bonaventure des Periers, valet de chambre de la Royne de Navarre. 16. A Lyon par Benoist Rigaud 1577. V

291. Lettres missives familieres entremeslees de certaines confabulations non moins utiles que recreatives. Ensemble deux livres de l'utilité du train de marchandise. le tout composé par Gerard de Vivre, à Coulogne chez Gerard Grevenbruck in 8. 1591. A

XXX. De Terramotu.

292. Discours du tremblement de terre en forme de dialogue, pris de l'Italien de Luccio Maggio gentilhomme Boulonnois. à Paris 1575. A

XXXI. Variae & eruditae lectionis.

293. Luc Apulee de l'asne doré xj. livres traduit en François par Jean Louneau d'Orleans. A Lyon par Jean Temporal. decimosexto. 1571. V

294. De la vicissitude ou varieté des choses en l'univers, & concurrence des armes & des lettres, par les premieres & plus illustres nations du monde, depuis le temps, ou a commencé la civilité, & memoire humaine jusques a present. Plus s'il est vray de ne se dire Rien, qui n'ait esté dict auparavant, & quil convient par propres memoires augmenter la doctrine des anciens, sans s'arrester seulement aux versions, expositions, corrections & abregez de leurs escrits. par Loys le Roy, dict Regius. in fol. A Paris 1577. V

295. Vingt & cinq fables des animaux, vray miroir exemplaire par lequel toute personne raisonnable pourra voir & comprendre avec plaisir & contentement d'esprit, la conformité, & vraye similitude de la personne ignorante, vivante selon les sensualitez charnelles, aux animaux & bestes brutes. Composé & mis en luminere par Estienne Perret Citoyen d'Anvers. in fol. A Anvers par Christophle Plantin 1578. A

296. Les colloques de Maturin Cordier en latin & en françois. 8. 1579. A

297. Essais de Messire Michel S. de montagne Chevalier de l'ordre du Roy, & gentilhomme ordinaire de sa chambre. A Bourdeaux par S. Millanges imprimeur ordinaire du Roy. 8. 1581. A

298. La joyeuse & magnifique entrée de Monseigneur Françoys de France frere unique du Roy, par la grace de Dieu Duc de Brabant, d'Anjou, d'Alençon, Berri, &c. & en sa tresrenomme ville d'Anvers. à Anvers 1582. A

299. Les oeuvres françoises de Jean de la Jessee 4. Antverpiae apud Christophorum Plantinum 1583. V

300. La Bibliotheque d'Antoine du Verdier S. du Vauprivas. A Lyon par Barthelemy Honorat fol. 1586 A

301. Discours & advertissemens notables faicts par le Lac Leman aux villes & jeux circumvoisins, escrit par A.Z. 1588. V

302. Academie des animaux par Gabriel Meurier. 1589. V

303. Des deux fontaines dites de Creysbach, & de Sainct Prier. A Strasbourg. Antoine Bertram. in 8. 1590 A

304. L'introduction ou traité de la conformité des merveilles anciennes avec les modernes: ou Traité preparatif a l'Apolog. pour Herodote composee en latin par Henry Estienne, reueu & corrigé de nouveau avec deux tables. A Lyon par Benoist Rigaud. 8. 1591. & 1592. V

FINIS

IMPRIME A FRANCFORT SVR LE MAINE, PAR Nicolas Bassé. 1592.

Index

St Andrews Studies in Reformation History